IRELAND'S
GREAT HUNGER

Silence, Memory, and Commemoration

QUINNIPIAC UNIVERSITY
STUDIES IN THE GREAT HUNGER

Edited by
David A. Valone
Christine Kinealy

University Press of America,® Inc.
Lanham · New York · Oxford

⊖™ The paper used in this publication meets the minimum
requirements of American National Standard for Information
Sciences—Permanence of Paper for Printed Library Materials,
ANSI Z39.48—1984

Contents

LIST OF TABLES AND ILLUSTRATIONS

Preface

Quinnipiac University and the Great Hunger

DAVID A. VALONE

As is the case with all major projects, this book has a long history. Unfortunately, the histories of works such as this more often than not are silenced, often without much thought, in the course of their production. After all, the product, not the process, is valued in academia and in publishing more generally. Such silencing, however, can leave works bereft of important contexts that might further the understanding of the material they contain. In the case of this book, some of the context and history of its creation are critically important. Giving a voice to some of this history seems particularly appropriate here, since this work deals extensively with the implications, both psychological and social, of silence. The story of this volume, and of the Quinnipiac University Great Hunger educational initiative, began in 1996. Around that time, Dr. John L. Lahey, president of Quinnipiac, was selected to serve as grand marshal for the 1997 New York City St. Patrick's Day Parade. Dr. Lahey realized that he would be serving in his post during the sesquicentennial commemoration of Black '47, the year that marked the worst period of the Great Hunger.

In the fall of 1996, I was still a relatively new instructor at Quinnipiac. I had met the president only in passing during the year or so I had spent on campus. I was rather surprised, therefore, when I received a phone call from Dr. Lahey's office asking me to meet with him immediately. It was with no small degree of trepidation that I stepped into the president's office on that day. Much to my surprise and, frankly, relief, Dr. Lahey wanted to ask me a very simple question: "Could you read something that I've written on the Great Hunger? I'd like you to take a look at it and give me your expert opinion." This query caught me somewhat off guard. First, I had no idea that the president was aware that I am a historian who specializes in nineteenth-century Britain. Second, I was loath to admit to him that I had precious little scholarly expertise about the Famine. Despite this, I agreed to read his essay and critique it. He asked me not to hold back and to be as honest (or, indeed, as vicious) as I felt appropriate. Before I even began to read his work, I headed to the university's library to begin educating myself more thoroughly about the Famine.

My own relative lack of knowledge about the Great Hunger speaks loudly about where the Irish catastrophe of the 1840s stood not only in the popular memory, but also within the historical discipline more broadly at that time. Based on my educational background, one might have expected me to know quite a bit about the Great Hunger. I was at that time still a relatively freshly minted Ph.D. in history; though my primary specialization was intellectual history, my main field of study was nonetheless nineteenth-century Britain. Further, I had written my dissertation on the educational and religious debates at the University of Cambridge in the 1820s and 1830s. A good portion of my work addressed controversies in political economy that spilled out of Thomas Robert Malthus's work on population growth, and the reaction to them by a group of conservative Anglican economists at Cambridge. It also touched upon the utilitarian and laissez-faire opponents of my Cambridge Tories. All of these issues might have led me to study the Great Hunger in depth, but none of them actually had.

Further, during my study at the University of Chicago, I had taken a course on Victorian Britain taught by an eminent historian of the Irish Church. Ironically, during that semester we talked very little about Ireland, and even less about the Great Hunger. Indeed I don't believe the issue ever arose in the class. My most striking memory of the course was of reading George Kitson Clark's epic survey of the era, *The Making of Victorian England*. Although published in the early 1960s, this work remains an essential book for historians of nineteenth-century England, particularly the period from 1850 to 1875. It masterfully blends a consideration of social, political, demographic, intellectual, and religious forces in Britain during the period. In reviewing that book now, I realize that both the question of Ireland and the issue of the Great Hunger are hidden and nearly silent in Kitson Clark's work, but are nonetheless present. For instance, prior to giving the lectures that would become *The Making of Victorian England*, Kitson Clark had published extensively on the repeal of the Corn Laws in 1846, an act that was undertaken in large measure as a response to the failure of the Irish potato crop and that had a tremendous impact on the course of Famine relief. Not surprisingly, Kitson Clark has much to say about the importance of the repeal of the Corn Laws in helping to define the later Victorian era politically, economically, and socially. Yet at least as far as he discusses the issue in his book, he has almost nothing to say about the immediate crisis of 1846 in Ireland that helped precipitate British Prime Minister Robert Peel's final push for the repeal.

Similarly, Kitson Clark devotes an entire chapter to the "Increase in Population" that was the demographic precursor to both the social and political revolution in England during the nineteenth century and, of course, the Great Hunger. Yet he devoted only parts of two pages to the Great Hunger itself, which he summarized as follows:

> In the autumn of 1845, and in 1846 and 1847, the potatoes which had made the increase in population in Ireland possible had been stricken by disease. When they were dug from the pits they proved to be black, rotten and inedible. It is calculated in these years about a million of the Irish died and about a million fled overseas. (G. Kitson Clark 75)

To be fair to Kitson Clark, he does spend several paragraphs before and after the above quotation assigning "moral guilt" to the English for the "horrible tragedy" of the Great Hunger. He excoriates the English for severely damaging the Irish economy during the prior century, for imposing on the Irish absentee English landlords who drained Ireland's resources and cared little for the land and less for their tenants, and for the shoddy relief efforts of the British government under Lord John Russell. In the end, however, he does fall back on a kind of Malthusian logic that when food is abundant, populations will necessarily grow until starvation becomes inevitable. All this takes place in the space of no more than a few hundred words.

That such an eminent historian could write a book on Victorian England yet almost entirely skirt the issue of the Famine goes a long way toward explaining, though not excusing, my own relative ignorance of the issue. This is not to say that a body of historical work on the Famine, both popular and scholarly, did not exist. But even in Ireland the Famine was not much discussed prior to the late 1990s, for reasons that psychologist Deborah Peck illuminates later in this

volume. Certainly there was relatively little public awareness of the
Great Hunger in the United States beyond a passing familiarity with the
fact that an "Irish Potato Famine" had taken place and had brought a
large number of Irish men and women to America as immigrants.

Both the relative neglect of the Great Hunger by professional
historians and the relative public ignorance of the event began to
change in 1995, the one hundred fiftieth anniversary of the beginning
of the Great Hunger. At that time, a groundswell of commemorative
efforts arose in Ireland, the United States, and Canada. By 1997, there
was an outpouring of books, articles, lectures, and commemorative
sites. The article that John Lahey gave me to review was just one of the
more visible efforts. I gave him my comments and suggestions based
on my rapid survey of the historical scholarship on the Great Hunger.
Not surprisingly, we differed on some points of interpretation, but he
took my comments in good spirit and produced a strong essay that was
published in Britain in the Guardian newspaper's *The Observer* during
December of 1996. After that, I didn't expect to have much contact
with issues of the Great Hunger, although I did include it as an
important and tragic part of my modern European history classes.

John Lahey's involvement with the Great Hunger did not end with
his duties as grand marshal of the parade, however, and eventually I
was also drawn back to Ireland and the Great Hunger even more
deeply. By 1997, Quinnipiac had undertaken a major capital campaign
to support a complete reconstruction of its library. As the campaign
progressed, Dr. Lahey became involved in a conversation about the
Great Hunger with Murray Lender, a Quinnipiac graduate and one of
its longstanding benefactors. When Dr. Lahey described his activities to
promote awareness of the Great Hunger as part of his position with the
St. Patrick's Day Parade, Lender realized that he did not know much
about Ireland during the Famine, and that he knew even less about the
Famine's causes and consequences. Lender decided to find a way to
better educate people about the Famine. Thus was born the Lender
Family Special Collection Room dedicated to *An Gorta Mor* (the Great
Hunger)—a Gaelic designation for the catastrophe experienced by the
Irish people during the late 1840s. Lender promised to fund the creation
of an educational site in the newly reconstructed Arnold Bernhard
Library, dedicated to raising awareness of the Famine.

In the fall of 1999, just after plans for the new library were
announced, I got another call from Dr. Lahey's office requesting that I
meet the president to discuss the Great Hunger. This time I felt much
better prepared to fulfill my role as a historical consultant. Dr. Lahey
revealed to me the plans for the Great Hunger Room in the new library
and asked my opinion on how to promote it as both an educational and

scholarly resource. We concluded that the best approach would be to hold a series of academic conferences that might also draw interested members of the public, and to publish the papers that resulted from the conferences in edited volumes. This book is the result of the first conference, which was held in September 2000. Held in conjunction with the ceremony dedicating the Great Hunger Room, the conference, titled "Ireland's Great Hunger: An Interdisciplinary Assessment," drew scholars from North America and Europe to Quinnipiac for a full day of discussion.

The breadth and quality of the papers presented at the conference are represented in this volume, grouped thematically into three parts. The first, "Silence," takes as its point of departure the ways in which the Great Hunger created silences, both at the time of the Famine and in the subsequent historical memory of the Irish people and, to some extent, within the historical profession. The second section, "Memory," addresses the lasting impact of the Famine on the lives and work of the generation that lived through it and those who came after, both in Ireland and among the Irish diaspora. The final section, "Commemoration," focuses on how the Famine has become a locus of attention during the past decade in the popular memory, particularly through various efforts to remember it and to integrate it into educational curricula.

The first section considers varies ways in which the Famine created silences, both through death itself and by way of the imaginative and psychological impact of those deaths. Edward McCarron in "Famine Lifelines" tries to make audible one of the most glaring silences that lingers in the wake of the Famine: the experience of the Irish cottier and landless laborers who suffered the greatest during the Hunger. His chapter recaptures some of their experiences and concerns through an examination of a rare archival collection of letters written before and during the Famine by James Prendergast of County Kerry. In "The 'Unborn and Unburied Dead,'" Robert A. Smart and Michael R. Hutchenson consider the rhetorical and imaginative possibilities created by another silence, that of the Famine dead. Their chapter leads us to reflect on the horror of the Famine for those who did and did not survive it, as well as on the literary possibilities the experience of the Famine created. In Mary Ann Matthews' chapter, "Irish Immigrants and African Americans," we see yet another area where the Famine led to a silence, in this case concerning the close relationships and tangled histories of Irish and Africans transplanted in the United States. Mary Lee Dunn, in her fine-grained analysis of the Famine experience of Kilglass Parish in County Roscommon, sheds further light on the local variations of the Famine experience across regions of Ireland, which have been largely muted by the overwhelming scope of the Famine. Her chapter not only details the experience of one group of families, but it also provides an agenda for researching parallel cases across the rest of the Irish countryside. Rached Khalifa explores another type of silence in his chapter on William Butler Yeats: the ways in which Yeats's failure to represent the Famine in his poetry represents a "strange occlusion." As Khalifa argues, however, this absence in Yeats's poetry is all the more telling about the nature of the Famine in the Irish literary and historical memory. Deborah Peck also addresses memory and silence in her psychological exploration of the enduring impact of the Famine on the psyche of the Irish people, both in Ireland and among the diaspora. For her, the Famine became a "silent hunger" as successive generations of Irish repressed the memory of their ancestors' experiences during the Famine, often with serious psychological consequences.

The second section looks at the degree to which the Irish remember the Famine and the impact of these memories and experiences. Thomas O'Grady opens this section with an analysis of the works of the contemporary Irish poet Seamus Heaney. His chapter forms an interesting counterpart to Khalifa's chapter on Yeats, as O'Grady uses Heaney's commentary on Yeats as his starting point for a consideration of Heaney's explicit efforts to discuss the Famine experience in his poetry. In "Easing Integration," historian David T. Gleeson considers aspects of the "psychological legacy" that the Famine created in the memories of Irish immigrants in the southern United States and how this legacy ultimately aided in easing the integration of the Irish in the antebellum South. Through an examination of the work of recent Irish playwrights, Jerome Joseph Day also explores how recent generations of Irish have begun to place more emphasis on remembering the Famine and its impact. Combining historical analysis with critical theory, Day explores the ways that the Famine has become an increasingly important cultural resource for contemporary Irish writers. William B. Rogers, through an examination of the controversy over the Famine as a case of genocide, looks at another aspect of how historical memory shapes and is shaped by contemporary issues. Using a case study based on students in a graduate seminar class on the Great Hunger, Rogers explores how perceptions of the Famine, and of more recent genocides, produced a contentious dialogue concerning whether or not the Great Hunger was an act of genocide. Finally, this section closes with a historical and personal study of the memory of the Famine in the life of a Famine survivor, Margaret Maher. By examining Maggie's extraordinary relationship with the great American poet Emily Dickinson, Connie Ann Kirk exposes the importance of the

Famine experience not only in two women's lives but also in the whole literary history of the United States.

The final section of the book addresses the important issue of the commemoration of the Famine both in the public memory, and in educational establishments. Over the past decade, the need to remember, to discuss, and to memorialize the Famine has achieved unprecedented levels. The section opens with a series of interrelated papers concerning the Irish Famine memorial recently established at Grosse Île in Quebec, Canada. The site of arrival, quarantine, and ultimately death for many thousands of Irish during the depths of the Famine, Grosse Île has become a tangle of historical, political, and artistic controversy. In her chapter on visual silences and visual dialogues, Kathleen O'Brien explores the varied dimensions of this tangle through an examination of the history of Famine commemorations at Grosse Île and a critical analysis of the process of commemoration itself. Sylvie Gauthier's chapter on Le Mémorial, the most recently created memorial on Grosse Île, compares the maneuverings involved in the creation of this memorial with the one completed in 1909 by the Ancient Order of Hibernians and concludes with a surprisingly personal, yet in many ways representative, connection to the site. Lorrie Blair, finally, undertakes an analysis of the "official" commemorative site created by the Canadian government. Her work explores the sometimes unintended messages that are conveyed in the establishment of government-sponsored commemorative sites and the way that mixed and often confused messages that visitors thus receive represents a tragic lost opportunity to create real understanding and dialogue.

The second part of "Commemoration" addresses the important issue of Famine education. The collaborative chapter by Karen Manners Smith, Holly Gillogly, and Jim Riordan discusses the innovative teaching methods used by Manners Smith and her graduate assistants in a course on Irish history. By urging their students to "relive" the Famine through imaginatively reconstructing the lives of those who lived at the time, Manners Smith not only provides her students with a valuable history lesson, but also gives them a real sense of the lives of Famine victims and survivors. The second collaborative chapter in this section, that by Maureen Murphy, Maureen McCann Militta, and Alan Singer, provides critical insights into one of the most significant developments to come out of the recent round of Famine commemorations: the decision to include the Famine in the teaching curriculums of several northeastern states, including New York, New Jersey, and Connecticut. These chapters make a convincing case not only for the importance of studying the Great Hunger itself, but also for understanding the multifaceted complexities of our shared past and the ongoing impact that the past has on the present.

The varied and fascinating chapters in this volume shed new light both on the experience of the Famine and on its impact on subsequent generations in Ireland and in North America. This collection reminds us that the Great Hunger is an episode that cannot be relegated to the past. The great human tragedy that occurred in nineteenth-century Ireland, and the issues both that created it and that it created, are very much alive today. Our understanding of ourselves, and of our world, is richer for our deepening understanding of the Great Hunger. To the degree that this volume contributes to that enterprise, it enriches us all.

Acknowledgments

In the production of a group project such as we have incurred many debts. Our greatest thanks go to the Lender Family, whose generosity and vision made the Quinnipiac University Great Hunger collection a reality. John L. Lahey, President of Quinnipiac University, has exhibited tremendous leadership both in creating the Great Hunger collection at Quinnipiac and in raising public awareness of the tragedy in Ireland during the 1840s. Many people at Quinnipiac made the Great Hunger Conference in the Fall of 2000 a success. Among them were Lynn Bushnell, Jean Husted, David Stineback, Betsy Delaney, Nicole Ellis, Kathy Cooke, Thea Mortiz, and Robin Utley. Thanks are also in order to the staff of Cheney and Company in New Haven for helping to create the artwork that graced both the promotional material for the conference and the cover of this book. Janet Reed undertook the heroic task of trying to unify the style, citations, and bibliography of various authors across two continents and various disciplinary traditions. Alan Bisbort gave the manuscript a final reading to smooth out many remaining peccadilloes.

The authors of the individual chapters in this volume also deserve thanks. Each of them persevered though the barrages of email and stacks of paperwork that were thrown at them as they drafted, revised, and finalized their essays. We are also grateful to Diane Lavery and Beverly Baum at University Press of America for helping to guide the book through the editorial and production process.

Thanks to Four Courts Press for quotation from Michael Huggins' work "A Secret Ireland: Agrarian Conflict in pre-Famine Roscommon," winner of the Four Courts Press J.C. Beckett Prize in Modern History, 2000. *Social Conflict in pre-Famine Roscommon*, a revised version of Huggin's work, will be published by Four Courts Press in September 2002.

Excerpts reprinted by permission of the publishers from *The Letters of Emily Dickinson* edited by Thomas H. Johnson, Cambridge, Mass.: The Belknap Press of Harvard University Press, Copyright © 1958, 1986 by the President and Fellows of Harvard College.

Quotations from Jay Leyda, *The Years and Hours of Emily Dickinson* reprinted by permission of Yale University Press.

Quotations from Aife Murray, "Miss Margaret's Emily Dickinson," *Signs* 24:3 (Spring 1999) reprinted by permission of the University of Chicago Press.

Portions of the chapter by Maureen Murphy, Maureen McCann Miletta, and Alan Singer were previously published by Alan Singer and Maureen Murphy as "Asking the Big Questions: Teaching about the Great Irish Famine and World History " in the September 2001 edition of *Social Education* and are reprinted by permission of the National Council for Social Studies.

Introduction

"The Famine Killed Everything": Living with the Memory of the Great Hunger

CHRISTINE KINEALY

Thainig blianta an ghorta agus an droch shaoghal agus an t-ocra agus bhris sin neart agus spiorad na ndaoini. Ní rabh ann ach achan nduinne ag iarraidh bheith beo. Chaill siad a' dáimh le chéile. Ba chuma cé a bhi gaoolmhar duit, ba do charais an t-é a bhéarfadh greim duit le chur in do bhéal. D'imthigh an spórt agus a' caitheamh aimsire. Stad an fhilidheacht agus a'ceol agus damhsa. Chaill siad agus rinne siad dearmad den iomlan agus nuair a bhisigh an saoghal ar dhóigheannái eile ní tháinig na rudaí seo ariamh arais mar a bhí siad. Mharbh an gorta achan rud.

Máire Ni Grianna, A famine survivor, from the Rosses,
County Donegal. (qtd. in Deane 203–4)

(The years of the famine, of the bad life and the hunger, arrived and broke the spirit and strength of the community. People simply wanted to survive. Their spirit of comradeship was lost. It didn't matter what ties or relations you had; you considered that person to be your friend who gave you food to put in your mouth. Recreation and leisure ceased. Poetry, music and dancing died. These things were lost and completely forgotten. When life improved in other ways, these pursuits never returned as they had been. The famine killed everything.) (trans. in Deane 204)

The Great Hunger was one of most lethal famines in modern history, accounting for a loss of 25 percent of the population in Ireland over a period of six years. Emigration accounted for approximately half of the decrease; once the Famine floodgates had been opened, the hemorrhage continued, and even by European standards the level remained remarkable. This was even more unusual perhaps given that by the mid-nineteenth century, famine had disappeared from Europe and, since 1801, Ireland had been part of the affluent United Kingdom. For the survivors who remained in Ireland or sought refuge overseas, the years of deprivation had taken a toll, and both their health and their expected lifespans were curtailed. The long-term demographic changes also made Ireland unique as the population never recovered from the disaster; it did not start to increase until the 1960s and then only slowly. In the late 1990s the growth accelerated, largely driven by economic factors. Nonetheless, at the beginning of the twenty-first century, Ireland remains singular in Europe in having a smaller population than it had in 1845.

As a consequence of the Famine, Irish society also changed in a number of ways: in the post-Famine decades many landlords disappeared or went into terminal decay; agriculture moved from tillage to pasture; the use of Irish language declined; emigration became even more embedded in the life cycle; the main churches grew stronger and more organized, and political allegiances increasingly split along both religious and geographic lines. Additionally, the survivors of the Great Hunger, both in Ireland and elsewhere, had changed in ways that were intangible and not easy to quantify or define. The Famine had helped to shape the identity of Irish people and that of their descendants throughout the world. Yet, despite people having an awareness of the Great Hunger, to a large extent the Famine remained hidden, unexplored, and unknown. No monuments existed and little had been written about it. The one million people who had died during the tragedy remained invisible and nameless; few graves had survived and the government had not kept records of death during the Famine. Furthermore, those who had attempted to forge a collective memory of the Famine were accused of being simplistic or politically motivated. These points are illustrated by Nell McCafferty's personal Famine recollection titled "Whatever You Say, Say Nothing" (in Hayden 160– 64). This title is, in turn, based on a poem of the same name by Seamus Heaney, which says:

O land of password, handgrip, wink and nod
Of open minds as open as a trap . . .
(Seamus Heaney, "Whatever You Say, Say Nothing")

Consequently, the impetus to remember was often strongest outside Ireland. Why did an event that, even by nineteenth-century standards, was cataclysmic in its impact and that had cast a long shadow over the Irish people, remain concealed for such a long time?

I. "Dehydrated History": Revisionism and the Great Hunger

Until the 1990s the history and memory of the Great Hunger had not been well served by Irish historians who had either ignored or marginalized it. Moreover, the Great Hunger was rarely taught in either schools or universities, and it did not appear as a topic of research in either learned journals or academic monographs. Before 1994, only two substantial publications were available: the sanitized and uneven *The Irish Famine* edited by R. D. Edwards and T. D. Williams, which had been commissioned by the then Taoiseach, Eamon de Valera—and which appeared eleven years after schedule and even in the words of the editors was "disappointing"; and the vibrant, thoroughly researched, but academically panned, *The Great Hunger* by Cecil Woodham-Smith. Also, despite having little basis in research, a number of orthodoxies had emerged regarding the reasons for, and the impact of, the Great Hunger. The revisionist interpretation, in varying degrees, suggested that the Famine was inevitable, that it was not a watershed in the development of modern Ireland; it also played down the relevance of Ireland's colonial relationship with Britain and argued that the British government did all it could to provide relief, in the context of the time.

These orthodoxies conformed to the dominant approach in Irish history known generically as revisionism. Since the 1930s, revisionists had been successfully rewriting the nationalist interpretations of history, which they viewed as simplistic and politically influenced. This was evinced by the absence of Famine research in the pages of the authoritative *Irish Historical Studies,* which had been founded in 1938. Its first authors, Theodore Moody and Robert Dudley Edwards, set the tone for subsequent decades in challenging what they regarded as received myths about Irish history and about Britain's relationship with Ireland. A main target of these historical revisions was the nationalist myths concerning the history of Ireland. James Donnelly has suggested that their anti-nationalism also may have been shaped by the fact that many of this generation of scholars were educated in British universities (*Great Irish Potato Famine* 12). These scholars, and those sympathetic to this view, also influenced the teaching of history in Irish universities, notably in Trinity College and University College, Dublin, where Moody and Dudley Edwards continued to teach up to the 1970s. Consequently, subsequent generations of Irish scholars who received their graduate training in Irish universities had been nurtured within the revisionist environment. Moreover, whereas historical debate in universities in Britain and elsewhere after the 1960s had been enriched by developments in the women's movement, Marxism, post-colonial studies, and so on, within Ireland revisionism not only remained in ascendancy but also had been invigorated by political developments in the north of Ireland.

Following the outbreak of the conflict in the six counties of Northern Ireland after 1969, politics and history became even more ideologically charged as the battle for hearts and minds took on a new significance. The most gifted champion of "new" revisionism was Roy Foster whose ideas found an outlet in the bestselling *Modern Ireland, 1600–1972.* This publication instantly became, in the words of the political commentator, Tim Pat Coogan, "the bible of revisionists" (qtd. in Hayden 167). In it, Foster defended the response of the British government throughout the Famine. He also averred that the Famine was not a significant turning point in Irish history, arguing:

> Traditionally historians used to interpret the effects of the Famine as equally cataclysmic: it was seen as a watershed in Irish history creating new conditions of demographic decline, large scale emigration, altered farming structures and new economic policies, not to mention an institutionalized anglophobia amongst the Irish at home and abroad. As a literal analysis, this does not stand up, at least insofar as economic consequences are concerned. . . . *If there is a watershed year in Irish social and economic history it is not 1846, but 1815,* with the agricultural disruption following the end of the French wars. (Foster, *Modern Ireland* 318, emphasis added)

The Famine's place in Ireland's social and economic development was of less significance, therefore, than the ending of the Napoleonic Wars. Moreover, by describing the Famine as a "Malthusian apocalypse" he suggested that overpopulation was the real cause of the Famine. Malthus himself, however, did not view Ireland as being on the brink of demographic disaster. Furthermore, Foster conveniently ignored the fact that the most densely populated county in Ireland was County Armagh, in the northeast of the country (an area that he describes as having "escaped lightly"). The ascendancy of the revisionist interpretation was also evident in Foster's provocative but self-reverential article "We Are All Revisionists Now," in which he described Woodham-Smith as a "zealous convert" (*Irish Review* 1986: 1–6). Only a few years later, however, Foster admitted that the nonrevisionist view had some support. In an interview published in *History Ireland* in 1993, he expounded on the motives of those who opposed revisionism, saying, "I think that there is very often an agenda behind this so-called anti-revisionism" (9-12). Revisionism, in contrast, claimed to have no agenda but to be objective, scientific, and value-free in its approach.

The stranglehold that revisionism had on history departments within Irish universities, and their supporters in the media, made proponents of revisionism virtually unassailable. Moreover, those who challenged the revisionist orthodoxies were likely to be branded as nationalists or republican sympathizers, which after 1969 was politically unacceptable in Ireland and Britain. Consequently, revisionism also imposed a form of unspoken censorship on its critics (Waters). An uncompromising critic of revisionism, however, was Brendan Bradshaw, an Irish academic based at Cambridge University. In 1989, in an article on "Nationalism and Historical Scholarship in Modern Ireland," he accused revisionists of avoiding writing on the cataclysmic episodes in Ireland's history, using the Famine as an illustration because it demonstrated "more tellingly than any other episode of Irish history the inability of practitioners of value-free history to cope with the catastrophic dimensions of the Irish past" (34–41). Bradshaw singled out Mary Daly, who had published a small overview of the Famine in 1986, for having failed to engage with the unpalatable reality of the catastrophe "by assuming an austerely clinical tone, and by resorting to sociological euphemism and cliometric excursi, thus cerebralising and thereby de-sensitizing the trauma" (34–41). Bradshaw's attacks on revisionism, in turn, resulted in his being castigated (both personally and professionally) by some fellow academics (Brady 246–52, 306–26).

The imprint of revisionism was indeed particularly evident in interpretations about the Famine, which were cautious, partial, and averse to engaging with the obscenity of more than a million people dying of hunger in the center of the richest empire in the world. Regardless of the significance of the Famine in the development of modern Ireland—and arguably, the subsequent development of Britain, Australia, and the United States—little had been written about it. The idea for a substantial study of the Great Hunger to mark its centenary in 1945 did not originate with Irish academics but was the brainchild of the then Taoiseach, Eamon de Valera. Despite his providing a subvention to two Dublin historians to produce a comprehensive narrative of the Famine, the end result was a collection of essays of uneven quality that took so long to produce (almost twelve years) that the centenary anniversary had passed. Furthermore the overall approach of the writers was so delicate that they conveyed little sense of loss, devastation, or trauma. The Introduction (which was ghost-written by a junior historian) set the tone for the overall placatory nature of much of the volume, especially in relationship to the role of the British government (Ó Gráda, "Making History" 87–97). It reproached folk memory for interpreting "the failure of the British government in a sinister light," explaining that "[t]he scale of the actual outlay to meet the Famine and the expansion in the public-relief system are in themselves impressive evidence that the state was by no means always indifferent to Irish needs" (Edwards and Williams xi). More damagingly perhaps, from the outset it was decided that the thorny issue of mortality should be sidestepped, although they admitted that "many, many had died" (Edwards and Williams xi). By avoiding the issues of mortality and culpability, controversy was averted. However, intellectual honesty also had been compromised. De Valera, who had commissioned the publication, was also disappointed, preferring the more robust approach of Woodham-Smith, while one of its editors described it privately as "dehydrated history" (Edwards in Ó Gráda, "Making History" 87–107; for debate on the historiography of the Famine, see also Kinealy, *Death-Dealing Famine* 1–15).

The Great Hunger by Cecil Woodham-Smith first appeared in 1962. The book became a bestseller, and it informed a generation of people about the tragedy. It also engaged directly with the thorny issues of the devastation caused by the Famine and the culpability of Irish landlords and the British administration. However, *The Great Hunger* did not receive academic acceptance within Ireland, even being described pejoratively as a "great novel" in an undergraduate exam in Dublin. Woodham-Smith was also savaged in a feral review by the Dublin historian F. S. L. Lyons (who subsequently became Provost of Trinity College in Dublin) who accused her of, *inter alia,* providing inadequate context and oversimplistic explanation. However, some of the criticisms made against her interpretations by Lyons could have also been directed at the Edwards and Williams volume. Lyons also chastised her for vilifying Trevelyan and exaggerating his importance in relief provision (Lyons 78–79). Ó Gráda has characterized the response of Irish academic historians to *The Great Hunger* as one of "indignant ridicule" (Ó Gráda, *Great Irish Famine* 10–11). The condescending approach to Woodham-Smith was also perhaps due to the fact that she was neither a professional historian nor Irish. In addition, she was a woman who had inadvertently exposed the deficiencies of some (male) professionals. Although her book was not well-received by the academic establishment in Ireland, reviews from scholars elsewhere were more positive, some even ascribing to the British government intentions not claimed by Woodham-Smith. For example, the English historian A. J. P. Taylor, a respected scholar of modern Germany, asserted that "all Ireland was a Belsen" (74). Despite being denounced or ignored by Irish historians, *The Great Hunger* sold massively and was reprinted frequently, making it one of the bestselling history books of all time. In addition to the dislike of Woodham-Smith's interpretations, less cerebral considerations may have been at work: Donnelly has suggested that "[t]hese academic historians no doubt envied the book's commercial success" (qtd. in Hayden 119).

The publication of *The Great Hunger* marked an end, rather than a beginning, to Famine research. The book had exposed the split between academic orthodoxy based on revisionism and popular memory, but no Irish historian seemed willing to provide either an explanation for, or bridge over, the gulf. However, the publication of the influential *Irish Agricultural Production: Its Volume and Structure* by Raymond Crotty in 1966 played down the significance of the Famine as an event of consequence in the development of the modern Irish economy. Crotty influenced the writing of a generation of Irish economic historians who gave little importance to the Famine in Ireland's development.

By the 1990s the domination of revisionism appeared unassailable, and it had enjoyed "a triumphal march, slaying one dragon of nationalist historiography after another" (Donnelly, qtd. in Hayden 117). Its advancement had been helped by the support of a number of powerful media figures in Ireland and Britain including Ruth Dudley Edwards, Kevin Myers, Conor Cruise O'Brien, and Eoghan Harris. The stranglehold of revisionism acted as a form of invisible censor, especially since to challenge the canon could be suicide for aspiring historians. Debate was therefore stifled, and those who questioned or disagreed with revisionism were denounced as nationalists or republican sympathizers (Waters). Not surprisingly, therefore, some of the most sustained and dynamic challenges to revisionism came from outside Ireland or from academics outside the discipline of history—led by James Donnelly, Terry Eagleton, Christine Kinealy, Joel Mokyr, and Cormac Ó Gráda.

But revisionist history had not convinced the wider public, and a gulf existed between popular and academic memory of the Famine. The approach of the 150th anniversary of the onset of the potato blight demonstrated a latent interest in the Famine that was both unexpected and unprecedented. Moreover, the Republic of Ireland was undergoing an economic boom and cultural renaissance (typified by the *Riverdance* euphoria) while in 1994 the IRA and the Protestant paramilitaries had declared a cease-fire. Official recognition was also given by the establishment of a government Famine Committee in 1994 with money available for promoting commemorative events.

The sesquicentenary also resulted in a wave of publications, many of which were not afraid to engage with the awfulness of the tragedy. Local studies also demonstrated the impact of the Great Hunger on communities, families, and individuals—adding a human dimension that had sometimes been lost when mortality had been reduced to a rounded-up statistic. A number of historians associated with revisionism also repositioned themselves: Mary Daly, in a preamble to a public lecture on the Famine in 1995, explained, "Now that we are in a cease-fire situation, we can talk about aspects of history which we may previously have felt uncomfortable with" (qtd. in MacAtasney xv). The challenge to revisionism, however, ignited an ideological conflict that tended to be most vitriolic among non-historians who were avowedly anti-nationalist. For example, Eoghan Harris, a political spin-doctor, journalist, and vehement opponent of republicanism, claimed during a televised discussion that because the IRA had lost the military war, they were using the Famine as propaganda to incite anti-British feeling in Ireland (*Davis Show*, RTE, February 1995). Similar accusations were made by Conor Cruise O'Brien on a British news program in June 1995 (*Newsnight*, BBC2, June 1995). In 1995, however, the journalist John Waters argued that as a consequence of the cease-fire, the political situation in Ireland had changed dramatically and that the revisionist argument could not be sustained in the new political context. His comments, together with those of Mary Daly, highlight that much revisionist writing was, in fact, underpinned by a political agenda. Waters also warned, however, that the "increasingly vicious attacks on those who advance alternative viewpoints demonstrate a kind of menopausal fear of their own impending obsolescence."

The peak of Famine publishing occurred between 1994 and 1997. More books were produced in those three years than in the previous 150 years. Significantly, the vast majority of these publications favored an interpretation that was closer to the traditional nationalist version than to the revisionist one. After 1997, however, "Famine-fatigue" had allegedly set in, and publishers believed that the marketplace was saturated with publications on the topic. Despite this commercial curfew some substantial Famine books did appear, by historians whose interest predated (and post-dated) the anniversary period, notably Ó Gráda's *Black '47 and Beyond* (1999), and Donnelly and Kinealy's *The Great Irish Potato Famine* (2001) and *The Great Irish Famine. Impact, Ideology, and Rebellion* (2002). These books contain fresh perspectives on the Great Hunger and each demonstrated that much remains unknown about the Famine and there still is a great deal to be explored or said.

II. An Official Memory?

The memory and commemoration of the Great Hunger makes it unique—perhaps no other single famine has received international recognition both at the time and 150 years after the catastrophe. A further remarkable feature is that even after the immediate experience of suffering had disappeared from Ireland and, more significantly, had been "written down" by Irish historians, the sesquicentenary triggered a response that was unparalleled in the history of the state and that had repercussions beyond Ireland. The hundredth anniversary of the Hunger had received little public attention from the state (despite de Valera's personal interest), while the fiftieth anniversary of the 1916 uprising had been largely ignored.

As the sesquicentenary approached it was unclear whether the government in the Republic would commemorate it and, if so, what form those commemorations would take. In May 1994, an inter-departmental committee chaired by Tom Kitt was established. When the government fell the committee remained, although Avril Doyle replaced Kitt at the beginning of 1995. In the wake of Doyle's appointment (and no doubt encouraged by the cease-fire), the scale and scope of the committee increased, and in June 1995, the Famine Commemoration Committee was officially launched, with Doyle as Chairperson. At the inauguration she announced, "The Irish government wholeheartedly shoulders its responsibilities in acknowledging the importance of the Famine, which so signally marked us as a people, which vastly expanded our diaspora, and in which modern Ireland itself was born." She described the program as "wide, varied, with heavy emphasis on education, on scholarships and famine relief projects in the modern world." Doyle also gave official endorsement to the notion that remembering could bring pain relief, stating that "For our own sakes we need the catharsis of a commemoration which fully recognizes the pain and loss the Famine represented. I am confident that the Government's Program of Commemoration will make a significant contribution to that process." The time scale for the catharsis, however, was limited as the official Famine commemorations were to end in 1997.

The Famine Committee had a budget of £250,000 (Irish) out of which £115,000 was made available to four historians to oversee new areas of research. The historians—all of whom were based in Dublin universities—were Mary Daly, David Dickson, David Fitzpatrick, and Cormac Ó Gráda (*Irish Times,* 3 March 1995). Only Ó Gráda had previously undertaken substantial research on the Famine and could be regarded as a nonrevisionist. To date, this group has not collectively published the results of the research project. Funding was also made available by the Committee for a television documentary on the Famine, and a number of local and national projects were financed, including a commemorative "Famine Suite" and the erection of a number of Famine monuments. A number of charitable organizations had hoped that a substantial part of the government budget would be set aside for overseas aid, especially Famine prevention programs. But the committee decided that overseas aid was not a priority (*Church of Ireland Gazette,* 13 January 1995; *Irish Times,* 3 March 1995). Avril Doyle also took her Famine message further afield as she, accompanied by a small group of historians, lectured on the Hunger in a number of selected venues in North America and Australia. The place of Northern Ireland within the "national" commemorations was more difficult. At the outset the Famine Committee recognized that the Famine was "an all-Ireland tragedy," and the first official ceremony took place in August in County Fermanagh, where blight had first been observed 150 years earlier. Following this event, however, the program relocated to the Republic, with little sensitivity shown to the memories of either nationalists or unionists in the north.

From the outset of the commemorations, the link between historical memory and current politics was evident. At the launch of the committee in 1995, Doyle asserted that "the Peace Process allows us all the more freely to explore the truth." The fact that a cease-fire had been declared by republican and loyalist para-militaries in 1994 was clearly significant, but the statement suggests that if there had been no cease-fire or Peace Process the "truth" would not have been explored fully. The Peace Talks also demonstrated that "[t]he relations between the two islands have now reached a maturity which allows us to look at our history objectively and to tell the story how it was. . . . After all, the Famine was not just an Irish event, it was just as much a British event, a shared experience" (launch speech by Doyle). Doyle's description of the Famine as a "shared experience" not only denied the uneven political relationship between Britain and Ireland, but also neutralized the unparalleled suffering of the Irish people during those years.

At the launch of the Famine Committee it was decided that the government's program would end in the summer of 1997, thus allowing a few months' gap before a new program of official commemorations for the 1798 uprising could begin. It was intended that the final Famine ceremony would be a National Service of Commemoration, which was to be attended by church leaders of the main denominations (launch speech by Doyle). However, by 1997, commercialization and tourism had overtaken the spiritual aspects of the commemoration, and it was decided that a "Great Irish Famine Event" should mark the closure of the official program. The event took place in Millstreet in County Cork. It was marketed widely in North America, but a number of Irish-Americans condemned the fact that the memory of the Famine was being honored with music and alcohol (*American Irish Newsletter* 1–4). During the course of the weekend event, various messages of condolence and commiseration were read, including a quasi-apology from British Prime Minister Tony Blair and a letter of sympathy from United States President Bill Clinton. Its overall celebratory tone led Joe Murray of the relief agency Afri to describe the event as "dancing on the graves of the dead." It marked an inglorious end to an intense period of remembrance and reflection. The premature ending to the commemoration also replicated the actions of the British government 150 years earlier when it declared the Famine to be over in 1847. On both occasions the date was chosen due to a combination of financial self-interest and political expediency.

At the time of the Famine, Ireland had been part of the United Kingdom and governed by a parliament in Westminster, so how did Britain fit into a process of commemoration? At an individual level, many Irish communities in Britain organized lectures and commemorative services, but appeals for government involvement or funding were turned down. At the commencement of the commemorations a number of calls were made for the British government—or occasionally Prince Charles—to apologize for the Famine, including one from the leader of the Opposition in Ireland, Bertie Ahern (*Irish Independent,* 7 June 1997). However, an open apology appeared unlikely. In 1995, a Conservative government led by John Major had been in power and it had distanced itself from local Famine events in Britain, refusing, for example, to give financial support to a Great Hunger monument to be erected in Liverpool (*Liverpool Daily Post,* 20 December 1997). During the Conservative Party's final period in office, their majority was so reduced that, in effect, a handful of Unionist MPs held the balance of power. The election of a Labor government in 1997, however, marked a new phase in Anglo-Irish relations, with Labor being less ideologically constrained and in possession of a large parliamentary majority. From the outset, Tony Blair had declared that Northern Ireland was a political priority. Blair used the opportunity provided by the final Famine event in Millstreet to issue a statement admitting that "[t]hose who governed in London at the time failed their people through standing by while a crop failure turned into a massive human tragedy." While the statement did not include the word *apology*, it clearly amounted to one. It was also the most unequivocal public admission of British government culpability ever made. He also acknowledged the long-term legacy of the Famine by saying, "It has left deep scars" (Blair 212). Unionists and revisionists hated Blair's statement, especially since they viewed it as a way of wooing Irish nationalists. Some members of the British press also condemned it. The *Daily Telegraph* accused Blair of giving succor to "the self-pitying nature of Irish nationalism" and "the grievance culture which allows nationalist Ireland to place the blame for all the country's ills at the door of the Brits, ultimately justifying terrorism" (qtd. in *Irish Times,* 5 June 1997). Even the moderate *Belfast News Letter* warned that Blair's "implicit apology" would "hardly remove the strength of feeling in nationalist Ireland" (Editorial, 3 June 1997). Blair's apology had exposed the fact that despite two years of concentrated remembrance, for some the Famine was not regarded as a national tragedy but rather as a nationalist grievance.

Inevitably, there were controversies and some of the most acrimonious ones took place outside Ireland, especially in the United States where sections of the diaspora were less ideologically constricted than people in Ireland or Britain when debating the Famine. Although Avril Doyle took a "Famine roadshow" to a number of selected venues in North America, many Irish Americans palpably wanted to extend the commemoration beyond the state-sanctioned limits of the Famine Committee. In 1995, for example, a Genocide Committee had been established in New York, and a number of reputable academics, church leaders, and business people signed their petition. Moreover, college students in the United States were encouraged to think creatively about the issue of genocide, even if few students ultimately agreed with this interpretation. Such a teaching strategy seemed improbable in Ireland. Refusal to engage with such issues, however, begs the question, Who decides what are the parameters of historical debate? Unfortunately, some advocates of the genocide theory demonstrated a similar zealotry and aversion to debate as had a number of revisionists. This attitude led James Donnelly—one of the first historians to challenge revisionism—to lament that:

> a scholar who seeks to rebut or heavily qualify the nationalist charge of
> genocide is often capable of stirring furious controversy and runs the risk

of being labeled an apologist for the British government's horribly misguided policies during the famine. (*Great Irish Potato Famine* 209)

The importance of the Famine—both as a human rights issue and as an event that had helped to shape modern America—was also recognized with the incorporation of a schools Famine curriculum by various state legislatures. New Jersey was the first state to pass a Famine curriculum and this was achieved with the support of many non-Irish educationalists. Its introduction provoked criticism in the British press, led by the conservative *Sunday Telegraph,* which described the Famine curriculum as "the work of hard-line Irish-American nationalists" (11 February 1996). The attempt to introduce a Famine curriculum into New York State proved to be even more controversial and demonstrated how contemporary Irish politics was restraining debate on Irish history. Again, support for the New York curriculum cut across racial divisions, with the American-Cuban Congressman who introduced it explaining that "[t]he Irish Famine teaches an important lesson about intolerance and inhumanity and the indifference of the British government to the potato blight that led to the mass starvation of one million people" (*Sunday Times,* Dublin ed., 16 October 1996). The conservative press condemned the legislation, with a number suggesting (incorrectly) that its supporters had likened the Famine to the Holocaust (*Wall Street Journal,* 10 November 1997). In Britain, John Major's Conservative Party responded swiftly and emphatically. The British Ambassador in the United States was recalled from leave. He registered an official protest with Governor George Pataki and asked that the curriculum should not be allowed to proceed further, arguing that "[u]nlike the Holocaust, the famine was not deliberate, not premeditated, not manmade, not genocide." Interestingly, the *New York Daily News,* which had opposed the introduction of the curriculum, nevertheless argued that "[e]ven after 150 years, the British still obviously fear the facts" (26 October 1996). The press in Britain was less restrained; the London *Times* accused the governor of New York of supporting the curriculum as a way of winning Irish votes, adding that his knowledge of Irish history was derived from "the Fenian propaganda version which ambitious American politicians tend to prefer" (13 October 1996). It took a further two years before the state legislature provided $300,000, which was given to Hofstra University to develop the curriculum. The New York Famine curriculum was introduced into 8,000 public schools in 2001. Ironically, its main detractors were members of other Irish-American groups who have accused the curriculum of being "[a] thousand pages of revisionist history" (*New York Daily News,* 1 April 2000). Nonetheless, the introduction of the Famine as a topic to be studied in a number of American schools will provide American students with a knowledge of this pivotal period in Irish history, unlike many students in Ireland or Britain.

When in 1997, the Grand Marshall of the New York St. Patrick's Day Parade, John Lahey, announced that its aim was to "draw attention to the British government's culpability in the Irish Famine," he was criticized in the British press for inflaming anti-British feelings (*New York Post,* 11 December 1996). A few months later, however, the new British Prime Minister Tony Blair issued a statement in which he also referred to the culpability of the British government. In 2000, John Lahey was responsible (funded by a Jewish benefactor) for opening a Great Hunger Collection in Quinnipiac University. The center not only houses a unique collection of secondary sources and Famine artifacts, but it has also provided an important legacy for future students of the Famine. Some of the most groundbreaking debates also took place in the United States. For example, in October 1997, a Famine conference called "Breaking the Silence" was held in New York. What made the conference unique was that, in addition to a number of academic lectures, the program included contributions from Mary Nellis of Sinn Féin and Billy Hutchinson of the Progressive Unionist Party—voices that had traditionally been silenced or unheard.

The Famine commemorations after 1995, both in Ireland and further afield, raised a number of issues that are central to the memory of any catastrophe. One of the remarkable features of the commemorations was the geographic range of, and the public involvement in, the ceremonies and events. Moreover, the activities were matched by a stream of publications, even by scholars who had previously shown little interest in the Great Hunger. Book sales undoubtedly benefited from popular interest in the anniversary of the Famine and a three-year program of commemorative events. The intensity that resulted was succeeded by "Famine-fatigue." For some, weariness came early; in December 1995, Eddie Holt, a journalist for the *Irish Times,* claimed that everything that needed to be known about the Famine had been said (30 December 1995). The scale and longevity of the Famine commemorations in Ireland and elsewhere, however, demonstrated that for many people a desire to remember and to mourn still existed.

In the 1990s, the rush to commemorate both the Famine and the 1798 uprising also led to accusations that Ireland was staging a "commemoration circus" that had become "another extension of the heritage industry, a provider of jobs and cash for all sorts of interest groups" (*Irish Times,* 21 January 1998). Yet, apart from returning the Famine to its central place in Irish (and possibly British and American) history, the commemorations provided fresh insights into the ongoing problem of famines in the world. This was recognized by the Irish President Mary Robinson who wrote, following a visit to Somalia, that the memory of the Great Hunger could best be honored "by taking the folk memory of this catastrophe into our present world with us, and allowing it to strengthen and deepen our identity with those who are still suffering" (Robinson 12).

III. Malignant Shame?

When did the Famine really end? Furthermore, what impact did the Famine have on those who survived it? The long-term impact of the Hunger on survivors is one that continues to divide academic history from popular memory. One of the most vociferous detractors of its commemorations was Roy Foster, who condemned the outpouring of survivor guilt that accompanied the anniversary of the Great Hunger and accused those who talked about healing of promoting "psychobabble" (*Guardian,* 23 October 2001). Nonetheless, as the work of Garrett O'Connor and Deborah Peck has demonstrated, the return of good harvests to Ireland did not mean an end to the suffering. The shame and the feeling of guilt experienced by the survivors have been carried on from generation to generation. This emotion has been identified by O'Connor as lingering or "malignant shame," and it can exist at either an individual, cultural, or community level (5). Both O'Connor and Peck employ a transgenerational model to understand the long-term psychological damage caused by the Famine. They also argue that the consequences of prolonged political abuse or colonialism are low self-esteem, dependency, self-misperceptions of cultural inferiority, and suppression of feelings. These feelings were reinforced by the attitude of the authoritarian Catholic church, which in the nineteenth century changed from being oppressed to becoming a major force in Irish politics. Peck's work has also demonstrated that such feelings were part of the emigrants' baggage and so spread in the late nineteenth century beyond the shores of Ireland. The post-Famine decades also coincided with the emergence of an increasingly organized, powerful, and authoritarian Catholic church, which cemented even further people's feeling of worthlessness. Consequently, O'Connor argued that "the psychological and spiritual price of survival was high; so high, in fact, that it is still being paid 150 years later by significant numbers of Catholics in Ireland, and by many more of the diaspora, including myself" (11). O'Connor, who was born in Ireland and became a successful M.D. and psychologist in the United States, suggests that personal and professional achievements can be eclipsed by the impact of an event that happened 150 years earlier and thousands of miles away.

Garrett O'Connor has also argued that the Famine has to be viewed in the wider context of a long history of colonial oppression, and he claims that even political independence did not end the damage done by centuries of colonialism. In 1991, the leading Irish psychologist, Dr. Anthony Clare, while noting the "extraordinary vigour and vitality of so much of Irish life" added that the Irish mind was "enveloped, and to an extent suffocated in an English mental embrace." At a societal level, this attitude had resulted in "an emphasis on physical control, original sin, cultural inferiority and psychological defensiveness" (qtd. in O'Connor 6). Outside of medical practitioners, the idea of malignant shame or post-colonial trauma has found resonance. The respected historian Professor Joseph Lee has explained the notion of cultural inferiority in post-colonial Ireland as lying in the "elusive but crucial psychological factors that inspired the instinct of inferiority" that were manifested in "feelings of self-deception, begrudgery, contempt for authority, lack of self-confidence and poor leadership" (qtd. in O'Connor 6).

The concept of transgenerational trauma induced by the Famine has also been embraced by a number of Irish artists, such as the controversial Irish singer Sinéad O'Connor. In her rap single "Famine," first released in 1994, she wrote:

> OK, I want to talk about the Ireland
> Specifically I want to talk about the 'famine'
> About the fact that there never really was one
> There was no 'famine'
> See Irish people were only allowed to eat potatoes
> All of the other food
> Meat fish vegetables
> Were slipped out of the country under armed guard
> To England while the Irish people starved
> And then on the middle of all of this
> They gave us money not to teach our children Irish
> And so we lost our history
> And this is what I think is still hurting me
>
> See we're like a child that's been battered
> has to drive itself out of it's head because it's frightened
> Still feels all the painful feelings
> But they lose contact with the memory
> ("Famine," *Universal Mother Album,* 1994)

Sinéad O'Connor's song aroused controversy, especially in Ireland. She was attacked both for her historical interpretation of the Famine and for linking it with many of the social problems within Ireland at the end of the twentieth century. The historian Mary Daly, for example, criticized the song on the grounds of historical inaccuracy claiming that "[t]he country suffered an enormous natural disaster through the failure of the potato crop and the only way the eight million plus population could have survived was through eating potatoes . . . no substance known could have fed eight million people, the number of calories lost was simply irreplaceable" (*Evening Press,* 26 September 1994). Daly's response, however, disregarded the fact that the whole of the Irish population did not depend on potatoes for a subsistence; potatoes accounted only for about 20 percent of total crop yield, and—if loss of calories is the principal measure—what about the calories lost through exports? Nonetheless, Mary Daly and, more significantly, Anthony Clare, agreed with Sinéad O'Connor's assertion that "the Irish nation had suffered a deep, psychological damage as a result of the Famine" (*Evening Press,* 26 September 1994). O'Connor defended her claims at a Famine conference organized by Afri, an Irish human rights group. A few weeks before the conference a Dublin newspaper reported that "Sinéad was recently spotted in a library reading files on the subject" (*Evening Herald,* 26 January 1995). O'Connor's assertions were also championed by John Waters, a writer and journalist, who commended the fact that she was "alive and well and determined not to be quiet" (*Irish Times,* 11 October 1994).

Notwithstanding the criticisms of Sinéad O'Connor's interpretation, her song did confront a number of issues that had been avoided by revisionist historians and others. The image of food being exported as people starved had been an evocative and enduring image of Famine memory, yet it had largely been ignored by historians. The fact that John Mitchel had written about ships loaded with food leaving the country in *The Last Conquest* gave the question an early association with a nationalist interpretation. The issue of food exports continues to be a contested area in Famine historiography, yet even nonrevisionists have shown reluctance to engage fully either with the archives or in debate. Consequently, it has been generally accepted by historians that there was not enough food in the country to feed the people (Donnelly, *Great Irish Potato Famine,* and Gray, for example, have concurred with this view). However, most of these historians base their conclusions on the flawed (by his own admission) tables of exports provided by Austin Bourke. They are also only concerned with corn, rather than the vast array of edible commodities that also left Ireland between 1846 and 1850, which included bacon, eggs, fish, butter, vegetables, and more than three million cattle. An examination of the records of ships' cargoes during this period demonstrates that while corn exports may have fallen, the exports of all other commodities remained buoyant or increased throughout the Famine years (for the debate on food supply and exports see, Kinealy, *Great Irish Famine,* 96–116).

Sinéad O Connor also suggested that the word *famine* was a misnomer; even though the potato crop had failed, sufficient quantities of other food was being grown and could have been used to feed the poor. For this reason, a number of people feel uncomfortable with the use of the term *Great Famine,* preferring to use the Irish translation *An Gorta Mór* or *Great Hunger.* But the reluctance to use the word *famine* only became an issue for nationalists at the end of the nineteenth century. This is evident in the writings of Jeremiah O'Donovan Rossa, whose family left Ireland as a consequence of the Hunger. He objected to such terminology on the grounds that "[w]e adopt the English expression and call those years the 'famine years,' but there was no famine in the land . . . the English took the food away to England and let the people starve" (111). However, nationalists and republicans in the 1840s, including John Mitchel, openly used the word *famine* to describe Ireland after 1845, whereas government officials were clearly uncomfortable with this designation, preferring to use words such as *distress, destitution, extreme destitution, calamity,* or *suffering* (O'Rourke 287). The use of both designations, the Famine and the Hunger, are justifiable. While the latter captures more of the human dimension of the tragedy, the use of the word *famine* more fully conveys the political dimensions of food shortages—especially in regard to food distribution and entitlements. Famine is never just about food shortages but is ultimately about political choices and decisions, and what happened in Ireland in the 1840s is a clear case of this (the politics of contemporary famines have been explored in the work of Amartya Sen on Indian famines).

John Waters, through his columns in the *Irish Times,* was one of the few people in the media to challenge the revisionist interpretation of history in the early 1990s. In 1994 he asked, "Why are we so afraid to confront the ghosts of our past?" He argued that Irish people were collectively in denial but that they needed to return to the past, and confront it honestly, so that they could move forward into the future. The Famine had a central place in this process because, as the most extreme example of tyranny by the colonizer, it was "the door by which that colonial experience can be assessed." Historians, by playing down Ireland's colonial past, had helped to keep the door shut because "[r]evisionist semantics about the source of the blight or the feasibility of aid efforts once the blight had taken hold are utterly irrelevant to the meaning of that experience . . . it is meaningless to discuss the Famine outside of the context of the colonial process in which it was rooted" (repr. in Hayden 28–30).

Sean Kenny, author of *The Hungry Earth,* also adopted the concept of transgenerational shame for his novel, but he felt that people in Ireland continued to be reluctant to identify with these feelings, leading him to write:

> So many Irish people who have read the story seem either to have failed altogether to see what was behind it or, worse, to have understood and then utterly dismissed the underlying premise— which is that we remain traumatized today by this cataclysm one hundred and fifty years ago. (qtd. in Hayden 181)

Kenny's reflections appear in *Irish Hunger: Personal Reflections on the Legacy of the Famine* edited by Tom Hayden, which provides a unique collection of essays on the long-term trauma. In the Introduction, Hayden explains, "This book stems from another Irish Hunger that still continues, a hunger for the meaning of the Great Hunger in our lives today." He further argues that there was a need to know because "a Famine repressed breeds an incipient hunger of its own, a hunger to know, to grieve, to hold accountable, to resolve and to honour" (11).

Garrett O'Connor has suggested that in order for such feelings not to be passed onto future generations, "a combination of psychological and spiritual recovery" is necessary (2). Since the production of Garrett O'Connor's paper, the Republic of Ireland has undergone a radical transformation, largely due to the birth of the "Celtic tiger" and the move toward secularization. Furthermore, cultural inferiority has been replaced by a confident, modern, pluralist state. Ironically, the "spiritual recovery" that O'Connor talked about appears to be rooted in the rejection and questioning of the formal structures of Catholicism. At the beginning of the twenty-first century it is widely accepted that the Irish Catholic church is "a church in crisis," while the moral authority of priests and bishops has been weakened by its inflexible stand on contraception in the 1970s and 1980s and a succession of well-publicized clerical scandals in the 1990s (Donnelly, "A Church in Crisis" 12).

Writing in 1995 the historian John Killen explained that the impact of the Famine on subsequent generations was that

> [a]nger, hatred, fear and compassion have mixed with shame to produce a reluctance, possibly an inability, to address the enormity of the national tragedy. It is possible that only now in the last years of the century and of the millennium have the people of Ireland the self-confidence to seek to understand fully the causes, progress and consequences of the famine decade. (9)

Arguably, the success of Ireland has enabled her to confront a painful chapter in her past relating to the Famine. But the wider issue of confronting the colonial past may not be so easy given the ongoing conflict in the six counties of Northern Ireland.

A feature of these interpretations and individual reflections is that they view feelings of post-Famine personal and cultural inferiority as being exclusive to Irish Catholics. The association of Famine trauma with Catholicism—identified by Garrett O'Connor as the "Irish-Catholic character"—ignores the long-term impact of the Famine on Irish Protestants. Historians also have tended to exclude the Protestant communities, especially in the northeast of Ireland, from their research. But to what extent has the memory of suffering *post facto* followed political divisions devised in the early twentieth century?

IV. A Catholic Disaster?

In 1995, the academic Irene Whelan wrote:

> Among the catalogue of grievances accumulated by the Irish Catholics during the catastrophic years between 1845 and 1852, few attracted such odium as the phenomenon known as "souperism," or the alleged attempts of evangelical missionaries to use hunger as an instrument to win converts to the Protestant faith. (qtd. in Póirtéir, *Great Irish Famine* 135)

Her comments raise the unpalatable issue of proselytism (or souperism) and suggest that the suffering of Catholics during the Famine was qualitatively different from that of Protestants, while reinforcing the different experience between Catholics and Protestants. There is no doubt, however, that the activities of Protestant churches have been blemished by the memory of proselytism. Although they made few converts, the legacy of souperism proved to be hard to dispel—for all denominations.

The association of Protestant churches during the Famine with souperism also proved to be a troublesome memory for those churches, especially during the Famine commemorations. In 1995, the *Church of Ireland Gazette* made a number of impassioned appeals for a reappraisal of their role during the Famine. One article suggested, "This is perhaps the moment to face squarely the charge of 'souperism' which is still levied against the Church of Ireland" (*Church of Ireland Gazette*, Dr. Robert McCarthy, 11 August 1995). The role of Protestant proselytizers was recognized generally to have been a damaging one and it was proposed that "[n]o attempt should be made to minimize their pernicious effects, particularly the lasting suspicion of the Protestant faith they bred in the Roman Catholic population" (*Church of Ireland Gazette*, 13 January 1995). Nevertheless, a historian of the Anglican church admitted that "one looks forward to an end to the blanket dismissal of landlords as callous perpetrators of eviction and of clergy as dispensers of soup at a price" (*Church of Ireland Gazette*, Dr. Ken Milne, 1 September 1995).

The emphasis on the suffering of Catholics has a long history. The first history of the Great Irish Famine was published in 1874 and was written by a Catholic priest (O'Rourke). The commercial success of *The History of the Great Irish Famine of 1847* meant that two reprints had to be made. More significantly, for almost eighty years, O'Rourke's publication remained the only major history of the Great Famine. The influence of O'Rourke's interpretation also spilled over into literature. Liam O'Flaherty's powerful novel *Famine*, first published in 1937, borrowed much of its historical detail from O'Rourke. This work of literature has been described as "the most successful famine narrative" (Kelleher in Póirtéir, *Great Irish Famine* 241). The timing of its publication was also significant as it was published in the same year as the Irish Constitution was being written and the Irish Free State was defining itself.

O'Rourke's publication provides a valuable insight into a late-nineteenth-century interpretation of the Hunger, which limited the Famine to one year—1847 (although O'Rourke does provide detailed accounts of earlier relief schemes). O'Rourke also suggests that anti-Catholicism played a major role in the response to the food shortages, arguing that "a not inconsiderable class of persons . . . discovered, beyond all doubt, that *Popery* was the true cause of the potato blight"

(Kelleher in Póirtéir, *Great Irish Famine* 264). But, in addition to punishing Irish Catholics for their idolatry, the Famine was also a punishment on the British government for allowing Catholicism to flourish. In August 1846 the *Achill Missionary Herald* (the journal of the proselytizing mission) averred that:

> to fill the measure of our national guilt, the prevalent idolatry is countenanced and supported by our government. The Protestant members of the House of Lords and Commons have sworn before God and the country that popery is idolatrous; our Queen, at her coronation, solemnly made a similar declaration, yet, all have concurred in passing a Bill to endow a college [Maynooth College, which received an increased grant in 1845] for training priests to defend, and practice, and perpetuate, this corrupt and damnable worship in this realm.

The providentialist interpretation of the Famine took a variety of forms and, within Lord John Russell's Whig government, it found favor with a small but influential group of evangelical Protestants. This moralist grouping included Earl Grey (Colonial Secretary), Charles Wood (Chancellor of the Exchequer), Sir George Grey (Home Secretary), and Charles Trevelyan (Permanent Secretary to the Treasury). They each viewed the potato blight as a God-sent opportunity to bring about social and economic change in Ireland. Their influence on policy formation was helped by the fact that Russell was a weak leader at the head of a minority government. Furthermore, the Treasury was placed in charge of the distribution of government monies, which made Wood and Trevelyan the final arbiters in the allocation of public funds. However, their moralist, redemptive views provided a prism through which to view the suffering in Ireland. Hence, Trevelyan wrote in 1846, on the eve of the period of greatest suffering, that the blight had been sent to remedy Ireland's social ills, stating:

> the cure has been applied by the direct stroke of an all wise Providence in a manner as unexpected and unthought of as it is likely to be effectual. God grant that we may rightly perform our part and not turn into a curse what was intended for a blessing.
> (Trevelyan to Monteagle, 9 October 1846, Monteagle Papers, NLI)

Overall, little research has been carried out on the impact of evangelical Protestantism on the day-to-day provision of either public or private relief, or on the role of proselytism—or souperism—during the Famine (exceptions are, Whelan in Póirtéir, *Great Irish Famine* 135–54; Kinealy and MacAtasney). Despite the lack of scholarly attention, souperism—and the stigma associated with it—provided one of the most enduring memories of the Famine in folk memory. But the emphasis on these aspects of evangelical Protestantism also overshadows the fact that many Protestant relief workers interpreted their duty in terms of the primacy of the Christian duty of charity. The interface between various denominations, however, was not one-dimensional or simply based on religious tension and proselytizing crusades. In contemporary records, the involvement of clergy of all denominations in providing relief was widely commended. The nationalist *Freeman's Journal* observed:

> The Catholic and Protestant clergymen vie with one another in acts of benevolence. They are the most active members of the relief committees—they confer together, remonstrate together, evoke together the aid of the dilatory government, and condemn together its vicious and dilatory refusals. (11 January 1847)

For the most part, however, the impact of the Hunger on poor Protestants has been ignored.

V. Invisible Protestants

Protestants are largely invisible in Famine narratives. The view of the Famine as a Catholic disaster has a long history. Indeed, one of the most enduring myths about the Famine, which was rarely addressed during the intense period of publication and commemoration after 1994, was the impact of the Hunger on the northeast of Ireland, especially on the local Protestant communities. To some extent this denial has its roots in the 1840s, but increasingly political factors have helped to shape collective memory regarding religious differences.

But to what extent did the religious dimensions of the relationship between Britain and Ireland, and between communities within Ireland, mold responses to the Famine? At the beginning of the nineteenth century, Britain regarded itself as a Protestant state. The British historian Linda Colley has suggested that it was the bond of Protestantism, together with wars against Catholic France, that had helped to forge a sense of "British national identity." More significantly:

> Protestantism coloured the way that Britons approached and interpreted their material life. Protestantism determined how most Britons viewed their politics. And an uncompromising Protestantism was the foundation on which their state was explicitly and unapologetically based . . . [and] the most striking feature in the religious landscape, the gulf between Protestant and Catholic. (18)

Catholic Ireland, joined to Britain by the Act of Union in 1801, clearly presented a problem; how could "an avowedly Protestant nation admit any of its Catholic subjects to a full share in civic life without irredeemably compromising its national identity?" (Colley 323). The issue was never resolved. The reluctance to grant Catholic Emancipation even after the Act of Union demonstrated the opposition to conferring Catholics full political rights. Although Catholics were finally permitted to sit in parliament in 1829, Catholic Emancipation was only introduced following a campaign by Daniel O'Connell, which brought the United Kingdom to the brink of civil war. At the time of the Famine, the House of Commons was overwhelmingly Protestant, while a small number of evangelical Protestants had a disproportionate influence within successive cabinets (Hilton 36–70).

The Famine, however, also coincided with a period of political regrouping among nationalists that resulted in the Young Ireland–led uprising in Ballingarry in July 1848. It was easily defeated, although the uprising was part of a republican tradition established in the 1790s, not only due to its willingness to use physical force tactics, but also because its leaders (most of whom were Protestant) were advocates of nonsectarian politics. The Famine also coincided with a revival of the Orange Order, and the uprising provided an opportunity for Orangemen to reassert their loyalty to Britain and to the Union. Militant Protestantism, therefore, became the main beneficiary of this period of political as well as social turmoil (Kinealy, *Great Irish Famine* 182–200). Ruth Dudley Edwards, however, claimed in her polemical defense of the Orange Order that, despite their defeat in 1848, by 1849 "the Ribbonmen (members of a Catholic secret society) were back in business; the privations and sufferings of the previous three years had exacerbated the loathing of the have-nots for the haves, or those they perceived as haves" (Dudley Edwards 198). Loyal Protestantism, however, gained in terms of both support and political standing following the failed nationalist uprising. The 1848 uprising also increased religious divisions as Catholics were portrayed as disloyal and untrustworthy while Protestants cast themselves as saviors of the Union by their role as a "native garrison." In 1849 middle-class Protestants in the north of Ireland were publicly claiming their cultural and religious superiority when defining their right not to pay a national tax for relief of famine in the west of the country. Their arguments were expressed in sectarian terms, one MP suggesting that the purpose of the proposed tax would be to support "an army of beggars, fed out of the industry of Ulster" (Joseph Napier, *Hansard,* 1 March 1849). One Protestant newspaper also protested:

> It is true that the potato has failed in Connaught and Munster; but it has failed just as much in Ulster; therefore, if the failure of the potato has produced all the distress in the South and West, why has it not caused the same misery here? It is because we are a painstaking, industrious, laborious people, who desire to work and pay our just debts, and the blessing of the Almighty is upon our labour. If the people of the South had been equally industrious with those of the North, they would not have so much misery among them. (*Newry Telegraph,* 6 March 1849)

As early as 1849, therefore, the seeds were also being sown for the creation of a myth: that the Famine did not affect the Protestant people of the north (an area never precisely defined).

Developments in the late 1840s also contributed to a political polarization in the post-Famine decades and the Hunger developed into a tool of claiming difference as it became viewed increasingly as a Catholic catastrophe; Catholics were victims while Protestants, on the other hand, were British statesmen or proselytizers. The history of the Famine in the northeast of Ireland has also been hampered by continuing political and religious divisions. For example, in the 1940s, the Unionist government in Belfast refused to allow participation in an all-Ireland survey of Irish folklore, which included a questionnaire on the Famine. Moreover, following the creation of Northern Ireland, Irish history was rarely taught in state schools, but the curriculum concentrated on British and European history (*History Ireland* 9.2: 11). The observations of a number of prominent historians has also contributed to a widespread acceptance of a famine-free zone in the northeast corner of the country. Roy Foster, for example has claimed, "Regions with varied local economies (notably the north and east coast) escaped lightly" (*Oxford History* 167). While Brian Walker, a historian based in Belfast, asserted, "The great famine, with its enormous human toll, affected Ulster far less than elsewhere in Ireland, thanks to northern industrialization and the availability of crops other than the potato" (18). The majority of Famine narratives, however, simply ignore the northeast, focusing particularly on the west. Even less has been written about the impact of the Famine on Protestants, although the assumption is that they suffered less than Catholics. Liam Kennedy, for example, has proposed that "Ulster fared better than the average experience of the island . . . the Protestant people of that province suffered less severely from famine" (Kennedy and Ollerenshaw 30). A similar claim has been made for a low level of mortality among Presbyterians, with Finlay Holmes, a historian and former Moderator of the Presbyterian Church, claiming "few members of the congregation died; those who died came mainly from an underclass who no longer had any church connection" (103). The exclusion of some parts of Ulster from the tragedy has also permeated public consciousness, hence, during a *Dail* debate on the Famine in 1995, one member proclaimed, "My ancestors, who came from Belfast, would have been very little affected by the Famine" (McDowell).

Contemporary evidence, however, demonstrates that the impact of the Famine in the north was not as trifling as had been suggested. Overall, loss of population in the province of Ulster was 17 percent, making it higher than the loss suffered in the province of Leinster. At a more local level, in 1847 the distress in parts of County Down led visiting Quakers to liken what they witnessed "to the horrors of Skibbereen"—a small town in County Cork that had already became a benchmark of human suffering (Transactions 190–92). In Belfast, the main Protestant cemetery was overflowing and unable to accommodate any further interments. The local Orange lodges also restricted their marching activities in that year, on the grounds that the Famine had "thinned out our local population and removed many of our loyal brethren" (*Belfast Protestant Journal*, 17 July 1847). One of the areas to suffer most in Belfast was the industrialized and Protestant area of Ballymacarrett, in the east of the town, where more than 40 percent of the population was dependent on private soup kitchens for subsistence. The distress of Ballymacarrett illustrates that no district or religion was exempt from suffering (Kinealy and MacAtasney 40–65). But even at the time, much of the suffering remained invisible. A local newspaper, the *Belfast Vindicator,* chastised the wealthy inhabitants of Ulster for having ignored the suffering on their doorstep, saying that they did so "because it is a disgrace to the province" preferring "the fine philosophy that would starve the poor for the honour of the rich" (22 April 1846).

A report written in 1872 from Newtownards in County Down—a town that was both Protestant and industrialized in the 1840s—also suggests that the impact of the Famine was deep and enduring. This recollection from a Protestant man provides a rare insight into the more intangible consequences of the Hunger:

> The weavers after the Famine were not the same men as they were before it. Saturday night squabbling had ceased: the public houses might as well have been closed for all the business done; prayer meetings were established in different localities, in out-of-the-way places where cock-fighting, dog-fighting and rat-hunting-on-Sunday characters had lived; and a tone of seriousness pervaded the people. Many of them felt that they had something else to live for than to eat, drink and be merry. Numbers of old Bibles, hymn books and Psalm books were fished up from all sort of places. (*Newtownards Independent,* 13 July 1872)

Nonetheless, the subsequent orthodoxy that the north of Ireland had escaped from the Hunger was most evident in the small level of commemorations within Northern Ireland between 1995 and 1997. The absence of commemoration—especially at an official level—served to reinforce the traditional view that the area had not suffered. At the beginning of 1997, the Northern Ireland Office announced that while it "recognized the special significance" of the Famine, it had "no current plans to commemorate the event at government level" (*Andersonstown News,* 15 March 1997). The debate moved into the public and political arena in Belfast when a Sinn Féin member of the City Council proposed to install a stained-glass window to commemorate the Famine in the City Hall—traditionally a bastion of Protestant supremacy. Although the proposal won some cross-party support, it was opposed by the Unionist Party and the Democratic Unionist Party, with Sammy Wilson of the latter claiming, "There is no evidence that the Famine played any part in the history of Belfast." He also claimed that to do so would give Sinn Féin, whom he described as "the monsters of manufacturing and media manipulation" a propaganda victory (*Irish News* and *Newsletter,* 4 February 1997). Politics, rather than history, informed his objection. The balance of political power within Belfast was changing, however, and a few months later, the first-ever nationalist Lord Mayor of Belfast was elected (*Newsletter,* 3 June 1997). A Famine window was eventually erected in the City Hall in 1999.

The Great Hunger was also remembered in Belfast at the community level, most visibly by the painting of a number of wall murals dedicated to its memory. However, the murals were located in Catholic west Belfast, with none being painted in Protestant east Belfast, the area that had probably suffered most during the Famine. The fact that the murals were situated in Catholic areas also reinforced the hypothesis that the Famine did not affect all denominations. Overall, the partial view of the Famine has proved hard to dispel, and Protestant suffering remained marginalized, even in the recent proliferation of Famine publications. Consequently, a distorted view of the Famine has emerged that— perhaps conveniently—suggests the impact of the Famine anticipated the boundary imposed by Partition. The work of MacAtasney on Portadown and Lurgan, and Kinealy and MacAtasney on Belfast (all of which were predominately Protestant towns) suggests a more complex picture and demonstrates that the Famine cut across religious and geographical divisions.

The denial of the Famine is an indication of a demarcation between Protestant and Catholic memory in Ireland, especially in Northern Ireland. The actor Stephen Rea, a Belfast-born Protestant, has explained that Unionist history has been the dominant discourse in Northern Ireland because "[t]here is an amnesia among Protestants in this town about their part in the creation and preservation of so much of the culture of Northern Ireland" (*Belfast Telegraph,* 16 November 1998). Similarly, Roy Garland, a writer who grew up in the Protestant Shankill area of Belfast in the 1950s, has written of his schooling that "Irish history was to me a closed book. The only aspects of my Irish past of which I was conscious were the siege of Derry, the Battle of the Boyne and St. Patrick." Moreover, in addition to his experience of formal education, he acknowledged that within his family and community "selective folk memory has shaped much of our thinking." As a consequence he believed "we have suppressed so much of our past because it didn't fit with later notions of who we were." Belatedly, Garland has began to learn about Irish history and asserts that learning about the past has been a crucial component of the "new thinking" of some loyalists, which has in turn facilitated a "new accommodations approach in politics" (*Irish News,* 3 August 1998). To what extent, however, have Catholics, especially in Northern Ireland, appropriated the memory of the Famine? A middle-class and, in her words, "middle-of-the-road Protestant" from County Down writing in 2000 admitted to feeling "a gaping hole" in her identity. She blamed Catholic nationalists for denying Protestants access to a rich culture and history, suggesting, "If you look at the Famine, the Irish have taken it over as if it was an anti-Irish phenomenon" (McKay 23). In the light of the fragility of the peace process, perhaps the increasing acknowledgment of a shared past would help to provide a more solid basis for a shared future.

VI. Famine Villains?

Memory and folk traditions are an important part of history. Historical memory is clearly selective in those it views as the heroes or villains. There has been general consensus about the positive role of the Society of Friends, and folk literature contains many instances of individual examples of generosity. The many people who contributed privately to Famine relief have also been remembered fondly, with some donations—such as the one from the Choctaw Nation of Oklahoma—having been widely celebrated during the Famine commemorations. As a consequence, Mary Robinson, the president of Ireland, visited the Choctaw people and was made an honorary chief, while representatives of the Choctaw Nation, including Gary White Deer, spoke movingly at a number of Famine events in Ireland, Britain, and North America.

A rich, if underused, record of the oral traditions of famine survivors and their descendants is available in the Irish Folklore Archive, held in University College in Dublin. The collection runs to thousands of pages of manuscripts and includes some very detailed answers, written in English and Irish. A large part of the archive is based on a project commenced in the 1930s to amass a written record of folklore traditions within Ireland. In 1945, a questionnaire regarding the Famine was distributed to mark the hundredth anniversary. The Unionist government in Belfast refused permission for the survey to extend to Northern Ireland; therefore, most of the records relate to what was then the Irish Free State.

Within the archive, local landlords or traders who behaved badly are identified by name, as are compassionate landlords who helped their tenants. Most of the recollections are strongly based within the local community, and little is said about relief measures at a national level. Individual members of the British government or Queen Victoria "rarely play a part in the thousands of traditions that were passed on orally within the post-Famine communities themselves" (Póirtéir, *Famine Echoes* 5). This omission is perhaps not surprising given that the majority of the victims of the Famine were separated by geographic distance, language, religion, and class from the policy makers in London. Instead, "the greatest odium seems to have been reserved for those members of the community who acted as agents for the landlords. They were often seen as having turned on their own" (Póirtéir, *Famine Echoes* 9). Some of the omissions or silences with the folk archive are eloquent. The worst aspects of famine (of any famine)—stealing from each other, hoarding, feuding, nakedness, cannibalism, and agonizingly slow and obscene deaths—rarely appear, possibly due to residual feelings of pain and shame, which are common among survivors of trauma. Also, a feature of folk memory is a universal denial that the Hunger was bad in their locality; it was always far worse elsewhere.

In Famine memory the roles of the British government and Irish landlords—and to a far lesser extent, merchants—have been remembered unfavorably—despite attempts by some revisionists to rehabilitate them. Some of the recent writing has also shown a more nuanced approach to these groups, identifying, for example, the opposition that existed within the British government by individual members such as George Poulett Scrope, William Sharman Crawford, and Lord George Bentinck, to policies being pursued (Kinealy, *Great Irish Famine* 47–52). The names of these defenders of the Irish poor, however, have largely disappeared from the Famine narrative. By the end of the twentieth century, two individuals had become indelibly associated with the Famine and widely remembered for their malignant roles, overshadowing even the roles played by the two Prime Ministers, landlords, or politicians. The villains of collective memory are Charles Trevelyan and Queen Victoria. The incorporation of Trevelyan and Queen Victoria into popular memory, however, is curious as individual members of government, the royal family, or relief administrators were rarely mentioned in recorded folk memories of the Famine. This would suggest that a number of oral traditions originated after the Famine and had their base in some nationalist narratives of the tragedy.

Trevelyan emerged as the main villain of the Famine in collective memory. One reason may have been that, although the Famine was rarely taught in schools or colleges, Woodham-Smith's analysis of Trevelyan had reached a receptive audience. The public memory of his role was kept alive in the stanzas of the popular ballad "Fields of Athenry," which in the last decades of the twentieth century was widely sung at social gatherings, during Catholic masses, and before sports occasions, especially among the Irish diaspora. It had also become one of the unofficial anthems of the Scottish Catholic soccer team, Celtic, and was sung by their supporters in the United States (see, for example, the Web page of Chicago Celtic Supporters Club). The first verse of the song is:

By a lonely prison wall
I heard a young girl calling
Michael they have taken you away
For you stole Trevelyan's corn
So your young could see the morn
The prison ship lies waiting in the bay

This popular song personalizes the withholding of corn from the poor and identifies Charles Trevelyan as being in charge of food supply. It is not a contemporary Famine song and its exact origins are unclear. Nonetheless, its evocative appeal is powerful, especially outside Ireland. Thomas O'Grady, the Director of Irish Studies at the University of Massachusetts-Boston, has referred to the "Fields of Athenry" as that "heartbreaking ballad about love's promise thwarted by the pitiless laws of the land during the Great Hunger." He has identified the power of the song as lying in its ability to transport listeners "to another place and another time . . . to the fertile plains of Galway almost a century-and-a-half earlier." If sung well, he argues, it can "recover briefly" an aspect of history in a way that is unique (*Boston Irish Reporter,* February 1998). For the diaspora in particular, music has been an important tool for shaping and preserving their collective memory of Ireland and Irish history. The popularity of the "Fields of Athenry" ensured that the name Trevelyan would be linked with government parsimony, just as "Revenge for Skibbereen" meant that the name of this small town has become indelibly linked with Irish suffering in the Great Hunger (Miller, qtd. in Gribben 180–95). Neither of these songs were written during the Famine but, like other forms of literature, they provided "space in the imagination for what cannot be said otherwise, for what has not been experienced directly but must be reconstructed or even invented" (Sicher).

But to what extent can any one individual be held responsible for policies over a period of years? Moreover, how influential was Trevelyan who, after all, was not a politician but a civil servant? Woodham-Smith's depiction of Trevelyan as a principal and reprehensible figure roused the ire of the influential historian F. S. L. Lyons. An even more comprehensive defense of Trevelyan was made by P. M. Austin Bourke, a meteorologist who has written extensively on agriculture, climate, and the potato blight. In an article titled "Apologia for a Dead Civil Servant," he takes Woodham-Smith to task for having "broken new ground by casting Trevelyan in the role of principal scapegoat for the British government's mishandling of the famine crisis." Instead, Austin Bourke argues against the

> transfer of guilt from a responsible minister of government to a public
> servant who faithfully implements and defends his master's policy
> without regard to his own opinions or preferences. (Bourke 170)

Instead, he lays much of the blame for inadequate policies at the feet of Russell whom he accuses of being dilatory and dead weight.

Subsequent interpretations, however, have tended to view Russell as a well-intentioned but ultimately weak prime minister, who persistently failed to stand up to various vested interests within parliament (Gray 31–35). Moreover, few recent histories have concurred with Austin

Bourke's defense of Trevelyan. But what was Trevelyan's role during the Famine?

As Permanent Secretary to the Treasury, Trevelyan was only answerable to the Chancellor of the Exchequer. In this role he served under both prime ministers and, although their relief policies varied, they both placed the Treasury in charge of deciding how government money should be allocated for relief. Trevelyan's role went far beyond a mere accounting one as, within a few months of blight appearing, he was advising on relief distribution, corresponding with all local relief officials, and taking charge of their day-to-day duties. Following the second appearance of blight in 1846, it was Trevelyan who chose the date at which food depots should be opened—contrary to the advice of local officials and despite the beginning of a period of mass mortality. He had also antagonized many of the relief officials in Ireland—a pattern that was to continue throughout the Famine (Kinealy, *This Great Calamity* 227–31). His central role was officially acknowledged at the time as, in April 1848, Trevelyan was knighted for his work in Famine relief.

In 1848 Trevelyan wrote his own account of the Famine years; he considered the Famine to be over by that stage. Trevelyan's *Irish Crisis,* which was published anonymously in the *Edinburgh Review,* was the only account of the tragedy written by a senior official, and consequently it provides a valuable insight into the workings of government. However, because of its uncritical defense of the government and its unrestrained praise of the various relief measures, a number of Trevelyan's colleagues felt uncomfortable with his account of events. The radical MP George Poulett Scrope opined:

> A stranger to the real events of the last two hundred years might read through the whole hundred pages without ever finding out that during the "Irish Crisis" several hundred thousand souls perished in Ireland of want, through the inefficiency of those "colossal" relief measures. (Scrope, qtd. in O'Brien 172)

Privately also, a number of Whigs expressed their disquiet at Trevelyan's upbeat assertion that the Famine was over in 1848. In that year, almost one-quarter of the population was dependent for survival on the minimalist Poor Law system. The evident continuation of famine led Lord Monteagle, a liberal Protestant landlord, to comment that Trevelyan should write a sequel titled "The Relapse" (Monteagle to editor of *Edinburgh Review,* Monteagle Papers, NLI, 3 October 1848).

Privately, within government also, Trevelyan's ideologically driven and imperious handling of relief provision was increasingly resented—but rarely challenged publicly. Some of the most clear and unequivocal criticisms of Trevelyan and his associates was made by a fellow Whig, the Earl of Clarendon. Within a few weeks of being appointed Lord Lieutenant, he admitted privately that the policies being pursued were adding to the death toll in Ireland. By 1848, he realized that his advice was being ignored and regardless of what he recommended "the doctrinaire policy of Trevelyan, reflected through C. Wood, and supported by Grey, would prevail" (Clarendon to Russell, Letter Books, Bodleian Library, 12 February 1848). By the beginning of 1849 Clarendon had become totally disillusioned with the policies of his colleagues in London attesting that:

> C. Wood, backed by Grey, and relying on arguments (or rather, Trevelyanisms) that are no more applicable to Ireland than to Loo Choo, affirmed that the right thing to do was to do nothing—they have prevailed and you see what a fix we are in. (Clarendon to Duke of Bedford, Letter Books, Bodleian Library, 16 February 1849)

In 1849 also, Edward Twistleton, an Englishman who had been placed in charge of Poor Law relief, resigned in frustration at the policies being pursued by the government. He and Trevelyan had clashed many times, usually because of the parsimony with which Trevelyan released treasury funds. Before he left office, Twistleton informed Trevelyan that due to the latter's refusal to provide even emergency funding he considered himself and his colleagues to be "absolved from any responsibility on account of deaths which may take place in consequence of those privations" (Twistleton to Trevelyan, 7 March 1849, BPP, 1849, xiviii, 14). He repeated similar sentiments before a parliamentary committee shortly afterward when he forcefully made the point that shortage of money rather than administrative incapability had caused many of the deaths in Ireland (Evidence of E. Twistleton, BPP, 1849, xvi, 699–714, 717). Clearly the identification of Trevelyan as an influential and officious figure in relief provision did not originate with Woodham-Smith, but Trevelyan was regarded as powerful and lacking in sympathy by his colleagues. This perspective predated even the first nationalist interpretation of the Famine written by John Mitchel in 1861. In *The Last Conquest (Perhaps)*, Mitchel provided a sustained polemical attack on the relief policies of the British (or, as he more commonly states, English) government during the Famine years, and he singled out the contribution of Trevelyan as being especially pernicious. During Mitchel's visit to the west of Ireland at the end of 1847, he described the children he saw thus: "their limbs fleshless, their bodies half-naked, their faces blotched yet wrinkled" adding "I saw Trevelyan's claw in the vitals of those children; his red tape would draw them to death; in his government laboratory he had prepared for them the typhus poison" (148). One hundred years later, Cecil Woodham-Smith in her powerful account *The Great Hunger,* ascribed to Trevelyan an importance that was more in keeping with contemporary viewpoints on him than with subsequent rehabilitations or revisionist appeals for restraint.

Queen Victoria is widely remembered as "the Famine Queen." Nonetheless, there are few direct references to her in the written folk archives, and they tend to be contradictory: in one she is described as having sent £50 "to relieve the Irish" and at the same time £5,000 for the Grand National Race Course in Liverpool; while another contrasts the parsimony of the government with the "generosity" of the Queen (Póirtéir, *Famine Echoes* 211–12). A widespread oral tradition, however, is that at the height of the suffering Victoria gave £5 to Famine relief and £200 to a London dogs' home. Ironically, it was Queen Victoria who gave the largest single donation of £2,000 to Famine relief, at the beginning of 1847. She also published two Queen's letters, which appealed for money to be sent to Ireland. The second letter was criticized in England on the grounds that Irish people should do more to help themselves (*Times,* 19 October 1847). Nonetheless, during a fund-raising tour in 1880, the nationalist leader Charles Stewart Parnell erroneously claimed that "in 1847 the Queen of England was the only sovereign of Europe who gave nothing out of her private purse" (*Times,* 14 January 1880).

During her long reign, Victoria only visited Ireland on three occasions. The first time was in 1849, largely at the behest of her ministers and as part of a propaganda campaign to demonstrate that the Famine was truly over. Her visit was short and limited to the east coast. She traveled by yacht, only stopping briefly in Cobh (which was renamed Queenstown), Dublin, and Belfast. During her visit she showed a determination not to give support to sectarianism by refusing to visit a Protestant-only Deaf and Dumb Institute in Belfast. For nationalists and the Catholic hierarchy, however, her visit caused a quandary: a number of moderate nationalists took part in the welcoming festivities, but the nationalist *Nation* opined that the celebrations in Dublin were "like illuminating a graveyard—like fireworks in Glasnevin, or like shutting out, with a gorgeous curtain, one half of a long ward of an hospital, crowded with all kinds of disease and suffering" (19 January 1850). For the most part the Irish and British newspapers reported that the visit had gone well and large crowds had turned out to see the young queen and her children. Instances of discord were rarely recorded, although a ballad that was allegedly sung at the time said:

> Arise ye dead of Skibbereen
> And come to Cork to see the Queen. (O'Neill 60–63)

John Mitchel, who had been transported to Bermuda in 1848 and was therefore absent during Victoria's visit, nevertheless wrote about it in his *Jail Journal* published in 1854. He mocked the fact that her itinerary was so restricted and excluded Famine-stricken areas such as Skibbereen or Westport, caustically suggesting:

After a few years, however, it is understood that her majesty will visit the west. The human inhabitants are expected by that time to have been sufficiently thinned, and the deer and other game to have proportionality multiplied. The Prince Albert will then take a hunting lodge in Connemara. (203)

Fifty years after her first visit, Queen Victoria, old and wheelchair-bound, again visited Ireland. The main purpose of her trip was to rally support and troops for the Boer War in South Africa. Her visit was condemned by nationalists. The nationalist Maud Gonne wrote an emotional article titled "The Famine Queen," published in the radical *United Irishman,* which the British government ordered to be confiscated. It said:

And in truth for Victoria, in the decrepitude of her 81 years, to have decided after an absence of half a century to revisit the country she hates and whose inhabitants are the victims of the criminal policy of her reign, the survivors of 60 years of organized famine, the political necessity must have been terribly strong; for after all she is a woman, and however vile and selfish and pitiless her soul may be, she must sometimes tremble as death approaches when she thinks of the countless mothers who, shelterless under the cloudy Irish sky, watching their little starving ones, have cursed her before they die. (Ward 61)

In folk literature, however, there are few direct references to Victoria or her meanness. The attribution of blame appears retrospective and she is singled out by Gonne largely because as a woman and mother, her pitilessness is more reprehensible than even that of her male politicians—who did control policies. Significantly also, Victoria's long reign coincided with a period of massive depopulation in Ireland, which had been triggered by the Famine. In the course of Victoria's reign from 1837 to 1901, the population of Ireland virtually halved. For nationalists at the end of the nineteenth century, the consequences of the Famine were still visible. The recollection of Victoria's alleged parsimony during the Hunger was evident following the declaration of the Irish Republic in 1949. On this occasion a statue of Victoria was removed from in front of the *Dail,* and in a much-used picture of its removal, a man in the foreground is waving "the fabled fiver" at the departing Victoria.

The longevity of the antipathy to Victoria was evident in 1995 when a sesquicentenary exhibition was opened at Cork University to mark the anniversary of the opening of the "Queen's" Colleges. The decision to dig up and include a statue of Queen Victoria (which had been buried on college grounds for more than half a century) caused controversy both locally and nationally (*Cork Examiner,* 14 June 1995). The tone of the dispute was frequently bitter, demonstrating that in collective memory Queen Victoria was a villain of the Famine narrative.

VII. Conclusion: The Process of Commemoration

During the intense two-year cycle of commemoration, a number of issues were raised, although not always resolved. In the twenty-first century, what is the place of the Great Hunger in Irish history? Was the tragedy unique in its awfulness or was it a further incident in a catalog of colonial misrule? To what extent has it shaped Irish identity not just in Ireland but also among the diaspora? Moreover, does the collective memory of a disaster overshadow the individual experience of suffering and trauma? Can such suffering ever be recaptured or represented, or does the Famine continue to be an "unspeakable and inexpressible reality" (Kelleher 3).

For some historians, the Famine commemorations forced them to confront a number of issues about their roles and responsibilities (*Irish Times,* 21 January 1998). For example, is it the scholar's role to intervene in the processes of memory in order to ensure that they are accurate, or is it sufficient simply to examine the dynamics of memory without concern for the relationship to historical "reality" ("The Memory of Catastrophe, Conference Report")?

Should they intervene if a popular myth is used as propaganda? Historians cannot endorse such a usage but neither should they ignore it. On the other hand, the David Irving libel case in Britain over his writings on the Holocaust provided an extreme instance of "a historian" who has "distorted history for the sake of political ideology, in the face of overwhelming evidence to the contrary" (*Sunday Times,* 16 April 2000). The issue of responsibility becomes more difficult if it is the state, or reputable historians, who are promoting the myth. This raises a further question. During the Famine commemorations of 1995–1997, to what extent did the Irish government attempt to mold a collective memory? In the same way, to what extent did Unionist politicians endeavor to perpetuate the view that Protestants were special and different from people in the rest of the island of Ireland?

A positive feature of the period of commemorations was that it renewed a debate about the legacy of the Famine and allowed differences to be aired publicly in Ireland in a way that would not have been possible twenty years earlier. One consequence was that the revisionist interpretation of the Famine was undermined, although not vanquished. For a number of people also, the commemorations helped to recapture the meaning of the catastrophe in a way that had resonance for the descendants of the survivors. The involvement of the British prime minister in the commemorations was welcome but fleeting. Should Britain follow the example of a number of states in the United States and ensure that the Famine is not forgotten but is made a compulsory subject in the school curriculum? Such a move would recognize the centrality of Ireland in the development of modern Britain.

One of the disturbing features of the Great Hunger is that despite the fact that it occurred so late in European history, and was so fully documented and chronicled, so many silences have remained. The silence of the victims is easiest to understand, but other silences are more difficult to comprehend, especially the silence of the generations born after the Famine. The silence of the historians before 1995 is one of the most striking abysses, not only in Famine historiography but also in the wider process of forging a collective memory. While the commemorations have helped to end the academic silence, some voices and stories remain under-represented, notably those of women, of survivors, of merchants, of unionists, and of Protestants.

Silence could take many forms and the memory of the Famine was sometimes hidden. Although photography had been introduced by the 1840s, there are no photographic records. Most of the images, therefore, come from the British press and from the perspective of outsiders—middle class and male. There was a lack of visibility in other ways—before 1995 no monuments had been erected to the Great Famine and the mass graves were largely unmarked. While the work of Kelleher and Morash has shown that although Famine literature and poetry does exist, most of it remains obscure or difficult to access. Much of it was also written by people who were separated by time or class from the actuality of hunger or starvation. This paucity of major works has led the literary critic Terry Eagleton to ask, Where is the Famine in the great revival of Irish literature at the end of the nineteenth century? But is language adequate to the task of representation or does the Famine's awfulness render it inexpressible? Eagleton concludes that it may be saying "the event strains at the limits of the articulable, and is truly in this sense the Irish Auschwitz" (Eagleton 11).

The final question is, How do you measure the impact of the Great Hunger? Historians have tended to use excess mortality as their benchmark. However, mortality is clearly too crude a measure and has served to dehumanize the Famine by making individual suffering into a convenient-to-remember statistic. It also does not convey the individual lives that lay behind the number or the impact that the deaths or emigrations had on those who remained behind. Adolph Eichmann, a German Nazi, is alleged to have said:

> If a hundred people die, it's a disaster
> If a million people die, it's a statistic.
> (Nazi Germany, Channel Five, 4 March 2001)

The descendants of Famine victims and survivors have helped to break the long silence surrounding the Great Hunger, and this made it possible for the first time in 150 years "to know, to grieve, to hold accountable, to resolve and to honour" (Hayden 11).

Works Cited

Abbreviations used
BPP: British Parliamentary Papers
NLI: National Library of Ireland
British Parliamentary Papers:
Further Papers relating to the aid afforded to the Distressed Unions in the west of Ireland, 1849, xiviii.
Select Committee on the Irish Poor Law, 1849, xvi.
American Irish Newsletter. 21.8 (August 1996): 1–4.
Blair, Tony. British Information Services, 31 May 1997.
Bourke, P. M. A. *'The visitation of God?' The Potato and the Great Irish Famine.* Dublin: Lilliput Press, 1993.
Bradshaw, Brendan. "Nationalism and Historical Scholarship in Modern Ireland." *Irish Historical Studies* 26 (1989): 34–41.
Brady, Ciarán, ed. *Interpreting Irish History: The Debate on Historical Revisionism.* Dublin: Irish Academic Press, 1994.
Church of Ireland Gazette. 13 January 1995.
Colley, Linda. *Britons Forging the Nation 1707-1837.* New Haven: Yale Univ. Press, 1992.
Crawford, E. M. *The Hungry Stream: Essays on Emigration and Famine.* Belfast: Belfast Institute of Irish Studies, 1997.
Crotty, R. D. *Irish Agricultural Production: Its Volume and Structure.* Cork: Cork Univ. Press, 1966.
Daly, M. E. *The Famine in Ireland.* Dublin: Dundalgan Press, 1986.
Deane, S., ed. *The Field Day Anthology of Irish Writing.* Derry: Field Day, 1991.
Donnelly, James S., Jr. "A Church in Crisis. The Irish Catholic Church Today." *History Ireland* 8.3.
---. *The Great Irish Potato Famine.* Gloucestershire: Sutton, 2001.
Doyle, Avril. Launch of Famine Commemoration Programme. 27 June 1995.
Dudley Edwards, Ruth. *The Faithful Tribe. An Intimate Portrait of the Loyal Institutions.* London: HarperCollins, 1999.
Eagleton, Terry. *Heathcliff and the Great Hunger: Studies in Irish Culture.* London: Verso, 1995.
Edwards, R. D., and T. D. Williams, eds. *The Great Famine: Studies in Irish history 1845–52.* Dublin: Browne and Nolan, 1956.
Foster, Roy. *Modern Ireland, 1600–1972.* London: Penguin, 1988.
---. "Our Man at Oxford." *History Ireland* 1.3 (Autumn 1993): 9-12
---. *Oxford History of Ireland.* Oxford: Oxford Univ. Press, 1989.
---. "We Are All Revisionists Now." *Irish Review* (1986): 1–6.
Goodbody, Rob. *A Suitable Channel: Quaker Relief in the Great Famine.* Bray: Pale Publishing, 1995.

Grace, Daniel. *The Great Famine in Nenagh Poor Law Union, Co. Tipperary.* Nenagh: Relay Books, 2000.

Gray, Peter. *Famine, Land and Politics: British Government and Irish Society 1843–1850.* Dublin: Irish Academic Press, 1999.

Gribben, Arthur, ed. *The Great Famine and the Irish Diaspora in America.* Amherst, Mass.: Univ. of Massachusetts Press, 1999.

Hayden, Tom, ed. *Irish Hunger: Personal Reflections on the Legacy of the Famine.* Boulder, Colo.: Roberts Rinehart, 1997.

Hilton, Boyd. *The Age of Atonement: The Influence of Evangelicalism on Social and Economic Thought.* Oxford: Oxford Univ. Press, 1988.

Holmes, Finlay. *The Presbyterian Church in Ireland: A Popular History.* Dublin: Columba Press, 2000.

Kelleher, Margaret. *The Feminization of Famine: Expressions of the Inexpressible?* Cork: Cork Univ. Press, 1997.

Kennedy, Liam, and Philip Ollerenshaw. *An Economic History of Ulster, 1820–1939.* Manchester: Manchester Univ. Press 1985.

Kerr, D. A. *The Catholic Church and the Famine.* Dublin: Columba Press, 1996.

Killen, John. *The Famine Decade: Contemporary Accounts 1841–1851.* Belfast: Blackstaff Press, 1995.

Kinealy, Christine. *The Death-Dealing Famine.* London: Pluto Press, 1997.

---. *The Great Irish Famine: Impact, Ideology and Rebellion.* New York: Palgrave, 2002.

---. *This Great Calamity: The Irish Famine 1845–52.* Boulder, Colo.: Roberts Reinhart, 1995.

Kinealy, Christine, and Gerard MacAtasney. *The Hidden Famine: Hunger, Poverty and Sectarianism in Belfast.* London: Pluto Press, 2000.

Lee, Joseph. *The Modernization of Irish Society, 1848–1918.* Dublin: Gill and Macmillan, 1973.

Lyons, F. S. L. "John Dillon and the Plan of Campaign, 1886-90." *Irish Historical Studies* 14 (1965): 313-47.

MacAtasney, Gerard. *"This Dreadful Visitation": The Famine in Lurgan/Portadown.* Belfast: Beyond the Pale Publications, 1997.

McDowell, M. *Parliamentary Debates of Dail Eireann.* Vol. 456, 5 October 1995.

McKay, Susan. *Northern Protestants: An Unsettled People.* Belfast: Blackstaff, 2000.

The Memory of Catastrophe. Conference Report, University of Southampton, 2001. <<http://www.soton.ac.uk/ˉko/>>

Mitchel, John. *Jail Journal.* 1854. Dublin, 1982.

---. *The Last Conquest (Perhaps).* Dublin: Irishman Office, 1861.

Murray, Joe. "Dancing on the Graves of the Famine Dead" *The Phoenix,* 23 May 1997.

Neal, Frank. *Black '47: Britain and the Famine Irish.* New York: St. Martin's Press, 1998.

O'Brien, George. *The Economic History of Ireland from the Union.* London: Longmans, Green, and Co., 1921.

O'Connor, Garrett, *Recognizing and Healing Malignant Shame: A Statement about the Psychological and Spiritual Recovery from the effects of Colonialism in Ireland.* Unpublished paper, 1995.

Ó Gráda, Cormac. *Black '47 and Beyond: The Great Irish Famine in History, Economy and Memory.* Princeton: Princeton Univ. Press, 1999.

---. *The Great Irish Famine.* London: Gill and Macmillan, 1989.

---. "Making History in Ireland in the 1940s and 1950s: The Saga of the Great Famine." *Irish Review* 12 (1992).

O'Neill, Thomas P. "The Queen and the Famine." *Threshold*, 1.2 (summer 1957).

O'Rourke, John. *The History of the Great Irish Famine of 1847, with Notices of Earlier Irish Famines.* Dublin, 1989.

O'Sullivan, Patrick, ed. *The Meaning of the Famine.* London: Leicester Univ. Press, 1997.

Peck, Deborah. *The Irish Famine: A Case of Cultural Trauma, Delayed Mourning, Disenfranchised Grief and Recovered Memory.* Unpublished Ph.D. Thesis, Mass, School of Professional Psychology, 2000.

Póirtéir, Cathal. *Famine Echoes.* Dublin: Gill and Macmillan, 1995.

---. *The Great Irish Famine.* Dublin: Mercier Press, 1995.

Robinson, Mary. *A Voice for Somalia.* Dublin: O'Brien Press, 1992.

Rossa, Jeremiah O'Donovan. *Rossa's Recollections, 1838–1898.* Shannon, Irish University Press, 1998.

Sen, Amartya. *Poverty and Famines: An Essay on Entitlement and Deprivation.* Oxford: Clarendon Press, 1981.

Sicher, Efraim. *In the Shadow of History: Second Generation Writers and Artists and the Shaping of the Holocaust Memory in Israel and America.* New York, 1998.

Taylor, A. J. P. *Essays in English History.* London: Hamish Hamilton, 1976.

Transactions of the Central Relief Committee of the Society of Friends during the Famine in Ireland in 1846 and 1847 Dublin: Hodges and Smith, 1852.

Trevelyan, C. E. *The Irish Crisis.* London: Longman, Brown, Green and Longmans, 1848.

Walker, Brian. *Dancing to History's Tune. History, Myth and Politics in Ireland.* Belfast: Institute of Irish Studies, 1996.

Ward, Margaret. *Maud Gonne: Ireland's Joan of Arc.* London: Pandora, 1990.

Waters, John. "One Year of Peace Means We are Forever Changed." *Irish Times,* 22 August 1995.

Woodham–Smith, Cecil. *The Great Hunger: Ireland, 1845–1849.* London: Hamish Hamilton, 1962.

PART ONE: SILENCE

Chapter 1

Famine Lifelines: The Transatlantic Letters of James Prendergast

EDWARD MCCARRON

Milltown [County Kerry]
20 November, 1846

My dear Children,

The state of this Country is almost beyond description. Nothing to be seen in all quarters but distress and destitution. Famine and starvation threatening everywhere unless God mercifully send some foreign aid. . . . The last remittance ye sent is out long since and we are considerably in debt. Therefore if ye can assist us as usual do not delay your usual relief.

I remain affectionately your Father,
James Prendergast[1]

During the past several years an impressive volume of scholarship has focused on the Great Famine, work that has contributed both new findings and new perspectives. Today, for example, we have a keen understanding into the demographic impact of the Famine, are privy to the providential mindset of British policy makers, and have witnessed the extent of economic and political mismanagement during the tragedy.[2] Despite these important advances there are several stones left unturned in the field of famine studies. Many of us, for example, still view the Great Famine from a wide-angle lens: we have read of crowded workhouses, the spread of famine fever, the millions who took ship to America. Yet, as historian Kevin Whelan asks, how do we grasp at the local and individual level the implications of a tragedy that wiped out one million people in half a decade and sent another two million to distant shores ("Bitter Harvest" 21)? Indeed, the voice of the smallholder and the laborer—those who experienced the era most intimately and tragically—is surprisingly silent in this flurry of scholarship.

This oversight, in part, stems from the existing historiography of the Famine. The Irish Famine was the first famine that was widely covered in the press and well documented by the British government. The voluminous paper trail left by government officials, parliamentary inquests, poor law unions, and policy makers has led historians, as one scholar has noted, to "adopt an essentially administrative or political approach to understanding the famine" (Whelan, "Interpreting" 67). While this perspective is important, we also need to move beyond the political focus to retrieve a social history of the Famine. We need to understand the tragedy not only through the observations of politicians and elite observers but also through the experience of everyday people: small farmers, cottiers, women, and the poor who made up the majority of its victims and survivors.

The question is how do we reconstruct the experience and perceptions of such ordinary folk? From what vantage point—from what sources—can we understand the profound chances that refashioned their personal and local world? Cormac Ó Gráda, for one, has employed Famine poetry to penetrate the mindset and anguish concerning a world crumbling around them. Kevin Whelan has teased out the Famine's multiple personality by exploring the social landscape and regional changes in Irish geography. Robert Scalley has utilized a unique set of inquests, estate papers, and parliamentary reports to reconstruct the life of one townland, Ballykilcline, in Roscommon.[3] Still another source that illuminates the social history of the Famine are the personal letters and family correspondence written by ordinary people. Such letters (while elusive and rare) provide an invaluable lens for magnifying the personal and communal experiences of families caught during the Famine. James Prendergast of County Kerry wrote one such collection of letters. This correspondence, written from a father to his children in Boston, opens a window onto a transatlantic community that straddled the Famine abyss: its worldview, its chain migration, and its collective strategies for survival.[4]

Sources such as these have revealed tantalizing glimpses of the Irish understanding of *An Gorta Mor* and offer perhaps the most authentic record of a disintegrating culture and way of life. But they provide a far more revealing perspective as well. As poet Nuala Ni Dhomhnaill (69) suggests, "Fixated as we have become by the overwhelming vision of the people of the Famine as victims, are we not forgetting something very important: that they are representatives of a culture as different to ours today as that of Brahmanic India?" The Prendergast letters open up a window onto this world—not only of death and destruction, but also of the centrality of emigration, the web of family and neighbors in local communities, and especially the world of words that was often beyond the ken of the bureaucrats, correspondents, and landlords who have provided our primary view of the Famine. Indeed, English travelers and outsiders normally viewed the Irish "peasantry" from the vantage point of their coaches—a distance separated by hedgerow and mudsill as well as the figurative barriers of discrimination and ethnocentrism. As students of the Famine we need to cross over these hedgerows—to broaden the boundaries of our understanding of the Famine, and to recover the mindset, the experience, and the "voice" of ordinary folk who lived then. One of these voices was that of James Prendergast.

The Prendergasts were an extended family of cottiers and smallholders working land in Milltown, a village between Killorglin and Tralee. In 1841, two younger sons, Thomas and Jeffrey, sailed for Boston where they joined their sister Julia, who had earlier settled in the Fort Hill District, a bustling Irish neighborhood along the waterfront. During the next ten years—a period spanning the Great Famine—their father James and mother Elizabeth sent close to fifty letters to their emigrant children. This correspondence sketches a remarkable story of community distress, family survival, and personal deliverance. It also chronicles a world that would be irrevocably changed by the Famine.

I. Milltown

Milltown, in the parish of Kilcoleman, was a busy market town and estate village near the head of Dingle Bay. During the eighteenth century its livelihood centered on linen manufacturing, and many of its inhabitants were engaged as spinners and weavers—one of several pockets of textile manufacturing that flourished in Kerry.[5] The collapse of this domestic cottage industry (brought on by economic recession following the end of the Napoleonic Wars) had a pronounced impact on Milltown. Unemployment and low wages spurred many laborers to leave the village during the early nineteenth century, some migrating to England in search of work, others journeying to Boston. Other Milltown neighbors—poor and middling alike—were squeezed out by diminishing opportunities at home. Jeremiah Connors, a publican in the village, sought a situation in Boston for his eldest son Patt, "a proper honest Boy and a very Proficient scholar." Connors confided that he had seven in his family and hoped to place his son "in some good way to get thro life [in America] than to have him in this miserable country in Poverty." Patrick Connors was one of scores who left Milltown on the eve of the Famine. This exodus, as we will discover, would have an important impact during the Famine decades.

Milltown was held by the Godfreys, a Cromwellian family who occupied an estate immediately adjoining the town. During the eighteenth century they had refashioned an earlier village—introducing a tannery and linen industry, building a central square, and directing the construction of houses that were slated and of a vernacular Georgian style—presenting a new and "improved" front for visitors traveling through the town. By the early nineteenth century, Milltown boasted a local market and was a busy crossroads town in Kerry. Yet Milltown had its ragged fringe as well—vacant houses, abandoned bleach works, and a smoky warren of laborers' cabins that ringed the town like a necklace. It was here that we would have found James Prendergast in 1841.

Prendergast and his wife, Elizabeth, lived on Bleach Road, a crowded district of thatch houses and cottiers cabins that may have originally housed some of the spinners and weavers associated with Milltown's linen trade. In 1841, James Prendergast worked as a laborer—holding a small plot and garden on the edge of town.[6] Even in the years prior to the Famine, comfort was hard won. In August 1842, he wrote to his children that "we have one comfort for the winter we have a good Reck of Turf in the Garden . . . also I have sufficient potatoes until Christmas for the little I sat this year." What additional subsistence Prendergast enjoyed was supplemented by his children in Boston. He wrote to his son Thomas, "I bought a pig which cost me the sum of one pound ten shillings. . . . I have bought same out of your last remittance" (27 July 1841). In return the Prendergasts sent news of their village along with myriad pairs of stockings "all knitted by your affectionate Mother" (28 April 1842).

During the early 1840s, James and Elizabeth were regularly visited by a close network of kin and relations. Besides their children in Boston, the Prendergast letters identify three sons and their families living in Kerry prior to the Famine: Michael, a cottier and ploughman in Curraghglass; Maurice, who was "jobing [jobbing] in pigs and cattle with the little money reserved him"; and John, a cottier "in low circumstances" near Tralee.[7] They were among the more than one million cottiers in Ireland in 1841—laborers who worked land for a large farmer in return for a small wage, a cabin, and a plot of potato ground. In times of prosperity, cottiers had some degree of economic independence, but during the Famine they were among the hardest hit. This was largely due to their dependence on the potato as their principal food source. Indeed, the tuber figured most importantly in cottier's lives in that they were essentially "paid" in potatoes. When the potato blight devastated Ireland in 1846, many cottiers, having lost their potato "wage," asked to be paid in cash. Many were subsequently evicted or turned out by callous or improving farmers.[8] Such would be the fate of at least one of the Prendergast sons.

James Prendergast was in his fifties when he composed his first letter to Boston in 1841. Although literate, Prendergast dictated all of his messages to a series of local scriveners or "writers" as he called them. These included Daniel Connel, the local schoolmaster, and land surveyor Patrick Mahoney, whom he referred to on one occasion as "the poor pedagogue."[9] Prendergast likely needed someone with a steady hand and good penmanship to frame his letters. Yet, despite the fact that he uses a variety of "writers," there is a clear consistency in the letters—a certain eloquence, a witty turn of phrase, a depth of emotion.

The early correspondence between James Prendergast and Boston talks of local issues: the burial of the local pastor, neighbors emigrating to Boston, the promise of a bountiful potato crop. Most striking, perhaps, is the political sentiment expressed in the letters. In 1843, for example, Prendergast voices his support for Daniel O'Connell, proclaiming to his children in Boston that "[w]e are all in this Country Repealers" (3 August 1843). When O'Connell was later indicted, James defended him in no uncertain terms in a letter to Thomas:

> Danl O'Connell the Liberator was on his trial in Dublin this time past for treason against the government for holding Repeal Meetings, for enticing the people at these meetings . . . and also for collecting money at home and from foreign Lands called America. They say for the dismemberment of the Empire but they are liers [sic]. Danl means no such thing, he means equal laws, eql justice and equal right to Ireland together with some means of support for the poor of all Ireland. (3 December 1843)

While Prendergast's opinions typify the groundswell of support that Irish folk brought to O'Connell's campaign, it is unusual to hear these words in the letters of a cottier. Indeed, his voice, and his awareness of issues, challenges the popular image of Irish laborers during the mid-nineteenth century—one that paints them as ignorant, impoverished, and far from the mainstream of politics and culture. Yet, we should remember that the rural underclass in Ireland was part of a vibrant culture that largely existed outside the reach of English and Anglo-Irish contemporaries. The Prendergasts and their neighbors were part of a rich communal world that was open and expressive; one where words, mental dexterity, and knowledge had great value.[10] We should also remember that Milltown was not an isolated backwater. It was a market town, and an important crossroads in Kerry, a place where one exchanged news along with other commodities. Such news and ideas naturally found their way to Boston.

II. The Famine
In October 1845, local news in the Prendergast letters took a dark and ominous turn:

> My Dear Children,

> The beginnings of this Harvest was very promising, the crops in general had a very rich appearance, and it was generally expected that next season would be very plentiful. But within the last few weeks the greatest alarm prevails, throughout the Kingdom. It is dreaded that nothing less than a famine must prevail next summer unless the Almighty Lord interpose. A disease has seized the potato crop which was the standing food of the Country. The Potatoes which were good and healthy a few days since are now rotten in the Ground. . . . The Newspapers teem with alarming Accounts of the same disease throughout the Kingdom. I cannot say whether the loss is equal to the alarm. But dread of the greatest nature pervades all classes. . . . (postmarked 25 October 1845)

In subsequent letters Prendergast tried to make sense of the rapid changes that were churning about him. His dispatches to Boston comment on local concerns such as food shortages, rising prices, and poor relief. With growing apprehension, he chronicles the failure of the potato crop and notes bitterly to his children on 20 November 1846 that "Potatoes are seldom in Market and the few that then come are bought by the rich as a rarity."

By 1847 and 1848, conditions had reached a desperate state in Milltown. Prendergast wrote to his children,

> We have no sort of employment for the poor. And the Workhouses are scarcely sufft to receive them. Farmers are oppressed with poor rates & other charges. Many are deserting their farms and flying to America as fast as they can, destitution is seen almost every where. (29 October 1848)

Indeed, Prendergast family letters describe a world turned upside down. Maurice Prendergast, writing to his siblings in Boston, noted that the poorhouse, normally the place of the infirm and destitute, was thronged with "many a desent [sic] person well reared."[11] Conditions in many of the workhouses had reached a deplorable state of overcrowding and were infested with disease. What should have been a refuge was looked upon by the poor as a place of last resort. Yet their options were few. Some neighbors sold their worldly possessions at the "pawn office here" which, as the elder Prendergast noted "are so stocked with goods that 10 shillings could scarcely be raised on the value of five pounds." Others turned to more drastic measures. As Maurice Prendergast remarked in 1848 even the jails were filled, "people only doing Crime to get something to eat or to be transported, preferring it to be a better life."

For many in Milltown poor relief and public works were not enough to sustain them. Prendergast letters to Boston contain news of friends and relations who were daily "falling [with] fever and dysentery." The Prendergasts themselves were not spared. Son John, a cottier outside Tralee, died of famine fever during the ravages of "black '47," leaving behind a young daughter, Julia. James and his wife Elizabeth likewise weathered bouts of relapsing fever. As Maurice noted, they "would be in their grave" if not for the assistance of our "family of friends" in America.

Milltown was hard hit by the Famine. One measure of the devastation that hit the district was the decline in townsfolk between 1841 and 1851. In that decade alone, the population in Milltown dipped from 797 people to 485 (close to 40 percent either dead or displaced).[12] Rural townlands in the parish were also devastated. Rathpook, the homeplace of several emigrants to Boston, boasted 17 inhabited houses in 1841, but only 3 a decade later (with a corresponding drop in population from 86 to 19 persons). *Rathpook* translates as "the Fort of the Fairies." In the years that followed, it was a lonely place, haunted by its Famine memories. Indeed, by 1861 only one person remained in the townland. Rathpook had turned into a ghost town—as many of its survivors took ship to America (Egan 93, 96–97).

III. Emigration
Besides death and the workhouse, emigration was the other great escape from the Famine. Indeed, it is a constant theme that appears in the Prendergast letters. In the pre-Famine years there are myriad references to voyagers leaving for, as James described it to Jeffrey, "that Yankee Country." This exodus out of Milltown accelerated during the potato blight as cottiers and farmers alike were "flying to America."

This transatlantic movement, however, presents something of a quandary. How were the poor—the cottiers and laborers described in the Prendergast letters (and those who had the least amount of resources)—able to emigrate during this time of destitution? The explanation is that emigration was *already* a notable feature of Milltown life well before the Famine because of the earlier erosion of the spinning and weaving industry. During the Famine era, remittances from these earlier emigrants, many of them established in Boston, provided the means by which their friends and relations were able to escape.[13] As Peter Gray reminds us, in rural districts without this established tradition of migration—west Cork, for example—the poor were reluctant or unable to leave "and they often died in their own villages as strength and resources became exhausted" (*Irish Famine* 100). This reluctance may have been all the more accentuated in Irish-speaking communities where an intimate, communal way of life held precedent.

The ability of family members to make the transatlantic leap was often choreographed at home by patriarchs like James Prendergast. Throughout the Famine his letters are a conduit of information—a lifeline—for family members at home in dire need of assistance. In 1847, for example, he appeals to his children in Boston for passage money for his grandson James, age fifteen, whose family was sick and destitute. Prendergast wrote that "the Boy himself is most anxious for the call . . . he is active, strong, and I think both graceful and grateful" (26 September 1847). When several months elapsed and still no passage money appeared, Prendergast persuasively added, "If he were over [in America] he ought to help his own family and free ye from a part of your cares here on this side" (18 June 1848). As David Fitzpatrick suggests, homeland appeals such as this were a key element in negotiating emigration during the Famine and were designed as a likely strategy to inspire the obligations and duties of relations abroad ("Flight from Famine" 178; *Oceans* 516–25).

Yet emigration, as seen through the letters of James Prendergast, was often fraught with uncertainty and danger. Dispatches to his children contain news of friends who never arrived at their destination or neighbors who suffered a worse fate at Quarantine Stations such as Grosse Isle on the St. Lawrence. In the summer of 1847, he wrote to his children:

> I am very sorry to hear that young Patk Heffernan of Rathpogue died
> within a few hours sail of Quebec and my poor friend Mary Connor, sister
> to Jerry Connor late of Milltown who was going to her Brothers

[in]Hamilton [Ontario], I heard died after landing. The accounts of death
daily received here are really terrifying. (21 August 1847)

This is one of the more emotional responses that one witnesses in the
letters of James Prendergast. Perhaps it was because his own son had
recently braved the Atlantic crossing. He wrote on 25 July 1847,

> your mother and I feel very uneasy on account of your Brother Michl.
> About the 27th of March last he left home, and delayed a few days, only,
> in Cork, before he sailed for St. Johns, New Brunswick, as we heard.
> Since that time we never heard from him. . . . We are really alarmed on his
> account. He left 4 Children and their poor Mother, with no more
> subsistence than Nine shillings.

Prior to the Famine Michael Prendergast worked as a cottier—
struggling to survive on a small wage and a thin patch of potato ground.
He supplemented his livelihood by plowing and hauling goods on his
donkey, which his father noted "was the poor boy's sole support." Yet
Michael suffered a string of reversals. His donkey was killed "thro the
means of some Blackguard's ill treating," and he slipped further into
poverty, a decline that was accentuated by the Famine (to Jeffrey, 7
March 1845). By 1847, there was no work to be had, his family
endured recurrent bouts of fever, and they clung precariously to a small
cabin on Bleach Road. It came as no surprise, then, when James wrote
to his children that Michael was planning to set off for America rather
than "remain the last of his days in misery" (21 April 1847). He
traveled alone, hoping to make money in Boston to send home to his
family.

Michael's journey to America paralleled the experience of many
Irish emigrants in 1847. With passage paid by his brothers in Boston,
Michael traveled to Cork, which was rapidly becoming the primary
Irish port of departure for Liverpool and America. Here Michael would
have found an exodus driven out of panic. In March 1847 (the month of
Michael's departure), the *Cork Examiner* noted: "The emigrants of this
year are not like those of former ones; they are now actually running
away from fever and disease and hunger, with money scarcely
sufficient to pay passage for and find food for the voyage."[14] Many,
like Michael Prendergast, took ship aboard older timber vessels bound
for Quebec or St. John, even though their eventual destination was "the
Boston States." This decision, of course, was motivated by inexpensive
fares. In 1847, the United States instituted a series of passenger acts
that imposed harsh regulations on emigrant shipping bound for
America and raised the price of transatlantic passage to more than 7

pounds per passenger—beyond the reach of most laborers and cottiers. This encouraged voyagers like Prendergast to choose the much cheaper route to the British Maritime Provinces.[15] The vessels that sailed this Canadian route are known popularly as the "coffin ships." Many of them were unregulated, overcrowded and poorly provisioned. Under such conditions disease—especially typhus and dysentery—often spread rapidly on board. Indeed, popular memory asserts that mortality was extremely high aboard the coffin ships—and that many traveling the Canadian route were buried in a line of unmarked graves upon the Atlantic.[16] Thus we have the context for James Prendergast's anxiety over Michael's voyage.

Having said this, however, there is an important distinction to be drawn between the popular image of the Famine exodus and its reality. New research, notably by Cormac O'Grada, asserts that fewer perished on the transatlantic crossing than has been implied in traditional accounts of the "coffin ships." While Canadian voyages in 1847 did encounter harsh conditions and excess mortality, it is a mistake, O'Grada claims, to assume that such mortality was the norm throughout the Famine. American-bound shipping, especially to New York, largely avoided the tragic conditions of fever, death, and disaster that prevailed in 1847. Instead, "the great majority of those forced out in the late 1840s made it safely to the other side" (105–6). One of them was Michael Prendergast.

After a long and painful silence, news came that Michael had arrived in St. John, New Brunswick, penniless and in need of help. His brothers sent him two five-dollar bills and the admonition to "lose no time in coming to Boston."[17] Indeed, many of the Famine Irish arriving in Canada journeyed south to New England. Some, like Michael, traveled aboard steamers via Eastport, Maine; others walked along the "emigrant trail," which cut a path through Bangor, Ellsworth, and Portland. In 1847 alone, more than 37,000 Irish newcomers arrived in Boston, increasing its population by one third and straining its housing and charitable resources to the breaking point (O'Connor 60).

IV. Boston

Irish immigrants coming to Boston in the 1840s settled in several distinct neighborhoods, each with its own character and identity. Many Irish—particularly those from Ulster and Connaught—peopled the streets of the old north end, a maritime district that was a heterogeneous mix of Yankee and immigrant. Others settled around Fort Hill, a tangled warren of streets and laneways along the waterfront that today comprises the financial district of Boston. In 1847 Fort Hill was far from prosperous. Here, newly arrived Irish entered the workforce near the bottom of the economic ladder, finding jobs as day laborers, dockworkers, and draymen. Irish-born women, likewise, worked in lower-scale positions as factory hands and home seamstresses. Some helped supplement family income by doing neighborhood laundry or taking in boarders. It was in this neighborhood of cobbled streets and wooden tenements that we would have found the Prendergasts.

Michael Prendergast settled in the vicinity of Fort Hill, living in a tenement on South Street with his brother Thomas and several other Kerry immigrants. During the mid-nineteenth century, Fort Hill and the South Cove district in Boston were meccas for Kerry immigrants and Milltown folk. They congregated on Atkinson, Pearl, Oliver, and South streets. This residence pattern wasn't a coincidence. Recent literature has underlined the importance of homeland networks in choosing precisely where to settle in the New World. As John Mannion and Fidelma Maddock have noted, "Tenements in the cities filled up with people from a particular parish across the Atlantic; entire streets came to be dominated by acquaintances, friends and relatives from home." Such communities were often self-perpetuating: "A pathfinder or pioneering family established a base; friends and kin followed through a system of information diffusion and remittances for fares." (Mannion and Maddock 371). Indeed, this serial migration was common throughout Irish-New England during the Famine era. Providence, Rhode Island, for example, had strong transatlantic links with parishes in south Tyrone (McCarron 145–61). The milltown of Dover, New Hampshire, likewise played host to a vigorous migration from handloom districts in Monaghan and Armagh, particularly the parish of Keady.[18] These migration chains in some cases stretched over several decades and provided needy emigrants with both a cushion of support and a ready destination. As Edward Senior asserted in 1855 in the wake of the Famine, "everyone has one leg over the Atlantic" (qtd. in Fitzpatrick, "Emigration" 607).

So it was in Boston. In his letters, James Prendergast alone makes reference to more than fifty different Milltown relations and acquaintances living in the city—many of them clustered in the streets and alleyways surrounding the financial district today. South Street is a case in point. Census data and city directories during the 1850s reveal that in a single block one would have found a cluster of kin and neighbors from home. Thomas Prendergast, a hostler, lived at 92 South Street with his wife Catharine Cotter. Although they were likely from the same region in Kerry, it was nonetheless in Boston where they met and married in 1847.[19] By 1850, Thomas and Catharine shared a wooden tenement crowded with forty-one other immigrants—most of them from Ireland and the Canadian Maritime Provinces. These included brother Michael and Michael Neville from Milltown. Several doors down were sister Julia and her husband Cornelius Reardon, a confectioner, as well as Jeffrey and Catharine Prendergast, who lived at 90 South Street. James Maurice, working as an apprentice machinist, boarded with his Uncle Jeffrey. He continued to send what little money he could over to his family throughout the 1850s.[20]

One of their neighbors on South Street was Dr. Francis Spring, a physician and son of an affluent farming family in Milltown. Despite the social divide between the Springs and Prendergasts, they shared kinship and deep roots on both sides of the Atlantic. When Maurice Prendergast was evicted from his cottier's cabin near Killarney, he found "a situation" with the Springs back in Milltown, strong farmers who provided him with a house and field.[21] The Springs were always treated with deference in James Prendergast's letters. He instructed his children "in your letters always I expect you will speak largely of the Springs in America as it would be [the] wish of these at home that it would be said that they were doing well and in great Situations" (21 March 1843). The Prendergasts in Boston most likely didn't volunteer the news that the Springs resided in the same humble tenements that they did.

The point to be underlined, however, is the deep layers of family association and community networks that existed in Boston during the Famine era. These ties are frequently voiced in the letters of James Prendergast. In the autumn of 1847 he noted that:

> A letter arrived here [from Boston] stating that Edmd Moriarty, Brother of John Murphy Of Ballyverane, was in a very bad state of health. He is the son of respectable Parents and a near relation of your own. . . . I would be glad that ye should enquire + let us know whether he is dead or alive. You will get every information from Maurice O'Brien, son in law to Farrel McHugh of Drominbeg. If you know not O'Brien you can hear where he is by applying to Daniel Buckley, No. 3 Broadstreet. (26 September 1847)

This recitation of familiar names and associations is significant for two reasons. First, one carries away from such letters the image of a man, not isolated in his Famine cabin, but instead having his finger on the pulse of a community far across the Atlantic. For him, Boston is peopled with familiar faces, the next parish across the Atlantic. On a deeper level, one also gets some sense for how those like Prendergast manipulated the strings of such emigrant communities. His recitation of family and neighborhood connections in the homeland was a poignant echo of recognition and memory for Boston immigrants—one that may have prompted them to send assistance home.

These lines of communication, orchestrated by transatlantic letters, were vital to the survival of villages like Milltown during the Great Famine. Between 1841 and 1850, for example, close to 150 pounds sterling was sent from Prendergast family members in Boston to relations in Milltown. This money was used to buy food, pay the landlord's rent, cover doctor's bills, and even purchase a cow to provide milk for Maurice's hungry family. Many families in Irish-America felt the same sense of obligation. In 1850, for example, more than one million pounds flowed back to Ireland, one of the greatest examples of transatlantic philanthropy during the nineteenth century (Fitzpatrick, "Flight from Famine" 178). Indeed, many of the rural poor who survived the Famine did so because of the charity and generosity of American relations. This point was not lost on the likes of James Prendergast. On the eve of the Famine he wrote to Thomas, "I and your beloved mother are well and strongly living still, tho in truth we would have died long since by all reason were it not for ye Dear children that are nourishing us in our old and feeble days" (6 December 1844).

Not all were as fortunate as the Prendergasts. Letters to Boston in the years surrounding the Famine make frequent reference to elderly parents in Milltown waiting for remittances and needy families forgotten by errant relations in America. In August 1845 James wrote to his children,

> If ye see either of your cousins, the Fords, tell them their Mother is really distressed in Cork. Thomas Kelliher the Carman told he met her [looking] worn and old . . . and endeavoring to work but unable to do so. She said that she had not the sign of a cloak and if she had she would return to Milltown that she could live more comfortably by begging among her neighbors. (9 August 1845)

Prendergast urged that "it would do them credit" to send their mother some assistance. In a sense, then, what we are seeing is not only a father writing to his children, but an extended community speaking across the Atlantic. Prendergast is a local clearinghouse of information, inquiry, and assistance for his neighbors. He is a go-between who passes on news and complaints to far-off acquaintances and attempts to breach the silence that so often descended over families separated by both tragedy and the wide Atlantic.

Throughout the Famine, the Prendergasts continued to send over news of Milltown and inquiries of Boston. In 1847, for example, they described the departure of their parish priest, Father Bartholomew O'Connor, who left for Boston on a mission from the diocese. He spent more than a year in America, raising money for the construction of a new Cathedral in Killarney (Egan 32–33). It was an assignment tinged with irony in the midst of the Famine. Upon O'Connor's return, according to Elizabeth Prendergast's letter to her children, "He said that all his countrymen shewed themselves as Irishmen ought . . . friends to the cause on which he went" (21 January 1850). On one level, O'Connor's efforts reflect the deep Kerry roots in cities like Boston. On another level, however, they help to illuminate the role of the church (or lack of it) during the Famine. Indeed, the Catholic church in Ireland has received mixed reviews for its actions to alleviate suffering during the Famine. While some bishops, such as Archbishop John MacHale of Tuam, drew attention to the plight of the poor and the neglect of the British government, other prelates were more moderate and conciliatory (see Gray, *Irish Famine* 158–59). Emblematic of this ambivalence was the unprecedented decision in 1847, at the height of the Famine, to raise money in America for a new Cathedral in Kerry rather than for the care of its sick and suffering. James Prendergast, perhaps, sensed this injustice. He remarked to his children, concerning Father O'Connor's mission to Boston, "If the Priest Mr. O'Connor should visit ye, ye need not lose much to him on our account. We were under no compliments to him" (26 September 1847).

V. Significance

The letters of James Prendergast are important for several reasons. First, as Kevin Whelan asserts, such letters suggest that beneath the seeming chaos of the emigrant experience there is a "deep grammar of stability" ("Interpreting" 99). They reveal the continuing links of communication and affection that bound families and neighbors separated by the Atlantic chasm. Such letters also suggest the ability of Famine emigrants in America to reconstruct families and build networks of community based upon Old World antecedents, homeland affiliation and local identity. As Whelan suggests, instead of the "lonesome lemmings" that have figured in earlier images of Famine migration, we need to recognize that some families, "seemingly fractured by emigration," were held "together by invisible but powerful filaments of affection and duty."[22]

In addition, the Prendergast letters are important in that they provide some clues into how the poor and the "voiceless" encountered the Famine. Certainly their experience, as viewed from the historical record, was one of grim misery and despair. But was that all? Letters such as James Prendergast's reveal that in the midst of difficulty there was also hope for the future. The fact that he knows his family is doing well in America gives him something to live for. Indeed, family news, marriages, and new grandchildren were food for the soul, even in the worst of times. In these letters one witnesses a depth of emotion that transported some—like Prendergast—beyond the confines of the Famine.

Finally, the Prendergast letters help to suggest new insights into Irish emigration in the years prior to the Famine. One of the surprising discoveries in the letters is a marked degree of return migration to Milltown during the early 1840s. Conventional wisdom on Irish migration asserts that very few immigrants returned to Ireland during the nineteenth century. While many left as "exiles" and perhaps dreamed one day of returning home, there was little incentive— economically or socially—for them to make the full circle. This argument, at least from a local perspective, is challenged in the letters of James Prendergast. Prior to the Famine he describes a number of Atlantic voyagers who returned to Ireland, particularly in times of economic hardship. In 1842, he asks his children "let me know in your next letter is America getting any improvement in the line of business as a great many of the neighbors who left this came home again" (20 August 1842). He also takes note of several immigrants who came home for a visit—carrying gifts and news from New England. The Spring family, for instance, journeyed home for five weeks in 1842. John Payne, likewise a resident of Fort Hill, returned with news of family and friends.[23] It is important to recognize that these returned "Yanks"—even those who came home to stay after failure overseas— reinforced the mechanics of migration that left Ireland's shores. They acted as a conduit of aid and assistance for aspiring emigrants and helped to diffuse information about life in the New World. As such they represent a "missing link" in understanding the process of chain migration from rural parishes like Milltown to the streets of Irish-America. Such return migration, of course, decreased considerably during and after the Famine. In the wake of the tragedy many emigrants had neither the means nor the inclination to return home.

VI. Aftermath

What was the ultimate fate of James Prendergast and his wife Elizabeth? From his letters we know that prior to the potato blight they were planning to join their children in Boston. This decision, of course, became more problematic during the Famine as hunger and disease ran roughshod from cabin to cabin. It was Prendergast's opinion that younger and hardier folk should emigrate first in order to help those who stayed behind. He also made the decision to divide his remittance among "old and young. We could not see them in want without sharing with them while we had it."[24] It was a communal strategy that enabled many of his extended family to survive the Famine. Prendergast himself, however, was not as fortunate. Bouts of relapsing fever and a weakened constitution brought him to his deathbed in December 1848. His final letter bid farewell to his family in Boston:

> Thanks to your goodness my dear Children I had every comfort hitherto, but now I am pennyless, the last of what I had is gone. A long illness in these times takes away money very quickly. If I die as I am sure I will before many days, there is not a shilling in the House to defray my funeral expenses, and your Mother must have recourse to credit from some neighbours until ye relieve her.

He added that "The only regret I feel in quitting this life is that of leaving your Mother alone, but I am reconciled to submit to the will of Heaven, as I know ye will not neglect her."[25]

Our story does not end here, however. Prendergast's widow, Elizabeth, continued to send letters to her children in Boston, providing news of the community and chiding far-off neighbors to send money to their Kerry relations. Despite entreaties from Boston, she at first resisted emigration herself, arguing that she had promised her husband she would "stretch my bones" next to his. In early 1850, however, she revealed a change of heart. Perhaps it was her concern for Julia, an orphaned granddaughter in her charge, and the hope of providing her with a new life.[26] In September 1850, Elizabeth and Julia left the village of Milltown accompanied by Florence Riordan, the brother of Cornelius Riordan in Boston (who was son-in-law to Elizabeth Prendergast). Taking a featherbed, clothes, and belongings they boarded a ship in Cork and made the crossing to England in the hold. Elizabeth's final letter leaves us as she is standing at dockside in Liverpool. In her letter (which is torn and much read over the years), she writes, "I wish to let you know that we are here 7 days under heavy Cost—waiting until the ship sails, her name is Noibe [Niobe] and her captain name is Soule which is to leave Liverpool on the 21st instant." She concluded with a wish and a prayer, stating, "Thanks be to God [we'll have the] courage to cross the [ocean]. . . . Your Loving Mother until Death, Elizabeth Prendergast."[27]

Significantly, this is the last letter in the Prendergast collection, and it raises several anxious questions. Did Elizabeth Prendergast and Julia meet their ship? Did they arrive safely at their destination in Boston? Such questions haunt the experience of many Irish voyagers during the Famine, especially those departing the port of Liverpool. Liverpool in the nineteenth century was a notorious hub of crime, poverty, and desperation. Prospective immigrants were prey to a host of dangers before they set sail: hucksters and petty thieves who sought to relieve them of their savings and crowded boardinghouses along the waterfront that were often unsavory and charged exorbitant rates. Indeed, some Irish never escaped the docks in Liverpool but joined the ranks of the poor and destitute that peopled the tenements and unlit cellars of the seaport (see Scalley 184–216; Neal 123–36).

And what of Elizabeth? Her ship, the *Niobe,* arrived in Boston from Liverpool on 26 October 1850. The passenger list, attested that day by Captain Freeman Soule, included Elizabeth Prendergast, age 60, Julia Prendergast, age 7, along with fellow traveler Florence Riordan ("Boston Passenger Lists"). In the years that followed Elizabeth lived on South Street, surrounded by a growing network of family and friends. She watched as son Michael was reunited with his wife Nelly and three children who journeyed from Ireland after the Famine. She also looked on proudly as Jeffrey opened a grocery on South Street in 1855 and eventually purchased the tenement building and premises. Yet in her last years her thoughts must have often turned to Ireland: to the medieval churchyard at Keel where her husband James lay buried, to the winding lanes and market square of Milltown, and to the cluster of cabins that lined Bleach Road. Once bustling with friends and neighbors, many of these landmarks were now silent—a lasting legacy of the Famine. Indeed, many of the survivors of this world, like Elizabeth Prendergast, had moved on to new lives in Camden town, Hells Kitchen, or Fort Hill—Irish communities that were surrounded by the cacophonous hum of factory, wharf, and waterside. For some emigrants this new world offered hardship and exploitation, but for others it held the promise of new beginnings. It was a world that James Prendergast would have embraced.

Notes

Thanks to Tom O'Sullivan, local historian in Milltown, County Kerry, for his hospitality and his assistance in the field identifying sites mentioned in the Prendergast letters.

1. James Prendergast to his Children, 20 November 1846, James Prendergast Letters (henceforth JPL), MS 86-141, John J. Burns Library, Boston College.
2. For new work on the Famine see O'Grada; Gray, *Famine, Land and Politics;* and Kinealy. Also see Gray, "'Potatoes and Providence'" and the essays of Donnelly in Vaughn 272–371.
3. See O'Grada, especially chapter 6 (famine memory), 194–225; Whelan, "Pre and Post Famine Landscape Change"; and Scalley. For new work on the Famine, also see Morash and Hayes; Crawford; and the essays in *Eire-Ireland.*

4. The Prendergast letters begin in February 1841 and run through September 1850. A selection of the letters (those written during the Famine years) have been published in "Bloodlines."

5. On Milltown's linen industry see Egan 40, 45; Galvin.

6. As evidenced from his letters, Prendergast was almost certainly a laborer or cottier. He writes to his children on several occasions regarding a new potato garden that he works. For example he comments, "I have taken a good new garden in addition to the redigging which I had. If [I] can seed and till what I have I may say I would be happy against next season" (25 February 1841). He later writes to Thomas, "I have double the quantity of Garden sat this year that I had last year" (29 May 1841).

7. On the occupations of the Prendergast sons, see James Prendergast to his children, 24 May 1844. On the eve of the Famine James informed his children in Boston that "Maurice removed on the first July last. He lives with Mr. John Lynch at Dromin near Killarney. He has a very good place with Constant employment. His wages are a house and garden, the grass of a cow, three sheep and his ass and six pounds yearly" (9 August 1845).

8. For a brilliant visual representation of the cottier's world see Aalen, Whelan, and Stout 74–75. On cottiers in general see Miller, 51–54.

9. James Prendergast to his children, 27 July 1844. Concerning the identity of scriveners see James Prendergast to his children, 20 August 1842 (Patrick Mahoney) and 15 December 1848 (Daniel Connell). Regarding Prendergast's literacy—he signs his letters and includes at least one post-script that he pens himself. See James Prendergast to Thomas Prendergast, 27 July 1841.

10. The experience of everyday people in nineteenth-century Ireland has been the subject of several recent works. See especially Scalley and Porteir.

11. Maurice Prendergast. Concerning the workhouses see Kissane 89–105.

12. Egan 96. Overall, the parish of Kilcoleman declined by 40 percent—from 4,740 (1841) to 2,844 (1851). These rates matched or exceeded many areas in Munster. See Kissane 173.

13. This point follows the insights of James Donnelly who identifies several areas of north Connaught and south Ulster with both excess mortality and a high incidence of migration. See "Excess Mortality and Emigration," Vaughn 354-55.

14. Quoted in O'Grada 107. Despite this bleak assessment in Cork, O'Grada asserts that many who left during the Famine had some means to do so and were not the very poorest in Irish society.

15. Gray, *Irish Famine* 103. Close to 100,000 left in 1847 for Canada. For emigration figures during the Famine see Miller 292.

16. In fact, upward of 30 percent of those traveling the Canadian route in 1847 perished—some at sea, others at Quarantine Stations such as Grosse Isle. See Kenny 103.

17. This comes from a fragment of a letter to Michael Prendergast in St. John, New Brunswick, that survives in the Prendergast collection. The salutation reads, "My dear Brother Michael" and is dated 14 June 1847.

18. Interestingly, this chain migration from Armagh continues into recent years. The folk singer Tommy Makem, from Keady, first arrived at Dover and continues to live there. On the Dover Irish see Bergen. Data on places of origin for Irish families in Dover comes primarily from headstones in St. Mary's cemetery, Dover.

19. Thomas Prendergast and Catharine Cotter were married at St. Patrick's Church in the South End on 2 September 1846. See St. Patrick's Church parish records.

20. The Irish community on South Street was reconstructed from state and federal records. See 1850 Federal Census 437–38. Also see 1855 State Census; and Boston City Directories, 1850–1855.

21. The Springs were strong farmers who farmed 97 acres in the townland of Ballyoughtragh South. In 1850 they occupied a house, orchard, and land and employed three cottiers, including Maurice Prendergast. See Griffith's Valuation (1850), County Kerry, Parish of Kilcolman, National Archives of Ireland, Dublin.

22. Whelan, "Interpreting" 99–100.

23. James Prendergast to his children, 20 November 1846.

24. James Prendergast to his children, 21 August 1847.

25. James Prendergast to his children, 15 December 1848. James Prendergast was buried at the family plot in Keel, County Kerry.

26. Elizabeth Prendergast to her children, 14 July 1850.

27. Elizabeth Prendergast to Thomas Prendergast [postmarked 20 September 1850]. On her preparations for the voyage, see Elizabeth Prendergast to her children, 19 August 1850.

Works Cited
Abbreviations used
JPL: James Prendergast Letters, John J. Burns Library, Boston College
MSA: Massachusetts State Archives, Dorchester, Mass.
NAW: National Archives, New England Records Center, Waltham, Mass.
Aalen, F. H. A., Kevin Whelan, and Matthew Stout, eds. *Atlas of the Irish Rural Landscape.* Toronto: Univ. of Toronto Press, 1997.
Bergen, Paul. "Occupation, Household and Family among the Irish of Nineteenth Century Dover, New Hampshire." M.A. Thesis. Univ. of New Hampshire, 1989.
"Bloodlines: Letters by James and Elizabeth Prendergast." *Boston College Magazine* 51.1 (Winter 1996): 26–33.
Boston City Directories, 1850–1855. MSA.

"Boston Passenger Lists, 1820–91." Microfilm M277, Roll 36 #879. NAW.

Connors, Jeremiah. Addendum to a letter written from James Prendergast to Thomas Prendergast. 21 May 1845. JPL. The addendum is signed by Connors.

Crawford, E. Margaret, ed. *The Hungry Stream: Essays on Emigration and Famine.* Belfast: Inst. of Irish Studies, 1997.

Dhomhnaill, Nuala Ni. "A Ghostly Alhambra." *Irish Hunger: Personal Reflections of the legacy of the Famine.* Ed. Tom Hayden. Boulder: Rinehart, 1997. 69.

Donnelly, James Jr. "Excess Mortality and Emigration." Vaughn 350–56.

Egan, Thomas, ed. *Milltown Parish: A Centenary Celebration.* Naas: Leinster Leader, 1994.

1850 Federal Census. Suffolk County Massachusetts. Ser. 432, Reel #337. NAW. 437–38.

1855 State Census. Boston, 8th Ward. Vol. 25. MSA. 151–52.

Eire-Ireland XXXII.1 (Spring 1997).

Fitzpatrick, David. "Emigration, 1801–70." Vaughn 562-607.

---. "Flight from Famine." *The Great Irish Famine*, Cathal Poirteir, ed. Dublin, Mercier Press, 1995: 178-184.

---. *Oceans of Consolation: Personal Accounts of Irish Migration to Australia.* Ithaca, N.Y.: Cornell Univ. Press, 1994.

Galvin, Michael. "Miltown Local History." *Cois Leamhna: Monuments, Milestones and Memories—Journal of the Killorglin History and Folklore Society* 1 (Summer 1984): 27–39.

Gray, Peter. *Famine, Land and Politics: British Government and Irish Society, 1843–1850.* Dublin: Irish Academic Press, 1999.

---. *The Irish Famine.* New York: Abrams, 1995.

---. "'Potatoes and Providence': British Government Responses to the Great Famine." *Bullan* 1.1 (Spring 1994): 75–90.

Kenny, Kevin. *The American Irish: A History.* New York: Pearson, 2000.

Kinealy, Christine. *This Great Calamity: The Irish Famine, 1845–52.* Boulder, Colo.: Roberts Rinehart, 1995.

Kissane, Noel. *The Irish Famine: A Documentary History.* Dublin: National Library of Ireland, 1995.

Mannion, John, and Fidelma Maddock. "Old World Antecedents, New World Adaptations: Inistioge immigrants in Newfoundland." *Kilkenny: History and Society.* William Nolan and Kevin Whelan. Dublin: Geography, 1990: 345-404.

McCarron, Edward T. "Altered States: Tyrone Migration to Providence, Rhode Island, during the Nineteenth Century." *The Clogher Record* (1997): 145–61.

Miller, Kerby. *Emigrants and Exiles: Ireland and the Irish Exodus to North America.* New York: Oxford Univ. Press, 1985.

Morash, Chris, and Richard Hayes, eds. *Fearful Realities: New Perspectives on the Famine.* Dublin: Irish Academic Press, 1996.

Neal, Frank. "Black '47: Liverpool and the Irish Famine." Crawford 123–36.

O'Connor, Thomas H. *The Boston Irish: A Political History.* Boston: Northeastern Univ. Press, 1995.

Ó Gráda, Cormac. *Black '47 and Beyond: The Great Irish Famine in History, Economy and Memory.* Princeton: Princeton Univ. Press, 1999.

Porteir, Cathal. *Famine Echoes.* Dublin: Gill and Macmillan, 1995.

Prendergast, Elizabeth. Letter to her children. 21 January 1850. JPL.

---. Letter to her children. 14 July 1850. JPL.

---. Letter to her children. 19 August 1850. JPL.

---. Letter to Thomas Prendergast. [postmarked 20 September 1850]. JPL.

Prendergast, James. Letter to his children. 25 February 1841. JPL.

---. Letter to his children. 20 August 1842. JPL.

---. Letter to his children. 21 March 1843. JPL.

---. Letter to his children. 3 August 1843. JPL.

---. Letter to his children. 24 May 1844. JPL.

---. Letter to his children. 27 July 1844. JPL.

---. Letter to his children. 9 August 1845 JPL.

---. Letter to his children. [postmarked 25 October 1845]. JPL.

---. Letter to his children. 20 November 1846. JPL, MS 86–141.

---. Letter to his children. 21 April 1847. JPL.

---. Letter to his children. 25 July 1847. JPL.

---. Letter to his children. 21 August 1847. JPL.

---. Letter to his children. 26 September 1847. JPL.

---. Letter to his children. 18 June 1848. JPL.

---. Letter to his children. 29 October 1848. JPL.

---. Letter to his children. 15 December 1848. JPL.

---. Letter to Jeffrey Prendergast. 7 March 1845. JPL.

---. Letter to Thomas Prendergast. 29 May 1841. JPL.

---. Letter to Thomas Prendergast. 27 July 1841. JPL.

---. Letter to Thomas Prendergast. 28 April 1842 (stockings). JPL.

---. Letter to Thomas Prendergast. 3 December 1843. JPL.

---. Letter to Thomas Prendergast. 6 December 1844. JPL.

Prendergast, Maurice. Letter to brother and sister's husband. 22 June 1848. JPL.

Scalley, Robert J. *The End of Hidden Ireland: Rebellion, Famine, and Emigration.* New York: Oxford Univ. Press, 1995.

St. Patrick's Church parish records. "Marriages, 1836–1881." Archives, Archdiocese of Boston. Brighton, Mass.

Vaughn, W. E., ed. *New History of Ireland, Vol. V: Ireland Under the Union, I, 1801–70.* Oxford: Clarendon, 1989.

Whelan, Kevin. "Bitter Harvest." *Boston College Magazine* 51.1 (Winter 1996): 21.

---. "Interpreting the Irish Famine." Unpublished paper.

---. "Pre and Post Famine Landscape Change." *The Great Irish Famine.* Ed. Cathal Poirteir. Cork: Mercier, 1995. 19–33.

Chapter Two

The "Unborn and Unburied Dead": The Rhetoric of Ireland's *An Gorta Mor*

ROBERT A. SMART
MICHAEL R. HUTCHESON

I am not at all appalled by your tenantry going. That seems to me a necessary part of the process. . . . We must not complain of what we really want to obtain.
Sir Charles Wood, Chancellor of the Exchequer (22 November 1848)

At the height of the Great Hunger, the year known now as "Black '47," several strange terms appear in the journalistic lexicon to describe the horrors of famine-bred disease and death in Ireland, including *the unborn dead* and *the unburied dead*. The unborn dead, in the journalistic and literary imagination, wait to be counted in the Famine victim lists, but are not actually born because of the physical deterioration of their "parents" (Kennedy et al. 36). This is a new variation on an old trope, the revenge tragedy convention of the blood of the buried victim accusing the murderer. The unburied dead are—literally—the walking dead. Both unborn dead and unburied dead are part of a cluster of related tropes employed repeatedly by witnesses of the Famine years. In the *Weekly Freeman's Journal* of 17 July 1847, Henry Brennan described the corpses left to scavengers and parasites outside his Kilglass home as "the Unburied Dead." The account is horrific, detailing the work of wild dogs and "worms" on the bodies of the destitute and dead as they lay in the "waste cabins and dykes" of the surrounding area (Killen 148).

Brennan's account of "the Unburied Dead" echoes similar articles from *The Nation* in January 1847, which describe "hundreds of thousands of doomed wretches" who were "now walking or tottering upon this land . . . who must surely die—for whom, as for the man of Uz, the graves are ready" (Killen 101). The image of the unburied dead walking through the village, waiting to be buried "out of sight . . . without coffins" (Killen 101) is provocative, given Ireland's claim as the chief provenance of the Gothic in nineteenth-century popular literature. More terrible still are the accounts of men, women, and children buried undead, not yet fully succumbed to the ravages of Famine fever and disease. Even the restrained historian Cormac O'Grada admits that claims "that people were taken away for burial or even dumped in graves while still not quite dead are plentiful" and are in the end "plausible" (202). Thus the wellspring of rhetorical tropes and figures is replenished by the wealth of popular "folk" references to those buried undead during the Famine. Their burial grounds are forever marked in the local imagination as places where one might come to harm, and they are rich with rhetorical and metaphorical meaning for Gothic literature. Consider the following story recounted by Thomas Gallagher:

> There was also the story of the driver who was only temporarily nonplussed when the "corpse" he was trying to bury protested, at the graveyard, in a barely audible voice, that he was still alive. The driver regained his composure as quickly as he realized that the man had been declared dead at the hospital from which he'd taken him. In the driver's eyes this made the burial legal and proper, an assignment he had the right and responsibility to complete. Besides, the man was dying; he was close to death and would certainly be dead by the time they returned to the hospital. So the driver buried him anyway and collected his fee. (109)

In this context, the trope of premature burial attracts a number of interesting political and social connections, particularly regarding the motives of successive English cabinets as they tried to deal with the growing Irish calamity. As Christopher Morash has noted in his landmark study *Writing the Irish Famine*, the deadly application of Malthusian and Darwinian ideas to the "Irish Problem" made the Irish dead more "alive" in the sense of their relative value as part of the "solution" than they had been as living beings (28). These stories ultimately serve both a sympathetic and a cynical end.

These images are part of the broader grammar that underlies English-Irish political dialogue, in which the walking dead, the prematurely buried, the unborn dead, and (eventually) the vampire can be studied rhetorically to shed new light on Ireland's colonial relationship with

England in the nineteenth century. In regard to the Great Hunger, two discrete and clearly connected motives, one practical and the other metaphysical, drive this language. Primarily, these rhetorical images describe accurately the inhumanity and hopelessness of these villagers' situations. However, the language has another powerful and subversive purpose: to expose English colonial rapacity in Ireland, especially during *An Gorta Mor*.

Even in recent historiography about the Famine, we find references to the metaphysical dimension of this imagery. In *Mapping the Great Irish Famine*, Kennedy, Ell, Crawford, and Clarkson note that many of the "upper-bound estimates" of Famine deaths include "those who *would have been born*" had the Famine and its attendant diseases not lowered the fertility rates of Irish women (36). These "averted births" are named the "Unborn Dead" and they help to form the same chorus of children and adults who walk the margins of Brennan's Kilglass, waiting for the grave. They also include those countless unfortunates who were buried alive. In the shadows of the Peel and Russell administrations, being buried alive because one has been declared "dead" certainly resonates against the providential rhetoric used by *The Times*, Trevelyan, and countless other officials. As Christine Kinealy noted, "A providentialist interpretation of the blight cut across social barriers and found resonance with pauper and politician alike" (60). This, at the same time that death "from starvation or disease became so common that a number of newspapers ceased to report on them" (93), helps drive the irony that many of those who died from Famine-related disease were in fact "dead" before they "died." To remain alive in such circumstances is to be "undead." From 1847 through the publication of Sheridan LeFanu's "Carmilla" in 1871 to Bram Stoker's *Dracula* in 1897, the language about those "unborn dead," those buried alive, and the undead forms part of a subversive rhetoric that becomes increasingly essential to understanding the colonial and post-colonial struggles of Ireland.

f

Posterity will trace up to that Famine . . . that on this, as on many other occasions, Supreme Wisdom has educed permanent good out of transient evil.

Charles E. Trevelyan (1847)

A rhetorical analysis of these oppositions requires a search for conflicted motives, notably for a difference between what the language says and what its context means. Philosopher Kenneth Burke called attention to such syntactical and lexical contradictions, in rhetorical study termed non sequitur, paradox, and parataxis. In her article "Teaching Deconstructively," critic Barbara Johnson provides a taxonomy of such contradictions:

> [The use of] ambiguous words; . . . undecidable syntax created by a suspension of the text's claim structure between two often incompatible possibilities; incompatibilities between what a text says and what a text does; incompatibilities between explicitly foregrounded assertions and illustrative examples; and [the use of] obscurity, usually deliberately, as part of the artifice of the text, thus offering multiple possibilities for interpretation. (6)

This last element usually creates irony, intentional or dramatic. So, when the *Times* said that "something like harshness is the greatest humanity" as regards the growing calamities in Ireland, we can detect two plausible motives in the statement (O'Grada 83). Overtly, the *Times* advanced the principles of laissez faire political economy. However, we can detect a second motive when we compare these statements to other utterances that ascribed the Famine to Providence, as a punishment upon the Catholic Irish for the continuing presence of the "Romish Church and its idolatry." Read this way, the statement by the *Times* suggested that the Irish were suffering a rightful punishment and that interference by London (in the form of expanded Famine relief) would be meddling in the affairs of Providence, an act that might invite its own retribution.

In the fiction of Sheridan LeFanu and Bram Stoker, as well as in the political speeches and writings of Theobald Wolfe Tone, John Mitchel, and Michael Davitt, these language structures and tropes work within a radical and subversive rhetorical strategy. LeFanu and Stoker were outsiders within the British colonial hegemony, making them acute observers of the realities around them. This is a central element in the psychology of the "Other," which accurately describes the position of both men within Irish and British society. These observed realities are taken into the novels (as landscapes, descriptions of peasant life, accounts of historical violence) through a variety of narrative devices (letters, telegrams, newspaper clippings, bills of lading, etc.) and are eventually made "unreal," through their articulation within a Gothic narrative, replete with vampires, ghosts, undead, curses, and the like. For this reason critics of both LeFanu's and Stoker's work have insisted that Ireland and its historical landscapes are the real objects of study, not England, Stygia, or Transylvania. The ontological claims made by the narrative are ahistorical and mythic, not positivistic and "real."

The crucial other side of this rhetorical strategy insists that the unrealities of the vampire stories are "real," as testified by either an outside, "impartial" observer or by a character within a novel who is in a position to demand our belief. Thus, in the preface to "Carmilla," a friend of "Dr. Hesselius" asks that we believe everything in the story on behalf of his learned but dead colleague, while in the opening note to *Dracula*, an unnamed narrator informs us that "all needless matters" have been eliminated from the following account, so that "a history almost at variance with the possibilities of later-day belief may stand forth as simple fact" (Stoker n.p.) The operative words here are *history* and *fact,* which have come to mean something opposite in these stories. In this context, perhaps Terry Eagleton is right when he suggests that "[h]istory itself is an effect of rhetoric" (309).

f

The destitution here is so horrible and the indifference of the House of Commons so manifest . . . a policy must be one of extermination.
     Attributed to Edward Twistleton, Chief Poor Law Commissioner (1849)

In his 1991 article, "The Imaginary Irish Peasant," Edward Hirsch described one of James Joyce's critical insights about early-twentieth-century Irish life, which he articulated through his protagonist Stephen Dedalus:

> Dedalus thinks of an emblematic peasant woman first as a "type of her race and his own" (thus associating himself with the woman) and then as "a batlike soul waking in consciousness of itself in darkness and secrecy and loneliness." In Dedalus' view, the woman is a figure of the Irish unconscious associated with something dark, lonely, beckoning, shameful. The engendering of the peasant is crucial here. Whereas the colonizer is associated with invulnerable masculine strength, the colonized is associated with a guilty and dangerous female secrecy and vulnerability. (1124)

The engendering of the peasant is indeed crucial here and has become a major tenet of post-colonial critical theory. Equally crucial to this discussion are Dedalus's description of the woman as "batlike" and her self-consciousness as "dark" and "secretive." Clearly, Stephen Dedalus's epiphany is drawn from a deep source of Irish cultural tropes and images. We can identify two different topical sources here: the words of such historical, political figures as Theobald Wolfe Tone, John Mitchel, and Michael Davitt and the literary works of Sheridan LeFanu (especially "Carmilla") and Bram Stoker, notably his immensely popular novel *Dracula*.

The polemics of political figures achieve their subversive intent in part by drawing upon some of the standard images of colonizers' rhetoric and inverting them, subversively turning them back upon the English. There was a florescence of colonial descriptions of Ireland in the late-sixteenth and early-seventeenth centuries. Common to these accounts is "the apparent need to think of Ireland as the sort of speculative problem best approached in a 'Treatise,' or a 'Discourse,' or a more rhetorically forensic 'View'" (Harrington 94). Typical of such works is Fynes Moryson's *Itinerary*, portions of which first appeared in English in 1617. As in many of these colonial "descriptions," Moryson provided an extensive catalog of the institutional and personal incivilities of the Irish: a corrupt landholding system, a barbaric kinship network, superstition, idleness, drunkenness, tumultuous behavior, inconstancy, nakedness, licentiousness, incest. The latter, more personal sins are progressively associated with women, who are described with a mixture of distaste, awe, and fear common in colonial literature: "the greatest part of the wemen are nasty with fowle lynnen, and haue very great Dugges some so big as they giue their Children sucke ouer theire shoulders. For the wemen generally are not straight laced . . . and the greatest part are not laced at all" (Kew 105).

Among the other diverse Irish customs criticized at the end of the *Itinerary* is that "most Commonly eate flesh [meat], many times rawe, and if it be roasted or sodd, they seldome eate bread with it." More startling, Moryson reported, is this culinary habit: "The[y] swallowe lumps of butter mixt with Oate meale, and often lett their Cowes blood, eating the congealed blood with butter" (Kew 110). This is the most direct of Moryson's numerous references to an Irish barbarism linked with blood—the corrupt bloodlines of the kinship system, the related corruptions of miscegenation and incest, the blood spilling of war and riot, and the ingestion of actual blood. Moryson stopped short of imputing to the Irish the blood-custom often adduced in colonial literature—namely, cannibalism—although he did revile the names of the Irish for "some rather seeming the names of *Devowring Giants* then *Christian* Subiects" (Kew 36). It seems fair to suggest that Moryson and other colonial commentators established a field of images that linked Irish barbarism with blood.

By the late eighteenth century, one can find indications that such blood imagery was being turned back against the English. One would expect to find the English cursed for corrupting Irish bloodlines and spilling Irish blood in conquest, and certainly the pamphlet literature is full of such condemnations. In the years immediately preceding the Rebellion of 1798, one additionally finds more visceral, sinister blood associations invoked, as seen even in the political rhetoric of Theobald

Wolfe Tone (1763–1798), who in terms of the sectarian pamphlet literature of the late-eighteenth century was a relatively equanimous voice.

Before 1795, both Tone's public and private writings were concrete and legalistic, inveighing against particular abuses by using the political language of human rights that had gained currency on both sides of the North Atlantic. Only once, in "On the State of Ireland in 1720," a 1790 address directed to the fellow members of a Dublin political circle, did Tone invoke the blood tropes of colonialism:

> Our benches were filled with English lawyers; our Bishoprics with English divines; our custom-house with English commissioners; all offices of state filled, three deep, with Englishmen in possession, Englishmen in reversion and Englishmen in expectancy. The majority of these not only aliens, but absentees, and not only absentees, but busily and actively employed against that country on whose vitals and in whose blood they were rioting in ease and luxury. (*Writings* 95)

The bitter humor of the first sentence quickly leads to a diabolical image, and the accusations of bloody barbarism ubiquitous in colonizers' accounts are reflected back on the colonizer.

In the revolutionary atmosphere leading to 1798, Tone more frequently resorted to such subversive metaphor, as exemplified in the pamphlet "An Address to the People of Ireland on the Present Important Crisis" (1796). According to the publisher's advertisement for a reprint edition, this writing "was found on board the French ship of war le Hoche, which was taken by the squadron under the command of Admiral Warren, in the action off Tory Island, in October 1798" (Tone, "Address" iii). Tone's purpose in the "Address" was clearly to rally as many Irish as possible to immediate armed insurrection. Although the unsympathetic publisher criticized Tone's approach as "declamation" rather than "general reasoning," Tone did begin with a defense of Republicanism and a systematic survey of the ills wrought by the English king and Parliament. He admitted, however, that "for Ireland, her cause is independent of the theory. . . . She has too many solid, substantial, heavy, existing grievances, to require much ingenuity, or subtle argument" (3). This allowed—and the historical circumstances required—Tone to replace reasoned argument with provocative polemic, and it is significant that in this rhetorical situation he stated,

> The Temple of your liberties is filled with buyers and sellers, with money changers and thieves; with placemen and pensioners; those unclean and ominous harpies, gorged with the public spoil, and sucking

still, like insatiable Vampires, the last drainings of the vital blood of
their country. (10)

The images tumble from Christian to classical to vampiric,
attributing corruption, paganism, uncleanness, and bloodsucking to the
English rulers and their Anglo-Irish placemen. This late writing by
Tone not only completes the rhetorical inversion of the blood trope, but
also links it to the vampire, increasingly in this era a fictive locus for
fears about diabolism, blood-lust, and the undermining of civilization.

The horrors of *An Gorta Mor* produced a number of similarly
striking rhetorical reversals. The Elizabethan accusation that Irish
savagery led them to consume raw meat and blood was transformed in
innumerable Famine accounts of the starving barely bothering to cook
food they came upon. For instance, among the accounts collected by
the Irish Folklore Commission in the 1930s and '40s was that of Hugh
Byrne of County Carlow, who remembered hearing "that a hungry man
used to draw blood from the first thing he'd met with. One man
attacked a fox but he was so weak the fox snapped at him and took his
arm off" (Póirtéir 61). Even the most damning colonial accusation—
cannibalism—became poignant, heart-rending rather than stomach-
churning, as in this memory recorded by the Folklore Commission: "I
heard my grandmother saying that the worst sight she saw was, she saw
a woman laid out in the street (in Kenmare) and the baby at her breast.
She died of the famine fever. Nobody would take the child, and in the
evening the child was eating the mother's breast" (Póirtéir 105). In the
spectral rhetorical arena created by the Famine, indictments were
turned on the accusers and the horrific was made sympathetic. The
nearly always metaphoric figure of the monster became actual, literal,
and horrifyingly real.

In the presence and aftermath of the Great Hunger, Irish political
agitators such as John Mitchel (1815–1875) and Michael Davitt (1846–
1906) added to the store of rhetorical inversions. The Famine
accelerated Mitchel's despair over the constitutional path to reform for
which his career as a lawyer had prepared him. His contributions to *The
Nation* in 1845 document this growing anguish, which led him to
conclude late in that year that the British government, and Charles
Trevelyan in particular, had used the occasion of the potato blight to
punish and further subjugate Ireland. In Mitchel's memorable phrase,
"The Almighty, indeed, sent the potato blight, but the English created
the Famine" (Brown 105). It is striking that in this frame of mind, in
which despair began to give way to insurrectionism, Mitchel, like Tone,
resorted to the vampire metaphor. When Mitchel learned that Charles
Trevelyan had suggested that the Queen set aside a day for raising

Famine relief funds, he wrote, "Keep your alms, ye canting robbers. We spit upon the benevolence that robs us of a *pound* and flings back a penny in *charity;* and if the English cared to show their compassion for the Irish, let them take their fangs from our throat" (Brown 105).

Perhaps the most famous political use of the vampire trope is from Michael Davitt. He not only observed and sympathized with the plight of the Irish rural Catholic population, but he also directly experienced it. He was, unlike Tone and Mitchel, baptized Catholic, and his family was evicted from its County Mayo home in 1850. In a speech in County Galway on 12 October 1879, Davitt uttered his much-quoted characterization of landlords as "the brood of cormorant vampires that has sucked the life blood out of the country" (Moody 323). The cormorant reference, rich in its suggestion of a black menace diving from above, is likely derived from Book IV of Milton's *Paradise Lost*, where Satan sits "in the shape of a Cormorant on the Tree of life." Rhetorically joined to the vampire, it resembles the conflation of Christian reference and the vampire image in Tone's 1796 "Address." Because Davitt's reference comes eight years after the publication of Sheridan LeFanu's "Carmilla," and after a great deal of other vampire literature as well, it is impossible to say whether political rhetoric echoed literary images, or vice versa. But clearly, by 1879, the practice of subverting British domination by seizing the arsenal of colonial tropes and rhetorically turning them back upon the accuser had become well established.

Roy Foster, in his seminal revisionist work *Modern Ireland, 1600–1792*, attacked such historical portrayals of Irish landlords, saying, "The picture of 'cormorant vampires' (Davitt) or 'coroneted ghouls' (Fanny Parnell) has long been disproved; if the post-Famine Irish landlords were vampires, they were not very good at it" (372). In his effort to criticize the fairness of the vampire trope, however, Foster missed both its inversion of colonial accusations of a diabolical savagery and the significance of how widespread the metaphor had become in Irish political rhetoric and literature, as can be seen in its apotheosis at the hands of Sheridan LeFanu and Bram Stoker.

ƒ

[H]ow charged this orifice [the mouth] is for the ambivalent representation of Irishness: the site at once of fluent speech and secretive silence, lament and laughter, intoxication and hunger, guile and guilelessness.

David Lloyd, "The Memory of Hunger," in *Irish Hunger*

Sheridan LeFanu published "Carmilla" in 1871 as part of a collection of Gothic short stories titled *The Dark Blue*. One passage early in the novella invites close examination:

> Her [Carmilla's] agitations and her language were unintelligible to me. From these foolish embraces, which were not of very frequent occurrence, I must allow, I used to wish to extricate myself; but my energies seemed to fail me. Her murmured words sounded like a lullaby in my ear, and soothed my resistance into a trance, from which I only seemed to recover myself when she withdrew her arms. In these mysterious moods I did not like her. I experienced a strange tumultuous excitement that was pleasurable, ever and anon, mingled with a vague sense of fear and disgust. I had no distinct thoughts about her while such scenes lasted, I was conscious of a love growing into adoration, and also of abhorrence. This I know is paradox, but I can make no other attempt to explain the feeling. (35–36)

The speaker is Laura, an Englishwoman in a strange land, Stygia. As a gesture perhaps indicative of Bram Stoker's debt to LeFanu, the original venue for the story of *Dracula* was Stygia, a trace of which remains in "Dracula's Guest," the introduction to the novel that Stoker abandoned and that his wife, Florence, published after his death. Laura maintains that her family is English despite their foreign home, a large castle surrounded by deserted stone villages. Critic Michael H. Begnal has noted that the landscapes of LeFanu's fiction, while almost never in Ireland, "are in actuality the Irish 'big houses' which were fast disappearing from the contemporary scene" (14). As a scion of the Anglo-Irish ascendancy—he is a descendant of dramatist Richard Brinsley Sheridan—LeFanu was indeed familiar with the "big houses," especially in the village of Abington, where his chaplain father lived on a salary paid from Catholic tithes to the Church of Ireland. We also know that "LeFanu in midcareer began giving his stories English instead of Irish settings owing to a direct demand from his London publishers, Bentley and Company, that he should do so" (McCormack 238). During the height of the Famine (1847–1848), his brother William, an engineer, had to rescue the bodies of Famine victims from marauding dogs at Burnfort near Mallow, and these dreadful reminders of Britain's "disastrous imperial policy" surely affected the younger Joseph Sheridan LeFanu (McCormack 102). Thus it is "feasible . . . to correlate the guilty past of LeFanu's fiction with the politics of his time, and particularly of his caste" (230).

So, for this son of a conservative Protestant clergyman, the terrors of the Famine created a troubling and troublesome tension between his distrust and dislike for the Catholic peasants and his horror at the rapacity of the British bureaucrats and politicians who were nominally in charge of Famine relief. After the death of Daniel O'Connell in 1847, whom LeFanu feared as "a kind of Dracula of Derrynane" (Eagleton 189), the increasingly radical turn of those who supported a repeal of the Act of Union caused LeFanu public embarrassment, and he retreated into a life of solitude in Dublin, especially after the death of his beloved wife, Susanna, in April 1858. While LeFanu withdrew from public life, his focus on Irish life—especially what he considered the corruption and decline of the aristocratic ascendancy—continued until his death, and virtually all his critics agree that in his best work, "Carmilla" and *Uncle Silas* (1864), the "actual subject . . . is Ireland" (Begnal 58).

If we return to the passage from Edward Hirsch's "The Imaginary Irish Peasant" cited above, Carmilla becomes "a figure of the Irish unconscious associated with something dark, lonely, beckoning, shameful," and thus we can read this classic vampire tale with new eyes. We note first the "unintelligible" speech and movements of Carmilla toward Laura, who nonetheless succumbs to the vampire's advances as a child does to its mother. Thomas Crofton Croker noted in his 1824 *Researches in the South of Ireland* that "the Irish language [is] . . . a sufficient cloak for the expression of seditious sentiments" (172–73). Irish is "beckoning" and "dark" from the vampiric Carmilla, mouthed lovingly and sinisterly into the ears of the unsuspecting, and very English, Laura. The encounter between Carmilla and Laura concerns power, in which the "guilty and dangerous female secrecy" (Hirsch) of the vampire threatens to undermine the innocence of Laura, who is, after all, only trying to extend her family's "care and tenderness" to the hapless visitor "from the West" (LeFanu 24, 35). Without the determined help of her father and nearby villagers familiar with the historical ravages of the Carnstein clan, LeFanu suggests, Laura would forever be in Carmilla's thrall. We can discern clearly here the tensions of LeFanu's Anglo-Irish politics. Critic Julian Moynahan traces this tension and suspicion to the peculiar relations of the Anglo-Irish and the Catholic majority: "one apparently in control but outnumbered; the other in servitude yet much larger and longer in the land; . . . the majority constantly watching the privileged minority, coming to haunt its dreams, which are of crumbling mansions under ghostly siege, or at the point of falling" (128).

Laura herself describes the chief rhetorical device of the passage— "[t]his I know is paradox"—and the feelings engendered in her by the vampire are uniformly bipolar: "excitement that was pleasurable . . . mingled with . . . fear and disgust"; "love growing into adoration, and also of abhorrence." This seems to be a trait universally associated with the vampire, as in Jonathan Harker's characterization of the breath of Dracula's wife, close on his throat in the vampire's castle as "honey-sweet . . . but with a bitter offensiveness, as one smells in blood" (Stoker 39). This "signifying conflict" brought into the story by the vampire points us toward the transformation of metaphor seen in Fynes Moryson, Tone, Mitchel, and Davitt, which first characterizes the Irish as parasites and then in a powerful "semantic slide" (Eagleton 33) represents England as a vampire, positioning the metaphoric hierarchy so that it correctly reflects the colonial, extractive relationship with Ireland. If we return to Barbara Johnson's taxonomy, these polarities suspend the "text's claim structure between two . . . incompatible possibilities"; this bipolarity is the chief structural venue of the Gothic novel. In the Protestant Gothic tradition of Ireland, the traumatic memory of *An Gorta Mor* is recoded into the two major vampire novels of the period, "Carmilla" and *Dracula*. The political ambivalences of both writers, one an Anglo-Irish Protestant with nationalist sympathies, the other an Anglo-Irishman with an ambivalent self-idenity, were finally resolved in the stories of Carmilla and Count Dracula, whose sinister and alluring kisses capture perfectly the powerful antipathies on both sides of the Famine relief debate.

f

Sometime after the turn of the century . . . Bernard remembered watching an old man of strange gait struggling up the boreen to the O'Regan house. . . . As a child during the Famine time, the man had collapsed from hunger and been taken for dead. Rather than see him consigned to a mass grave, the boy's Mother consented to his legs being broken so he could be fitted into the only coffin that was available. When his legs were snapped the pain forced out a deep moan that saved him from being buried alive.
　　　　　Peter Quinn, "In Search of the Banished Children," in *Irish Hunger*

In *Dracula*, the invader came from the east, not the west, and his aim was the conquest of London, capital of what Prince Albert called "the workshop of the world." In the novel, Stoker used virtually the entire lexicon of colonial metaphors and figures. All the protagonists are male, with one possible exception, Mina Harker, who very early on shows a propensity for sexless or male behavior. She is, Dr. Van Helsing tells us, "a woman with the brain of a man" (Stoker 209). One only need compare her to her sexualized "sister," Lucy Westenra, to see the difference: while Mina marries Jonathan Harker because he needs her to, Lucy wishes to marry all three of the men who propose to her. She is doomed, we know, because she so perfectly plays out the expectations of the gender stereotype of the time, while Mina, we also know, will succeed because she only comes to this female stereotype after she has played a masculine role in the narrative.

The count arrives in London via some surreptitious dealings through the Bank of London and works very quietly to plant himself and then his minions in this new feeding ground. He is very clear that he wishes to pass for an Englishman, not a foreigner who speaks English "with a strange intonation." He has fifty coffins with him, so we know that he has ambitious plans. His aim is total, not partial, control over the people and their environment, much as a colonizer would desire. The intended victims are all feminized, even the indomitable Jonathan Harker, who faints through three-quarters of the novel. Mina is far more "masculine," at least until the men get enough money together to chase the count back to Transylvania. Then she recedes into the third person objective and is spoken about rather than speaking for herself, which she has done for nearly the entire novel.

In addition to borrowing the gender roles that serve the purpose of the colonizer, *Dracula* utilizes the process of infantilization, which makes the victims like children: trusting, unknowing, and completely open to suggestion and possession. The stereotyped roles demand that the victims become silly clones of the vampire, completely in his thrall until they either die or become vampires. One has to note in this connection the regular stereotyping of the Irish by the British popular press as childish and infantile (cf. Foster, *Paddy & Mr. Punch* chap. 9). The terror of Dracula is masked by the clownish figure of Renfield, who desires a bird or a kitten as he moves his way up the food chain. The novel, however, shows the danger from the count to be all too "real." Lucy Westenra, the name of "the Anglo-Irish Barons of Rossmore in County Monaghan" (Milbank 20), is drawn consistently as a child: she cannot make up her mind about anything remotely adult, is spoiled like an overindulged Victorian child, and is exasperated by anything that demands adult perseverance or perspicacity. The scene after her death when she arrives at her tomb, as the "bloofer lady," is nearly unbelievable: a monstrous child victimizing other children. Soon, however, we see why. Once she has been made to drop the child, she turns on her fiancé, Arthur Holmwood, with the capital hunger of the archetypal vamp, mouthing, "Come to me, Arthur," in a seductive kiss he has never seen from his young fiancée. Behind this monstrous child's face lurks the "dark, lonely, beckoning, shameful" love of Stephen Dedalus's peasant woman. But it's a sham; she is still a child and once staked by the vampire hunters, regains her innocent demeanor in death. This scene recalls some of the passages recorded about the ravages of the Famine, detailing the "childlike" qualities of the dying and the peace that it was assumed came to them after they died (cf. Nicholson 88).

In terms of Ireland and the Famine, the landmarks of Stoker's "troubled relationship to the Irish question" (Glover 13) seem transparent. Transylvania is really Ireland (Milbank 20), and the racial fears expressed by Jonathan Harker and the vampire hunters mirror the fear that many Englishmen had after the waves of Famine immigration: the "barbarian" and atavistic Irish peasant would cause English workers to regress away from the progressive ideals of the Protestant ethic of work and moral improvement (Sage 51–52). All of the vampire's victims "regress" to a state where their basest emotions are dominant and the rational sentiments espoused by the Protestant ascendancy are violated and demeaned. This is in fact connected to the colonial feminization and infantilization of the Irish in the fiction of the Protestant ("Anglo-Irish") Gothic, in which the Irish peasants are regularly ruled by overweening sentiment. "The idea of the Irish as 'essentially emotional,' when taken together with references to tears as 'unmanly signs of emotion,' seems to suggest [in Stoker's works, *The Snake's Pass* and *Dracula*] that the unguarded outflow of affect is a source of racial and cultural weakness" (Glover 46).

The feminization and infantilization of the victims becomes the most common means by which the work of the vampire is done. Culturally, these roles need no translation, since they offer the most unambiguous metaphors for the mastery and power of the monster or the colonizer. Once the culturally acceptable roles have been fitted to the intended victims, it remains only to justify them historically. Such "imperial" narratives have long been used to articulate the work of the colonizer as the natural and inevitable product of the forces of history, progress, and biological survival. This reconstruction is not without its risks: "To achieve hegemony, colonial rule must be refracted through the traditions of those it governs, miming their cultural gestures and conforming itself to their customs. In order to flourish, such power must court *kenosis*, risk a loss of being in order to come into its own" (Eagleton 41). In Stoker's *Dracula*, this process is split between two speakers, the monster and Van Helsing, his alter ego. The monster tells Jonathan Harker about his "proud people" in what is evidently an attempt to recall the real-life exploits of Vlad Tsepes, Vlad the Impaler. Quickly, the reader realizes something odd: it was all to no point. The history lesson provides no link in the narrative, it explains no part of Dracula's present plans, and it clarifies nothing for Jonathan Harker, who is merely hungry and thirsty after his long ride. The same is true later in the story, when Van Helsing recounts in even greater detail the history of the vampire, reputedly gleaned by Stoker from a talk by historian Arminius Varbery. Then, inexplicably, Van Helsing leaps to Dracula's exploits as a supernatural monster. These have no connection to the Tsepes story: the exploits of Vlad the Impaler bear in no way on the impending story, either for the vampire hunters or for us. And this is the point. The "real" story of the Rumanian nobleman makes an overt claim for authenticity against the "unreal" activity of the fictional count, but for no discernible purpose and toward no historical end. Stoker did not simply transcribe the historical figure of Vlad the Impaler into an Anglo-Irish Gothic tale: he "emphasized the multiple natures of the vampire and also placed the vampire squarely in the modern world. Furthermore, he was the first writer to use the vampire to suggest the intersection of myth and science, past and present" (Senf 7). By doing this, he completes the process of recreating the vampire metaphor as a familiar trope in the rhetoric of colonization. Seen in this new context, Van Helsing's syntax becomes problematic, as several critics have noticed, since it seems to have no real resemblance to the Anglo-Dutch it's intended to suggest. After what we've already said about language and about Irish especially, Van Helsing's contorted speech must be related to the question of Irish language illegitimacy, of which Stoker would certainly have been aware. In speaking about another Anglo-Irish fictional character (Maria Edgeworth's Kit Rackrent), Terry Eagleton notes that his

> loquacity is a kind of artlessness, an unstaunchable excess of speech; but it is also, so we may suspect, the rhetorical strategy of the "lower Irish," disarming authority by its rumbustious spontaneity and wrapping unpalatable truths in endless parataxis. Truth and artifice are thus interwoven in his discourse, as they are in the form of the text itself [which is also true of Stoker's *Dracula*]—a palpable piece of invention which nonetheless claims the status of a historical document. (162)

Raising the metaphorical elements of the story to the narrative surface blocks the process of imperial storytelling, which usually masks this system of exploitation from the reader. While the Victorian era is filled with examples of stories that cast the victims as unwitting and sometimes unwilling recipients of the benefits of "higher" civilizing, these monster stories "lay bare" the reality of this relationship for all to see. The anecdotal (and thus "nonhistorical") accounts of the peasants who have suffered at the hands of the vampire speak much more loudly than a story about Vlad Tsepes ever could. As critic David Glover astutely remarks about Jonathan Harker's comment that the Transylvanian peasants "were just like the peasants at home," "we might pause at this sentence to wonder exactly where home was" (35).

By playing overtly with the metaphors of colonization, Stoker made the usual business of imperial historiography impossible. Thus the tidbits about the "real" historical prince are pointless, while the invented stories of the villagers and victims are poignant and contextually viable. In this rhetorical strategy, the ontology of writing history is inverted. The invented becomes more "real" than the real, illustrating Barbara Johnson's example of "incompatibilities" between two different but equal assertions within the text. A reader familiar with "folk" accounts of the Famine would certainly recognize similarities to Stoker's story. Early in his travel diary, Harker even notes that the historical devastation of the area around the Borgo Pass was "assisted by famine and disease" (Stoker 6), a provocative detail from an Anglo-Irish writer whose ambivalent position in Irish society as "both colonizer and colonized" made England's response to the Famine difficult to accept. In Irish letters, the "Protestant Gothic might be dubbed the political unconscious of Anglo-Irish society, the place where its fears and fantasies most definitively emerge" (Eagleton 187). The two acknowledged leaders of the Protestant Gothic are Sheridan LeFanu and Bram Stoker, whose fears about its degeneracy produce "festering guilt and persecutory terror" and whose fantasies about a pluralistic solution to the "Irish Question" imbue their present reality with "a kind of spectral insubstantiality" (Eagleton 194). This is why Dracula is much more complex, more ambivalent than the earlier figure of Carmilla. This point brings us back to the work of Mina Harker, by far the most compelling character in the story, for it is she—not one of the vampire hunters—who tells the story of the count's capture and demise.

In a crucial reversal of narrative prerogatives, Mina Harker combines the disparate stories of the characters who encounter the vampire into a coherent narrative that becomes the single most important weapon in the arsenal of the vampire hunters. Once she hands the neatly typewritten manuscript to Van Helsing, Dracula is doomed. It may take weeks of chasing and the expenditure of large sums of money ("Oh the wonderful power of money," Mina croons at one point), but the Transylvanian count is dead once one of his victims forges the narrative that will catch him. By this one act, the vampire hunters know his patterns, uncover his strategies, and spoil his conquest. As the center of this subversive rhetorical "net," the vampire has to be vanquished: his elimination allows this transformation into a more powerful metaphoric threat to be completed. Under hypnosis, Mina speaks the vampire's words and reveals his thoughts and sensations. Explained in narrative terms, the vampire hunters can now see ahead of him, not merely behind him. In rhetorical terms, the vampire figure then becomes ambivalent, contradictory, and seditious. Mina's ability to "become" Dracula under hypnosis symbolizes this reversal.

The death of the American Quincey Morris also becomes important in the context of the Famine rhetoric we have described, not only because he is emblematic of those Irish who emigrated to America, but also because he is later "reborn" as the new son of Jonathan and Mina Harker. In the final "Note" to the novel, Jonathan tells the reader that little Quincey's "bundle of names links all our little band of men together," as though he represented in fact a genealogical and biological history of the vampire hunters (Stoker 332). They are, of course, not related, and the only characters whose names suggest Stoker's Irish heritage are either dead (Lucy, Quincey) or married off to a progressive and wealthy Englishman (Mina to Jonathan) whose future is ensured by their "rigorous process of self-development as a result of their experiences" (Glover 49). As with other Anglo-Irish writers, Stoker seems to suggest that out of the terrifying devastation of the Famine, at the heart of which lies the powerful and multifaceted image of the vampire, came something good. Given the conflicting motives embedded in the larger narrative, Stoker is free to suggest this, since there is evidence in the story to support both views. The final "Note" of the novel, written by Jonathan Harker seven years after the death of Dracula, reveals this double intent: "We were struck by the fact, that in all the mass of material of which the record is composed, there is hardly one authentic document; nothing but a mass of type-writing. . . . We could hardly ask anyone, even did we wish to, to accept these proofs of so wild a story. . . . We want no proofs; we ask none to believe us!" (Stoker 332)

f

> There is an unspeakable foulness at the very heart of civility; but if this frightful paradox is not to shatter the mind it must be rationalized by the image of the divided self, the vampiric victim who is sweetly unaware in waking life of the unspeakable horror he or she perpetrates at night.
>   Terry Eagleton, *Heathcliff and the Great Hunger*

Many writers have remarked on the peculiarities of Anglo-Irish ambivalence and fears, particularly regarding the ascendancy's liminal status vis-à-vis England. This sense of becoming both victim and victimizer pervades not only the literary language of nineteenth-century Protestant Gothic literature in Ireland, but politics as well. "Language," Eagleton writes, "is strategic for the oppressed, but representational for their rulers" (171–72). For a class that feels it occupies both positions (however much this "divided self" is the product of "fear and fantasy"), the language it uses to represent itself to others (or Others) will be fractious and paradoxical. In the novels of Sheridan LeFanu and Bram Stoker, this complexity is centered on the figure of the vampire and is refracted in the ambivalence that surrounds the vampire's victims. Lucy Westenra is both innocent and corrupt; Dracula is first victimizer and later a figure whom Mina Harker pities, after she is certain that the money and energy that the vampire hunters have dedicated to Dracula's destruction cannot fail. This is why we have isolated these particular tropes and figures from the literary and political discourse of the age. Eagleton is accurate when he suggests that "[p]aradox, metonymy, oxymoron: it is in terms of such tropes that the relationship between imperial Britain and colonial Ireland has to be read" (125), but he does not go far enough. These "signifying conflicts" (Johnson) have to be placed within the larger rhetorical strategy of the writers and pamphleteers working in nineteenth-century Ireland. By inverting the usual political meaning of the vampire lexicon, Tone and Davitt effectively turned this term against the British, who had introduced blood barbarism into the political dialogue. By using the vampire figure to invert the ontology of "real" and "unreal," LeFanu and Stoker deconstruct the imperial rhetoric of nineteenth-century England and affirm the "seditious" and "unofficial" history of Famine Ireland.

Works Cited

Begnal, Michael H. *Joseph Sheridan LeFanu.* Lewisburg: Bucknell Univ. Press, 1971.

Brown, Malcolm. *The Politics of Irish Literature: From Thomas Davis to W. B. Yeats.* Seattle: Univ. of Washington Press, 1972.

Croker, Thomas Crofton. *Researches in the South of Ireland.* London: John Murray, 1824.

Eagleton, Terry. *Heathcliff and the Great Hunger.* London: Verso, 1996.

Foster, RoyF. *Modern Ireland, 1600–1792.* New York: Penguin, 1988.

---. *Paddy & Mr. Punch: Connections in Irish and English History.* London: Penguin, 1996.

Gallagher, Thomas. *Paddy's Lament.* New York: Harvest, 1987.

Glover, David. *Vampires, Mummies, and Liberals: Bram Stoker and the Politics Of Popular Fiction.* Durham: Duke Univ. Press, 1996.

Harrington, John P. "A Tudor Writer's Tracts on Ireland, His Rhetoric." *Éire-Ireland* 17.2 (1982): 92-103.

Hayden, Tom, ed. *Irish Hunger.* Boulder: Roberts Rinehart, 1997.

Hirsch, Edward. "The Imaginary Irish Peasant" *PMLA* 106 (1991): 1116-1143.

Johnson, Barbara. "Teaching Deconstructively." *Writing and Reading Differently: Deconstruction and the Teaching of Composition and Literature.* Lawrence: Univ. Press of Kansas, 1985: 140-148.

Kennedy, Liam, et al. *Mapping the Great Irish Famine.* Dublin: Four Courts, 1999.

Kew, Graham, ed. *The Irish Sections of Fynes Moryson's Unpublished Itinerary.* Dublin: Irish Manuscripts Commission, 1998.

Killen, John, ed. *The Famine Decade: Contemporary Accounts, 1841–1851.* Belfast: Blackstaff, 1985.

Kinealy, Christine. *A Death-Dealing Famine: The Great Hunger in Ireland.* London: Pluto, 1997.

LeFanu, Sheridan. "Carmilla." *The Dracula Book of Great Vampire Stories.* Ed. Leslie Shepard. Secaucus: Citadel Press, 1977.

McCormack, W. J. *Sheridan LeFanu and Victorian Ireland.* Dublin: Lilliput, 1991.

Milbank, Alison. "Powers Old and New: Stoker's Alliances with Anglo-Irish Gothic." *Bram Stoker: History, Psychoanalysis and the Gothic.* New York: St. Martin's, 1998: 12-28.

Moody, T. W. *Davitt and the Irish Revolution, 1846–82.* Oxford: Clarendon, 1982.

Morash, Christopher. *Writing the Irish Famine.* Oxford: Clarendon, 1995.

Moynahan, Julian. *Anglo-Irish: The Literary Imagination in a Hyphenated Culture.* Princeton: Princeton Univ. Press, 1995.

Nicholson, Asenath. *Annals of the Famine In Ireland.* Dublin: Lilliput, 1998.

O'Grada, Cormac. *Black '47 and Beyond: The Great Irish Famine.* Princeton: Princeton Univ. Press, 1999.

Póirtéir, Cathal. *Famine Echoes.* Dublin: Gill and Macmillan, 1995.

Sage, Victor. *Horror Fiction in the Protestant Tradition.* New York: St. Martin's, 1988.

Senf, Carol. *Dracula: Between Tradition and Modernism.* New York: Twayne, 1998.

Stoker, Bram. *Dracula.* Ann. by Leonard Wolf. New York: Ballantine, 1975.

Tone, Theobald Wolfe. "An Address to the People of Ireland on the Present Important Crisis." Belfast. 1796.

---. *The Writings of Theobald Wolfe Tone 1763–1798. Tone's Career in Ireland to June 1795.* Ed. T. W. Moody, R. B. McDowell, and C. J. Woods. Vol. 1. Oxford: Clarendon, 1998.

Chapter Three

The Tangled Roots of Irish Immigrants and African Americans: Historical and Contemporary Perspectives

MARYANN MATTHEWS

Both African Americans and Irish Americans had a significant impact on the development of American society. Starting from the lowest places in America, uneducated and poor, each group became influential in literature, sports, business, and politics. Their achievements grew while they labored to become accepted in a society that was hostile to their presence. The history of each group's struggle and success is increasingly documented. Less well-examined is the shared history of the two groups. From the mid-nineteenth century, when more than a million Famine immigrants arrived in America, there were a significant number of events that joined the two groups, including the worst riots of the nineteenth century. The shared history, however, is larger than hostility between the two groups.

During the nineteenth century, two powerful spokesmen, Daniel O'Connell and Frederick Douglass, recognized similar goals and aspirations in the two groups and hoped they would unite. A political union did not happen, however, and, after the post–Civil War Reconstruction era, the Jim Crow laws left African Americans behind as Irish Americans were elected to political power. Shared aspirations did bear fruit in other cultural areas, however. Both groups preserved their cultural identity in literature and music; they faced a similar dilemma, "namely that the dominant culture in large measure refused to recognize their heritage, or at least its validity" (Gallagher 14). Writing about the relationship between the Irish and Harlem renaissances, Mishkin noted that in his 1922 preface to *The Book of American Negro Poetry* James Weldon Johnson wrote, "What the colored poet in the United States needs to do is something like what Synge did for the Irish; he needs to find a form that will express the racial spirit by symbols from within rather than by symbols from without, such as the mere mutilation of spelling and pronunciation" (16).

In the later twentieth century, the tangle continued. Martin Luther King Jr.'s call for civil rights gained the support of the first Irish Catholic elected to the presidency, John Kennedy. Many other Irish Americans actively supported the civil rights movement. In Ireland, King's nonviolent demonstrations were a model for Northern Irish Catholics in their struggle for equal rights.[1] In the United States, hostility between Irish and African Americans rose again in urban areas. In 1974, in South Boston, Massachusetts, angry Irish Americans rioted against the desegregation of their neighborhood schools. In 1998, black college students who visited Northern Ireland saw pictures of Dr. King in classrooms and talked easily with Irish students who had been taught African-American history. They came back to the United States asking why Irish Americans did not seem to know as much about their past history with African Americans.[2]

Educators and researchers who were asked to consider the students' question suggested two reasons why Irish Americans seem to know little about the shared history.[3] First, American students are often taught the history of specific groups, such as African Americans and Irish immigrants, as separate histories, rather than as part of an integrated narrative of a historical period. This limits their understanding of how groups interacted. Second, there is a discomfort among Irish and African Americans with what they know about past conflict between Irish and blacks. The material presented here is research developed for a project to document this shared history and to investigate how Irish and African Americans think about their common legacy. The shared history began before the Irish arrived in America and continued after the Irish had settled in America. Irish citizens who fled to America during the Great Hunger were the largest part of an unprecedented influx. In 1840, there were fewer than 600,000 immigrants in the United States, including those from Ireland. From 1840 to 1850, immigration swelled to 1.7 million; 780,000 came from Ireland; the next largest group, 435,000, came from Germany. In the next ten years, another 2.5 million immigrants arrived; 952,000 from Germany and 914,000 from Ireland (U.S. Bureau of the Census). The Irish immigrants were different from those emigrating from other European nations in the same time period in several respects. They were poorer, less educated, and more malnourished. Nearly 60 percent of the Famine immigrants came from rural areas of Ireland; many were Catholic and Irish-speaking. Other immigrants of the period did not come from all classes or regions; most were lower middle class citizens. They emigrated as farms and trades were industrialized and often arrived with sufficient funds to travel beyond major ports and to purchase land.[4]

Because of their poverty, the majority of Irish immigrants settled in major cities along the East Coast of America, rather than moving farther west. Their low economic status placed them in competition for the lowest level of work and existence with the already established lowest rung of American society—free black men. In Boston in 1850,

> no other nationality depended so heavily upon unskilled work. There were 1,545 (of 7,007) unskilled laborers in the city other than Irish, but in no (other) group did they form a significant proportion. Among the natives, no more than 5 percent were so employed and only the Negroes and Germans had as much as 10 percent. But even in these cases, the actual number was small: 115 Negroes and 107 Germans. (Handlin 60)

Some Catholic leaders tried to relocate Irish immigrants to rural areas to preserve their faith, but John Hughes, Archbishop of New York, and other eastern prelates "argued that the urban concentration of the Irish permitted the Church, with limited financial and human resources to best minister to their spiritual needs, and to protect them from American secularism and Protestant proselytism."[5] In Philadelphia in the 1850s, "a Catholic world emerged, not only to threaten a traditional Protestant one, but to intensify working class divisions. Irish Catholics and Irish Protestants established separate neighborhoods, and separate fire companies, gangs and voting blocs" (McCaffrey 69). Isolated from other immigrants by their poverty and religion, Irish immigrants shared a low status with black competitors for jobs, creating a dual struggle for acceptance, both between them and against the established American society.

I. Abolition and Emancipation

In the earlier decades of the nineteenth century, Frederick Douglass and Daniel O'Connell had hoped for an alliance between the two suffering groups. In 1833, O'Connell said of slave owners, "In the deepest of hell, there is a depth still more profound, and that is to be found in the conduct of American slave owners" (Cusack). O'Connell supported Douglass and the cause of freedom for slaves, and he usurped the images of slavery and British support for the abolition of slavery. He pressed England to support freedom for the slaves of Ireland. He compared the peasants to slaves, as Douglass himself did on several occasions, and wondered how the British could allow oppression of the Irish in Ireland while supporting abolition of slavery in America. In a speech in 1838 delivered against the Tithes in Ireland, O'Connell spoke of "a paltry and a hollow hypocrisy" that he saw among Englishmen.

> There is a kind of morbid humanity abroad; it is to be found amongst men who affect philanthropy—who are tenderly alive to all the evils which may be endured by those who are not of an agreeable colour, and who are to be found in distant regions; they are men who overflow with milk of human kindness for black men and women, but who can with patience, with equanimity, and even with approbation, look on and see all the injuries you inflict upon Irishmen, and all the injustices you do to Ireland. I wish the Irish were Negroes, and then we should have an advocate in the hon. Baronet. (Cusack 521)

When Douglass visited Ireland in 1845, he praised O'Connell's work on behalf of abolition, saying:

> I cannot proceed without alluding to a man who did much to abolish slavery, I mean Daniel O'Connell. I feel grateful to him, for his voice has made American slavery shake to its centre—I am determined wherever I go, and whatever position I may fill, to speak with grateful emotions of Mr. O'Connell's labours. I heard his denunciation of slavery. I heard my master curse him. In London, O'Connell tore off the mask of hypocrisy from the slave-holders, and branded them as vilest of the vile and the most execrable of execrable, for no man can put words together stronger than Mr. O'Connell. (Blassingame 45)

Douglass acknowledged the shared conditions but challenged Irish audiences to recognize the unique degradation experienced by American slaves. Speaking in Limerick, on 10 November 1845, Douglass drew cheers from his audience when he said he'd been told there was no reason to explain slavery in Ireland since slavery existed there. He went on to say, "If slavery existed here, it ought to be put down." Again, there were loud cheers. "But there was nothing like American slavery on the soil on which he now stood. Negro-slavery consisted not in talking away any of the rights of man but in annihilating them all" (Blassingame 77, 78). Like O'Connell, Douglass appropriated England's ending the slave trade as benefited his cause. "He could at one moment play upon British chauvinism and contempt for America . . . then, in the next breath, he could appeal to Britain's responsibilities to America, citing her original introduction of slavery to the American colonies."[6] Douglass and O'Connell shared a vision of freedom that was greater than skin color or religious belief. Both were morally committed to freeing the oppressed from their oppressors. In each other, they found a moral ally, but their union was weakened by their political goals. In many ways, their relationship was a kind of template for the Irish and African American experience of the ferment surrounding the abolition of slavery.

An American broadside, a woodcutting from the late 1830s titled *The Results of Abolitionism!*, provides an example of how immigrants were manipulated by political factions in the controversy. The woodcutting depicts a construction site where a multilevel building has been framed. Standing on the ground are two big-bellied managers, one white skinned, the other black. The white supervisor calls out to a black worker, "Sambo, hurry up those white laborers"; the black boss yells, "White man. Hurry up them bricks." Singled out are the Irish workers. "You bogtrotters, come along with them bricks" (Yellin and Van Horne 224). The broadside addressed social and economic status, two important issues for Irish immigrants. In the same time period, members of anti-slavery associations were themselves divided about the inclusion of Irish emancipation in the anti-slavery movement. In 1835, E. Bickersworth, a member of the British Anti-Slavery Committee, resigned from the work rather than continue to be allied with the likes of Daniel O'Connell. Writing from Walton Rectory, Ware, 20 May 1835, to the Secretary of the London Anti-Slavery Society, Bickersworth said,

> I have been, I believe, almost from the beginning a member of the Anti-Slavery Society though I have always regretted the union with men of the avowed principles of Lord Brougham & Mr. O'Connell. . . . The object of the society I consider to be most truly Christian & benevolent: but the course of public events has more deeply than ever impressed upon my mind the importance of attention to the plain Christian principle, "Be not unequally yoked with unbelievers." The Committee having therefore chosen to call Lord Brougham & Mr. O'Connell to take so leading a part in the proceedings of its Anniversary, I must beg them to withdraw my name from the members of an Institution so completely under such influence.[7]

In America, abolitionists thought other immigrants were more likely to support the anti-slavery movement than the Irish. At their 1840 meeting, the Anti-Slavery Society reported, "There has been the diffusion of anti-slavery principles and intelligence among the portion of our countrymen who use the German language . . . the general passion of the Germans for liberty, gives the assurance that nothing is wanting but light to range them against oppression in this country, as they have fled it in their fatherland" (Am. Anti-Slav. Soc. *Proc. of 7th Ann. Mtg.*). Others argued to include Irish liberation in the anti-slavery objectives. At the 1850 Anti-Slavery Meeting, celebrating the twentieth anniversary of the society, William Lloyd Garrison's opening remarks included "Our movement is not sectional or geographical, but world-wide in its principles, affecting all the hopes and interests of humanity, and indisolubly connected to the freedom of mankind. It does not relate to the color of skin, but to the value of a man" (Am. Anti-Slav. Soc. *Proc. at Its 2nd Dec.* 4). In a later speech at the meeting, Joseph Baker, a delegate from Ohio, took up the theme of a worldwide movement and spoke about oppression in Ireland. Baker said

> that if the Aristocracy of Great Britain and Ireland were not as bad as our Southern slaveholders, they were at least the next bad set of men on the face of the earth, and if he could not prove that the conduct of the English and Irish Aristocracy had been as purely selfish, unfeeling and cruel, toward the working classes as the conduct of Southern slaveholders to their victims, he could prove that the difference to say the least, was one in degree only, and that the effect of the misconduct of the English and Irish aristocracy have been more ruinous than the effects of the selfishness and cruelty of the Southern slaveholder. (Am. Anti-Slav. Soc. *Proc. at Its 2nd Dec.* 38)

Baker believed that "their [the anti-slavery society's] object should be to endeavor to find where they could stand together, and in what way they could cooperate most harmoniously for the overthrow of oppression in this land, and in all other lands" (Am. Anti-Slav. Soc. *Proc. at Its 2nd Dec.* 47).

Several other delegates rebutted Baker's view, arguing that Catholics were proslavery. In a speech addressing the failure of established religions to support abolition activities, Wendell Phillips spoke about Catholics' allegiance to Rome:

> Take Catholics, for example. The Catholic, whether he freezes with Fenelon in the snows of Canada or burns with Xavier in the torrid zone, represents always the Pope. A young man goes out from Rome and his brow never loses the impression of that Bishop's hand at Rome; because the created always has the form of the creator. And the priest . . . is still

the reflection of Rome, his creator." (Am. Anti-Slav. Soc. *Proc. at Its 2nd Dec.* 86)

Philip's view that Catholics did not support abolition was held by many of the period; a nineteenth-century history text quoted a Catholic saying, "For us Catholics, the fugitive slave law presents no difficulty. We are taught as we have said, to respect and obey the government as the ordinance of God, in all things not declared by our church to be repugnant to the divine law" (Von Holst and Lalor 228). Phillips went on to say that he had little reason to hope for anti-slavery support from immigrants, "as all history shows us that no oppressed class of one nation has ever been able to sympathize cordially, or to any thing effectively, for the sufferers of a different oppression under another government" (Am. Anti-Slav. Soc. *Proc. at Its 2nd Dec.* 86). Alienated from abolitionists on one side, Irish immigrants were also scorned by many who worked to preserve slavery. In its 1857 platform, the American Party supported the rights of states to maintain slavery and called for a change in the laws of naturalization, which would exclude all paupers. In defense of the exclusion of paupers, the American Party quoted a supporter who wrote, "To believe that a mass so crude and incongruous, so remote from the spirit, the ideas, and the customs of America, can be made to harmonize readily with the new element into which it is cast is, to say the least, unnatural."[8] As the abolition movement and nativism intensified, the continued arrival of immigrants from Ireland increased the tangle between African and Irish Americans.

II. Conscription and the Draft Riots

By 1860, New York City's population was nearly split between American (404,469) and foreign born (383,717). Irish-born residents (203,740) were 23 percent of the city's population; another 56,710 Irish-born lived in Brooklyn (*8th Census* Tab. II). The large number of Irish immigrants further separated them from the American born. Immigrant living conditions were miserable. Sickness and disease were common; the city's death rate was the highest on the continent.[9] Irish immigrants created severe demands for housing, medical services, and jobs. Although only 49,005 free blacks lived in the state of New York, they were competition for available work. The movement to emancipate the nearly four million slaves into free labor increased the likelihood for further economic pressure and barriers. In March of 1863, Congress enacted a National Conscription to induct male citizens of the United States, and those of foreign birth who intended to become citizens, into the Union Army. Included in the act was the right to purchase a substitute for a 300-dollar payment, which meant men of wealth might avoid serving (*Cong. Rec.* Sec. 13).

When the New York City draft began enrolling men in July of 1863, rioting exploded. Irish men, women, and children took to the streets of New York City in protest against the Civil War Draft. They attacked individual black men on the street, stoned the homes of abolition sympathizers, and burned the Negro Asylum—a black orphanage—to the ground. Black adults and children were lynched. The *New York Times* and the *Herald* reported the daily atrocities. On Wednesday, 16 July 1863, the *Times* reported that

> at a late hour on a Tuesday night, the mob made an attack upon the tenement houses, occupied by colored people, in Sullivan and Thompson Streets. For three hours, and up to two o'clock yesterday morning, there was what may be truly said to be a reign of terror throughout that portion of the city. Several buildings were fired and a large number of colored persons were beat so badly that they lay insensible in the streets for hours after. Two colored children at no. 59 Thompson Street were shot and instantly killed.

The week's death toll rose to more than a hundred. The most conservative estimates included eleven blacks, eight soldiers, two policemen, and more than eighty rioters. Claims for damages rose to over one and a half million dollars. Twenty percent of the black population fled and never returned.

Late in the week, Archbishop Hughes of New York City addressed the mob and asked them, "Would it not be better for you to retire quietly? Not to give up your principles on conscription but to keep out of a crowd where immortal souls are launched into eternity, and at all events get into no trouble until you are at home. Would it not be better?" Hughes then said, "There is one thing in which I would ask your advice. When these so-called riots are over and the blame is justly laid on Irish Catholics in what country could I claim to be born?" Hughes was a stalwart defender and protector of Irish immigrants; early in his address he identified himself as an Irish man and a Catholic, to a response of great cheers from the assembled. Given his concern for the people, his public acknowledgment that the Irish were culpable was particularly significant as it confirmed what less sympathetic newspapers and police had already reported. His appeal to cease the rioting joined religious belief with a civics lesson for the new immigrants. "In this country, the Constitution gives the right to the people to make a revolution every four years. But it is a different kind of revolution; the battles of our revolution are not battles of blood and violence, nor are they the bullets of lead" ("Archbishop").

A *New York Times* editorial from Saturday of the same week more severely chastised Irish rioters and denied that competition for jobs was an excuse for hostility against African Americans. "On all sides labor finds more than it can do. The Irish man might as well quarrel with the black man for taking up too much of the atmosphere as for encroaching against the labor market. Every willing hand, white or black is now, more than ever, in demand, and more than ever too, a public benefit." The editorial reminded the rioters that they had been protected themselves in earlier times. "In other days we did what we could to shield the Irish when they were fleeing before frantic mobs—mobs which we may say were instigated by one at least of the very Presses which have instigated the population which were then the victims, to make the present attack upon a race which never did them injury" ("Aid for the Injured").

Nearly a year later, the memory of the New York Irish and the riots continued to affect black and Irish interactions. In April of 1864, the *Christian Recorder* printed a letter from a member of the Fifty-Fifth Massachusetts Regiment, Volunteer Infantry. He wrote to tell of an incident that occurred while the troops were boarding ships on Folly Island, South Carolina, in preparation to report to Jacksonville, Florida. In his words,

> While we were waiting with patience for the long looked for morning to dawn, some of the men got to rambling about, as is common among soldiers, when one of them happened, either by chance or otherwise, to get a little too near one of those mean contemptible scamps, notable for no greater crime than having burned the colored Orphan Asylum, in the city of New York, less than a year ago, who took on himself the prerogative of calling one of our men a nigger: this not going down well with the soldier, he was for using the stock of his gun over Pat's head; but Pat, being very sensible of his danger, soon found his way to the hull of the ship that lay near the dock. The soldier . . . well knew that if he reported the case to Col. Fox, that he would get justice; for Col. Fox is not one of those men who will let his men be run over by a lot of mobcrats who deserve to die than live. . . . Col. Fox ordered Pat to come out . . . ordered him under arrest and sent him, accompanied by at least two files of good, brave colored soldiers, to report to the Provost guard.

Although the Sixty-Ninth Irish Regiment had been the second to leave New York when the Civil War began and 175,000 Irish served in Federal armies,[10] the reputation of the Irish as scamps and rioters remained vivid throughout the war and endured in political cartoons of the post–Civil War era. An 1867 Thomas Nast cartoon depicted St. Patrick's Day as "The Day We Celebrate Rum and Blood." Nast drew Irish caricatures with heavy boots, worn frock coats, and simian facial features. Some had a leg poised, jig-like, with a glass in one hand. Some were swinging at policemen who raised billy clubs to quell the crowd. In an 1876 cartoon, "The Ignorant Vote—Honors Are Easy," Nast placed an African American and an Irishman on the two sides of a scale, swinging in balance. The barefooted black wore pants that did not reach his ankles and a too-small wide-brimmed field hand hat. The Irish man wore a ragged frock coat, heavy boots, and a worn-looking stovepipe hat with a knocked-in top. The black man grinned widely at the scowling ape-faced Irishman. In 1883, Rogers drew "The balance of trade with Britain still seems to be against us" depicting a Galway poorhouse, a large stone building, tipped toward the ocean, with its poor Irish inhabitants falling toward the United States. In these and other cartoons of the period, African Americans and Irish immigrants continued to be shown as problems, disrupters of American politics and culture.

III. Contemporary Perspectives

Interviews with living Irish and African Americans provided some insight into the present perceptions of this relationship and how these perceptions have been learned. Those interviewed talked about their personal experiences and what had been passed on in family histories. They included members of the clergy, ministers and religious Brothers, college administrators, secondary educators, and retired blue-collar workers. Males and females were included; all lived within three states: New York, Connecticut, and New Jersey. Their ages ranged from fifty to ninety-two. All of the Irish Americans interviewed were Catholic.[11] Their personal narratives presented details concerning what they learned about acceptance and how they negotiated their place in America. The following remarks are excerpted from lengthier interviews.[12]

A ninety-year-old African American is the grandson of a slave, who was brought to America from Barbados in 1820. When the grandfather was freed, he married a Native American and became a bricklayer. His wife's family had purchased the land that they lived on. Owning the land was made possible because of advice given by an Irish family. The Irish Americans had told the Indians to change their tribal name to one sounding more Anglo-Saxon. The same neighbors had introduced them to other residents. When asked about his experience of discrimination, he said he had few problems with anyone about his being black. He had learned two methods of dealing with difficult people from his father. The first was to anticipate: "If someone might be a problem, we avoided them, didn't mingle, and kept our word." The second was to protect himself: "Always give them ten steps, and when they turn around, always have something strong with you."

A college administrator, also African American, said he thought that the Irish, like all European Americans, had lost touch with their history. He thought that the Irish had been anesthetized by success and had forgotten their early background. However, he had seen a different view of the Irish experience when he'd visited Northern Ireland. He felt an empathy with the Northern Irish Catholics because they were daily as aware of their separations as blacks were in America. He thought the British army in Northern Ireland was comparable to the Ku Klux Klan in the United States (Mazon).

A black minister, who served an inner-city parish, talked about the isolation of Irish Americans from the black community in America. He said that he had attended the funeral of a prominent Irish Catholic politician in a Connecticut town. The minister was the only black person in attendance at the funeral. He said that he was surprised to be the only black man. The Irish mourners seemed even more surprised by his presence. His experience was that acceptance for a black man was the acceptance of exceptionalism. As a minister, he worked among largely white civic organizations and was invited into the homes of some of these leaders. He believed that his welcome did not broaden anyone's tolerance. He was thought to be the exception to their more negative ideas about African Americans. One of the methods he used to evaluate the level of a group's acceptance in American society was through their representation in the media. He noted a wide difference in present perceptions of Irish and African Americans. Speaking about media portrayal of both groups, he thought that stereotypes of both groups continued to occur. He differentiated between the credibility of the two stereotypes. "When an Irishman portrays a crook or an alcoholic on a television show, I think viewers of the show know that the actor is playing a role. When African Americans play those roles, I'm less certain that the viewers think it's a performance only."

When Irish Americans spoke about their histories, they spoke more easily about how they had become accepted than about their relationship to any other race or group in America. An Irish-American teacher took strong exception to any negatives about her heritage. She would not believe that her ancestors had been dirty or poor. She thought Irish Americans who wrote stories about dirty living conditions or ignorance among the Irish were not telling the truth. She would not believe that Irish immigrants had ever fought against African Americans. She said simply, "Not my Irish."

A retired Galway-born woman, who came to America in her early twenties, had preserved her Irish identity by helping found and maintain an active Irish community club in her area. All members of her family are active as officers of the club and volunteers in Gaelic festivals. She came to America because she needed work and had stayed close to relatives still living in Ireland. She saw a distinction between whom she worked with and whom she socialized with. As she said, "You worked with different kinds but returned to your own at night. Each culture had its own club. You were taught to stick to your own kind and I did and so did my husband." She had encountered no discrimination but drew no attention to herself or her Irish roots when not among her own. Her family had taught her to "keep the glad side out" in public, and that's what she had done. Her husband, also Irish born, was present at the interview and said that he'd left New York as soon as possible after his arrival there. "Many Irish had drifted off in New York after they'd arrived; hundreds got lost on the Bowery," a reference to Irish who became drunkards and joined other homeless in the Bowery section of New York. He went on to say, "A nurse who worked with me asked me to help locate her brother who had gone to New York. He was from Cork. I contacted the president of the Corkmen's Association who could trace for someone all over the world. He was never found. Maybe he was lost on the Bowery."

An elderly man, also born in Ireland and now retired, had lived in New Haven, Connecticut, on Goat Hill, an Irish section of the city. Having a decent job was important to him because his father had had told him that in previous years, "Irish Need Not Apply" signs had been placed in the windows of many businesses. Through other relatives, he'd been able to get a railway job. He had been an active politician and continued to be active in church-related activities. In his experience, the Irish always took care of their own through organizations like the Knights of Columbus and did not bother with other groups. He had maintained his Irish culture with Irish music and dance in his home and had passed those on to his children. His daughter pressed him to talk about the changes in his own neighborhood that had occurred when blacks had moved into some houses. He said that he had seen no problems, although he did remember a period of street rioting in New Haven during the civil rights movement. His daughter remembered that when black neighbors played music or danced, her mother pulled down the curtains to keep her daughter from watching.

Seven retired De LaSalle Christian Brothers talked together about their early histories. All were the children of parents born in Ireland who had come to the United States during the 1920s. Six had grown up in New York City, one in Boston, Massachusetts. The discrimination they experienced was focused on their being Catholic more than Irish, although they believed that an Irish surname was cause for suspicion. One said, "When my uncle gave his [Irish] name during a job interview, the first thing out of the interviewer's mouth was, 'Do you drink?'" In their neighborhoods, blacks were never far away, but none of those interviewed remembered having any association with them. "In our parish there was one block where blacks lived, but we never communicated with them. We were not prejudiced; we were ignorant."

One said, "My father would speak about them in a generous way; he didn't think blacks as minstrels was putting them down." Another then said that in his first school teaching assignment he'd been in charge of the annual minstrel show. His students performed in Black Face. He said that at that time, the 1940s, no one knew any better. He and several other Brothers remarked that their formation as religious had included nothing about prejudice against African Americans.

Two men interviewed were of African American and Irish heritage. Both family histories were mixed heritage by choice; that is, an Irish ancestor in each family had married a free black ancestor. Both men grew up as African Americans. Neither had been raised as Irish Americans although both had known that they had a white Irish ancestor. Growing up, neither had participated in any Irish celebrations, nor had they considered themselves Irish.[13] One said that he was a Black American with an Irish paternal grandfather. "Being born and raised in the racial 'salad bowl' of Brooklyn, New York from the 1930s to the 50s, there were white people around me all of my life. Many of my friends, like myself, were multiracial. So I was never the object of direct discrimination until I was fourteen years old: I was with my father, a truck driver who, because his father was Irish, looked as if he was anything but a 'Negro.' One day while on the truck with him, we stopped in a restaurant to eat. They wanted to serve him but not me— and this was right outside of Atlantic City." He believes that "if we Irish/African Americans are unwilling to acknowledge them [events of a shared history], somebody else will and it may be somebody who does not have our best interests at heart."[14]

In general, where African Americans saw division, Irish Americans saw nothing. Where African Americans spoke of unnatural separation, Irish Americans described "staying with one's own." Several of those interviewed presumed a common understanding of the identity of "one's own," an implied meaning of a specific racial or ethnic identifier, although none was overtly stated. Frederick Streets, psychologist and chaplain at Yale University, believes that studying history as a shared story "clearly confronts the reality of interracial relationships and furthers the destruction of race as identifier." Streets, an African American, noted that blacks as well as Irish experience a confusion of identity when confronted by tangled historical events.[15]

Afterword

The research included in this paper comes from a larger work, *Tangled Roots, A Project Exploring the Histories of Americans of Irish Heritage and Americans of African Heritage.* With the support of the Gilder Lehrman Center, the project seeks to investigate the history of American slaves and immigrants from Ireland and to consider the links between them. It grows from the mission of the Gilder Lehrman Center for the Study of Abolition, Resistance and Slavery at Yale University to investigate and disseminate information concerning all aspects of the Atlantic slave system and its destruction.

A collection of primary documents from the seventeenth century to the present provides portraits of people and events from the history of African and Irish Americans. Documents can be accessed at http://www.yale.edu/glc/tangledroots/index.htm. The objective of the project is to foster an understanding of the tangled roots of the shared history. The project is dedicated to an understanding of race and ethnicity in America.

Notes

Mary Ann Matthews is a research affiliate of the Gilder Lehrman Institute. She and her research partner, Thomas O'Brien, were developers of the site.

1. Brian Dooley, *Black and Green* (London: Pluto, 1998). Dooley provides detailed information about the influence of the American civil rights movement on the civil rights movement in Northern Ireland.

2. Larri Mazon, personal interview, 1999. Mazon was organizer of the student trip to Northern Ireland.

3. Respondents to the question included D. Gregg, Connecticut Department of Education; L. Mazon; F. Streets, Yale University; and L. Huggins, Manhattan University.

4. Oscar Handlin, *Boston's Immigrants 1790–1880* (1941; Cambridge: Belknap, 1991). In his chapter, "The Process of Arrival," Handlin discusses the difference in status and skills among European immigrants to suggest why many would not settle in urban areas, particularly Boston.

5. L. J. McCaffrey, *The Irish Catholic Diaspora in America* (Washington, D.C.: Catholic Univ. of America Press, 1997). McCaffrey argues that just as pre-Famine Irish immigrants were beginning to blend into Anglo America, the arrival of the Famine Irish disrupted their acceptance.

6. B. Soskis, *From Bondage to Freedom: The Making of an Abolitionist* (New Haven: Yale Univ. Press, 1998). In another section of his work, Soskis quotes from an Irish newspaper about Douglass's light features and narrow lips. He suggests that these less prominent features may have influenced his reception.

7. Heloise Abel and Frank J. Klingberg, eds., *A Side-Light on Anglo-American Relations, 1839–1858.* Furnished by the Correspondence of Lewis Tappan and Others with the British and Foreign Anti-Slavery Committee. Lancaster, PA (1927). Yale University microform collection. Reference to the resignation is found in Joshua Leavitt's letter to Tappan, dated 19 October 1839 (n 6).

8. S. W. Tisdale, ed., *The True American's Almanac* (New York: 1857). Also included in the *Almanac* is an article, "Rome and America Eternal Opposites," which documents the nativist bias against the Catholic Church.

9. "The Sanitary and Moral Conditions of New York City," *Catholic World* (April–September 1869). The article provides information from the 1866 New York City Board of Health Report, including housing and sanitary conditions. Comparison of conditions in different city wards shows a relation of death rate to living conditions.

10. D. P. Conygham, *The Irish Brigade and Its Campaigns,* ed. L. F. Kohl (New York: Fordham, 1994) 5, 8. In his introduction, Kohl suggests the early enthusiasm for the war was to demonstrate Irish loyalty to the Union. Conygham makes the same point in his preface.

11. Mary Ann Matthews has interviewed Catholic Irish Americans because the historical research for the Tangled Roots project has focused on Irish Famine immigrants who were largely Catholic.

12. Mary Ann Matthews and Thomas O'Brien have recorded interviews over a four-year period. All persons interviewed have given permission for use in published work. Complete transcripts of most interviews can be accessed at: http://www.yale.edu/glc/tangledroots/index.htm.

13. Mary Ann Matthews contacted Michael S. Harper to ask about his African and Irish heritage. Harper suggested that his poems were a source of this information. His father, W. Warren Harper has published an extensive family history, *I'm Katherine, A Memoir,* which offers more detailed biographical information.

14. James McGowan is author of *Station Master of the Underground, the Life and the Letters of Thomas Garrett* and editor of *The Harriet Tubman Journal.*

15. Frederick J. Streets, personal interview, November 1998. Streets is Chaplain and Pastor of Church of Christ in Yale, and Assistant Professor in the Divinity School at Yale.

Works Cited

Abel, Heloise, and Frank J. Klingberg, eds. *A Side-Light on Anglo-American Relations, 1839–1858*. Furnished by the Correspondence of Lewis Tappan and Others with the British and Foreign Anti-Slavery Committee. Lancaster, PA (1927). Yale Univ. microform collection.

"Aid for the Injured." *New York Times* 18 July 1863.

American Anti-Slavery Society. *Proceedings at Its Second Decade.* (Philadelphia.) New York: 1854.

---. *Proceedings of Seventh Annual Meeting.* New York, 1840. Anti-Slavery Collection. Yale Univ. microform collection.

"The Archbishop and His Flock." *New York Times* 18 July 1863.

Blassingame, J., ed. *The Frederick Douglass Papers.* Vol. 1 New Haven: Yale Univ. Press, 1979.

Bodnar, J. *The Transplanted.* Bloomington: Indiana Univ. Press, 1987.

The Christian Recorder [Philadelphia] 2 April 1864.

Cong. Rec. 3 March 1863: ch. 74, 75.

Conygham, D. P. *The Irish Brigade and Its Campaigns.* Ed. L. F. Kohl. New York: Fordham Univ. Press, 1994.

Cusack, M. F. *The Speeches and Public Letters of the Liberator.* Vol. 1. Dublin: McGlashan & Gill, 1875.

Dooley, Brian. *Black and Green.* London: Pluto, 1998.

The Eighth Census 1860.

Gallagher, B. *About Us, For Us, Near Us: The Irish and Harlem Renaissances.* Eire-Ireland: 1981.

Handlin, O. *Boston's Immigrants 1790–1880.* 1991 ed. Cambridge: Belknap, 1941.

Harper, M. S. *Images of Kin.* Chicago: Univ. of Illinois, 1977.

Mazon, Larri (Dir. of the Fairfield Univ. Multicultural Center, Fairfield Univ.). Personal interview. December 9, 1998.

McCaffrey, L. J. *The Irish Catholic Diaspora in America.* Washington, D.C.: Catholic Univ. of America Press, 1997.

Mishkin, T. *The Harlem and Irish Renaissances.* Gainesville: Univ. Press of Florida, 1998.

Nast, Thomas. *Harper's Weekly* 17 March 1867.

---. *Harper's Weekly* 9 December 1876.

New York Times 12–16 July 1863.

Rogers, W. A. *Harper's Weekly* 1840.

"The Sanitary and Moral Conditions of New York City." *Catholic World* April–September 1869.

Soskis, B. *From Bondage to Freedom: The Making of an Abolitionist.* New Haven: Yale Univ., 1998.

Tisdale, S. W., ed. *The True American's Almanac*. New York: 1857.

The United States in 1860. vol. 19. New York: Norman Ross, 1990.

U.S. Bureau of the Census. *Historical Statistics of the United States: Colonial Times to 1970*. Bicentennial Ed., pt. 1. Washington, D.C.: GPO, 1975.

Von Holst, H., and John J. Lalor. *The Constitutional and Political History of the United States*. Chicago: Callaghan, 1881. Yale Univ. Microform collection.

Yellin, J., and J. Van Horne, eds. *The Abolitionist Sisterhood*. Ithaca: Cornell Univ. Press, 1994.

Chapter Four

An Agenda for Researching the Famine Experience of Kilglass Parish, County Roscommon

MARY LEE DUNN

Of all the green fields of Ireland, the fields of Kilglass Parish in County Roscommon may be the most fertile for Famine-related research as a result of recent efforts to memorialize that singular catastrophe. Perhaps no other locality in Ireland has produced so many Famine incidents that have attracted national or international attention.[1] As a result, studies of the families and history of Kilglass in the hundred or so years before the Famine and afterward should help us understand how and why that great convulsion shook Ireland in the 1840s with such force that it not only changed the lives of millions of people in Ireland, but also altered the social, political, and economic landscapes of at least five other countries.[2]

In the context of this paper, *memorials* refer to institutions, publications and other media, and unique initiatives that remember, investigate, or focus in whole or in part on Kilglass people and their Famine experience. Much recent activity centers on Kilglass in Famine time, producing major new resources. The potential of their collective impact to generate knowledge about Ireland's calamity may not be widely recognized since most of these efforts have been developed independently as single projects.

This paper is organized in three sections: the first part describes new aids for researching the history and families of the parish; next is a synopsis of the local history to provide context for the research suggestions that follow; the last section describes six areas of Kilglass research that merit attention, provides new information about the Kilglass Famine story, and offers suggestions for targeted new research strategies. The paper deals with three central events during the worst year of Famine: first, the murders of two local landlords in 1847— Major Denis Mahon of Strokestown and the Rev. John Lloyd of Aughrim; second, the eviction by Major Mahon of thousands of tenants and his "assisted" emigration of hundreds of them in 1847 to Quebec where they landed at Grosse Ile; and finally, the Ballykilcline tenants' twelve-year battle with Crown authorities and their forced emigration in 1847 to the United States.

I. The Memorials

County Roscommon is unique in having so many historical and genealogical memorials related to the Famine.

The Famine Museum was opened in 1994 at Denis Mahon's former home in Strokestown. Mahon was a leading landowner in Roscommon when the Famine began, and his estate covered much of Kilglass Parish. He also was a leader in county affairs and his murder in November 1847 upset the countryside.[3] The museum published Stephen Campbell's book, *The Great Irish Famine* (1994), which is based on records from Mahon's estate, considered an important archive of an Irish "big house" though one that is so far largely unexplored. Also related to the Mahon estate, Robert Scally's book, *The End of Hidden Ireland*, was published in 1995. Scally, taking off from Eilish Ellis's 1983 essay about state-aided emigration from Crown properties, examines the land battle between the tenant farmers of Ballykilcline in Kilglass and Crown authorities and the eviction and "assisted" emigration of the townspeople. Descendants of the Ballykilcline farmers who read Scally's book organized as the Ballykilcline Society in 1998 to locate their counterparts and collaboratively research their stories, their families' emigrant experiences, and the earlier history of Kilglass Parish and the Famine as it happened there.[4] In doing so, the Society is building a records archive and is receiving help from a group in Kilglass called the Friends of Ballykilcline. The Society uses an approach articulated by co-founder Maureen McDermott Humphreys: collaborate to research families from the same area, pool your findings and histories, share the strategies you employ and the records you acquire, and contribute to collective data sets. Paralleling the Society's work is the ongoing development by Ed Finn and Laurie McDonough of a comprehensive and ambitious Internet web site devoted to Roscommon people and history that includes a bulletin board where researchers can connect to share their knowledge.[5] The site is a resource unmatched for other parts of Ireland. Its archive of messages holds much otherwise undocumented Kilglass and personal history, and it identifies and makes accessible individuals who know pieces of it.

Dr. Charles Orser of Illinois State University has for several years conducted archeological studies in Kilglass Parish, including in Ballykilcline where he has excavated Famine-era sites. Orser has established an educational organization there called the Center for the Study of Rural Ireland, focused on life before the Famine.[6]

Strands of the Kilglass story also have been developed elsewhere, where the parish's Famine emigrants traveled and settled; valuable work is occurring outside of Roscommon to explain the Kilglass history. The development of Canada's Grosse Ile Irish immigrant memorial in Quebec and publication of the quarantine station's death records are important advances for Kilglass history since a number of Mahon's evicted tenants arrived there and died there (Charbonneau and Drolet-Dube). The publication of *The Search for Missing Friends,* edited by Ruth-Ann Harris, Donald M. Jacobs, and Emer O'Keeffe, makes it possible to trace the early paths of dozens of Kilglass people in the United States. This multi-volume set extracts the Famine refugees' ads in search of lost family and friends that appeared in the *Boston Pilot* over decades in the nineteenth and early twentieth centuries. At least seventy-eight of the ads were placed by former residents of Kilglass.

Two recent books, four journals, and a prize-winning essay are worth mentioning for the important insights they provide to what transpired in Kilglass and nearby areas and ways to research these events. The books are Coleman's short work, *Riotous Roscommon,* and the *Roscommon and Leitrim Gazette, A Chronicle of the 19th Century,* edited by Mullaney and Lombard, which briefly summarizes selected news stories covering six decades, 1822–1887. The journals are Betit and Radford's *The Irish at Home and Abroad,* O'Beirne's *The O'Beirne Family Journal,* the *County Roscommon Historical and Archaeological Society Journal,* and the *Moylfinne Journal* of the County Roscommon Family History Society. In addition, Michael Huggins won the J. C. Beckett Prize (2000) for his essay on pre-famine agrarian conflicts in Roscommon, which contains examples drawn from life in and near Strokestown.[7] Finally, when the Public Broadcasting Service created its Irish immigrant documentary *Long Journey Home* a few years ago, Denis Mahon and his estate were featured prominently, bringing part of the Kilglass story to the public.

II. The Local History

Kilglass Parish's population exploded between 1749, when the Synge Census recorded it at 2,105, and 1841, when it exceeded 11,300 people (Coyle 23, 36). Repeated sub-division of the land meant that as the Famine began, 45 percent of the "farms" were smaller than five acres (Campbell, *Strokestown* 4).[8] For several decades before the Famine, a significant transition was underway from tillage farming to grazing in some areas of the county, threatening the conacre system that produced food for the Irish people. Conacre allowed a man who had no land to negotiate each spring for a parcel just big enough to grow the store of potatoes for his family's table. Potatoes had become the primary foodstuff of the native Irish by the late 1700s; they were easy to grow on a patch of poor land and they would keep over the winter. By the 1840s, a number of landlords were refusing to set land for conacre because they felt they could do better by using their land for tillage or grazing (Coleman 26). This and other pressures fed the Ribbon movement and the Molly Maguires, the secret societies that sought to help the poor by using force, such as turning up land to compel owners to let it out for conacre. Roscommon experienced serious disturbances after 1820. Emigration from the county proceeded at a moderate pace even before the Famine, and significant numbers of these emigrants went to England and Scotland (Duffy 90, 91).

In 1845, Major Denis Mahon inherited the two hundred-year-old Mahon estate based in Strokestown. Mismanaged until then, the property had more than 13,000 tenants on its 27,000 acres, including much of Kilglass and nearby parishes (Coleman 8). Mahon determined to make it succeed and hired his cousin, John Ross Mahon, as agent. The agent appraised all aspects of the estate and recommended that Major Mahon evict large numbers of tenants so that small farms could be joined to make bigger ones where Protestants could grow grain crops.[9] In autumn 1847, landlords were made responsible for financing relief for the poor; in consequence, the incentives to evict small holders on their properties increased. Thereafter, it became cheaper to "assist" tenants to Canada than to pay their costs in the workhouses as British poor law required. Mahon took that course of action earlier that year. He sent nearly 1,000 evictees to Quebec where the survivors arrived at Grosse Ile in such appalling conditions that Canada protested loudly to England (Donnelly). Approximately 511—that is, more than half—of his former tenants died en route to or on arrival there, and the two ships that carried solely Mahon's tenants had the highest death rates of hundreds of immigrant-laden vessels arriving at Quebec that season.[10]

A few months later, Denis Mahon was ambushed and killed on the road in Doorty. Police conducted a massive manhunt and the murder drew international news coverage. The Rev. John Lloyd was killed in nearby Lissavilla only three weeks later. As a result, Roscommon was officially proclaimed as a disturbed area by the authorities in Dublin Castle and nervous landowners fled with their families (Coleman 40). At the same time, the twelve-year-old "combination"—that is, rent strike—and legal battle between the Crown authorities and hundreds of Ballykilcline farmers ended with eviction and emigration of nearly the whole population. Authorities believed that their strike had touched off other rent strikes as well.[11] The situation concerned the Queen's top administrators in Ireland, including the Attorney General and the Lord Lieutenant of Ireland.[12] In the end, the Crown paid the tenants' way to New York, satisfied to get rid of these troublemakers who had fought them on the land and in the courts where a jury acquitted the Defendants of criminal charges in a stunning verdict that later was overturned (Scally 98). During the Mahon murder investigation, police initially focused on the Ballykilcline strikers. But others eventually were arrested, convicted, and either executed or transported (Coleman 47, 49).

As these cases were settled locally in the summer of 1848, the national scene erupted in the tragi-comic Rising by the Young Ireland nationalists who had been producing a popular Dublin-based newspaper called *The Nation*. The uprising was small and easily defeated. The British put it down in "a cabbage patch" in County Tipperary and transported its leaders. Though they had failed, the patriots had nonetheless excited the Irish with their "cultural nationalism."

When the Famine abated after 1850, Kilglass Parish was a very different place, reeling after losing in some places more than 60 percent of its people to death and emigration (Coleman 54). The Famine toll there was among the highest in Ireland.

III. A Research Agenda

The Famine history of Kilglass is complex but its complexity offers many points to access the story. What follows are descriptions of research approaches and targets that seem especially promising.

The records of the Mahon estate hold great interest for any serious family or local historian of the Kilglass Parish area. Nicholas Mahon arrived in Strokestown in the middle 1600s and the estate operated for hundreds of years, generating a great volume of records. The family was landlord to thousands of local Catholic tenants and the estate archives document those Irish people in their activities as lessees, workers on the Mahon property, and, in some cases, as tithe-payers, voters, or charity cases. It is possible that the estate records may hold the only documentation that exists about some generations of local families. During the Famine, Mahon was an important local figure and his actions affected the lives of thousands of people; some of the estate papers explain or at least shed light on actions Mahon took in a quasi-public capacity.

Records of the estate are held by both the Famine Museum and the National Library of Ireland (NLI, where they are known as the Pakenham-Mahon Papers). An archivist at the NLI, however, was not able to state whether the library's collection from the estate duplicates what the Famine Museum holds (although he said there is substantial overlap) or whether each site has some unique holdings. No complete index as yet exists.

One writer has had full access to the estate records. The museum has published Campbell's book about the Famine, which uses the estate records as a major source. Campbell also has written a manuscript entitled *The Strokestown Famine Papers,* which relies on the Mahon records of the 1840s. A careful reading of his references shows the kinds of sources contained in the archive and, importantly, discloses that there was much correspondence between Denis Mahon and his agent concerning how to make the estate profitable once again and the actions they took to do so.

The NLI holdings include numerous items of family and estate correspondence that cover the period from 1729 to 1865. These documents cover a diverse range of topics and a significant number of them are from the eighteenth century. Many represent unique vantage points or insights on local events. Letters were written to and from the first Lord Hartland between about 1800 and 1820. Some describe the election of 1799. Particularly interesting to family historians might be "seven letters to Lord Hartland re the Strokestown Yeomanry" dated 1806–7.[13] There are ninety items addressed to Denis Mahon from 1833 to 1847; five others were written by Mahon himself. Seventy-three letters between Mahon and his agent-cousin are dated 1846 and '47. Others from 1846 to 1849 deal with emigration, including the exodus of his evictees to Quebec.[14]

Manuscript collections in the archive appear to hold significant interest for family and local historians of the Kilglass and Strokestown area. For instance, there are estate maps from 1734 to 1895 and a 1721 copy of a county survey that was made from one done in 1636.[15] There are rent books and hundreds of deeds, some dating to 1654. There are quit-rent receipts and lists of wages-earners, tithe-payers, and freeholders, as well as genealogies of the Mahons and other families.

The Mahons even recorded to which servants they gave their old clothes and which people they fed meals to one day during the Famine.[16] John Ross Mahon described how he managed his cousin's property during the first year he worked for him. Family records give an account of the linen industry in the county for more than 100 years. Denis Mahon's emigration account book is included in the records.[17] In short, a wealth of primary evidence can be examined in these documents that appear so far to have received only limited attention.

Another point of access to the local history is the landlord murders—the killings of Mahon and Lloyd. As with any criminal activity, these cases generated official documents as well as extensive news coverage. These two deaths and the investigations that followed, with their class, religious, and political implications, had major impacts nationally and internationally. Indeed, it has been said that the murder of Mahon helped turn British public opinion against the Irish people during the worst year of the Famine (Kinealy 132).

Denis Mahon was shot dead on 2 November 1847. Patrick Hasty of Doorty was hanged for the murder in August 1848; James Cummins was executed later. But early in the police hunt, authorities focused suspicion on the troublesome tenants of Ballykilcline. What do we really know about who killed Denis Mahon and why?

As Coleman points out, a police document that November names John McGann [sic] as a suspect in the murder and describes him as a "kind of country schoolmaster" (Coleman 49). In April 2000, family historians Michael and Helen Brennan located a police document at the National Archives that states that the suspect lived in Ballykilcline, a fact that Coleman did not report. The record found by the Brennans, dated Dec. 28, 1847,[18] referred to "a man named John Magan [sic] of the Townland of Ballykilcline in the Parish of Kilglass, a person of that name having been mentioned as being concerned in the murder of Major Mahon."

Confusion ensues because there were two men in Ballykilcline with similar names that were spelled differently and police records used both spellings. It is not clear which of the two—John Magan, 34, or John McGann, 24—is the subject of the police records. However, the older man left for America on the *Creole* in September 1847 and was not present in Kilglass weeks later when Mahon was killed, although it is still possible that he could have been the suspect if he had been implicated in early planning of the murder. But Coleman uses the spelling of the younger man's name, presumably reflecting the way it was recorded in her source (49). More importantly, she says that police had the suspect's family under surveillance *after* the murder, which seemingly must refer to the younger McGann, the one who still lived there. Police recorded that the suspect was single and a teacher.

It is not known what evidence turned suspicion on the Ballykilcline striker or why, under the circumstances, he was able to leave Ireland, as recorded by police.[19] It might be rewarding to look in Ireland or Liverpool for evidence of an interrogation of McGann whose leave-taking quickly followed the murder. In March, the ship *Channing* left Liverpool for New York; McGann, courtesy of the Queen, was listed as a passenger. The last word from John McGann was recorded as he waited to board the *Channing* in Liverpool. He signed an affidavit after fellow emigrants complained about Johnny Cox, the Crown's agent who had escorted the emigrants to Dublin. McGann added a postscript in defense of Cox: "All the complaints that were got up were for the purpose of injuring Johnny Cox." In reporting this footnote to the story, Scally described McGann as "one of the smaller cottiers who had not been prominent in the rent strike" (175). McGann apparently did not hesitate to step forward to defend Cox, which hardly seems like the action of a man on the run. On the other hand, perhaps he was indebted to Cox or wanted officials to see plainly that he was headed to America (and out of their reach). Or Cox may have been a relative since McGann's mother had been born a Cox.[20]

Testimony was given at Hasty's trial that the prisoner had discussed killing Mahon during a stop at a Strokestown pub where a number of Kilglass men were present. No Ballykilcline suspect was named during the trial, at least not in the report about it that appeared in a local newspaper.[21] There are some who believe that Hasty may have been a "hired gun" contracted through a Ribbon or Molly Maguire organization.[22] Coleman, who looked at both the Mahon murder and the killing of Lloyd, found that a single source gave police information in both cases. She subscribed to the Ribbonman theory when she said: "It is evident that someone highly placed in the Ribbon movement betrayed his colleagues. . . . Neither is it surprising that both assassinations had the same source" (48).

Campbell, who wrote with access to the Mahon estate records, contended that the murder had its source in the middle class, a view that may still dovetail with the theory that the men prosecuted were only the "hired guns." He said:

This [murder] appears first and foremost as a middle class enterprise, of reasonably prosperous farmers or tradesmen who could subscribe funds and employ assassins, who might be said in some sense to benefit from the terrorizing of landlords. Killing a landlord could hardly be said to improve the lot of a struggling cottier-tenant who could command little economic force of his own; but rather might be seen to benefit those to whom the land passes at a bargain rate once the landed gentry flee their property and throw their estates on the market. (*Strokestown* 50, 51)

Campbell suggested that Mahon was a random target who was marked for death to scare off property owners so that others could buy land at low prices. He pointed to one instance where the auction of a 288-acre estate was interrupted with the news of Mahon's murder nearby and described the startling effect of that news, which forced a postponement of the sale (*Strokestown* 24). It would be interesting to test Campbell's theory by studying what property changed hands under what circumstances in the months after the murder. But it is worth noting that the Mahons held on to theirs.

Many motivations were possible for the murder of Mahon. The Irish had cause for bitterness against him: in particular, people to whom he had refused conacre or those whose families and friends he had evicted and sent to their deaths in Quebec. A false rumor had circulated around Strokestown that fall that many of Mahon's evictees had died by shipwreck en route to Canada because Mahon had not properly planned for their passage. The true story came to Ireland in September when a Galway newspaper reported the awful state of passengers aboard the *Virginius* as it landed at Grosse Ile (Scally 39; Campbell, *Strokestown* 21). The local Catholic priest, the Rev. Michael McDermott, subsequently gave his view in a letter to *The Evening Freeman* that it was Mahon's evictions that had led to his murder.[23] But the priest's statement was self-serving in that he also was attempting to quell any notions that Catholic conspiracies were involved. Perhaps the motivation for the killing was a private grudge; a modern-day Cox has suggested that Mahon may have fathered a child with a local woman of the Cox line (O'Neill). It is also possible that Mahon's death was related to his argument with the local Catholic clergy over managing help for the starving poor in and around Strokestown, a dispute serious enough that the Vatican eventually paid attention (Campbell, *Strokestown* 22, 23, 26–31). Perhaps the secret societies targeted him themselves rather than acting as middleman on behalf of others; they may have seen him as a threat. In 1843, following the attempted murder of a magistrate, Mahon had convened a panel of justices that urged coercive measures against crime in the county (Campbell, *Strokestown* 6). Mahon certainly took a leading role in the county's affairs and thus may have been held to blame for the disorder that prevailed in that place at that time.

Despite the apprehension, conviction, and punishment of several men in the case and the massive amount of news coverage that it generated, there is no certainty that justice was done. This is only underscored by the words of Denis Kelly, a relative of Mahon's, in a letter to Henry Pakenham Mahon, the victim's son-in-law:

> The "on dit" is (I know not how true) that . . . the jailor admitted a strange priest to [name illegible, presumably one of the chief witnesses] when dying from whom he wrung a declaration of the innocence of the parties he had charged. (Campbell, *Strokestown* 44)

Apparently a report had circulated that a witness on his deathbed at the jail had told a priest not known to the jailer that authorities had arrested the wrong men.

Papers at the National Archives, at the Famine Museum, or even in the Public Record Office in London, which houses the records of the Home Secretary, or private correspondence may yet yield more clues. But no obvious motivation seems to stem from the Ballykilcline events unless a private grievance concerned a farmer there.

In the other murder case, the Rev. Lloyd was killed at Lissavilla, near Kilglass, only a few weeks after Mahon died. Owen Beirne was convicted and was hanged alongside Hasty. In timing, in tactics, in punishment, and some say in source, the Mahon and Lloyd cases are similar and perhaps related. But there are few—if any—studies of Lloyd's evictions at Caldra, even though they were cited as the cause of his murder (Coleman 49). What were the circumstances of his evictions? How many people were evicted and who were they? Is it possible to link them with Owen Beirne? What else in Lloyd's history may have provided a motive for his death, such as, for example, the incident involving wages for a servant that caused three armed Molly Maguires to visit him in the spring of 1846 or the role a Lloyd relative had played in apprehending Molly Maguires some time earlier?[24]

A further link with the Kilglass Famine narrative occurs in Quebec where more than fifty Roscommon children were orphaned in 1847 on landing at the quarantine station at Grosse Ile. The search for descendants of the Ballykilcline families, and for their stories, has been made possible because the tenants' identities are known—a list of the families was compiled at the time of their evictions. Similarly, in the case of Mahon's evictees who were sent to Canada, there exist three lists that, when studied together, provide rough pictures of what happened to at least a few of these families. They are the list of heads of households evicted by Mahon that was compiled by the Bishop of Elphin and published in *The Freeman's Journal* in April 1848;[25] the list of those who died en route to Grosse Ile or at the quarantine station that has been published by Parks Canada (Charbonneau and Drolet-Dube);

and the list of more than 600 children orphaned at Grosse Ile that summer, which was kept by nuns in Quebec and published by Marianna O'Gallagher (117-43). Some families appear on all three lists, captured at different points in time during their passage from the old world to the new. But it is the third list —the orphans' list—that contains sufficient detail to illuminate the story and tie the lists together since in some cases it gives both parents' names (sometimes including the mother's maiden name), the county and locale they emigrated from, and the name of the ship on which they traveled. Since the names of the ships chartered by Denis Mahon are known, this is an important clue to identify his evictees and match them up with the bishop's newspaper record. Taken together, the lists achieve a revelatory power that none has individually, and together they offer a rough picture of what happened to some of the families sent out of Strokestown. In particular, the list of orphans includes a number who emigrated from Lissonuffy and others from Bumlin, both near Strokestown.

The Sheridan family makes a good example. According to the bishop's list, eleven members of the James Sheridan family were evicted from the townland of Curhownaugh in Lissonuffy civil parish. Along with others he evicted, Denis Mahon considered the Sheridans "surplus population" on his estate. In June 1847, the Sheridan family boarded Mahon's chartered ship, the *Naomi*, in Liverpool, bound for Quebec. Only six of them survived the voyage and quarantine at Grosse Ile. One unidentified Sheridan must have chosen to remain either in Ireland or England or must have died between Roscommon and Liverpool since eleven family members were evicted but only ten are listed in Canadian records. The father, James, age 60, his son John, 22, and Bridget Sheridan, age and relationship unknown, all died at sea or in quarantine on the island. The wife and mother, Mary Connor Sheridan, then 60, died in the hospital at Grosse Ile during the last week of August 1847. Six Sheridan children—Catherine, 20, Mary, 19, Ann, 15, Owen, 14, Ellen, 12, and Pat, 10—were sent to the nuns at a Catholic orphanage in Quebec. On 2 October, the children left there for Lockport (presumably near Buffalo, New York). It is likely that they had family or friends in New York.

The Sheridans' story was pieced together by picking family members out of the three record sets and interpreting the evidence. One or more of the Sheridans appears on each list and each list adds details to their story. Together, they allow us to see at least the outline of their sad tale in which nearly half of the family members died during those frantic few months when they first lost their home and then embarked on an Atlantic passage on a coffin ship where 196 of the several hundred passengers died by the time it was halted at Grosse Ile.

The convent list names at least fifty-six Grosse Ile orphans who came from Roscommon. Since hundreds of Mahon's former tenants arrived at Grosse Ile in the same way on ships whose names are known, it might be a productive undertaking to study the list of orphans and compare the information about each of the Roscommon children with the other two sets of records. There also is the suggestion that either the bishop's list of evicted families was incomplete or relatives of some evicted families chose to leave Ireland together with the evictees, unwilling apparently to have their families separated. For instance, the orphan list shows that at least two families named Campbell from "Lisanuffy" traveled aboard the ship *Virginius*, but only one of the families (William Campbell's of Kilmachaneny townland) was identified by the bishop as evicted by Mahon; the family of the other orphaned Campbell child was not listed there. (The bishop does, however, list additional Campbell families who were evicted from the same townland.)

While Mahon was evicting and transporting those thousands of tenants, the Ballykilcline rent strike was ending. In Kilglass, the strike was a major parish event during the 1830s and 1840s, subject to gossip, speculation, and forceful action on both sides. But is it possible that the strike had national significance as well? Calls by the radical Young Irelanders James Fintan Lalor and John Mitchel for a national rent strike early in 1848 came just as the Ballykilcline tenants left Ireland and only weeks after the notorious landlord murders in Roscommon (Hachey, Hernon, and McCaffrey 90). The coincidence of tactic and timing raises questions: Did coverage of the murders extend to coverage of the Roscommon rent strike and vault it to the attention of Lalor and Mitchel? Lalor, in particular, given his great concern for agrarian reform, could hardly have failed to be attracted by the events in Roscommon. It would be worthwhile to comb his writing and issues of *The Nation* during those crucial weeks or months to see whether any evidence shows that the Roscommon events affected the calls in Dublin for a national rent strike. At least two potential conduits of information existed between Ballykilcline and the Dublin activists: first, the striking tenants' lawyer, Hugh O'Ferrall, had an office in Dublin and, second, both the Attorney General and the Lord Lieutenant of Ireland were pressing to resolve the Ballykilcline problems (Scally 73; Campbell, *Strokestown*). The radicals may have uncovered the story from political or governmental sources in the Irish capital or from the local or national press. It is an important point. Lalor's and Mitchel's calls for a rent strike created a rift in Young Ireland that caused Mitchel to break away and establish the incendiary newspaper called *The United Irishmen* (Hachey, Hernon, and McCaffrey 90). The rest of the story is well known: Mitchel's arrest and transportation; the hopeless Rising of 1848; more trials and sentences to penal colonies.

But it is not only the ending of the Ballykilcline strike that warrants study. Where did the tactic come from? What is the history of strike action in Ireland?

In his essay on agrarian conflict and emergent class consciousness among pre-Famine rural Roscommoners, Huggins saw conflict produced as "commerce brought change to the subsistence-oriented peasant community" (12). The secret societies developed to defend peasant interests and their actions focused "on all aspects of economic life in order to ensure the satisfaction of subsistence needs" (7). Their goals of curbing prices for land, provisions, tithes, and so on showed

a consciousness that was able to make general conclusions about the need for working people to pursue collectively held interests, and it identified the enemies of those working people precisely as the landlord and employers. (28)

Threatening notices sometimes aimed at "reasonable prices for land," as was the issue in Ballykilcline. But precedents for collective action turned up in other local contexts as well, such as in the laboring relationship: in June 1823 workers who were building a road near Strokestown protested a plan to pay them a fixed fee by destroying a ditch at the site. "A combination exists amongst the workmen . . . that employment might be afforded the longer to the labouring classes," an observer explained. Industrial actions took place in mills at Roscommon town and Athlone about the same time (Huggins 8, 9). A few years later, the *Roscommon Journal* gave substantial coverage to the Captain Swing disturbances and related conflicts in England. Notions of class and protest also returned from England along with seasonal Irish migrant laborers who, an 1831 select committee was told, saw their British counterparts "swear to be true to each other, and join to keep the people upon their ground" (Huggins 32–34).

The earliest local rent strike reference though appears to be from *The Roscommon and Leitrim Gazette* only a year before the start of the strike at Ballykilcline. It suggests that Lawyer O'Ferrall may be a pivotal, if neglected, figure in this story. Serious disturbances at Gillstown and Ashbrook in Roscommon were reported by the newspaper in spring 1834. The *Gazette* said demonstrators had pressed for action against landlords.[26] Gillstown was on the edge of Kilglass Parish, near Strokestown. Ashbrook was not far from there in Lissonuffy and was the home of O'Ferrall (Scally 73). This fact makes it tempting to ponder O'Ferrall's role, if any, in both events and to wonder whether the seed of the Ballykilcline strike came out of this fracas or directly from the lawyer. Is it germane that the first time any Ballykilcline tenants withheld their rent was the following year and O'Ferrall represented the tenants?[27] The lawyer, his political views, his Dublin practice, and his role in the Ballykilcline strike are worth more investigation. The inquiry is important not only in the context of local history but also because it may have wide national implications.

Evidence shows strikes against other local landowners in the 1840s; the success of the Ballykilcline strike likely encouraged them, a development that had worried officials. A combination aimed at the Rev. Lloyd in 1845 at Carrick-on-Shannon (Coleman 47). Strikes affected the Mahons around 1845. Denis Mahon's agent later reported that the strike pre-dated the Famine and was not due solely to the people's increasing distress (Campbell, *Strokestown* 6, 7). The Crown's overseer in Ballykilcline reported that Mr. Blakeney's and Mr. Balfe's tenants were withholding rents. These landowners, he said, "have suffered severely from the example of those [Ballykilcline] tenants, and are not paying their rents as hitherto" (Scally 102). By 1848, Patrick Browne, the brother of the Bishop of Elphin, also was targeted by "a regular combination and conspiracy against the payment of rents" (Campbell, *Strokestown* 35). Some evidence of strikes in other counties at that time exists as well; Foster says that "there were rent strikes and intimidatory tactics in Clare and elsewhere" (343). What were they and when did they occur? Was a rent strike a well-used tactic then or was it only just being introduced in the theater of protest action?

Three decades later, Michael Davitt, who was intrigued by Lalor's ideas about rural issues, and Charles Stewart Parnell, who stepped in to head the Irish National Land League, urged the Irish to combine against the unfair landlord system (Inglis 148), much as the Ballykilcline farmers had done. The people's compliant response to their call eventually led to the Land Act of 1881, supported by Gladstone, the leader of the Liberals, under which the British conceded much to the Land League. "The state of Ireland made it impossible for them to reject it," Inglis said (150), much as the British could not and did not ignore the strike in Ballykilcline.

British authorities forcibly emptied Ballykilcline and sent hundreds of its residents to New York. The townland's farmers thus became a small but visible segment of the estimated 40,000 Irish who were "helped" out of Ireland by subsidies from landlords or the government.[28] By the time the British imposed their solution on Ballykilcline, one wonders whether the tenants—despite their long battle to preserve their rights to the land—were willing or unwilling emigrants. The tenants had long been viewed around Strokestown as stubborn people and troublemakers. The early suspicions that fell on them when Mahon was murdered attest to their reputation. They fought back against the system repeatedly—in withholding their rents individually and then as a group, hiring a lawyer, re-possessing their holdings after eviction, resisting in court, clashing with police on the land, sending memorials to Crown officials, and for some perhaps by conniving to stay in Ireland even after receiving the Crown's bounty to leave (Scally 225). Yet in late 1846, when the Crown offered them an easy settlement that demanded little in the way of arrears (seemingly the tenants' major goal during most of their strike), they did not respond. Ballykilcline was disturbingly and uncharacteristically quiet then. The question is, Why? Had the tenants' goals shifted eleven years into their strike? Were they demoralized by the Famine and their land battle? Had the Famine turned their eyes abroad? Did they know that during the winter and spring of 1847 officials were considering an "assisted emigration"? Did that idea start in Ballykilcline and go through O'Ferrall to Dublin authorities or was it the other way around? In the end, was passage to America what they came to want in the face of Famine in Ireland?

By that time, some of them surely had gained a view to America through a window opened across the Atlantic. Fresh evidence shows that Kilglass sent at least two dozen people to Vermont alone in the ten years before the Famine; tenants from Ballykilcline also had gone, some of them quite early. John and Sabina Brennan Hanley of Ballykilcline had settled in Rutland, Vermont, by 1835. The Hanleys' descendants possess letters that they wrote to Ireland in which they described the land they bought, two tracts totaling nearly 100 acres, part of which they called Hanley's Mountain.[29] Soon, more Kilglass emigrants arrived in Rutland and, by the early 1840s, many of them were U.S. citizens.[30] Their letters home must have opened a window on emigration for the families who received and read them in a place of social chaos where people around them lay dying. When a jury's July 1844 verdict favoring the Ballykilcline tenants was overturned months later, perhaps some of them looked ahead to an inglorious end to their long protest. And by Black '47, Ireland was a very different place than when their strike began and their united stand was only a memory.

No more than 298 of nearly 500 Ballykilcline tenants identified in 1846 landed in New York under the Crown's emigration scheme, Scally reported. This was far fewer than the 409 who had taken the Crown's travel allowance and far fewer than the number recorded as boarding the ships in Liverpool.[31] It is a reasonable assumption that a number of them had died and an unknown number remained in Ireland, whether by choice, fear, or family obligation. Further, Scally speculated plausibly that some of them may have sold or bartered their "place in the line" to neighbors or relatives who wanted to go to America (224, 225). More research is needed to substantiate the theory, but the existence of an underground Kilglass market for the Crown's passages to America, as Scally said, would be "yet another conspiracy in Ballykilcline [for some tenants] to remain where and what they were" (225). At the same time, it would have camouflaged some local people's way out of Ireland to America. In any case, the Crown's final solution for Ballykilcline bought passage to America for hundreds of local people. It seems certain that some of them got what they wanted when they headed out of Strokestown. Finding their descendants may uncover personal papers or oral history that tells how the emigrants saw or negotiated their leave-taking.

Finally, the early experience of Ballykilcline people in America may be a lens to retrospectively view their behavior during the rent strike in Kilglass. People do not change their natures by crossing an ocean. If the records of Ireland do not tell us what we want to know about them, perhaps American records and experience can do so.[32] Thus, following the Ballykilcline people in their life in America may be one way to gain insight to what they were like in Kilglass and the strike decisions they made there. Some questions are worth asking to learn about their behavior, their psychic baggage (if any) from Famine and eviction, their sense of self, and their capacity to navigate the economy and social setting of the United States: Did they remain a community in any sense in the United States (Scally 226-227)? How literate were they? How many of them could read and/or write? How soon, if at all, did they become American citizens? How quickly did they accumulate personal goods, property, and money, as an index of their accommodation to their new surroundings? Did they prosper or go under? Answers should provide clues to their purposefulness and intentionality as tenants in Kilglass.

Ads in *The Boston Pilot* after 1850 show that some Kilglass immigrants kept in touch with each other after they landed in New York. The Ballykilcline Society has found several places where numbers of Ballykilcline and Kilglass people settled: Baltimore and Texas, Maryland; LaSalle County, Illinois; West Rutland, Vermont; Providence, Rhode Island; Chicago, Illinois; Albany and Lockport, New York; and areas of Pennsylvania and Tennessee.[33] Already we know that they maintained some sense of community in the United States, that while they did not settle in one place en masse, numbers of them settled in several locations where they remained neighbors, intermarried, and helped each other. We also know now that some of them prospered. One who did so is Richard Padian who went with his family to Texas, Maryland, which developed an enclave from Roscommon where, as in Ballykilcline, Padian was a leading figure.[34] The Ballykilcline Society now counts about seventy-five members in four countries. It is conducting an internet search for other descendants—"the lost children of Ballykilcline."

As the knowledge base builds, we can expect more insight and answers to these puzzles out of Famine Ireland.

Acknowledgments

I am deeply indebted to the Ballykilcline Society and its members, especially Maureen McDermott Humphreys, Lynne Sisk, Tom Shanley, Anne Marie Bell, Maureen Hanley Cole, Mary Ellen Valenty, Liz McDermott Condon, Cassie Kilroy Thompson, and Jim Padian; also to Michael and Helen Brennan, Robert Scally, Luke Dodd, Sean O'Beirne, Ruth-Ann Harris, Ed Finn, and above all to my mother, Frances Dunn, and my sister, Jane Dunn Millett, for sources, insight, and inspiration. Thanks go also to Quinnipiac University's president, John Lahey, for his interest in fostering knowledge about the Irish Famine; to David Valone who organized its September 2000 conference, *"An Gorta Mor*, Ireland's Great Hunger: An Interdisciplinary Assessment"; to the Lender Family who funded the conference; and to Christine Kinealy and Valone for their insightful suggestions to strengthen this paper.

Notes

1. Any list of noteworthy events affecting Kilglass Parish in Famine time must include the Ballykilcline rent strike; the mass evictions by Denis Mahon and deaths of some of his former tenants in Quebec; the murder of Denis Mahon and the police investigation, trial, and execution that followed, as well as the linked killing of the Rev. John Lloyd; and, as a backdrop, the disturbed state of the countryside, the unfolding of the Famine itself and efforts to alleviate it, and massive emigration.

2. The countries are Ireland, Scotland, England, Canada, the United States, and Australia.

3. Numerous works recount this history. Three primary books are Stephen J. Campbell, *The Great Irish Famine* (Famine Museum, 1994); Robert James Scally, *The End of Hidden Ireland* (Oxford UP, 1995); and Anne Coleman, *Riotous Roscommon*, Maynooth Studies in Local History (Irish Academic Press, 1999).

4. The Ballykilcline Society has a Web site at www.ballykilcline.com. It held its first Reunion in Roscommon in August 1999, attended by approximately one hundred people from four countries. Its second Reunion took place in July 2000 in Lowell, Massachusetts. Co-presidents are Maureen McDermott

Humphreys, whose ancestor is Hugh McDermott of Ballykilcline, and Mary Lee Dunn, a descendant of John Riley who was born in 1822 the oldest of seven known children of Michael and Ann Colligan Riley of Kilglass Parish. Riley emigrated to Providence, Rhode Island, in April 1848.

5. The Leitrim-Roscommon web site is at www.leitrim-roscommon.com. In addition to the mentioned bulletin board, databases of Griffith's Valuation and the 1901 Irish Census are being added to the site, which contains various maps and other information, family histories, and a link to the on-line telephone book of Ireland.

6. *The Bonfire*, the newsletter of The Ballykilcline Society, Spring 2000. Orser is a faculty member at Illinois State University. His Web site is at www.ilstu.edu/~ceorser/Kilglass.htm.

7. Quotations from Michael Huggins' "A Secret Ireland: agrarian conflict in pre-Famine Roscommon," winner of the Four Courts Press J.C. Beckett Prize in Modern History, 2000. *Social conflict in pre-Famine Roscommon*, a revised version of Huggins' work, was to be published by Four Courts Press in September 2002. I am grateful to Huggins for sharing his essay before publication.

8. Thanks to Luke Dodd, former curator of the Museum, for a copy of this paper.

9. Campbell, *Strokestown Famine Papers*, Ms. Famine Museum, rev. 1990, 32. Campbell says that Mahon advertised for Protestant tenants in Scottish newspapers without result. Also, Christine Kinealy, *A Death-Dealing Famine* (Pluto, 1997), 126.

10. Two sources were used to calculate the number of Mahon's former tenants who died in passage: Campbell's *The Great Irish Famine* and Charbonneau and Drolet-Dube in *A Register of Deceased Persons at Sea and on Grosse Ile in 1847*, as indicated below.

	No. of Mahon Evictees Aboard[a]	Total No. Passengers[b]	Total No. Who Died[c]
Erin's Queen	100	518	136
John Munn	55	452	188
Naomi[d]	3501/2	334	196
Virginius	476	476	268

[a] Campbell; in *Strokestown Famine Papers*, Campbell gives a somewhat different account, stating that Mahon emigrated 490 in the first batch, 390 of whom boarded the *Virginius*, the rest took the *Erin's Queen* (19). In this calculation, it is assumed that the later published version is the most authoritative.

[b] Charbonneau and Drolet-Dube

[c] Charbonneau and Drolet-Dube

^d The sources disagree on the total number of passengers aboard the *Naomi*.

Thus, the 464 passengers on the *Naomi* and *Virginius* who died were all former tenants of Mahon's. On those two ships alone, Charbonneau and Drole-Dube calculated a death rate of 56 percent (2). If the Mahon passengers aboard the *John Munn* and *Erin's Queen* died at the same rate as all passengers on those two vessels, then 47 more of Mahon's people died on those ships, making a total of 511 deaths among his former tenants. Campbell counted 981 former Mahon tenants boarding the four ships. The numbers then mean that at least 52 percent of Mahon's tenants died in passage. More of them undoubtedly carried undetected disease with them as they left Grosse Ile and died inland (where tracing them is harder). The epidemics that subsequently developed in Quebec and Montreal and the great number of deaths among immigrants inland showed that the island quarantine station had not prevented all disease from entering Canada with its new residents.

In their work, Charbonneau and Drolet-Dube present a table that includes, where known, the number of passengers and number of deaths for each of the 442 ships that landed at Grosse Ile, making the calculation of death rates a straightforward matter.

11. Coleman, *Riotous Roscommon* 47; Quit Rent Office (QRO), Official Correspondence of the Commissioners of Woods and Forests, Lands of Ballykilcline, County Roscommon 76; Campbell, *Strokestown* 6, 7, 17, 35.

12. *The Times*, May 31, 1848, and letters of the Earl of Bessborough and the Attorney General for Ireland, 17 and 18 February 1847, 79. Thanks to Dr. Ruth-Ann Harris of Boston College for this source. During the waning months of· the Ballykilcline strike, Lord Bessborough was succeeded as Lord Lieutenant by Lord Clarendon.

13. National Library of Ireland (NLI), 10.097. These and subsequent references to NLI Pakenham-Mahon Papers are from Hayes, *Manuscript Sources*.

14. NLI, 10.101, 10.102, 10.104, Pakenham-Mahon Papers.

15. NLI, 16 M.14-16; Pakenham-Mahon, Family of. NLI, #3119.

16. NLI, #10,131, Pakenham-Mahon Papers. NLI, for instance, #D. 11,707–24; D. 11,725–11,868; D. 11,869–12,001; D. 12,002–12,089; D. 12,935–13,047; D. 12,207–12,360; Pakenham-Mahon Papers. NLI, #10,136, 1844; Pakenham-Mahon Papers. NLI, #10,137; Friday, 19 January 1846; Pakenham-Mahon Papers.

17. NLI, n. 558, p. 928; 8 November 1847; Pakenham-Mahon Papers. NLI, #10,126; 1780–1890; Pakenham-Mahon Papers. NLI, #10,138; Pakenham-Mahon Papers.

18. National Archives of Ireland (NAI), Outrage Papers, 1848, Roscommon, 25/862. H.W. Blakeney to Stephen Burke, Dec. 28, 1847. Personal communication with Michael and Helen Brennan, April 2000.

19. NAI, Outrage Papers, 1848, Roscommon, 25/862. Michael Fox to Thomas Blakeney, Dec. 28, 1847. Personal communication with Michael and Helen Brennan, April 2000.

20. NAI, Outrage Papers, 1848, Roscommon, 25/__. Confidential memo from Michael Cox, 26 November 1847. Personal communication with Michael and Helen Brennan, April 2001.

21. "Crown Court—Wednesday/Murder of Major Mahon." News account of the trial of Patrick Hasty, *The Roscommon Journal and Western Reporter*, 15 July 1848. Thanks to Sean O'Beirne, editor of *The O'Beirne Family Journal*, for a transcript of this account.

22. Personal communication with Sean O'Beirne, who explained to me the ways in which the secret organizations were thought to operate, including the notion that hiring someone from a distance away was thought to afford protection.

23. Campbell, *Strokestown* 27, 28.

24. Mullaney and Lombard, eds. *Gazette, 1822-1887*, Report for 16 May 1846; Coleman 47.

25. *The Freeman's Journal*, Letter from the Bishop of Elphin, Dublin, 29 April 1848, 1. In *Strokestown Famine Papers*, 41, Campbell says that John Ross Mahon, in defending his slain cousin's reputation, contended that "most of the people on the bishop's list had surrendered their holdings or been evicted *since* [emphasis added] the murder of Major Mahon" (i.e., after 2 November 1847). The bishop's letter does not date the evictions.

26. Mullaney and Lombard, Report for 19 April 1834.

27. QRO, Official Correspondence of the Commissioners of Woods and Forests, Lands of Ballykilcline, County Roscommon, 10–13. This is a table of rents paid by the landholders of Ballykilcline between 1 May 1834 and 1 November 1841 and clearly shows when individual tenants stopped paying rent.

28. David Fitzpatrick, "Flight from Famine," in Póirtéir, 178. Fitzpatrick says, "All told, less than 40,000 emigrants are known to have received subsidies from either landlords or the state between 1846 and 1850."

29. Personal Correspondence with Anne Marie Bell and Mary Ellen Valenty, Hanley descendants and members of the Ballykilcline Society, 1998–2000.

30. Anne Marie Bell and Maureen Hanley Cole, both members of the Ballykilcline Society, found naturalization records of approximately 60 Kilglass immigrants who, in the 1830s–50s, lived at or near Rutland, Vermont, in the records office at Middlesex, Vermont, in July 2000. Many of these Kilglass people became U.S. citizens in the early 1840s.

31. Scally 121, 172.

32. The idea came out of communications exchanged with Dr. Ruth-Ann Harris of Boston College in Spring 2000.

33. These locales were identified through research by members of the Ballykilcline Society who, knowing where their own families settled in the United States, then looked for other Ballykilcline and Kilglass surnames and records in the same areas. Chicago was identified as a place of settlement by searching Tom Cook's Chicago Irish database at the Web site of *The Irish at Home and Abroad* <www.IHAonline.com>.

34. Research by James Padian and family members, who are descendants of Richard Padian and members of the Ballykilcline Society; also, evidence from a parish history of St. Joseph's Church, Texas, Maryland, furnished by Cassie Kilroy Thompson, a member of the Ballykilcline Society, to the Society.

Works Cited

Betit, Kyle J., and Dwight A. Radford, eds. *The Irish at Home and Abroad*. Privately published; publication now suspended.

The Bonfire (newsletter of the Ballykilcline Society), spring 2000.

Campbell, Stephen J. *The Great Irish Famine*. Strokestown: The Famine Museum, 1994.

---. *The Strokestown Famine Papers: The Mahon Family and the Strokestown Estate, 1845–1848*. Ms. Famine Museum, Strokestown, Co. Roscommon, rev. 1990.

Charbonneau, Andre, and Doris Drolet-Dube. *A Register of Deceased Persons at Sea and on Grosse Ile in 1847*. Ottawa: Parks Canada, 1997.

Coleman, Anne. *Riotous Roscommon*. Maynooth Studies in Local History. Dublin: Irish Academic Press, 1999.

County Roscommon Historical and Archaeological Society Journal. ISSN 0790-9306.

Coyle, Liam. *A Parish History/Kilglass Ruskey Slatta*. Kilglass Gaels; Boyle: *Roscommon Herald*, 1994.

"Crown Court—Wednesday/Murder of Major Mahon." *Roscommon Journal and Western Reporter,* 15 July 1848.

Donnelly, James S., Jr. "Mass Eviction and the Great Famine: The Clearances Revisited." In *The Great Irish Famine* ed. Cathal Póirtéir, pp. 155-73. Chester Springs, Penn.: Dufour Editions, 1997.

Duffy, Sean, ed. *The Macmillan Atlas of Irish History*. New York: Simon, 1997.

Ellis, Eilish. *Emigrants from Ireland, 1847–1852, State-Aided Emigration Schemes from Crown Estates in Ireland*. Baltimore: Genealogical Publishing Co., 1983.

Fitzpatrick, David. "Flight from Famine." In *The Great Irish Famine* ed. Cathal Póirtéir, pp. 174-84. Chester Springs, Penn.: Dufour Editions, 1997.

Foster, R. F. *Modern Ireland 1600–1972*. London: Penguin, 1989.

The Freeman's Journal. Letter from the Bishop of Elphin, Dublin. 29 April 1848.

Hachey, Thomas E., Joseph M. Hernon Jr., and Lawrence J. McCaffrey, eds. *The Irish Experience*. London: M.E. Sharpe, 1996.

Harris, Ruth-Ann, Donald M. Jacobs, and Emer O'Keeffe, eds. *The Search for Missing Friends*. 8 vols. Boston: New England Historic Genealogical Society, 1989–99.

Hayes, Richard J. *Manuscript Sources for the History of Irish Civilization*. Boston: G.K. Hall, 1965.

Huggins, Michael. *Social Conflict in pre-Famine Roscommon*. Dublin: Four Courts Press, forthcoming.

Inglis, Brian. *The Story of Ireland*. London: Faber, 1956.

Kinealy, Christine. *A Death-Dealing Famine*. London: Pluto, 1997.

Moylfinne Journal. County Roscommon Family History Society, Irish Connections, Bealnamullia, Athlone, quarterly.

Mullaney, Thomas, and Pat Lombard, eds. *Roscommon and Leitrim Gazette, 1822-1887 A Chronicle of the 19th Century*. Bromell Family, 1999.

National Library of Ireland (NLI). Pakenham-Mahon Papers.

O'Beirne, John (Sean), ed. *The O'Beirne Family Journal*. Privately published <www.obeirnefamily.mcmail.com>.

O'Gallagher, Marianna. *Grosse Ile/Gateway to Canada 1832–1937*. Quebec: Carraig, 1984.

O'Neill, Helen, "A Neighborhood, Wiped Out More Than a Century Ago in Ireland, Is Rediscovered in America." Associated Press 2 August 1998.

Póirtéir, Cathal, ed. *The Great Irish Famine*. Chester Springs, Penn.: Dufour Editions, 1997.

Scally, Robert James. *The End of Hidden Ireland*. Oxford: Oxford Univ. Press, 1995.

The Times 31 May 1848.

Chapter Five

W. B. Yeats's Politics of Proximity: or The Famine's Absence in Yeats's Poetry

RACHED KHALIFA

Finding a correlation between W. B. Yeats's poetry and the Great Famine is by no means evident. The poet, I am sure, would himself be outraged by this attempt to link his aesthetics to *phytophthora infestans*. Yeats talked about "cabbage" as an ideological symbol of modernity's utilitarianism and philistinism (of course epitomized in England), but never had he said anything about the "potato," which is a highly charged cultural symbol in the Irish tradition. This absence places the poet outside an Irish poetic tradition extending, say, from James Clarence Mangan to Seamus Heaney.[1] Yeats is broadly known as poet, dramatist, folklorist, anthologist, essayist, and definitely not as a historian, in spite of his many attempts at historiography. His writing of history is nebulous, inaccurate, and most often dissimulated in a strange mix of mythology and fact. His reading of major historical moments works within his theosophical philosophy of history. These moments are, according to Yeats, apocalyptic encounters between the supernatural and the natural, the otherworldly and the worldly. "Leda and the Swan" illustrates best his theory of universal history. His Irish version of a history in which myth and fact are interwoven is found in the Easter Rising in 1916:

When Pearse summoned Cuchulain to his side,
What stalked through the Post office?

Although Yeats tried during his poetic career to narrate crucial events in Irish history, he, very strangely, failed to incorporate into his text a tragedy of such a catastrophic consequence on the nation as the Great Famine. For a poet who defined himself as nationalist, who placed himself and his work in the mainstream of post-Famine Irish nationalism, be it aesthetic or romantic, this occlusion seems all the more strange and definitely calls for more investigation. There are some timid references to famines in Yeats's works, but these remain negligibly scant in comparison with the literature he devoted to Irish nationalism, history, and politics. The play *The Countess Cathleen* is Yeats's only explicit text where he hints to a famine-stricken land, where "the graves are walking" (55). The imagery of the play might have been culled from the memories of the Famine, as Margaret Kelleher argues, but this is by no means an explicit reference to the Great Hunger as a historical event. If the events of the play are geographically placed in Ireland, its historical background is then nebulously located in some "old times," suggesting, as Kelleher remarks, "Yeats's deliberate distancing of the play from well-known historical events" (*Feminization* 116-17). As such the famine is generic and not specific, symbolic and not metonymic. Yeats sees in the story of the Countess selling her soul to save her starving people "a symbol of all souls who lose their peace or their fineness of soul or the beauty of their spirit in political service" (Kelleher, *Feminization* 118). The statement of course refers to Yeats's *femme fatale*, Maud Gonne, who not only impersonated the Countess Cathleen in his play, but more important, came to symbolize in the poet's paradigm a woman's loss of "soul" and "fineness"—aristocratic values highly prized in Yeats—for political ends. This is not only emptying the Famine of its political meaning but also a clear rejection of female political militancy.[2] Such a rejection would gain more vehemence in the later poetry and even borders on misogynism in "A Prayer for my Daughter."[3] After ironically asserting that "fine women eat / A crazy salad with their meat / Whereby the Horn of Plenty is undone," Yeats takes up the same theme of aristocratic "loveliness" and "plentiness" to attack an ever "opinionated"—and thus degraded, "mobbified"—Maud Gonne:

> Have I not seen the loveliest woman born
> Out of the mouth of Plenty's horn,
> Because of her opinionated mind
> Barter that horn and every good
> By quiet natures understood
> For an old bellows full of angry wind?

Yeats's poetry as such embodies no allusion whatsoever to the Great Hunger. Yet his essay on "Edmund Spenser" stands probably as his most interesting text, showing the poet's awareness of the connection between starvation and colonial politics. In this essay he quotes at length what might be called Spenser's "final solution" to the Irish problem. This solution consists of what might be called in modern understanding simply genocide through deliberate starvation. In his *View on the Present State of Ireland,* Spenser advances a scheme by means of which Irish resistance ("the wandering companies that keep the wood") can be reduced to naught by cutting it off from all sources of "sustenance"—that is, deliberate starvation. The scheme postulates that the rebel's

> moste sustenaunce shall be wasted in preying, or killed in driving, or starved for want of pasture in the woods, and himselfe brought soe lowe, that he shall have no harte, nor abilitye to indure his wretchedness, the which will surely come to passe in very short space; for one winters well following of him will soe plucke him on his knees that he will never be able to stand up agayne. (Yeats, *Essays* 373-74).

Spenser's scheme, as he self-complacently defines it, is also highly economical. It would not cost a penny to Queen Elizabeth. To get rid of Irish recalcitrance, Spenser proposes the politics of depopulation and extermination, that is, the politics of demographic *tabula rasa.* In short, he proposes genocide. Spenser is persuaded that owing to his stratagem "in short space there were none allmost left, and a most populous and plentifull countrey suddaynely made voyde of man or beast; yet sure in all that warre, there perished not many by the sword, but all by the extremitye of famine" (Yeats, *Essays* 374).

To what extent this politics of depopulation had seeped into the metropolitan mind calls for more investigation; yet there is enough room to argue that this politics seems to work within a broader political tradition that had always underlain Britain's handling of the Irish Question. This tradition extends from the early conquests of Ireland to the well-known political economist Thomas Malthus, who envisaged that "a great part of the [Irish] population should be swept from the soil," as a measure not to solve Ireland's economic problems only, but mainly to protect Britain's own economic interests.[4] People as different as Spenser, Cromwell, and Nassau Senior may well be added to the list.[5] In spite of the willingness of politicians such as Sir Robert Peel to help hungry Ireland, the inefficiency and reluctance of the subsequent governments to intervene in the Irish crisis gave rise to an assertive nationalist sense of victimization and martyrdom. John Mitchel's statement that "the Almighty sent the potato blight, but the English created the Famine" (Ó Gráda, *Great Irish Famine* 11), and Maud Gonne's "picturesque" depiction of starved Ireland as "heroic in her suffering" (Kelleher, *Feminization* 112) are good examples of this rhetoric. It is precisely this nationalist sentimentalist rhetoric that Yeats critiqued. He undermines Maud Gonne's speech on the Great Famine on the grounds that it is

> the kind of speech, both in its limitations and in its triumphs, which could only be made by a woman. From first to last it is emotional and even poignant, and has that curious power of unconsciously seizing salient incidents which is so distinguishing a mark of the novel writing of women. Its logic is none the less irresistible because it is the logic of the heart. (Kelleher, *Feminization* 113)

Not only is Maud Gonne's account of the Famine sentimentalized, feminized, but it is also fictionalized, emptied of its factuality.

Yeats would not go so far as to accuse the British government of genocide, nor would he accept sentimentalized and romanticized versions of Irish famines. Famines are not his ideal of heroism. But this is by no means to accuse the poet of cynicism. In the same essay on Edmund Spenser, Yeats denounces the Spenserian scheme with the charge of political pathology, or better still, pathological politics. He attributes Spenser's scheme of deliberate starvation to the ethno-centrism of an Elizabethan "official" reporting from, and about, a colonized Ireland:

> Like an hysterical patient [Spenser] drew a complicated web of inhuman logic out of the bowels of an insufficient premise--there was no right, no law, but that of Elizabeth, and all that opposed her opposed themselves to God, to civilisation, and to all inherited wisdom and courtesy, and should be put to death. (Yeats, *Essays* 361)

Ironically enough, Spenser's politics of extermination-through-starvation ended up with his own death "for lack of bread." Yeats reports quasi-jubilantly: "The Irish . . . with . . . *The Present State of Ireland* sticking in their stomachs, drove Spenser out of doors and burnt his house, one of his children, as tradition has it, dying in the fire. He fled to England, and died some three months later in January 1599, as Ben Jonson says, 'for lack of bread'" (Yeats, *Essays* 363).

Yet it is important to point out here that Yeats wrote his introduction on Edmund Spenser not out of retaliation against a ruthless Elizabethan "official" who envisaged the decimation of the Irish population—

though there is some of this—but rather for other reasons which fall beyond the scope of this paper. In fact, Yeats finds Spenser even interesting because he was "king of the old race . . . of a time before undelighted labour had made the business of men a desecration" (Yeats, *Essays* 377). The Spenserian poetic text is valued because it records a crucial "moment of change" in history. The change is from aristocracy to modernity, from nobility to what Yeats pejoratively refers to as the "triumph of the Puritan and the merchant," or "the modern filthy tide." Spenser's problem is that when he "wrote of Ireland he wrote as an official, and out of thoughts and emotions that had been organised by the state." He is a poet that has been corrupted by colonial politics. Spenser's genocidal politics, one must observe, is not explicitly debunked in the essay, but is rather critiqued obliquely—ambiguously.

Apart from this ambiguous allusion to Spenser's genocidal politics *vis-à-vis* Elizabethan Ireland, Yeats's reference to the more immediate Great Hunger in Victorian Ireland is, strangely enough, virtually absent in his works. This occlusion is not only strange on the part of a poet who, less than a couple of generations after the Famine, concentrated his de-colonizing project on exploring Irish history, mysticism, culture, and landscape. This occlusion, or absence, however, is all the more significant and telling. I think it is so because it reveals more than conceals the problematic presence of the Great Hunger in the post-Famine imagination, namely in the literature of the Revivalists.[6] Or rather, because it conceals the crisis it reveals more about it. It is precisely in the *non-dit* of the Yeatsian text that the Famine, as a black spot in the history of the nation, acquires its full significance. This absence, in other words, is determined by a complex mixture of both psychological and ideological agencies and mechanisms. The Famine was not only emotionally and physically ravaging to its survivors, but it also seems to have profoundly affected the psychology of subsequent generations. Devastating tragedies such as the Irish Famine or the Holocaust, wherein the communal sense is emptied of its communality, especially in matters related to the quasi-sacred notions of death, communal and familial bond and solidarity, engender a psychic reaction that most often results in collective amnesia, or simply in resistance to narrate or exteriorize the trauma. The repression is partly governed by shame and partly by guilt: shame because the community is emptied of its communal sense and essence; guilt, related to an intricate psychology specific to those who survive great tragedies. The Holocaust survivors represent a good example of such a complex psychology of survival. In addition to this psychological element, repression, or silence, is also engendered by a consciousness of the failure of language to render the reality of truth, or rather by a consciousness of the impossibility to represent and reify imaginatively and physically, the truth of reality. Representation is paralyzed; language is emptied of its essence—that is, its *expressibility*. George Steiner therefore suggests "silence" as probably the only mode of expression that could possibly render the *unspeakability* of the Holocaust: "The world of Auschwitz lies outside speech as it lies outside reason. To speak of the *unspeakable* is to risk the survivance of language as creator and bearer of humane, rational truth."[7]

Yeats's occlusion of the Great Hunger could possibly be interpreted as part and parcel of this post-Famine psychological legacy, in which repression, silence, and amnesia formed basic mechanisms and reactions. This absence could then be contexualized within what Cormac Ó Gráda has called "the silences of popular memory" during and after the Famine. "Shared memories about the tragedy were very distressing and sometimes traumatic for those who endured it," stresses Ó Gráda. Famine survivors were taciturn about narrating the tragedy:

> Those who had witnessed the horrors of the famine were reluctant to give details. . . . Elsewhere, survivors were reluctant to admit their dependence on the soup kitchen or *min déirce* (beggar's meal), or to confess that a member of their own household had died of starvation (*Black '47* 11, 212).

The horrors of the Famine were still too vivid and fresh in the collective memory of the community to be spoken out without resistance, guilt, and shame.

If a historio-critical assessment of the Famine had only started long after the disappearance of the Great Hunger, then Irish folklore memory was replete from the outset with references to its outbreak, to its unfolding, and to the ravaging socio-economic impact it had on the community.[8] Though these references came most often either amplified or atrophied, sentimentalized or repressed, they are as yet highly important. They are so not so much because of *what* they say about the Famine, but mainly because of *how* they narrate the tragedy. It is precisely within these narratological maneuvers and strategies, strategies oscillating between inflation and deflation, promotion and demotion, exaggeration and understatement, presence and absence that new insights could be gained into the Famine.[9] Within the gaps and absences of this folklore historiography one can re-assess the Great Famine. The Famine's absence in Yeats is likely to be governed by the same psychological mechanisms that great calamities subsequently engender in the collective psyche of the community. As an argument, it is quite tempting. Yet I think this is hardly the case in Yeats. The poet was among the first to be interested in textualizing the Irish oral folklore. By the turn of the century he had already published—with the help of Lady Gregory—three anthologies in which he tried to present "representative" tales and legends of Irish folklore. Yet though his project was spurred by nationalism at this early phase of his career, he was as yet hardly interested in tales recounting the Great Hunger. The Famine is virtually absent in what he advances as "representative" compilations of the nation's memory. Could these compilations be so when archives have clearly shown the cataclysmic impact the Famine had on the collective memory of the Irish people? What appealed most to Yeats—and to the Revivalists in general—was the spirituality and not the historicity, the occultism and not the realism embedded in this oral tradition. In this tradition Yeats discovers an inexhaustible mine of poetic themes, themes that would serve him to the end of his poetic career.

My argument is that the Famine's absence in Yeats is determined by the poet's own idea of an ideal "imagined community" as well as by his concept of nationalism. He defines nation and nationalism as purely "imaginative," "cultural," and "romantic." In his paradigm, they are essentially aesthetic categories, wherein literary and cultural sobriety is fundamental. His philosophy of nationalism combines romantic idealization with O'Learyan political composure and sobriety. From John O'Leary[10] he learned that "There are things a man must not do to save a nation." Worst of all is "to cry in public" to save a nation (Yeats, *Essays* 246). As such Yeats demarcates his nationalism from the "sensationalism" and "sentimentality" of his precursors, the Young Irelanders, such as Thomas Osborne Davis (1814–1845), James Clarence Mangan (1803–1849), and Sir Samuel Ferguson (1810–1886). In the poem "To Ireland in the Coming Times" Yeats draws the line of demarcation quite intransigently: his nationalism is more profound, more mystical, and therefore more useful to the nation than the Young Irelanders', namely Davis's, "superficial" and flamboyant nationalism.[11] His philosophy of mystical nationalism would "make love of the unseen more unshakable, more ready to plunge deep into the abyss, and would make love of country more fruitful in the mind, more a part of daily life" (Yeats, *Essays* 210). Though Yeats validates his affiliation with this nationalistic literary movement, he as yet dissociates his idea of Art and nationalism, aesthetics and politics, from this tradition:

Know, that I would account be
True brother of a company

That sang, to sweeten Ireland's wrong,
Ballad and story, rann and song...
Nor may I less be counted one with Davis, Mangan, Ferguson,
Because, to him who ponders well,
My rhymes more than their rhyming tell
Of things discovered in the deep,
Where only body's laid asleep.

Dwelling on the Famine, it is clear, clashes with the poet's idea of suffering, a suffering he conceptualizes ideally as active, heroic, and tragic. In the Yeatsian philosophy of suffering, the individual/nation must bravely face, or rather, must heroically anticipate and will his/its own destruction—Death. Yeats's celebration of "tragic joy," or ecstasy in death, is, to be sure, far from the submissive and passive suffering of a starved-to-death individual or community. To perish is not to die in Yeats's aesthetics of death or philosophy of the sublime. The only form of anemia he tolerates is that of the mystical ascetic—and definitely not of those emaciated faces cramming kitchen soups. As such the Irish Famine can by no means provide the poet with an archetypal model of tragic suffering—of mystical death. The Famine, in other words, does not offer an ideal archetype of heroic death, a perfect model of an aestheticized Death. Tragic heroism in Yeats must in essence be self-sacrificial, self-destructive. It happens when the subject is conscious from the start of his lost battle against the unknown—against death itself. The poem "An Irish Airman Foresees His Death" in which the narrator impersonates the death of Major Robert Gregory whose plane was shot down in the First World War, and who Yeats dubbed in a previous poem "a perfect man," "soldier, scholar, horseman"—"all life's epitome":[12]

A lonely impulse of delight
Drove to this tumult in the clouds;
I balanced all, brought all to mind,
The years to come seemed waste of breath,
A waste of breath the years behind
In balance with this life, this death.

Yeats's heroic archetypes are culled from battles and not from famines, from aristocratic healthy bodies and not from rotten corpses, strewn unburied amid roads and fields. In the death of Major Robert Gregory Yeats sees something of a cyclical reincarnation of the Cuchulainian mythical archetype of tragic heroism. The hero's drive to his own death is subliminal and aesthetic precisely because it is *driveless.* Or rather, the only drive is the death-drive itself, just "a lonely impulse of delight." Death is sought just for the sake of the aesthetics of the *memento mori.* The moment of death becomes a moment of utter change, of radical self-transubstantiation. The self is transformed into "terrible beauty," into a work of art, as Yeats says in "Easter 1916." The *memento mori* in the poem becomes the zero-degree of Time, the imperturbable changeless moment in historical flux. In short, it becomes the moment of non-Time.

This aestheticization of the moment of death, one must observe, seems to rehearse the same idea expressed in "Easter 1916," a poem written nearly two years before "An Irish Airman Foresees His Death":

> We know their dream; enough
> To know they dreamed and are dead;
> And what if excess of love
> Bewildered them till they died?
> I write it out in verse—
> MacDonagh and MacBride
> And Connolly and Pearse
> Now and in time to be,
> Wherever green is worn,
> Are changed, changed utterly:
> A terrible beauty is born.

Yeats's assertion that "tragedy must be joy to the man who dies" (Yeats, *Essays* 522–23) stands in sharp contrast to—though shockingly oblivious of—the atrocities and horrors of the Great Hunger. The Great Famine is not "great" in Yeats's paradigm, not only because it does not conform to his idea of "greatness" as tragic nobility, but also because the Famine had infused the nation with a sense of self-victimization and self-shame. This sense of self-victimization is diametrically antithetic to the poet's oxymoronic idea of tragic triumphalism, or better still, heroic self-destructiveness. Yeats's philosophy of nationalism distances itself from this post-Famine psychology of victimage, a psychology mostly expressed by more and more confident Catholic voices. Yet Yeats's repudiation of this psychology, we must observe, is by no means governed by sectarian ideology. His theorization of the nation at this early stage of his career rather sought to define the nation as an organic entity, something based on what he advances as the three fundamental unities: Unity of being, Unity of culture, and Unity of Image. Yeats's sectarianism, however, began to surface only later when he, as Anglo-Irish, found himself paradoxically marginalized by the very same politics of essentialism and homogenization he launched with such Revivalists as Lady Gregory and John Synge.[13] Irish Revivalism, as he defines it, must be first and foremost based on the excavation of the "old confident joyous world" of Ireland, that is to say, must revalorize and reestablish the precolonial pristine world of the nation. In such precolonial cultural heritage Yeats finds Ireland's originality, its specificity, and its power as a nation. In "The Celtic Element in Literature," Yeats exalts the nation's contribution to European—if not universal—literary culture. The poet is adamant that Irish history is "fuller than any modern history of imaginative events." Here Yeats places the Irish nation among the giants of universal literary powers. That the aim is to empower the nation by revalorizing its cultural heritage is obvious. Narrativizing the Famine would certainly blemish such a self-aggrandizing image. It would in short shatter the myth around which Irish Revivalism constructed its *raison d'être*. Yet such an essentialist reading of the nation's past, though important in its proper historical context, does reflect something of a willful blindness on the part of the poet with regard to the deprivations of the present moment. Writing a couple of generations after the Famine, Yeats not only failed to narrate the crisis of the present but also ignored the horrors of the past—that is, the Great Famine. But the irony is that if the Yeatsian text had failed to narrate the Great Hunger, then it did not prevent the Famine stealing into his sub-text, opening inroads in his textual subconscious. The Famine, in other words, had erupted into his text not by virtue of its presence as phenomenon, as a historical event, but rather by virtue of its impact on the subsequent history of Ireland. The Famine occupied the space of the *non-dit* in Yeats's text. It becomes present by virtue of its absence. If the Great Hunger did not provide the poet with an ideal form of tragic suffering, then it had shaped quite substantially his philosophy of communality and territoriality, nation and landscape, nationalism and art.

There is truth in T. K. Hoppen's argument that "the quarter century after the Famine was in fact a time in which a complicated *mélange* of developments sustained a species of politics in which the locale, the immediate, and the everyday provided important contexts for interactions and interventions" (111). Yeats's textual aesthetics probably stands as the best example of such a post-Famine "species of politics." His romanticization of Irish proximity—ie. culture, politics, and geography—should be interpreted as such. From the beginning of his poetic career, Yeats is well aware of the priority and urgency of the aesthetics and politics of proximity, that is to say, revalorizing Ireland's landscapes and literary, mystical, and cultural heritage.[14] In fact he sees a dialectical correlation between narrating the nation and nationalism, aesthetics and politics: "there is no great literature without nationality, no great nationality without literature" (Yeats, *Letters* 174). The project is defined from the start. Irish mythology, landscape, and peasantry, henceforth, became central issues from which the Yeatsian poetic text would never detach itself.

Yeats's new conception of communality and geography is determined by the Famine's ravaging impact on both community and territory, nation and landscape. This impact had of course exacerbated an already deep-seated consciousness of the colonial condition. Yet if the Famine had consolidated the sense of communality in its aftermath, it did so not so much because it reinforced the anti-colonial feeling within the community, but rather more importantly because it alarmingly unraveled the fragility and vulnerability of this sense of communality. This fragility would in fact be further exposed during the Civil War—and henceforward remain endemic to Irish politics until today.[15] The Great Famine showed quite explicitly the precariousness of the sense of community on which the Irish nation was based. It clearly demonstrated the likelihood of the nation's disintegration at any moment of crisis. The Irish Famine, like all famines, disrupted the community from within. Jane Wilde's "The Exodus" captures forcefully the dissolution and "decay" of the social fabric from within the nation-body itself:

> "A million a decade!" Count ten by ten,
> Column and line of the record fair;
> Each unit stands for ten thousand men,
> Staring with blank, dead eyeballs there;
> Strewn like blasted trees on the sod,
> Men that were made in the image of God . . .
>
> "A million a decade!" What does it mean?
> *A Nation dying of inner decay—*
> A churchyard silence where life has been—
> The base of the pyramid crumbling away—
> A drift of men gone over the sea,
> A drift of the dead where men should be.
> (Kelleher, "Irish Famine" 238; emph. added)

Famines put at stake communal unity. They supplant the sense of community with crude social Darwinism. Communal bond is most often replaced by the primeval individualistic struggle for survival. Liam O'Flaherty sums up the idea powerfully in his narrative *Famine:* "under the pressure of hunger, as among soldiers in war, the mask of civilisation quickly slips from the human soul, showing the brute savage beneath, struggling to preserve life at all costs" (347). The community in such circumstances is deeply struck in its communality. "Hardship and hunger broke the communal spirit of the people, who became preoccupied with struggle to survive and lost their sympathy for each other," R. J. McHugh's eighty-year-old woman from Rosses recalls (434). McHugh gives forceful accounts of how the Great Hunger and famine-related diseases had shattered communal unity and ancestral tradition:

> Not only did disease take its toll of the population but it helped to disrupt the people's social life and to destroy their customs and observances. Victims would be left unburied or would be buried where they fell and relatives would sometimes deny the identity of their dead brethren for fear of having to bury them. Neighbours shunned each other's houses even in districts where communal help and sharing was traditional. Against tradition too, the "wandering man" was often turned from the door or was shunned. (419)

Not only did the Famine disrupt the inter-subjective bond, but it also destroyed the cultural heritage and life of the community. The same eighty-year-old woman recalls: "Sport and pastimes disappeared. Poetry, music and dancing stopped. They lost and forgot them all and when the times improved in other respects, these things never returned as they had been. The famine killed everything" (435). The Famine engendered not only biological but also aesthetic amenorrhea, so to speak. Yet these absences, or silences of the Muses, as O'Gráda suggests in *Black '47 and Beyond*, should be read as history too (11). A couple of generations after the Great Famine, the Irish literary movement took upon itself the project to restore the voice of the silenced Muses and to sing again the forsaken "soil." Yeats was well aware of this revivalist project:

> John Synge, I and Augusta Gregory, thought
> All we did, all that we said and sang
> Must come from contact with the soil, from that
> Contact everything Antaeus-like grew strong

If colonial condition fortifies communal sense because the enemy is by definition external—an intruder—then famine's impact on the community is rather more complex. A famine is after all an internal crisis, in which not only traditional continuity but also communal inter-subjectivity is put at stake. Though the colonial power is often implicated in the crisis, as was Britain in the Great Famine, this implication does not as yet help prevent the process of communal dissolution under the impact of the crisis. To put the argument differently, if colonialism consolidates what Benedict Anderson calls the "imagined community," famines rather disrupt and tarnish the idealism of this imagination. They do so simply because they destroy the foundations on which the "imagined community" is based—that is, homogeneity, continuity, and totality. It is revealing to remark here that accounts of communal solidarity or hospitality during the Irish Famine are scarce and sporadic in comparison with the horrendous amount of spine-melting tales of communal disunity, dis-solidarity, resentment, thuggery, agoraphobia, betrayal, abuse, misery, opportunism, souperism, exploitation, shame, crime, stinginess, usury, monopoly, and so forth.[16] Individuals who are involved in acts of benevolence and generosity are most often inflated with mythological dimensions in the Famine memory.

Yeats's revivalist project should be construed as an attempt to reconstruct a sense of communality that had been dramatically threatened by the Famine as well as by colonialism. The project is to reimagine the community anew, to recast the nation in a prelapsarian ideal form. The project is to rediscover and revalorize this prelapsarian sense of communality. Yeats's politics of aesthetic nationalism aims to accentuate Ireland's singularity, or better still, insularity. Such a de-colonialist stance is cogently analyzed by Edward Said in *Culture and Imperialism*. "One of the first tasks of the culture of resistance," Said argues, "was to reclaim, rename, and re-inhabit the land. And with that came a whole set of further assertions, recoveries, and identifications, all of them quite literally grounded on this poetically projected base" (273). Yeats's remappings of Irish landscapes abound in his early collections of poems. Local locales are overdeterminedly aestheticized, narrativized, and romanticized. Consider for instance his poem "The Hosting of the Sidhe" wherein references to local geography and mythology are incorporated into the text as part of this cartographic mapping of national culture:

> The host is riding from Knocknarea
> And over the grave of Clooth-na-Bare;
> Caoilte tossing his burning hair,
> And Niamh calling *Away, come away:*
> *Empty your heart of its mortal dream.*

Yeats's ideal examples of communal unity are culled from western Ireland. It is by no means far-fetched here to argue for a link between the poet's idealization of this geography and its own reality and history. It is well known that the Famine's impact was most dramatically felt in this part of Ireland. This is partly because of the area's long history of poverty as well as its distance from the centers of industrial powers—that is, Dublin and Belfast. Yeats's overdetermined romanticization of these localities invites us to investigate the correlation between this idealization and the socioeconomic realities of these geographies—in short, between his ideal idea and historical fact. The correlation lies in Yeats's own *ideation* of these places, that is, his imagining of them as pure *a-historical* geographies—as "place[s] of authenticity," as Deane would put it.[17] The project is to romanticize geographies and communities that had been ravaged not only by colonialism's systematic politics of regional disparity, but also by sporadic natural calamities. The Great Famine is definitely one of the most devastating to the collective memory. Yeats's romanticization of the Sligo community, for instance, could be interpreted as an anti-dote, as a counter-memory, to the Famine's dark history still poisoning communal conscience by the end of the nineteenth century. If by then the *phytophthora infestans* had been controlled by means of a mix of copper and sulphate, then the Famine's black memories had by no means been totally erased from collective conscience by the time Yeats and the Revivalists were theorizing the Irish nation. By idealizing Sligo, Yeats certainly celebrates a place so dear to his childhood memories. But inasmuch as this celebration does reflect a personal interest it also aims to reconstruct aesthetically a sense of unity for a community where the very sense of communality itself had been profoundly shaken by the Great Hunger. During the black years of the Famine in Sligo "if somebody died in a house, the corpse was left unburied unless there was somebody in the house able to carry in one way or another the corpse to the graveyard and do the burial."[18] As such Yeats's aesthetic project should be interpreted as an endeavor to re-establish imaginatively a sense of communality of a community that had been fragilized and de-fertilized, so to speak, by *phytophthora infestans*.

Like Sligo, Galway is also depicted in Yeats's poetry and prose as a *locus classicus* of communal organic unity. The poet is persuaded that "there is still in truth upon these great level plains a people, a community bound together by imaginative possessions, by stories and poems which have grown out of its own life, and by a past of great passions which can still waken the heart to imaginative action" (Yeats, *Essays* 213). Yet Yeats's statement here is history-blind. The poet seems to have forgotten that the "past" of Galway and of western Ireland in general narrates not only stories of "great passions," of what sounds like pastoral communities, but also tells unsettling stories of communal and familial conflicts, dislocations, and dissolution. In the following quotation McHugh shows the disastrous impact of the Famine on the filial and communal bond:

> The upheaval which the famine caused in the family and social life of the people is best seen in the tradition of parts of Ireland where there was much communal life in pre-famine days, notably in parts of Donegal, Mayo, sligo, Galway, Cork and Kerry. . . . In such districts communal sharing of work was general. . . . Such communities were often almost completely self-contained; wheat would be grown to pay the landlord, flax to make clothes and linen, while sheep would provide frieze and thread. . . . *The famine blasted many of these communities out of existence.* (433-34; emph. added).

Yet Yeats's occlusion, or better still, his willful forgetfulness of this Famine reality is understandable from a poet who from the start based his philosophy of nationalism on a homogenized and tension-free idea of the community. In "Ireland and the Arts" he vehemently calls for celebrating a homogenized Ireland, an Ireland he wants not only in tune with its geography and culture, but also in perfect harmony with its traditional history. The emphasis is on the history of the Irish tradition and not on the tradition of the nation's political history. Yeats's "Romantic Nationalism" postulates remembrance of cultural tradition and oblivion to historical tension. His call for celebrating the national and the local—the proximate—borders on fanaticism:

> The Greeks looked within their borders, and we, like them, have a history fuller than any modern history of imaginative events. . . . I would have our writers and craftsmen of many kinds master this history and these legends. . . . I admit, though in this I am moved by some touch of fanaticism, that even when I see and old subject written of or painted in a new way, I am yet jealous for Cuchulain, and for Baile and Ailinn, and for those grey mountains that still are lacking their celebration. (Yeats, *Essays* 205-9)

Celebrating the grey mountains of Ireland became something of a lifelong commitment for Yeats. From his early poeticization of Knocknarea to his late celebration of Ben Bulben in the last poems, the poet's politics of cartographic celebration is articulated with almost the same cultural "fanaticism."

Along with the mountain-as-symbol of nationhood, the "island" as geographical space becomes Yeats's most celebrated metaphor for Irish insularity. The "island" becomes in Yeats's symbolic system—and the Revivalists's in general—a synonym for Ireland, or rather for an ideal Ireland, autonomous, insular, and self-contained. Ireland and island are homonymized and homologized in Yeats's "The Lake Isle of Innisfree." Written in London, the poem embodies something of a "monochromatic" idealization of the "imaginary homeland," to put it Salman Rushdie's words:

> I will arise and go now, and go to Innisfree,
> And a small cabin build there, of clay and wattles made:
> Nine beans-rows will I have there, a hive for the honey-bee,
> And live alone in the bee-loud glade.
>
> And I shall have some peace there, for peace comes dropping slow,
> Dropping from the veils of the morning to where the cricket sings;
> There midnight's all a glimmer, and noon a purple glow,
> And evening full of the linnet's wings.

Though this is one of Yeats's most known poems, it is not his best. However, the poem is significant. It is so not so much by virtue of its aesthetic value as by virtue of its symbolic importance—its metaphoricity. Though the poem occludes political tension, it nonetheless articulates a substantial change in the poet's early conception of unity. The shift is from an aesthetic idea of unity to a more political theorization of the concept. Though the poem reiterates a Thoreauistic exaltation of landscape, this unity is infused with an implicit political intent and meaning. The landscapic experience is now rather lived in Irish geography. It is appropriated—nationalized. It is celebrated as a purely national experience, following which not only national geography is celebrated but communal identity is also highlighted. The personal experience of insularity in the poem reads like a metonymic celebration of communal insularity. The island becomes something of a utopian space for his ideal community.

If the isle of "Innisfree" is Yeats's *insula sacra* of poetic originality, the Aran Islands are then not only that but also ideal places of the perfect community. By urging John Synge in Paris to go home and write about the Aran Islands, Yeats in fact perpetuated a Young Irelanders' tradition, in which the Islands are not only celebrated as the *locus amoenus* of an ideal Ireland but are also invested with a highly charged political meaning. The Aran Islands came to symbolize in the nationalist imagination autonomy, authenticity, unity, solidarity, communality, and most important of all, invincibility to hunger and to colonial politics of cultural effacement. When advising Synge, Yeats had certainly in mind Samuel Ferguson's imperturbable conviction that "the islanders have had the singular good fortune never to have been visited by the potato blight; never to have had a death from destitution, and never to have sent a pauper to the poor house" (Ó Gráda, *Ireland* 118). Ó Gráda debunks this "idyllic" idea of the Islands on the grounds that it is a blind reading of the history and reality of the Islands (*Ireland* 119). The Famine in fact badly affected the Aran Islands.

Writing within the tradition of the Young Irelanders of the 1840s, the Revivalists seem to have perpetuated the same idyllic and essentialist idea of the Irish nation. Synge's *The Aran Islands* and Yeats's western landscapes are examples in point. Paradoxically enough, this essentialist reading and writing of the nation proved in the long run self-corrosive and self-defeating to both writers. Yeats's recourse to historicizing the so-called organic past and culture of Ireland, for instance, ended up by his own exclusion from this history. The cultural and historical hyphenation of his own identity—Anglo-Irishness—had been exacerbated, discredited, and marginalized in the process. Yeats's non-reading of the Great Famine and Synge's rewriting of Ireland in his most controversial play, *The Playboy of the Western World*, had to be taken with suspicion in a post-Famine Ireland not because they represent mis-representations of the country, but rather because they are blind mis-readings of Ireland's new reality after the Great Hunger—that is, its "ripeness" to integrate modernity. The Famine's most cataclysmic impact on the nation, Seamus Deane says, is that it "ended the possibility of Ireland's conceiving of itself as a distinct nation in traditional sense since one of its most remarkable effects was to alter the national character and with that, the whole question of the national territory and language" (50). Post-Famine Ireland was now "more susceptible than it ever had been to reorganization and rational reform [and was] ripe now for integration within the system of empire and capital" (Deane 50). Yet such a process of modernization and rationalization, Deane goes on, had been simultaneously accompanied by literary, political, and religious movements, the aim of which was to counter this process by claiming and insisting on an "archaized"—that is, pre-modern—idea of Irishness. Movements as different as Young Ireland, the IRB (Irish Republican Brotherhood), the Irish Revival and the Catholic Church had all claimed and asserted, Deane argues, "some form of Irish exceptionalism that would retain the category of national character . . . through legend rather than through history" (50–51). The Yeatsian text is well aware of these transformations in the social, economic, and cultural structures of post-Famine Ireland. And it is precisely against this process of modernization and rationalization of the nation that the Yeatsian text rebelled. Dublin became the epitome of this process of transmogrification, alienation, and philistinization of the community.[19] It was, so to speak, being "Londonified," to the poet's utter disappointment. Yeats's poetry not only was an uncompromising stance against this process but also presented itself as a continual cultivation and consolidation of an "Irish exceptionalism" against modernity's rampant and homogenizing "filthy tide":

> We Irish, born into that ancient sect
> But thrown upon this filthy modern tide
> And by its formless, spawning, fury wrecked,
> Climb to our proper dark, that we may trace
> The lineaments of a plummet-measured face.

Notes

1. See especially Margaret Kelleher, "Irish Famine in Literature," *The Great Irish Famine,* ed. Cathal Póirtéir, (Dublin: Mercier, 1995).

2. For more knowledge about Maud Gonne's political activism with regard to the issue of the Great Famine, see Kelleher "Impersonating the Past: Twentieth-Century Irish Famine Literature," *The Feminization of Famine: Expression of the Inexpressible* (Cork: Cork Univ. Press, 1997).

3. Consider, for instance, Yeats's following entry in a diary in 1910: "Women because the main event of their lives has been a giving of themselves give themselves to an opinion as if it were a stone doll . . . women should have their play with dolls finished in childhood for, if they play with ideas again it is amid hatred and malice" (Jeffares, *Commentary* 246).

4. See Christine Kinealy, *This Great Calamity: The Irish Famine 1845-52* (Dublin: Gill, 1994). Kinealy argues that "the political economists generally paid relatively little attention to Ireland, except when it impinged on Britain." Malthus is a case in point. One of his main concerns "was that the excess population in Ireland would eventually have serious implications for Britain, due to proximity of the two islands. The surplus Irish population would be tempted to emigrate to Britain, especially as wages were higher on the mainland. Malthus warned that the outcome of this would be to depress both wages and moral standards within Britain. The need to protect Britain was obvious. Malthus, however, offered a solution. The population of Ireland, particularly in the poorest part of the agricultural sector, had to be reduced" (16).

5. Consider for instance Nassau's outrageous cynicism and disregard for the suffering of the Famine victims for the sake of the "valuable illustrations" and "precious" results the tragedy can provide to economic theory. Ireland is transformed into a laboratory: "We are to have committees in each House on the Irish poor laws. They will contain illustrations valuable to a political economist. Experiments are made in that country on so large a scale, and pushed to their extreme consequences with such a disregard to the suffering which they inflict, that they give us results as precious as those of Majendie" (Ó Gráda, *Ireland* 112–13).

6. The Famine is almost absent in the literature of the Revivalists. The main concern of the movement was first and foremost to cultivate and intensify Irish differentness. Seamus Deane claims that this intensification was largely achieved "by the remarkable feat of ignoring the Famine and rerouting the claim for cultural exceptionalism through legend rather than through history" (51).

7. George Steiner, *Language and Silence: Essays 1958–1966* (London: Pelican, 1969), 165. For further ideas on the crisis of language, its "failure" and inadequacy to render the reality of the Great Famine, see M. Kelleher "'Appalling Spectacles': Nineteenth-Century Irish Famine Narratives," *The Feminization of Famine.*

8. See especially Roger J. McHugh, "The Famine in Irish Oral Tradition," *The Great Famine: Studies in Irish History 1845-52,* ed. R. D. Edwards and T. D. Williams eds. 1956 (New York: Russell, 1976).

9. Cormac Ó Gráda endorses the idea of re-assessing the Famine through studying folklore memory, not by mere compilation of this heritage, but rather through what sounds like an application of Freudian hermeneutics onto this oral tradition, that is to say, by analysing its textual and narratological structures, its gaps and silences, its semantic profusion and its penury, in order to gain new insights into the Famine.

10. John O'Leary (1830–1907) was one of the founding fathers of Fenianism. He was arrested in 1865 and condemned to twenty years penal servitude, but was released after serving five years on condition he did not return to Ireland for at least fifteen years. He spent his exile in Paris. O'Leary greatly influenced Yeats's concept of Irish nationalism. The "Old Fenian," as O'Leary was called, belonged, says Yeats, "to the romantic conception of Irish Nationality on which Lionel Johnson and myself founded, so far as it was founded on anything but literature, our art and our Irish criticism." He seemed to Yeats the last "to speak an understanding of life and nationality, built up by generation of Grattan, which read Homer and Virgil, and by the generation of Davis, which had been pierced through by the idealism of Mazzini, and of the European revolutionists of the mid-century" (*Essays* 246). Yeats declares in "September 1913" "Romantic Ireland's dead and gone / It's with O'Leary in the grave."

11. Comparing Alligham to Davis, Yeats reaches the conclusion that they "are two different kinds of love of Ireland. In Alligham I find the entire emotion for the place one grew up in which I felt as a child and which I sometimes hear of from people of my own class. Davis was possessed on the other hand with ideas of Ireland, with conscious patriotism. His Ireland was artificial, an idea built up in a couple of generations by a few commonplace men. This artificial idea has done me as much harm as the other helped me" (*Memoirs* 153).

12. That Robert Gregory came to represent Anglo-Irish aristocratic ideal in Yeats's poetry is obvious. For further discussion of Yeats's use and systematization of Robert Gregory as a romantic image of an ideal heroic death, see Frank Kermode, *The Romantic Image* 1957 (London: Routledge, 1961.

13. The riots triggered by Synge's *première* of *The Playboy of the Western World* had a devastating impact on Yeats's ideal of an Irish nation bound up by "Unity of Culture, of Image, and of Being." The incident, however, exposed, to Yeats's disappointment, the growing gap between "genius" and moralism, between artistic freedom and a more and more exclusionist audience.

14. See especially his "Ireland and the Arts" in *Essays and Introductions*.

15. In *Nation and Nationalism Since 1870* (New York: Cambridge Univ. Press, 1990), Eric Hobsbawm argues that "the assumption that a single Irish nation existed within a single Ireland, or rather that all inhabitants of the island shared the aspiration of a single, united and independent Fenian Ireland, proved mistaken, and while, for fifty years after the establishment of the Irish Free State, Fenians and their sympathizers could dismiss the division of the country as a British imperial plot and Ulster Unionists as misguided dupes led by British agents, the past twenty years have made it clear that the roots of a divided Ireland are not to be found in London" (135).

16. O'Flaherty's novel *Famine* compellingly relates this black socioeconomic reality during the Great Famine.

17. For the Revivalists, argues Seamus Deane, "the west [of Ireland] became the place of Irish authenticity, the place that was not yet subject to the effects of administrative, governmental rules and laws, and which therefore preserved among its population the national character in its pristine form or, at least, in such a state of preservation that the pristine form could be inferred from it. It was not only geographically distinct; it was historically precedent to the rest of the country which, especially in Dublin, had been reduced to a colonized space of imperial administration" (52).

18. Ó Gráda, *Black '47* 200. See also McHugh's compelling stories about communal isolation and fragmentation in Sligo and in many other counties. Consider especially the harrowing story of the baby sucking at its dead mother in *The Great Famine* (420).

19. Dublin is dubbed a "blind and ignorant town" in "To a Wealthy Man who promised a second Subscription to the Dublin Municipal Gallery it were proved the People wanted pictures"; "emasculated" and philistinized in "On Those that hated 'The Playboy of the Western World,' 1907"; and described as an "unmannerly town" in "The People."

Works Cited

Anderson, Benedict. *Imagined Communities: Reflections on the Origin and Spread of Nationalism*. London: Verso, 1983.

Deane, Seamus. *Strange Country: Modernity and Nationhood in Irish Writing since 1790*. Oxford: Clarendon, 1997.

Hobsbawm, Eric. *Nation and Nationalism Since 1870*. New York: Cambridge Univ. Press, 1990.

Hoppen, K. T. *Ireland Since 1800 Conflict and Conformity*. London: Longman, 1989.

Jeffares, N. *A Commentary on the Collected Poems of W. B. Yeats*.

Kelleher, Margaret. "'Appalling Spectacles': Nineteenth-Century Irish Famine Narratives." *The Feminization of Famine*. Cork: Cork Univ. Press, 1997.

---. *The Feminization of Famine: Expression of the Inexpressible*. Cork: Cork Univ. Press, 1997.

---. "Irish Famine in Literature." Póirtéir.

Kermode, Frank. *The Romantic Image*. 1957. London: Routledge, 1961.

Kinealy, Christine. *This Great Calamity: The Irish Famine 1845–52*. Dublin: Gill, 1994.

McHugh, Roger J. "The Famine in Irish Oral Tradition." 1956. *The Great Famine: Studies in Irish History 1845–52*. Ed. R. D. Edwards and T. D. Williams. New York: Russell, 1976.

Ó Gráda, Cormac. *Black '47 and Beyond: The Great Irish Famine in History, Economy, and Memory*. Princeton, NJ: Princeton Univ. Press, 1999.

---. *The Great Irish Famine*. London: Macmillan, 1989.

---. *Ireland Before and After the Famine*. New York: St. Martin's; Manchester Univ. Press, 1988.

O'Flaherty, Liam. *Famine*. London: Gollancz, 1937.

Póirtéir, Cathal, ed. *The Great Irish Famine*. Dublin: Mercier, 1995.

Rushdie, Salman. *Imaginary Homelands: Essays and Criticism, 1981–91*. London: Granta, 1991.

Said, Edward. *Culture and Imperialism*. London: Chatto, 1993.

Steiner, George. *Language and Silence: Essays 1958–1966*. 1966. London: Pelican, 1969.

Yeats, W. B. *The Countess Cathleen*. London: Benn's Essex Library, n.d.

---. *Essays and Introductions*. Dublin: Gill, 1961.

---. *Letters to the New Island*. Ed. Horace Reynolds. Cambridge: Harvard Univ. Press, 1970.

---. *Memoirs*. Ed. Denis Donoghue. London: Macmillan, 1972.

---. *The Poems*. Ed. Richard Finneran. New York: Macmillan, 1983.

Chapter Six

Silent Hunger:
The Psychological Impact
of the Great Hunger

DEBORAH PECK

"The Hunger, there's a long telling in that, it is a thing will be remembered always"

Lady Augusta Gregory—Galway, Ireland, 1926

I. Introduction

The Great Irish Hunger is, indeed, a story—as Lady Augusta Gregory predicted—with a "long telling" (Glassie). To tell it right, the story must include its pre-Famine and post-Famine political and social contexts. It's a story with a long prologue and an equally long afterword, without which one cannot discern its true scope and transgenerational impact. But Lady Gregory was wrong about one thing: predicting that the Hunger would "be remembered always." For the more than a century in which it was all but forgotten is far longer than the more recent period in which memories of the Great Hunger have exploded across continents (Mullan).

The events preceding, during, immediately following, and long after this dramatic nineteenth-century event ended have never been placed in a psychological context. And yet, almost all those who have recently recounted this event—historians, economists, academics, and laypersons—allude to the significance and inevitable psychological impact the Famine must have had on its immediate survivors and subsequent generational descendants. The purpose of this article is to offer a theoretically grounded psychological reinterpretation of the Great Hunger in order to highlight the long-neglected transgenerationally transmitted emotional aspects of the most significant event in modern Irish history.

II. An Unthinkable History

Unlike psychology, history has well-established methods, models, and formats for understanding and organizing the monumental chaos and destructive impact of events such as the Irish Famine into understandable narratives. At the time of the Great Hunger, 1845–1852, psychology was in its infancy. Thus, there was no language or structural method for understanding the psychological impact of this tragedy across generational time. In essence, the long-term emotional impact of the Famine was an "unthinkable history" (Trouillot). Therefore, the powerful emotional impact felt, but unspoken, lay hidden deep in the bone of all the survivors and their descendants. It remained inaccessible to consciousness for generations of Irish Hunger survivors. Only now, more than a century and a half later, can the unspoken psychological story of the Great Hunger be reconstructed and told.

III. Purpose of Study

If people today were asked to name the most traumatic political acts of the twentieth century, lethal and devastating famines would be unlikely to top the list. And yet, the prevalence of almost continual famines throughout the twentieth century has led some historians to dub it "The Famine Century" (Cahill). The tendency to minimize nutritionally catastrophic occurrences, when compared to the more dramatic and proactive destructive forces of war, is a common occurrence. For example, the numbers of those who perished in famines are often remembered, like many genocidal victims even today, in the inexact and awful arithmetic of atrocity. In this perverse form of feigned mathematical incompetence, the guilty parties are frequently at a loss as to the precise number of victims. Both perpetrators and victims, for differing psychological reasons and motivations, often vaguely remember the events of genocidal acts. And yet, this curious inability to accurately count famine victims persists even in today's highly sophisticated numerically obsessive age. In some cases, the historical existence of entire famines have been denied by the governments in charge—for example, the Armenian (Kupelian, Kalayjian, and Kassabian), Ukrainian (Dolot), and Chinese famines

(Becker) during the twentieth century, with death tolls from these silenced catastrophic events (Anonymous Scholar, Chinese History and Waal) totaling in the tens of millions of victims (Cahill).

And yet, if these seemingly preventable and repetitious nutritional tragedies are to be prevented, the dead must be acknowledged and counted accurately. Lessons must be learned as to who was responsible. Who had the power to prevent the loss of life and who, instead, left it up to God's indirect machinations to feed the hungry? In addition, and more important, the complex biopsychosocial aspects of these tragedies must be analyzed and reviewed from interdisciplinary perspectives.

This paper and others like it from the academic disciplines of sociology, economics, history, law, biology, and anthropology are attempting to integrate these varied perspectives into a comprehensible whole. It is hoped that through these combined multidisciplinary efforts at analysis and narrative the cyclical nature of these recurrent tragedies can be broken in the twenty-first century. Accountability may be, finally, ascribed to the guilty parties and appropriate reparations and justice, long denied, provided to the millions of silenced victims and the aggrieved survivor descendants. For it is ultimately in seeking some sort of international justice and remedies for these egregious overt or neglectful acts that humankind may have any hope of being rid of one of the four great horsemen of the Apocalypse: famine.

IV. Overview of Proposed Psycho-Historical Theoretical Model

This theoretically based study is organized using psychological theories of trauma, recovery, and memory as the overall framework for understanding the Great Irish Hunger. This section is backed by the works of a dedicated international group of both individual and collective trauma specialists (Bergmann; Booth; Caplan; Danieli; Flannery; Frankl; Herman, "Crime and Memory" and *Trauma and Recovery*; Krugman; Last; Leach; Lindemann; Pearlman; Rosenheck and Nathan; Sack, Clark, and Seeley; Seligman; Shabad; Sigal and Weinfeld; Simpson; Steinglass and Gerrity; van der Kolk and Kadish; Waites; Wilson and Raphael; Zinner and Williams). Theories on the psychological effects of colonialism/oppression and liberation are also used to inform this particular Irish Famine trauma model (Alschuler; Brabeck et al; Bulhan; Clarke; Doolin; Fanon, *Black Skins*; Fanon, *Dying Colonialism*; Friere; Hickman; Institute of Irish Studies; Martin-Baro; Moane, *Gender and Colonialism* and *A Psychological Analysis*; O'Connor; Prilleltensky and Gonick; Sands; and Trouillot)

These theories provide the psychological foundation and social context within which this cataclysm occurred. The historical context (Kinealy, *Death-Dealing Famine*) for these psycho-social dynamics are presented along with the effects of these events during each successive generational and historical period of pre-trauma, trauma, post-trauma, recovery, and future implications.

The dynamics of the collective memory for political events is also reviewed as a way of providing a psychologically based explanation for the official historical neglect of this event among Irish academics during the previous four and five generations (Baumeister and Hastings; Connerton; Coser; Dodd; Halbwachs; Heimannsberg and Schmidt; Jung; Marquez, Paez, and Serra; Lira; Middleton and Edwards; Morash; Pennebaker; Schacter; Schuman and Scott; Schuman; Thompson; and Waters).

V. Psycho-Historical Narrative of the Great Hunger
The Psychological Divide

The psychological divide between the British government and the Irish people is reflected in the different labels given to the event by the participants in the disaster. The English government would always refer to it as the Famine or, more frequently in the nineteenth century, as the Great Calamity (Kinealy, *This Great Calamity*), an act of God, and not their fault (Trevelyan). On the other hand, the Irish would remember it in the psychologically traumatic language of individual suffering. They labeled it simply, *An Gorta Mor*, which is Gaelic for the "Great Hunger" (Robinson). It earned the distinction of being "great" primarily to differentiate its size from the forty smaller previous Irish famines that had occurred since A.D. 900 under colonial rule (Crawford). It was remembered as well as that "Great Calamity" for many of those witnessing its devastating course across its seven-year duration during the nineteenth century

An Gorta Mor is ultimately the story of individuals, families, inter-group conflicts, and societies. It reaches across oceans, whole continents, and the great social and interpersonal divides of both race and class. It is a tale of unimaginable suffering and the triumphant reconnection of a people with themselves and their homeland. But the story begins with a name in a language that time has almost forgotten: Gaelic.

Psychological and Historical Timeline

The information in Table 1 provided below summarizes much of the information that will be discussed in more detail throughout the remainder of this article. It is organized so that the psychological stages of trauma and oppression/liberation are listed concurrently with their historically significant events. The effects of the disaster that occurred during each historical period are also provided below each specific psychological stage/theory. Finally, the population/demographics of

SILENT HUNGER

Psychological-Historical Timeline of The Great Irish Hunger

(1169 AD-2000 AD)

	1169 AD	1845	1852	1860	1916	1922	1960	1981	1994	2000
						Historical Stages of Silent Hunger				
Events:	Strongbow arrives in Ireland	Potato Blight Appears and Disappears ...		American Civil War	Irish Revolt	Ireland partitioned	JFK elected Amer. Pres.	Bobby Sands Hunger Strikers	Great Irish Hunger Commemoration IRA Cease Fire	Northern Irish Peace Process Ongoing...
						Psychological Stages and Theories of Silent Hunger				
Stages: *Pre-Trauma*	*Pre-Trauma*	*Trauma Theory* *Trauma*		*Post Trauma*		*Memory/Dissociation*			*Recovery*	*Future*
Stages: *Acritical*	*Acritical*	*Oppression/Liberation Theory* (Prilleltensky and Gonick) *Adaptive*		*Pre-Critical*			*Critical*		*Liberation*	*Implications*
Stages: *Oppression*	*Oppression*	*Collective Memory Theory* *Collective Trauma*		*PTSD/Recovery*		*Collective Traumatic Memory*			*Liberation Narrative*	*International Connection*
						Trauma and Recovery: Irish Population Statistics:				
Evidence:	Conditioned to accept suffering, helplessness, poverty	1,000,000 deaths 1,500,000 emigrate 250,000 evictions society disintegrates		Mass emigration continues... marriages decline increased addictions, mental illness, stunted physical growth		Forgetting/silence/break in narrative transmission across the generations assimilation/loss of identity/shame PTSD without the memory			Remembering commemorating forgiving search for meaning	Reconnecting survivors worldwide justice/food
Population:	4,800,000	8,175,125	6,552,385	3,139,688		2,971,992	2,818,341	3,443,405	3,623,087 3,836,400	4,052,000

(Bittles, 1994), (O'Brien, 1953), (Crawford, 1995 #288), (Office, 1997)

TABLE 6.1

Ireland, throughout the entire 150-year period from pre-famine to post-famine recovery are listed as an epidemiological barometer of trauma and recovery from this historically significant event.

Pre-Trauma—The Psychology of Oppression

Ireland, on the eve of the Great Hunger, was immersed in the psychologically toxic and pervasively traumatic environment of colonialism. In addition to its more well-known economic and politically devastating consequences, colonialism is psychologically significant for its peculiar ability to recruit individuals to participate in their own destruction (Bulhan). The primary economic hallmark of this system of exploitation is a gross inequity in the allocation of resources. The resources of one designated group of devalued people are systematically transferred to a group of societally valued people. It is a system universally recognized for sharp differences in political rights, economic access, and cultural control (Moane, "Psychologial Analysis").

Societies based upon these sharp differences in equality could be called "borderline societies." The term *borderline* is taken from the *Diagnostic and Statistical Manual (fourth edition) DSM-IV* of mental disorders, which is widely used in current mental health facilities and by mental health practitioners. It is a term attributed to a pathological condition for individuals hovering on the border between reality and psychosis. It describes a pathological condition characterized by a tendency to perceive and react to the world in emotional extremes, that is, as all good/all bad. Hence, borderline refers to the demarcation between sanity and insanity.

In Ireland, during the mid-nineteenth century, religious and class differences formed these "borderline societal separations" between the groups of valued and devalued citizens (Bulhan). In many contemporary societies race is this characteristic that defines the border between the haves and have nots (White), both politically and economically, for example, South African Apartheid (Fanon, "Black Skins"). The key ingredient is that there must be an easily identifiable characteristic or border that whole groups of people can recognize and respond to in psychologically stereotypical ways (Bulhan). It is these psychologically determined roles and responses that are at the heart of these oppressive systems. Once established they operate automatically and with ruthless efficiency. In addition, the pervasive and unquestioned acceptance of these stereotypes makes them impervious to change, as the psychological dynamics of oppression are not widely or consciously understood. The mechanisms for reversing these stereotypical responses are even less well understood.

The psychological roles of the oppressor and the oppressed are the same regardless of the conditions that sustain the oppression. It includes the self-identifying assumptions that are characterized in table 2 below:

Psychological Characteristics of the Oppressor and Oppressed

Profile of the Oppressor	Profile of the Oppressed
☐ All good	☐ All bad
☐ A sense of agency and competence	☐ A sense of inadequacy and incompetence
☐ Morally superior	☐ Morally inferior
☐ Sexually appropriate	☐ Sexually inappropriate
☐ Gendered as male	☐ Gendered as female
☐ Positive self image	☐ Negative self image
☐ Clean	☐ Dirty or unhygienic
☐ Healthy	☐ Diseased
☐ Hard working/industrious	☐ Lazy
☐ Intellectually superior	☐ Intellectually inferior
☐ Parent with both good and bad qualities	☐ Childlike
☐ Attractive human qualities	☐ Unattractive human qualities
☐ Model for humanity	☐ Inhuman animalistic

(Moane, "Psychological Analysis")

TABLE 6.2

In addition to these polarizing roles, certain predetermined psychological mechanisms are used by the oppressors to operationalize and maintain the system of exploitation. In response to this exploitation, the oppressed develop certain psychological defenses in order to survive emotionally as well as physically. The psychological well-being of the oppressed is under constant pressure, from birth till death, from the systematically oppressive environment. These mechanisms of oppression and their antagonistic defenses of the oppressed are listed below in table 3:

Behaviors of the Oppressors and the Oppressed

Mechanisms of Oppression	Defenses of the Oppressed
☐ Fear and physical control	☐ Passive resistance
☐ Sexual exploitation	☐ Refusal to give up religion
☐ Control of language	☐ Persistence of a separate language
☐ Control of education	☐ Great capacity for sharing
☐ Control of religion	☐ Mutual assistance
☐ Control of historical narrative	☐ Emotional connection
☐ Control of land usage	☐ Humor used as indirect anger
☐ Economic transfer of resources	☐ Art, music, and literature
☐ Exclusion from power	☐ Able to survive on the few resources
☐ Viewed as a problem	☐ Great capacity to endure suffering
☐ Annihilation of the oppressed is a wish of the oppressed either overtly or covertly	☐ Ongoing insurrection

(Moane, "Psychological Analysis")

TABLE 6.3

Finally, there are also psychological stages that societies may undergo on the path from unacknowledged and passive acceptance of oppression to eventual physical and psychological liberation and self-determination. These theoretical stages from oppression to liberation include five distinct phases: (1) The Acritical stage—sharply defined power inequities are accepted as the "natural order of things" and unchangeable; (2) The Adaptive stage—there is a belief that things are unjust but unchangeable; (3) The Pre-Critical stage—shows an emerging belief and yearning for a change in these inequities; (4) The Critical stage—reveals a deeper understanding of the sources of oppression and the beginnings of a willingness to work toward change; (5) The Liberation stage—the oppressive system becomes obvious and actual involvement in confronting injustice becomes a reality (Prilleltensky and Gonick).

Judy Herman, a Harvard psychiatrist and eminent trauma theorist, calls trauma an "affliction of the powerless" (*Trauma and Recovery*). The Great Hunger was traumatic biologically and psychologically. However, the actual traumatic experience of hunger was experienced differently by different classes of society. It was primarily a physical and psychological trauma for the most powerless members of Irish society, the landless peasants (Kinealy, *Death-Dealing Famine*). All others were secondarily affected through the mechanisms of "vicarious traumatization" (Pearlman). This is primarily the experience of trauma through observation rather than through direct experience of the traumatic event itself.

The Psychological Historical Timeline, provided earlier, identifies the stages of trauma and oppression/liberation defined above. It also identifies the historical path taken during each theoretical stage. The combination of these theories with actual historical events provides a new psycho-historical narrative of *An Gorta Mor*.

Trauma—An Gorta Mor

On 13 September 1845 the potato blight, *Phytophthora infestans*, arrived in Ireland (Lindley). This plant disease devastated the communal, agrarian, Irish lifestyle as it had been practiced for centuries. It brought to Ireland an "avalanche" of a disaster that was of unimaginable proportions to all those who experienced its long depredations (Murphy). The multitude of names given to this disaster by the many participants is a testament to its enormous physical and psychological impact: *An Gorta Mo*r, the Great Hunger, the Great Starvation, the Irish Famine, the Year of the Small Potato, the Hungry Forties, the Potato Famine, the Visitation from God, a Fearful Reality, a Nation of Beggars, the Irish Hecatomb, Black '47, the Great Calamity (Kinealy, *This Great Calamity*), the Irish Holocaust (Gribben). In its wake, the disaster would claim more than 1,200,000 lives and leave a "burnt hole" in the hearts of all the Irish who survived the disaster (Danieli, *International Handbook*).

Psychological disaster theories state that there are three levels of response to any disaster (Barton). The first level is the immediate response of the individual victim, the second is that of the entire society, and third is the response of those attempting to act as rescuers. The first level of psychological response, that of the individual survivor, includes the following psychological reactions to a disaster:

Individual Response to Disaster

- Immobilization—Survivor-victims report feelings of shock, numbness, denial, inability to concentrate, and feelings of unreality.
- Multiple Losses—The survivors may wonder when the death and dying will end. Multiple losses can lead to "bereavement overload," severely taxing the individual's ability to cope.
- Helplessness—Survivor-victims may feel overwhelmed by the destruction and loss and may become suicidal or develop the Learned Helplessness Syndrome (an inability to act on one's own behalf in a pro-active manner).
- Focus on Survival—The acquisition of adequate resources (food, shelter, and clothing) becomes the survivor's sole preoccupation. Biological survival protects the survivor-victim from attending to overwhelming emotions that could compromise the person's survival efforts (Sprang and McNeil).

The historical record of the Irish Famine is replete with examples of participants' reactions of shock and disbelief at each successive potato crop failure. The Irish peasants knew that with each failed harvest came eviction, emigration, or death on a massive scale. Eyewitness accounts say that the people would wail and keen at the sight of potatoes discovered rotting in their fields (Póirtéir). The Irish experienced not just the loss of loved ones but also the loss of burial rites and rituals. The sheer numbers of deaths, along with the oppressive behavior of those in power, prevented the Irish from acknowledging death in their customary ways. Examples of an inability to maintain burial rites and traditions speaks to the psychological phenomenon of "multiple losses" and a bereavement overload (Caplan).

The most heartrending examples of the psychological symptom of "learned helplessness" (Seligman) come from Irish Famine reports of entire families closing themselves off from the world to die within their homes (Hayden). This action bespeaks suicidal loss of hope. These individuals and families no longer believed that they were capable of obtaining food or medical attention and perished from the combined effects of psychological immobilization, starvation, and disease. In the disaster's aftermath, the work of the Famine survivors both within Ireland and throughout the world would become an almost obsessive "focus on survival" (Sprang and McNeil).

Collective/Societal Response to Disaster

Three stages of collective social response to nutritional disasters have been identified as the "General Adaptation Syndrome" (Selye). These stages are described as follows:

- Alarm—hyperactive phase when people and systems mobilize to sustain the traumatized system.
- Resistance—energy conservation strategy focus; normal societal functions are disrupted and an attempt is made to re-establish equilibrium.
- Exhaustion—Victims and rescuers become demoralized as the ongoing trauma takes its toll.

The Irish case, at least in part, followed these collective disaster response phases. During the Alarm phase, there certainly was an attempt to sound the alarm when botanists warned Irish politicians and British officials of the coming threat of widespread mortality due to famine within Ireland. This chorus of Cassandras was joined, after the second crop failure, by the Quakers or the Society of Friends, who provided much nongovernmental relief during this middle phase of the Famine. Initially, the relief response was largely successful, as the British government under Prime Minister Peel imported American corn to feed the Irish. However following the second crop failure of 1846, this was replaced by a less enlightened government policy of laissez-faire economics and the end of food imports to feed the hungry. In the areas most affected by the Famine, people focused almost solely on coping with the enormity of the disaster. There are countless examples of tenants and landlords alike attempting to manage the disaster through public works projects and emigration, with mixed results (Kinealy, *Death-Dealing Famine*).

In the Resistance phase, energy conservation strategies and a disruption in normal societal functions were paramount. The governmental relief strategy that required the Irish to work for their food rations was abandoned at the beginning of 1847. This failed Famine relief strategy proved costly, inefficient, and resulted in the lethal human cost of rising mortality rates (Kinealy, *Death-Dealing Famine*). In areas hit hardest by the disaster, all normal societal functions were disrupted and replaced with a focus on locating and eating anything available. The accounts of victims with "mouths stained green" from eating inedible and non-nutritional grass is vivid testimony to this desperate search for sustenance (Póirtéir). In addition, the peculiar phenomenon of "unusual wanderings" when people, during famine conditions throughout the world, are noted to begin to abandon their homes and take to the highways in search of food (Dirks).

In the final stage, exhaustion overcame both victims and the rescuers (private and public relief agencies) as the cumulative effects of seven years of protracted crop failures set in. In this phase we see many of the relief efforts abandoned and the Irish are left to fend for themselves.

Psychological Factors Affecting Relief Efforts

The psychology of relief workers has its own dynamics and stages. These factors impact the behavior of those attempting to save the victims. The survival of victims depends upon the motivation of their rescuers. If the rescuers succumb to physical and mental exhaustion or "vicarious traumatization" during a disaster, the effects of the original trauma are exacerbated (Pearlman). The psychological factors affecting rescuers' ability to maintain their life-saving efforts until the crisis ends are as follows:

- Knowledge/communication of the extent of the disaster.
- Victim's willingness to discuss the extent of the deprivation/trauma.
- Sympathetic identification with the victim.
- "Victim blaming" to explain the disaster.
- Relative deprivation mechanisms between groups.
- Prior negative stereotypes of the victimized group (Barton).

Unfortunately for the Irish, most if not all of these predisposing psychological factors affecting relief workers were not in their favor. These factors worked against the ability of the British government, the Quakers, and other nongovernmental rescuers, like the remarkable American philanthropist Asenath Nicholson (Murphy), from maintaining the massive efforts needed to save hundreds of thousands of Irish peasants in the latter stages of the disaster.

There was knowledge and communication of the extent of the disaster available to the rescuers. The Irish Famine has been called the first famine to be covered by the international news media. Knowledge of the Irish Famine was widespread. It has been reported that groups as far away as the American Cherokee Indian tribe were so moved by news accounts of the starving Irish that they sent funds to assist in the relief efforts (Fitzpatrick).

The victims were willing to discuss their needs for food but were prevented from resisting the false promises of food that often came too little and too late by the religious and political authorities of the day.

An immense body of starving and angry peasants marched into Macroom, West Cork, and gathered outside the workhouse seeking work and food. What was to become of their wives and children 12 or 13 miles off, who could not come to the workhouse for a meal, they demanded. Despite the presence of soldiers and armed police, a riot was avoided, it was alleged, only by the influence of the parish priest, Thomas Lee (Kerr 35).

It is well documented that the British government and many of the upper classes within Irish society did not sympathetically identify with the victims (Woodham-Smith,). Firsthand accounts by the great American abolitionist ex-slave, Frederick Douglass, who happened to be visiting Ireland on an abolitionist fundraising tour during the first year of the Famine (1845–1846), recounts the way the upper classes within Ireland ignored the plight of the starving Famine Irish while championing the eradication of slavery in America.

On his way through Ireland, Douglass saw what his antislavery hosts seemed blind to. Reports of famine—the grim result of the first of the rotted potato crops—were in the newspapers. Thin-armed children and their defeated mothers huddled at door-stoops as fathers tried, often unsuccessfully, to earn passage out of the ports of Wexford, Waterford, and Cork. The antislavery people stepped around these Irish poor as they made their way into Douglass's lectures about mistreated Africans in America. Abolitionists were generous in their concern for those who had been wronged, but in the late 1840s, a curious deafness to suffering at home accompanied their sympathetic response to what was endured across the Atlantic (McFeely 126).

In addition, the Irish were blamed for their plight. In one instance, a British official stated that the Famine was their fault for having willingly chosen to subsist on a single crop. Sir Charles Trevelyan wrote, "The consequences of depending upon the potato as the principal article of popular food, had long been foreseen by thinking persons . . ." (Killen). This curious psychological phenomenon is called "Blaming the Victim" (Ryan). It often occurs in situations of oppression when the oppressed are labeled as being responsible for their own suffering. It allows oppressors and bystanders to avoid the uncomfortable emotions associated with taking responsibility for assisting victims. It also allows nonvictims to avoid the "vicarious traumatization" that comes from sympathetically identifying with victims and attempting yet failing to rescue them (Pearlman).

Everyone, both victims and British and Irish upper classes, were desensitized to Irish hunger and endemic poverty from forty prior Irish famines dating back to A.D. 900 (Crawford). It was hard to shock anyone with images of Irish poverty, as it was only a matter of degrees to most observers. Only the victims would understand the lethal difference between subsistence poverty and nonsubsistence poverty.

Finally, the Irish had been negatively stereotyped as being racially inferior and animalistic for centuries (Ignatiev). Charles Kingsley, traveling in Ireland during 1860, would write of the Irish he saw on this trip: "I am haunted by the human chimpanzees I saw along the hundred miles of horrible country . . . to see white chimpanzees is dreadful; if they were black one would not feel it so much" (Robins 126).

Psychologists have identified the use of these types of negative stereotypes as a psychological precursor to genocidal acts (Staub). These stereotypes will also reduce the psychological motivation needed to sustain such a massive and protracted relief effort as was required during the Irish Hunger. The effects of these stereotypes were felt as one relief agency after another gave up and declared victory over the Great Hunger or succumbed to "vicarious traumatization" long before there was sufficient food provided to the hapless victims.

Post Trauma—A Silent Hunger

The longer-term post traumatic story of the Great Hunger is complex and multilayered. There are the physical and psychological responses of individual victims that occur over time to such large-scale disasters. There are also collective or social responses and how individuals react as groups to such events. There is the impact of trauma on family dynamics—the most intimate and sensitive of all social systems. Finally, there are the psychological dynamics of transgenerational transmission of trauma and how it is identified and expressed in hidden, silent, and enduringly traumatic ways.

V. Individual Physical Impact

The individual physical impact of the disaster would be written in the very bones of future generations, who had little awareness of the original event. Its impact has been described in the brutal statistics of ill health, disease, and early death in the immediate survivors and first- and second-generation survivors of the Great Hunger (Kinealy, *Death-Dealing Famine*). Less well known is the fact that there was a physical reduction in the height of subsequent generations of Irish Hunger descendants (O'Brien). This is a well-documented genetic and biological human response found in populations after repeated and extended periods of nutritional crises (Livi-Bacci). A people will actually become shorter as a way of reducing the nutritional requirements of a society. The Irish were just such a people having experienced forty famines since A.D. 900 (Crawford). In fact, the Irish people were among the tallest in Europe prior to the start of the Great Hunger (Kinealy, *Death-Dealing Famine*). This suggests that they had a fairly reasonable, if bland, and perhaps more than adequate diet prior to this event.

VI. Individual Psychological Response

The immediate survivors of large-scale disasters can, in addition to suffering short-term post traumatic stress symptoms, develop long-term characterological symptoms. These more enduring psychological symptoms include:

- Death imprint
- Psychic numbing
- Conflict over intimacy and nurturance needs
- Impaired formulation of the causes of the disaster
- Increased rates of mental illness
- Increased rates of addiction
- Survivor's guilt (Lifton)

A death imprint can be described as leaving survivors with nightmarish images that become intrusive and pathologically unforgettable (Lifton). The Irish Famine survivors were haunted by gruesomely graphic images of death by starvation (Woodham-Smith). The written and oral history of the Great Hunger is replete with haunting and spectral images of death (Póirtéir).

The human psyche is capable of protecting us from overwhelming emotions. However, when this barrier is breached, people can become either hypersensitive or completely desensitized to similar experiences. In an attempt to manage an uncomfortable, anxiety-producing reaction, survivors often develop a protective coping mechanism that numbs them to a wide variety of emotions, blunting and severely restricting their emotional experience of the world in the aftermath of the trauma (Leach).

Interpersonal relationships are often affected adversely. Individuals become obsessed with, and have conflicting attitudes toward, acknowledging and meeting their needs for nurturance and intimacy. In addition, trust is severely compromised, especially if betrayal is associated with the traumatic experience (Herman). The Irish, surely, felt betrayed by their British colonial rulers (Woodham-Smith). However, as the Famine progressed, severe deprivation degraded even the many formerly personal and positive intimate relationships between neighbors and relatives as people were forced to turn away from helping each other in order to survive. The oral history accounts are full of references to instances of fever victims being shunned for fear of contagion (Póirtéir). Many elderly and sick persons were abandoned as the young emigrated in order to survive (Lash). Their emigration created a sense of abandonment among those who remained in post-Famine Ireland (Kinealy, *Death-Dealing Famine*). And a sickening homesickness and longing remained among the immigrants who fled (Emmenegger-Hinden). Heart-rending accounts of both of these symptoms are readily available in the countless letters written between these surviving groups in America and Ireland (Harris, O'Keefe, and Pickett).

A curious psychological symptom of overwhelming disasters like famines and epidemics is that individuals struggle to rationalize how and why the event happened to them, specifically (Lerner). These formulations or causative explanations are frequently erroneous but serve as the foundation for adapting future behavior to survive in a world that is forever changed and experienced as dangerous and unpredictable (Leach). These basic assumptions and beliefs about the world and one's place in it are colored in subtle but devastatingly enduring ways. The Irish began to have a more pessimistic worldview after this disaster struck.

There are countless examples of this Irish pessimism in modern-day Irish colloquial speaking patterns. For example, "Murphy's Law" states, "If things can go wrong they inevitably will." Such statements are meant humorously, yet they formed the bedrock of the modern Irish character for generations following the Famine (Lennon). Upon hearing of the death of John F. Kennedy, Irish-American senator, Daniel Patrick Moynihan was heard to say, "There is no point in being Irish unless you understand that the world will eventually break your heart" (Mitchell). This belief in the inevitability of tragedy and loss remained well into the latter half of the twentieth century.

In the decades following the Irish Hunger, rates of mental illness skyrocketed (Robins). In particular, there has recently been a clearly identified increase in the rates of schizophrenia among children of famine. These rates come out of studies done on the offspring of women who were pregnant during the World War II Nazi blockade of Amsterdam (Susser et al.). Among this group, the expression of this devastating illness is 100 percent higher than among children born to mothers who did not experience a severe nutritional crisis during pregnancy. It has been an inexplicable and controversial fact that the generations following the Great Hunger have been, according to epidemiological statistics, among those with the highest rates of schizophrenia, affective disorders (bipolar and depression), and in-patient mental hospital admissions (Finnane). These rates are not readily understandable and are under constant critical review and dispute by more contemporary epidemiologic researcher studies

(Kinsella; Nuallaine, O'Hare and Walsh; Scully; Youssef; and Waddington).

In addition to increased rates of schizophrenia and affective disorders, there is a documented increase in anti-social personality disorders following famines (Neugebau, Hoek, and Sisser). This most assuredly fits with the historical case of the Irish Hunger. The Irish experienced an obvious increase in food and materially related crime (theft) during the Famine (Póirtéir). However, in the decades following the crisis, on both sides of the Atlantic, rates of violent crime and interpersonally violent crime rose dramatically, prompting one author to state that the Harlem River in New York City ran red with Irish blood due to these violent episodes.

The rural Irish, entering an urbanized and industrial culture, arrived in much worse shape than most immigrants and bore the psychic marks of an increasingly sick and violent society back home. They were quickly identified in the public mind with poverty, disease, alcoholism, crime, and violence.

Much of this was an accurate portrait of the Irish at the time. Irish violence was often astounding. Bodies floated in New York City's East River almost every day. At one point, the city jail population was 90 percent Irish. Police vehicles that rounded them up were called "paddy wagons," the wagons that carried all the hopeless Paddys to their natural home. Good citizens wondered about a permanently unfit underclass and the possibility of genetic inferiority (Leo).

That the Irish have long been identified with high rates of addictions and substance abuse pre- and post-dates the Great Hunger (McGoldrick) and is also a symptom of the psychology of oppression/colonialism described earlier (Bulhan). However, whether hunger can increase the cravings for substances that increase an individual's ability to dissociate from a traumatic situation is not as well known. Studies of World War II prisoner of war inmates reveals that soldiers would often choose addictive substances over food if hunger was a chronic condition (Brozek).

Finally, the survivors immediately following *An Gorta Mor*, were, like others in similar situations of extreme stress, unable to act in ways that met their pre-traumatic experience expectations of themselves. Even among those who might be objectively considered to have behaved heroically, a corrosive sense of guilt emerges, as even a hero would have been incapable of saving everyone (Sprang and McNeil). Famines, in particular, are enormously guilt producing as survivors who were capable of sharing their food with others must have chosen on some level to not share their life-sustaining resources. In informal conversations, international relief workers indicate that of all the disasters they encounter, famines are the most personally devastating (Lautze).

Famines create a situation of deep moral ambivalence in which it appears as if it is within everyone's power to at least share their food. It's easy for famine survivors, in desperate circumstances, to translate this simple fact into an irrational self-statement or belief that reads something like, "I wouldn't have survived without eating and yet my eating ensured the deaths of those who did not get the food I ate." In cognitive behavioral terms, this is called a cognitive distortion. The simple act of eating can turn people's sense of self into that of a having been complicit in a mass murder that they did not initiate. It is a heavy psychic burden to bear and one not easily borne by famine survivors, be they Irish, Russian, Armenian, Korean, Ethiopian, or Somalian living in any country and at any time in history.

VII. Collective Psychological Response

Collectively, recent disaster psychological theorists have identified three periods or phases of social and interpersonally significant patterns of behavior following large scale disasters. These phases are:

- Emergent phase—Increased social contact between participants, obsessive thoughts, and talking about the event.
- Inhibition phase—Reduced talking but no reduction in obsessive thoughts; participants also choose to stop listening to other victims.
- Adaptation phase—Obsessive thoughts are reduced and talking about the event returns to normal (Pennebaker and Harber).

Immediately following the Irish Famine, during the Emergent phase, there was a lot of talking about the disaster among the survivors. In Ireland and America, newspapers were full of stories and reports of the Famine and its emigration impact (Coffey, Galway, and Terry). There was also a great deal of assistance provided by emigrants to Famine survivors in Ireland during this period.

However, this phase was rather quickly replaced by the Inhibition phase, which is the beginning of the silent hunger that became the longer-term coping style of the survivors. During this long-term phase, survivors become overwhelmed with information on the gruesome details of the traumatic experience. It is during this phase that they began to voluntarily censor their own talking about the traumatic experience. Even more significantly, during this phase, they also choose to ignore the testimonials of their fellow survivors in subtle but effective ways (Pennebaker and Harber). For the post–Great Hunger

Irish, this Inhibition phase could be considered to have continued across more than one generation of famine survivors and their descendants. The reasons for this self-censorship in the aftermath of this disaster will be reviewed more extensively during the Recovery section of this article.

Finally, the Adaptation phase is a period in which rates of verbal expression related to the event return to normal and obsessive thoughts about the event return to normal. In the Irish case, this Adaptation phase did not occur until generations after the event (Pennebaker and Harber).

VIII. Post-Trauma Family Types

The most basic collective and societal unit is the family. Just as individuals respond to extremely stressful situations with characteristic post-traumatic behaviors, families appear to choose similarly identifiable and patterned psychological coping styles to manage traumatic situations. Recent psychological literature on the formation of four post-trauma family types following the Jewish Holocaust during World War II are described below:

- Victim Families—identify themselves as victims and have a family system that looks inward and is closed to outsiders.
- Numb Families—these systems are noncommunicative, shut off from their feelings and insular.
- Fighters—are counter-phobically risk-taking, have anti-social tendencies, and are intolerant of weakness.
- Assimilationists—focus on obtaining the external signs of success; in the process they suffer from a loss of identity and confusion. There is an attempt at passing or pretending to be someone or something else. There is a conflict between external and internal emotional states (Danieli, "Treatment and Prevention").

Almost all Irish families can find themselves in one of these four post-disaster family types. Probably the most famous transgenerational Irish Hunger family coping style can be found in the Irish-American Famine survivor descendants of Patrick Kennedy. His many generational descendants include the forty-third president of the United States, John F. Kennedy, and his extended family of siblings, nephews, and nieces. This famous politically dynastic Irish-American family can be described as having followed a combination of the Assimilationist and Fighter post-disaster family type. It is not the purpose of this paper to psychoanalyze or pathologize the family, and yet, in retrospect, some of these family patterns seem to fit their tragic trajectory both physically and psychologically.

For example, the patriarch, Joseph Kennedy, took enormous risks to get ahead and was not above bending the rules to accomplish his goals. In addition, there are innumerable biographical accounts of third- and fourth-generation family members taking inordinate and tragic risks with their own lives—at times, merely for fun; at others, for personal ambition and compassionate political causes. However, their internal family dynamics were often marked by a lack of compassion for themselves and an intolerance of weakness among family members that crosses several generations.

My own fourth-generation post–Great Hunger family experience seems to approximate the common Assimilationist family type. My family's experience includes a family narrative that obliterates the disaster completely from our personal transgenerational experience. The story begins in American with no narrative connection to Ireland, per se. In fact, my family's very name, Peck, is decidedly non-Irish. We had engaged in the common emigrant coping style of choosing to pass as something that we were not, namely British. Earlier generations of my family chose to adopt the surname of an ancient and bitter enemy to deal with the extreme forms of discriminational pressures they must have encountered both within Ireland and in America. This coping style has obvious advantages for reducing ethnic surname pressures exerted by an oppressor (employment opportunities and so on).

However, psychologically, the cost can be devastating as it confuses the identity of its participants and their descendants. Among the more insidious and hidden but devastating costs for some of the more vulnerable family members is that it creates a conflict between internal and external emotional states that can reach intolerable levels. All forms of passing as something that we are not requires that individuals present a positive, ambitious, and successful surface that may not always be authentic or congruent with internal psychological states. This was certainly true for those who chose this coping style after the Irish Famine. These families have, tragically, among the highest rates of suicide of the four post-trauma family types (Danieli, "Treatment and Prevention").

IX. Transgenerational Transmission of Trauma

Psychological researchers have documented the existence of post-traumatic stress symptoms across three generations of Nazi Holocaust survivors and their children (Bergmann and Jucovy, *Generations of the Holocaust* 194). The symptoms identified as transgenerational are different than the more immediate and easily identifiable post-traumatic symptoms of nightmares, intrusive thoughts, and the like. Transgenerational transmission dynamics revolve, primarily, around the initial symptom of "survivor's guilt." Most genocide or massive trauma survivors suffer from guilt about what they did or did not do during the disaster. This guilt about specific behavioral actions or inactions during the event become, over time, translated into a more globalized feeling of shame about oneself as a person and collectively as a people or nation (Leach; Lifton; Sprang and McNeil).

Shame becomes, for purposes of genocidal events, a generalized psychologically transmissible virus. It's present in almost all transgenerational descendants of these massive historic tragedies. It is a powerfully corrosive emotional state that causes such psychological discomfort that its victims may be prone to violent emotional outburst if the shame is exacerbated by totally disconnected stressors in completely separate nontraumatic and transgenerational circumstances. Obviously, similar retraumatizing experiences can also elicit powerful reactions among the immediate survivor generation. However, for subsequent transgerational survivor descendants, the shame is disconnected from the original traumatic events and is generalized to totally separate shame-producing situations, far removed across time and distance from the original guilt-producing event (Last). An excellent and, I believe, as yet unpublished article by Dr. Garret O'Connor, psychiatrist, describes the psychologically based phenomenon of "malignant shame" among contemporary Irish (O'Connor). He does not connect this shame to the Famine but rather to the pervasive effects of colonialism. The Famine was the ultimate expression of this colonial system of oppression and therefore a significant blow toward creating this possible vulnerability among contemporary Irish Famine descendants.

X. Memory—*Deep in the Bone*

One contemporary article on the Great Hunger asked, "Where are the Famine dead buried?" (Cozzens) How could a million bodies have disappeared in a country the size of Massachusetts? Why are there no markers? Surely, the British government did not prevent the Irish from marking their graves . . . so where are they, these lost souls of our collective past? One author describes the missing victims of *An Gorta Mor* as residing in all of our collective unconscious memories: "In Ireland, people still talk of the 'hungry grass,' the sod that covers the forgotten victims of the Great Potato Famine of 150 years ago. Those who tread on this grass are supposed to feel the wrenching of those who perished" (D. C. Daly 6).

XI. Post-Famine Memory Periods

The historical memory of *An Gorta Mor* can be divided into three phases of transgenerational memory: memory in conflict (1852–1900), dissociative memory (1960–1994), and reconstructive memory (1960–1994).

Memory in Conflict (1848–1900)

During the first historical period following the Great Irish Hunger, there were primarily three main conflicting memories of the Irish Hunger: the British governments' (Trevelyan), Irish nationalists' (Mitchel), and Famine survivors' versions of the event (Póirtéir). In the British government's version, the memory's purpose was to shift blame for massive loss of life to someone other than the colonial administrators. This official British governmental version framed the story by blaming either the victims or God/nature for the Famine as evidenced by these historical quotes:

And so the story begins with a version of events that are provided by the perpetrators. In the article, Trevelyan portrays the efforts of the guilty party, the British government, in a favorable light. The first official historical account of the Irish Famine begins with a treatise on holocaust denial. (Trevelyan)

But what hope is there for a nation which lives on potatoes? The consequences of depending upon the potato as the principal article of popular food, had long been foreseen by thinking persons. (Killen 175)

The second narrative, that of the Irish nationalists/independence movement leaders, chose to use the Famine for political purposes to channel the post Famine rage into the cause of independence and an Ireland free of British rule. (Mitchel)

The last narrative has been largely neglected and remained invisible for almost a century to official historical post-Famine accounts. However, these emotionally laden oral history accounts were preserved and transmitted across generations. They lay deep within the resentful memories of family survivor descendants for generations toward the British government even while the specific events of the tragedy were being transgenerationally repressed.

The purpose of the immediate Famine survivor's tale was to provide a rational explanation for *An Gorta Mor*. This search for meaning (Frankl), which is found universally among all survivors of such mass tragedies, erroneously attributed the disaster to the superstitious belief that the Irish had offended God in some way prior to the Famine's arrival (Póirtéir).

Afterward it was said that the Famine was a just retribution from God for the great waste of food. A local saying that may refer to this is: "A willful waste makes a woeful want" (Póirtéir).

Following this event, many post-Famine Irish would see God's hand in every disaster and every blessing. This type of thinking would become one of the primary psychological coping mechanisms that Irish survivor descendants would employ during many subsequently tragic events that occurred long after the Great Hunger (Ardagh). In addition, a great sense of fatalism about the world begins to take hold in the Irish psyche (Coffey et al.). One could say the syndrome of a post-Famine traumatic coping style or "silent hunger" begins here.

Dissociative Memory (1900–1960)

In this period the personal and familially transmitted memory of the great disaster of the nineteenth century begins to fade into a kind of oblivion. The second- and third-generation Irish Famine descendants would lose contact with the tragedy. This is called a "break in the generations" by social psychological theorists (Butterfield). The silence was both official and unofficial and spanned the entire sixty years. The reasons for this extensive and pervasive silence are many, but chief among them is that Ireland remained a society under British rule throughout this period. The memory of this event remained a dangerous memory and was discouraged by the authorities from being actively remembered and commemorated as it could lead to rebellion, which it eventually did (Scally).

However, the "conspiracy of silence" (Gray) about the Irish Hunger among the Irish themselves needs a separate psychologically based explanation. It cannot be entirely blamed upon the theory of British authorities' fear of the Famine memory. In the 1920s, Ireland would win partial independence from Britain. It was partitioned and remains so to this day. Psychological and social memory theorists have found that ongoing conflict within a society will inhibit the collective ability of a society to remember painful events (Schwartz). Ireland, in spite of her independence, remains painfully divided. It has interrupted the ability of succeeding Irish Famine descendants from forming a nonconflictual, safe, and collectively agreed upon narrative of this highly charged event for generations. There are other examples of this phenomenon of dissociated collective memory being documented in similar genocidal transgenerational memory experiences today (Danieli, *International Handbook*).

Reconstructive Memory (1961–1993)

During this last phase, the fourth generation of Irish Hunger descendants began to seek a remembrance of this long-hidden event within their own lives (Hayden). The process of historically reconstructing a new narrative of the original traumatic events had begun (Gray; Kinealy, *This Great Calamity*; O'Grada, *Ireland Before*; Woodham-Smith). This phenomenon is called "remote transmission" (Schuman), the transmission of memory that has skipped at least one generation. It is rediscovered in the absence of a living connection to the original memory. It is in this period that the official written historical memory of the Great Hunger re-emerges in the debate between the revisionist and counter-revisionist schools of narrative. Revisionists tended to reinforce the British view that they were not to blame for the deaths that occurred, and the counter-revisionists tended to state a more sympathetic view to the plight of those who suffered (M. Daly). The counter-revisionists were also less squeamish about assigning blame to the governmental authorities of the day.

X. Formal and Informal Memory

There are primarily two types of memory: formal and informal. The formal memory tends to be written and objective. The informal memory is oral and tends to be more subjectively rendered. The written memory transmits facts and dates more accurately but is not as good at capturing the emotional content or impact of an event. In order to get a reading on the emotional impact of an event, informal and oral history is a better mechanism, but it tends to be less accurate on dates and factual information. Both types of memory are needed for an accurate, more mature, and complex rendering of large-scale societally significant events (Thompson). The Irish Hunger memory was primarily maintained during the dissociative memory phase by informal and folkloric methods (Póirtéir).

There is a direct correlation between the use of more informal means of remembrance over formal if the memory is being officially repressed (Schwartz). In this case, the Famine was in some ways repressed first by the British Government for obvious reasons to discourage rebellion. However, the Irish themselves repressed the memory after independence, as it was not a memory that fostered nation building; therefore, it went unacknowledged by the newly independent Irish in the twenty-six counties in the south. It is in this proud post-independence nation-building phase that the historical accounts of the Famine were submerged for generations as well. However, the memory never receded entirely. It lay hidden in oral history and was recounted among the decreasing reservoir of Gaelic-speaking Famine survivor descendants in informal unrecognized ways. Unfortunately, Gaelic was increasingly dying out (Freine). As the years and generations passed, it had had fewer and fewer listeners, and the meaning of the Famine was nearly lost as well.

XI. Individual and Collective Memory

Individual memory has five stages: perception, retention, rehearsal, reinterpretation, and recall (Edwall). Large-scale disasters like the Great Hunger are difficult to perceive accurately at the time of the event. The sheer size of the disaster makes it difficult to comprehend for most victims and survivors. Retention of information during traumatic events is interrupted and distorted due to psychological symptoms of Post-Traumatic Stress Disorder (PTSD). Dissociation, which can foster temporary or permanent amnesia regarding the original event, is one of the primary symptoms of PTSD. It works cognitively against remembering painful events in the short term. In addition, rehearsal of a memory of the Great Hunger story was prohibited and discouraged for politically repressive reasons. Reinterpretation of this event, also a key ingredient to forming a transmissible memory, was delayed and conflicted. The conflict over the partition of the country into north and south continues to make Ireland's history a minefield of self-censorship. This collective self-censorship is motivated by internally divisive political reasons. Finally, transgenerational recall can occur but only after the previous stages have been worked through and resolved (Edwall). This process has taken several generations for the Irish Famine descendants on both sides of the Atlantic to successfully complete.

Collective memory requires that certain common features be present before a community will select an event to reside in a societally agreed upon place in their shared historical narrative. These common features include that the event must be: "Unique, provoke emotional reactions, . . . actively rehearsed, and . . . associated with subsequent changes in behaviors of beliefs" (Bellelli and Amatulli 4).

The Irish Hunger certainly met the first condition for collective memory formation as it provoked highly emotional reactions in its participants. Unfortunately, due to psychological reasons discussed in the individual stages of trauma section of this article, the opportunity and motivation to rehearse the story was interrupted by a variety of political and emotional reasons. The third condition, that it be associated with changes in behavior, was met as the Famine resulted in massively changed behavior; the mass emigration that followed is but one example of the radically altered behaviors that followed the disaster. Therefore, at least two out of three of the necessary conditions were present for the formation of this collectively held memory by the Irish people.

XII. Memory Distortion and Confabulation

Historical narratives are psychologically important to collective groups because all social groups need to form positive images and a group identity that fosters the psychological and physical well-being of the greatest number of its members. Like individuals, groups will use psychological defenses to guard against emotionally dangerous memories that threaten this group equilibrium, "As a result, social groups (again like individuals) will sometimes gradually distort their memories in systemic ways" (Baumeister 277). Here we see the intergenerational dynamics of the transmission of the victim's guilt feelings about the original event turned into the survivor descendant's shameful feelings about the powerlessness of the victims. The result is the omission of certain facts from the collective memory of the original event.

In addition, groups can fabricate a history that never occurred almost as a cover story for what did occur. This is often called "myth making" (Thompson 8). There are numerous examples of Great Irish Famine descendants creating myths about how the Famine happened somewhere else and did not affect them or their family in any significant way. My own family Irish immigration narrative comes primarily from a letter recalling my famine survivor ancestor's arrival in America during Black'47.   The letter was written by a second generation cousin (Cunningham) as a commemoration of the 100th anniversary of the famine survivors' safe arrival in New York City from Ireland.   In this 2nd generational retelling of that event the reasons for their migration to America are quite vague and unspecific. Mainly they include leaving Ireland due to "unjust laws and taxes" with scant references to any personal experience of hunger either within Ireland or on the journey over in a coffin ship. The famine was mentioned once in the letter but immediately distanced from our collective experience by saying that "it wasn't as bad in their county (Tipperary) as in other counties to the north." It goes on to say that the, "eats were not too plentiful on board the ship." However, the letter does say that when they landed in Battery Wharf, New York City the first thing they did was go to mass as it was "the Feast of the Epiphany or little Christmas."

All signs of a desperate nutritional struggle, if there was one, have been silenced in the generational re-telling of the tale.   And yet, what is left unspoken, is that they left Clonmel County during a time of reported rioting to obtain food from British soldiers as they shipped it out of Ireland (Woodham-Smith). In addition, omitted is any mention of the terror that my forebears must have experienced on board the ships with a six month old infant in tow. My family has no conscious remembrance of our origins as boat people and would deny having been starving refugees and not just immigrants motivated for higher political purposes like freedom, better employment and educational opportunities. One would think my family came to America for the sole purpose of finding better colleges to attend than those available to them in Ireland. It is a harrowingly silenced tale with all its psychological traumatic details washed out. And yet, my family's version of their personal and familial beginnings echo a common and almost universal minimization of historical facts. My conversations with other Boston famine Irish descendants about their families' origins universally minimizes any personal connection to the true motivations for such bravery amidst a wintery trans-Atlantic crossing. The famine Irish share a common silence, shame and amnesia about our humble and heroic Irish past (Hayden).

This curious tendency to distance one's own past from *An Gorta Mor* is not just an Irish-American Famine descendant phenomenon. This group tendency to fabricate a history to replace a more painful one has been documented within Ireland, as well. This is often called, by social psychologists, "myth making." It serves an important group psychological function to protect the identity or self esteem of whole groups of people collectively. Here are some Irish examples of this form of psychologically defensive posture about the famine that always happened elsewhere or to someone else:

> Again, popular memory suggests that Newcastle West in Limerick escaped lightly during the Famine. (O'Grada, *Black '47* 205)

> In 1938 a schoolchild was told by a relation in nearby Cil Mail Ceadair that the Famine was not as bad here as in other places. (O'Grada, *Black '47* 204)

> There is a strong local tradition on the Aran Islands that its people were spared the worst of the Famine, partly because the potato blight was less severe there. (O'Grada, *Black '47* 204)

The Irish descendants appear to have, each in their own way, embraced the myth of nameless Famine victims while disowning any particular Famine victim within their own respective and nameable family trees. Although this process could not be accurately termed unconscious, as the original memory was within conscious memory, it is not a process that individuals or groups are aware of or would readily admit to being a willing participant in.

XII. Recovery/Remembrance—*Breaking Silence*
Recovery Environments—Irish and American

The primary requirement for recovery from any traumatic experience is a safe environment. If the victim/survivors cannot find a safe place to heal, recovery will not occur (Herman). I argue that, within a societally unsafe environment, recovery can even be postponed across several generations. How many generations of recovery are required is still being researched. It remains a controversial topic as to whether it can extend beyond three generations (Moane, pers. conv.). I would argue that it is certainly possible that recovery can be prolonged beyond three generations. In fact, the entire field of transgenerational and transcultural trauma has only been able to scientifically observe and study three generations of victims and their descendants. It is at least, at this time, not disproven that the recovery period can go to a fourth and possibly a fifth generation, depending on the conditions provided to these succeeding generations of survivor descendants.

The search for safety becomes the primary goal of the survivor generation. Whether survivor descendants reach that goal will determine the psychological well-being of their unsuspecting offspring. These countless unborn generations may or may not ever comprehend that their collective and individual pasts include a world of silent pain. And yet, they will feel a "silent hunger" to be made whole. This silent hunger stems from an unexplainable and free-floating sense of loss that is unexplained by their own experiences of trauma. It is the grief of an entire people residing in the souls of isolated and disconnected individuals, who feel the Great Hunger but cannot recall the specifics of the event.

In Ireland and America the search for recovery and safety from physical and psychological hunger would take entirely different paths, and yet, in neither place would safety be found until the latter half of the twentieth century. In each country, the psychological environments were not conducive to psychologically healing the deeply traumatic wounds of *An Gorta Mor*. Instead in each place the recovery environments would contain elements of continual re-traumatization from new sources. The following table lists but a few of these historically recurring traumatic events that the Irish had to continued to survive, at great cost to their emotional well-being, for generations:

Irish and American Recovery Environments

American Recovery Environment	Irish Recovery Environment
☐ Atlantic Crossing—coffin ships	☐ British oppressor remains in power for sixty years
☐ Competition for scarce resources	☐ Renewed threat of famine and evictions in 1880s
☐ Racism/religious discrimination	☐ War for Independence
☐ American Civil War	☐ Divided Ireland
☐ Political struggle for power	☐ Civil War—ongoing conflict
☐ World War II	☐ World War II

TABLE 6.4

In America, the defining moment of having reached the elusive goal of safety was finally reached when John Fitzgerald Kennedy became the president of the United States. It heralded a new era of Irish-American identity that was no longer ashamed but proud and increasingly politically and economically powerful. The generation of President Kennedy brought a great sense of safety to all subsequent generations of Irish on both sides of the Atlantic. The Irish had finally arrived at the world's table of power and plenty. Oddly enough, President Kennedy was probably only minimally aware of his Irish Famine past (Mitchell).

In Ireland, a society that remains divided in the new millennium continues to struggle with ongoing conflict in the North. The crucial moment of resolution of the painful past came with the nonviolent Hunger Strikes of Bobby Sands in the early 1980s (Beresford). This highly charged political event acted as an almost unconscious reminder of the Irish relationship to British oppression and starvation. Many would not see it as having been part of Ireland's ability to finally come to grips with the Irish Hunger past, but it is this author's opinion that it did. Psychologically the world's reaction to Bobby Sands's sacrifice through voluntary starvation were both visceral and almost universally anti-British or at least anti-Thatcher. Curiously, many Irish in southern Ireland were opposed to the IRA and Sands's methods of nonviolent martyrdom, as it resulted in the deaths of ten young Northern Irish IRA prisoners. However, a great international moral victory was won during this supremely sacrificial act. It exposed British cruelty and indifference to Irish Hunger for all the world to see just a decade before Ireland would finally accept its Irish Famine past and commemorate it with dignity and without shame. The Hunger Strikers' nonviolent sacrifice deserves a lot of credit for this psychological reversal of sentiment.

Psychology of Liberation

It is during this last phase of recovery from Famine trauma and centuries of colonial oppression that we see the Irish in the fourth and fifth generations engaging in the final liberatory phase of recovery. In this period of liberation, oppression becomes obvious, and involvement in action to change and eradicate injustice becomes a reality (Alschuler). The commemorative Great Hunger memorials that are being erected internationally by the Irish Hunger diaspora descendants almost universally make reference to modern-day famine victims throughout the world (Mullan). In addition, Ireland continues to be an effective agent for providing relief to Famine victims around the globe. It allows the once disempowered and helpless Great Hunger survivors to regain a sense of power and agency by helping similarly oppressed groups in today's famine-stricken Africa (Tufts).

In addition, in a few significant areas Irish authors, scholars, and grassroots political advocacy groups are making the connections about Irish traumatic past and inter-group racial violence. Noel Ignatiev's book *How the Irish Became White* and Michael Patrick MacDonald's *All Souls* both try to sort out Irish and African American relationships of distrust and suspicion. There is more on the way as others begin to connect the darker side of this recovery by including the dots that scapegoat other groups unconsciously for past wrongs that have never been fully acknowledged by whole groups of people. It is in examining the more complex good and bad aspects of transgenerationally determined patterns of trauma and recovery that the real hope for significant change lies.

The ultimate signs of liberation are the reversal of the mechanisms of oppression. Signs of this recovery abound as the Irish appear to be at the top of their game socially, politically, and economically and have come close to achieving the long-deferred dream of a united Ireland. In addition, the Irish have reversed the effects of their colonial past and no longer suffer from the abiding sense of inferiority that accompanied their economic enslavement during most of their past. A new confident, educated, more hopeful, and culturally proud Irish identity has replaced that old crippling legacy. The transgenerational shame and silence that followed the Irish is being replaced with commemoration and reconnection. The ultimate sign of recovery is that the Irish are not only reconnecting with themselves and their history but have also reached out to similar groups with similar psychological profiles at earlier stages of traumatic recovery around the globe. This sense of recognition and solidarity, with similarly oppressed groups, is based upon recent psychological research that states that all human beings react in similar ways, no matter what their racial, religious, class, or ethnic background, to severely traumatic events and ongoing and toxically oppressive conditions. For no one knows better than the Irish how much these impoverished conditions can thwart the psychological recovery of individuals, families, and entire groups of traumatized peoples for generations.

XIV. Conclusion

If, as many have said, the Irish Hunger commemorations were meant to exorcise the ghosts of a million Irish Famine victims from our souls, I would argue that it is not the haunting of the ghosts of our past that we should fear, but the living spectral images of today's modern-day genocide victims. Our collective "silent hunger" will continue to haunt us if we fail to heed the desperate cries of the homeless, the poor, and the hungry that surround us each day. For in the end the legacy we write in this next chapter of the Great Irish Hunger story must be that each and every one of us is committed to caring about the fate of all those who "[h]unger greatly in today's world of plenty" (O'Connor).

Finally, what the Irish are learning to do after 150 years of recovery from *An Gorta Mor* is to see, hear, and have compassion for their own hidden but enduring silent hunger. A silent hunger not just for the sustenance of the simple potato that rotted in the fields so long ago, but also for relief from the psychological pain that lays "deep in the bone" of all the Irish no matter where they fled and how they struggled to forget *An Gorta Mor*.

Works Cited

Alschuler, L. "Oppression and Liberation." *Journal of Humanistic Psychology* 32.2 (1992): 8–31.

Anonymous, scholar, Chinese History; and A. D. Waal. *Starving in Silence: A Report on Famine and Censorship.* London, England: Article 19, 1990.

Ardagh, J. *Ireland and the Irish: Portrait of a Changing Society.* London: Penguin, 1994.

Barton, A. H. Communities in Disaster. Garden City, N.Y.: Doubleday, 1969.

Baumeister, R., and S. Hastings. "Distortions of Collective Memory: How Groups Flatter and Deceive Themselves." *Collective Memory of Political Events.* Ed. J. Pennebaker, D. Paez, and B. Rime. Mahwah, N.J.: Lawrence Erlbaum, 1997.

Becker, J. *Hungry Ghosts: Mao's Secret Famine.* New York: Free Press, 1996.

Bellelli, G., and M. Amatulli. "Nostalgia, Immigration, and Collective Memory." *Collective Memory of Political Events.* Ed. J. Pennebaker, D. Paez, and B. Rime. Mahwah, N.J.: Lawrence Erlbaum, 1997.

Beresford, D. *Ten Men Dead: The Story of the 1981 Irish Hunger Strike.* London: Grafton, 1987.

Booth, A. "Responses to Scarcity." *The Sociological Quarterly* 25 (Winter 1984): 113–24.

Brabeck, M., L. Brown, L. Christian, O. Espin, R. Hare-Mustin, A. Kaplan, E. Kashak, D. Miller, E. Phillips, T. Ferns, and A. V. Ormer. *Feminist Visions: New Directions for Theory and Practice.* Ed. J. Worell and N. Johnson. Washington, D.C.: APA, 1997.

Brozek, J. "Effects of Generalized Malnutrition on Personality." *Nutrition* 6.5 (September/October 1990): 389–95.

Bulhan, A. *Franz Fanon and the Psychology of the Oppressed.* New York: Plenum, 1985.

Butterfield, H. S. "The Discontinuities between the Generations in History." Paper presented at the The Rede Lecture, Cambridge, England, 1971.

Cahill, K. M., ed. *A Framework for Survival: Health , Human Rights, and Humanitarian Assistance in Conflicts and Disasters.* New York: Basic Books and Council on Foreign Relations, 1993.

Caplan, G. "Loss, Stress, and Mental Health." *Community Mental Health Journal* 26.1 (1990): 27–47.

Clarke, L. "Mental Illness and Irish People: Stereotypes, Determinants and Changing Perspectives." *Journal of Psychiatric and Mental Health Nursing* 5.4 (1998): 309–16.

Coffey, M. and Terry Golway, eds. *The Irish in America.* New York: Hyperion, 1997.

Connerton, P. *How Societies Remember.* Cambridge: Cambridge Univ. Press, 1989.

Coser, L. A., ed. *On Collective Memory.* Chicago: Univ. of Chicago Press, 1992.

Cozzens, C. "Tracing Tragedy in Ireland." *New York Times,* June 1, 1997: 13, 20.

Crawford, E. M., ed. *Famine: The Irish Experience 900–1900.* Edinburgh: John Donald, 1989.

Cunningham, M. Family Letter on Burke/Mahoney Family Migration, 1847. 1947.

Daly, D. C. "Famine's Ghost." *Natural History* 105 (January 1996): 6.

Daly, M. "Revisionism and Irish History: The Great Famine." *The Making of Irish History—Revisionism and the Revisionist*

Controversy. Ed. D. George Boyce and Allen O'Day. New York: Routledge, 1996.

Danieli, Y., ed. *International Handbook of Multigenerational Legacies of Trauma.* New York and London: Plenum, 1998.

---. "The Treatment and Prevention of Long Term Effects and Intergenerational Transmission of Victimization: A Lesson from Holocaust Survivors and Their Children." *Trauma and Its Wake: The Treatment and Prevention of Long Term Effects.* Ed. Y. Danieli. New York: Bruner/Mazel, 1982.

Dirks, R. "Social Responses During Severe Food Shortages and Famine." *Current Anthropology* 21.1 (1980): 21–40.

Dodd, L. "Famine Echoes." *The South Atlantic Quarterly* 95.1 (1996): 97–101.

Dolot, M. *Execution by Hunger.* New York: Norton, 1985.

Doolin, N. "The luck of the Irish?" *Nursing Standard* 8.46 (1994): 40–41.

Edwall, G., ed. *Comments on "Believe It or Not Rethinking the Historical Interpretation of Memory."* Lanham, MD: U Press of America, 1994.

Emmenegger-Hinden, I. *The Experiences of Culture Loss, Grieving/Mourning, and Acculturative Stress Associated with Depressive Symptomatology Among Adults in Cultural Transition.* Unpublished paper, Massachusetts School of Professional Psychology, Boston, Mass., 1993.

Fanon, F. "Black Skins, White Masks." *The New York Library/Book of Twentieth Century American Quotations.* Ed. S. Donardio, J. Smith, S. Mesner, and R. Davison. New York: Warner, 1952.

---. *A Dying Colonialism.* New York: Grove Press, 1967.

Finnane, M. *Insanity and the Insane in Post-Famine Ireland.* London, England: Croom Helm, 1981.

Fitzpatrick, M.-L. *The Long March.* Hillsboro, Ore.: Beyond Words, 1998.

Flannery, Raymond, Jr. "From Victim to Survivor: A Stress Management Approach in the Treatment of Learned Helplessness." *Psychological Trauma.* Ed. B. van der Kolk. Washington, D.C.: American Psychiatric Association, 1987.

Frankl, V. *Man's Search for Meaning.* Trans. Ilse Lasch. Boston: Beacon Press, 1992.

Freine, S. D. *The Great Silence.* Dublin and Cork: Mercier, 1968.

Friere, P. *Pedagogy of the Oppressed.* New York: Seabury, 1968.

Generations of the Holocaust. New York: Basic, 1982.

Glassie, H., ed. *Irish Folktales.* New York: Pantheon, 1987.

Gray, P. *The Irish Famine.* New York: Abrams, 1995.

Gribben, A., ed. *The Great Famine and the Irish Diaspora in America.* Amherst, Mass.: Univ. of Massachusetts Press, 1999.

Halbwachs, M. *On Collective Memory.* Chicago: Univ. of Chicago Press, 1992.

Harris, Ruth-Ann, Donald Jacobs, B. Emer O'Keefe, and Dominique Pickett, eds. *The Search for Missing Friends: Irish Immigrant Advertisements Placed in the Boston Pilot.* Vol. I–VII. Boston: Irish Studies Program and the Department of History at Northeastern University, New England Genealogical Society, 1989.

Hayden, T., ed. *Irish Hunger.* Boulder, CO: Roberts Rinehart, 1997.

Hayden, T. *Irish on the Inside: in search of the soul of Irish America/Tom Hayden.* New York: Verso, 2001.

Heimannsberg, B., and C. Schmidt, eds. *The Collective Silence.* San Francisco: Jossey-Bass, 1993.

Herman, J. "Crime and Memory" in *Trauma and Self.* Ed. Charles B. Strozier and Michael Flynn. Lanham, Md.: Rowman and Littlefield, 1996.

---. *Trauma and Recovery.* New York: Basic, 1992.

Hickman, M. "The Irish in Britain: Racism, Incorporation and Identity." *Irish Studies Review* 10 (1995): 16–19.

Ignatiev, N. *How the Irish Became White.* New York: Routledge, 1995.

Institute of Irish Studies, L. U. *Not Taken at a Glance: The Invisibility of Irish Migrants in British Health Research.* Unpublished ms., England, 1999.

Jung, C. G. *The Archetypes and the Collective Unconscious.* Trans. R. F. C. Hull. Vol. 9. New York: Pantheon, 1959.

Kerr, D. A. *A Nation of Beggars.* New York: Oxford Univ. Press, 1994.

Killen, J., ed. *The Famine Decade.* Belfast: Blackstaff, 1995.

Kinealy, C. *A Death-Dealing Famine: The Great Hunger in Ireland.* London: Pluto, 1997.

---. *This Great Calamity.* Colorado: Roberts Rinehart, 1995.

Krugman, S. "Trauma in the Family: Perspectives on the Intergenertional Transmission of Violence" in *Psychological Trauma.* Ed. Bessel A. van der Kolk. Washington, D.C.: APA, 1987.

Kupelian, D., A. S. Kalayjian, and A. Kassabian. "The Turkish Genocide of the Armenians." *International Handbook of Multigenerational Legacies of Trauma.* Ed. Y. Danieli. New York and London: Plenum, 1998. 710.

Lash, J. P. *Helen and Teacher, The Story of Helen Keller and Annie Sullivan Macy.* New York: Delacorte Press, 1980.

Last, U. "The Transgenerational Impact of Holocaust Trauma." *The Nazi Concentration Camps and the Conditions of Jewish Prisoners.* Ed. Gutman. Jerusalem: Yad Vashem, 1984.

Lautze, S. Personal Communication. 1998.

Leach, J. *Survival Psychology.* London: Macmillan, 1994.

Lennon, T. *Long Journey Home* [Video, Television Series]. New York,: PBS, 1998.

Leo, J. "Of Famine and Green Beer." *U.S. News and World Report* 122 (24 March 1997): 16.

Lerner, M. J. *The Belief in a Just World: A Fundamental Delusion.* New York: Plenum, 1980.

Lifton, R. *Death in Life: Survivors of Hiroshima.* New York: Random House, 1967.

Lindemann, E. *Beyond Grief: Studies in Crisis Intervention.* USA: Aronson, 1979.

Lindley, J. *Gardener's Chronicle and Horticultural Gazette,* 13 September 1845.

Lira, E. "Remembering: Passing Back Through the Heart." *Collective Memory of Political Events: Social Psychological Perspectives.* Ed. J. Pennebaker, D. Paez, and B. Rime. Mahwah, N.J.: Erlbaum, 1997. 299.

Livi-Bacci, M. *Population and Nutrition.* Trans. Tania Croft-Murray. Vol. 14. New York: Univ. of Cambridge Press, 1991.

Marquez, J., D. Paez, and A. Serra. "Social Sharing, Emotional Climate, and the Transgenerational Transmission of Memories: The Portuguese Colonial War." *Collective Memory of Political Events: Social Psychological Perspectives.* Ed. J. Pennebaker, D. Paez, and B. Rime. Mahwah, NJ: Lawrence Erlbaum, 1997.

Martin-Baro, I., ed. *Liberation Psychology.* Cambridge, Mass.: Harvard Univ. Press, 1994.

McFeely, W. *Frederick Douglass.* New York: Norton, 1991.

McGoldrick, M. "Irish Families." *Ethnicity and Family Therapy.* Ed. John Pearce and Monica McGoldrick. New York: Scribner, 1996.

Middleton, D., and D. Edwards. "Conversational Remembering: A Social Psychological Approach." *Collective Remembering.* Ed. K. J. Gergen and. J. Shotter. London: Sage, 1990.

Mitchel, J. *The Last Conquest of Ireland (Perhaps).* Glascow, Scotland: 1861.

Mitchell, A. *JFK and his Irish Heritage.* Dublin, Ireland: Moytura, 1993.

Moane, G. *Gender and Colonialism: A Psychological Analysis of Oppression and Liberation.* Dublin, Ireland: St. Martin's, 1999.

---. *Geraldine Moane.* Paper presented at the Association of Women Psychologists, Providence, RI, 1999.

---. Personal Conversations/Thesis discussant. Massachusetts School of Professional Psychology, 2000.

---. "A Psychological Analysis of Colonialism in an Irish Context." *The Irish Journal of Psychology* 15.2 and 3 (1994): 250–65.

Morash, C. "Literature, Memory and Atrocity." *The Meaning of the Famine.* Vol. 6. Ed. P. O'Sullivan. London: Leicester Univ. Press, 1994.

Mullan, D., ed. *A Glimmer of Light: An Overview of Great Hunger Commemorative Events in Ireland and Throughout the World.* Dublin, Ireland: Concern Worldwide, 1995.

Murphy, M., ed. *Annals of the Famine in Ireland.* Dublin: Lilliput, 1998.

Neugebau, R., H. W. Hoek, and E. Sisser. "Prenatal Exposure to Wartime Famine and Development of Antisocial Personality Disorder in Early Adulthood." *American Psychological Association Convention* 282.5 (1999): 455–62.

Nuallain, M. N., A. O'Hare, and D. Walsh. "The Prevalence of Schizophrenia in Three Counties in Ireland." *Acta Psychiatrica Scandinavia* 82 (1990): 136–40.

O'Brien, J. A., ed. *The Vanishing Irish.* New York: McGraw-Hill, 1953.

O'Connor, G. *Recognising and Healing Malignant Shame.* Unpublished ms., 1995.

O'Connor, J. *Irish Famine Memorial* (pamphlet). Cambridge: Irish Famine Memorial Committee, 1997.

O'Grada, C. *Black '47 and Beyond.* Princeton: Princeton Univ. Press, 1999.

---. *Ireland Before and After the Famine.* Manchester, England: Manchester Univ. Press, 1993.

Pearlman, L. M. *Psychological Trauma and the Adult Survivor.* Vol. 21. New York: Brunner/Mazel, 1990.

Pennebaker, J. Introduction. *Collective Memory of Political Events.* Ed. J. Pennebaker, D. Paez, and B. Rime. Mahwah, N.J.: Lawrence Erlbaum, 1997.

Pennebaker, J. W., and K. Harber. "A Social Stage Model of Collective Coping: The Loma Prieta Earthquake and the Persian Gulf." *The Society for the Psychological Study of Social Issues* 49.4 (1993): 125–45.

Póirtéir, C. *Famine Echoes.* Dublin: Gill and Macmillan, 1995.

Prilleltensky, Isaac and Lev Gonick. "Polities Change, Oppression Remains: On the Psychology and Politics of Oppression." *Political Psychology* 17.1 (1996): 127-148.

Robins, J. *Fools and Mad.* Dublin: Inst. of Public Admin., 1986.

Robinson, M. *Speech at the Cambridge Irish Famine Memorial Commemoration Ceremony,* Cambridge, Mass., 1997.

Rosenheck, R., and P. Nathan. "Secondary Traumatization in Children of Vietnam Veterans." *Hospital Community Psychology* 36 (1985): 538–39.

Ryan, W. *Blaming the Victim.* New York: Random House, Vintage Books, 1971.

Sack, W. H., G. N. Clarke, and J. Seeley. "Post Traumatic Stress Disorder across Two Generations of Cambodian Refugees." *Journal American Academy Child Adolescent Psychiatry* 34.9 (1995): 1160–66.

Sands, B. *Bobby Sands: Writings from Prison.* Boulder, Colo.: Roberts Rinehart, 1997.

Scally, R. J. *The End of Hidden Ireland: Rebellion, Famine, and Emigration.* New York: Oxford Univ. Press, 1995.

Schacter, D. L., ed. *Memory Distortion: How Minds, Brains, and Societies Reconstruct the Past.* Cambridge: Harvard Univ. Press, 1995.

Schuman, H. "The Generational Basis of Historical Knowledge." *Collective Memory of Political Events.* Ed. J. Pennebaker, D. Paez, and B. Rime. Mahwah, N.J.: Lawrence Erlbaum, 1997.

Schuman, H., and J. Scott. "Generations and Collective Memory." *American Sociological Review* 54 (June 1989): 359–81.

Schwartz, Barry and Robin Wagner-Pacific. "The Vietnam Veterans Memorial: Commemorating a Difficult Past." *American Journal of Sociology* 97.2 (1991): 376–420.

Seligman, M. E. *Helplessness.* San Francisco: Freeman, 1975.

Selye, Hans. "The Stress of Life." *Perspectives in Biology and Medicine* 2. (1956): 403-416.

Shabad, P. "Repetition and Incomplete Mourning: The Intergenerational Transmission of Traumatic Themes." *Psychoanalytic Psychology* 10.1 (1993): 61–75.

Sigal, J. S., and M. Weinfeld. *Trauma and Rebirth: Intergenerational Effects of the Holocaust.* New York: Praeger, 1989.

Simpson, M. A. "The Second Bullet: Transgenerational Impacts of the Trauma Conflict within a South African and World Context." *Intergenerational handbook of Multigenerational Legacies of Trauma* Ed. Y. Danieli. New York: Plenum, 1998.

Sprang, G., and J. McNeil. *The Many Faces of Bereavement.* New York: Brunner/Mazel, 1995.

Staub, E. *The Roots of Evil: the Origins of Genocide and Other Group Violence.* New York: Cambridge Univ. Press, 1989.

Steinglass, P., and E. Gerrity. "Natural Disasters and Post Traumatic Stress Disorder: Short-Term versus Long-Term Recovery in Two Disaster-Affected Communities." *Journal of Applied Social Psychology* 20.21 (1990): 1746–66.

Susser, E. M., Neugebauer, R., Hoek, H., Brawn, A., Lin, S., Labovitz, D., and Gorman, J. M. "Schizophrenia After Prenatal Famine: Further Evidence." *Archives of General Psychiatry* 53 (January 1996): 25–31.

Thompson, P., ed. *Believe It or Not: Rethinking the Historical Interpretation of Memory.* Lanham, Md.: University Press of America, 1994.

Trevelyan, S. C. "The Irish Crisis." *Edinburgh Review,* January 1848.

Trouillot, M. *Silencing the Past.* Boston: Beacon, 1995.

Tufts University Exhibit Brochure. *Famines Yesterday and Today: The Irish Experience in a Global Context.* Cork: Department of Geography, University College Cork, 1996.

Van der Kolk, B. *Psychological Trauma.* Washington, D.C.: APA, 1987.

---- "The Role of the Group in the Origin and Resolution of the Trauma Response." *Psychological Trauma.* Washington, D.C.: APA, 1987.

---- and William Kadish. "Amnesia, Dissociation, and the Return of the Repressed." *Psychological Trauma.* Ed. Bessel van der Kolk. Washington, D.C.: American Psychiatric Association (1987): 173–90.

Waites, E. *Memory Quest—Trauma and the Search for Personal History.* New York: Norton, 1997.

---. *Trauma and Survival.* New York: Norton, 1993.

Waters, J. "Troubled People." *Irish Hunger.* Ed. T. Hayden. Boulder, Colo.: Roberts Rinehart, 1997.

White, Aaronette. *A Course in the Psychology of Oppression: A Different Approach to Teaching About Diversity.* Teaching of Psychology. Vol 21, No. 1. February. 1994.

Wilson, J. P., and B. Raphael, eds. *International Handbook of Traumatic Stress Syndromes.* New York: Plenum, 1993.

Woodham-Smith, C. *The Great Hunger.* London: Penguin, 1991.

Youssef, H., P. Scully, A. Kinsella, and J. Waddington. "Geographical Variation in Rate of Schizophrenia in Rural Ireland by Place at Birth vs. Place at Onset." *Schizophrenia Research* 37 (1998): 233–43.

Zinner, E., and M. B. Williams, eds. *When a Community Weeps: Case Studies in Group Survivorship.* Philadelphia: Brunner/Mazel, 1998.

PART TWO: MEMORY

Chapter Seven

Seamus Heaney's "At a Potato Digging" Revisited

THOMAS O'GRADY

Discussing, in his book of essays *The Place of Writing*, William Butler Yeats's Thoor Ballylee—the Norman tower that Yeats refurbished for his wife in 1919—Seamus Heaney offers an illumination of Yeats's literary inscription of place that inevitably casts meaningful light on Heaney's own variously place-centered poems. Contemplating first how Thoor Ballylee eventually took on a primarily symbolic function in the poet's imagination—eventually "entered so deeply into the prophetic strains of his voice that it could be invoked without being inhabited" (24)—Heaney reiterates with a clarifying conciseness the conventional reading of Yeats's literal tower as a metaphorical "place of writing":

His other addresses were necessary shelters but Ballylee was a sacramental site, an outward sign of inner grace. The grace here was poetry and the lonely tower was the poet's sign. Within it, he was within his own mind. The posture of the building corresponded with the posture he would attain. The stone in all its obstinacy and stillness, the plumb bulk and resistant profile of the keep, the dream form and the brute fact simultaneously impressed on mind and senses, all this transmission of sensation and symbolic aura made the actual building stones into touchstones for the work he would aspire to. (24–25)

As Heaney shows further, however, in his analysis of Yeats's poem "My Descendants" (the fourth section of his magisterial "Meditations in Time of Civil War"), this conventional reading can be extended to consider the significance of the very form by which Yeats gives literary "being" to his tower. Admiring Yeats's mastery of the *ottava rima* stanza that he employs in "My Descendants," hearing in the stanza's "unshakably affirmative music . . . the formal correlative of the poet's indomitable spirit," appreciating how "The complete coincidence between period and stanza . . . compounds utterance with architecture," Heaney asserts that "Here the place of writing is essentially the stanza form itself, that strong-arched room of eight iambic pentameters rhyming *ababbcc*" (29).

Contending, in short, that "utterance and being are synonymous" (30) in Yeats's poetic elevation of his tower to iconic stature, Heaney actually provides crucial insight into many of his own poems in which poetic form affords essential reinforcement of thematic emphasis. In particular, his attention to the symbiosis of form and place in Yeats's poetry helps to elucidate the subtle workings of "At a Potato Digging," Heaney's principal poetic engagement with *An Gorta Mór*. Clearly provoked by the same awareness of "a racial memory" described by playwright Tom Murphy (xi), whose powerful drama *Famine* (1968) post-dates its publication by two years, "At a Potato Digging" is an ambitious poem, an evident product of Heaney's desire, which he articulated in 1974, to produce not only "poetry as divination, poetry as revelation of the self to the self," but also more resolutely poetry "as restoration of the culture to itself; poems as elements of continuity, with the aura and authenticity of archaeological finds" ("Feeling into Words" 41). Or as Heaney put it in "Digging," the now-famous opening poem of his first book of poems, *Death of a Naturalist*: "Between my finger and my thumb / The squat pen rests. / I'll dig with it" (14). Sharing with a number of Heaney's early poems—"The Barn," "Churning Day," "The Diviner," "The Outlaw," "The Forge," "Thatcher," "The Wife's Tale"—a fascination with the details of farm husbandry and other aspects of rural life, "At a Potato Digging" reads as an acutely observant record of an activity that epitomizes the cultural continuity between twentieth-century Ireland and the country in the troubled middle years of the nineteenth century. The poem also represents, as Edna Longley suggests, Heaney's "first embryonic fusion of Catholic experience in the North with the longer national history" (143).

Yet, by virtue of its very ambition, by the very nature of Heaney's attempt to register in verse the indelibility of the Famine in the collective memory of the Irish people, "At a Potato Digging" also differs significantly—in both its rhetorical and its formal strategies—

from many of Heaney's signature poems, especially those that engage intimately with place. "I think there are two ways in which place is known and cherished," Heaney wrote in "The Sense of Place" in 1977, "two ways which may be complementary but which are just as likely to be antipathetic. One is lived, illiterate and unconscious, the other learned, literate and conscious. In the literary sensibility, both are likely to co-exist in a conscious and unconscious tension" (131). Establishing early in his writing career his close identification with specific place, invoking and evoking his boyhood world by name (Toner's bog, Mossbawn, Anahorish, Moyola, Broagh, Derrygarve), Heaney clearly knows both experientially and cerebrally the local landmarks, the townlands, the very landscape of his native south County Derry in Northern Ireland. Thus, while purporting to locate its speaker and, vicariously, its audience "at" a seasonal undertaking that literally "Recurs mindlessly as autumn,"[1] "At a Potato Digging" is immediately conspicuous within Heaney's body of work as a poem utterly lacking in place *specificity*.

As such, the poem embodies the "tension" that Heaney himself embodies as an urbane pen-wielding poet of rural spade-wielding stock facing the challenge of expressing a communal consciousness of the Famine. For as much as "At a Potato Digging" is infused with details that authenticate the poet's apparent familiarity with the activity he records, the "place of writing" that the poem inscribes, while not as ultimately metaphorical as Yeats's tower, yet has the same sort of aura about it that Heaney describes in his "parable" of the space left after a familiar chestnut tree has been felled: "The new place was all idea, if you like; it was generated out of my experience of the old place but it was not a topographical location. It was and remains an imagined realm, even if it can be located at an earthly spot, a placeless heaven rather than a heavenly place" ("Placeless Heaven" 4). The result of Heaney's desire in this instance to speak not just for himself as lyric poet but also for an entire cultural community, the written "place" of "At a Potato Digging" is also, in effect, more imagined than actual—or at least more literary than "literal" in its "being."

ſ

Indeed, the literariness of the poem begins to emerge within the first few lines as Heaney's description of the rustic laborers following behind the mechanical digger to gather the potatoes—"Like crows attacking crow-black fields, they stretch / A higgledy line from hedge to headland"—reads readily as an allusion to the opening lines of Patrick Kavanagh's major opus "The Great Hunger," first published in 1942:

> Clay is the word and clay is the flesh
> Where the potato gatherers like mechanized scarecrows move
> Along the side-fall of the hill—Maguire and his men.
> . . . .
> Here crows gabble over worms and frogs
> And the gulls like old newspapers are blown clear of the hedges, luckily.
> (*Complete Poems* 79–80)

Of course, although many of the interrelated social ills—late marriages, sexual repression, poverty of purse and of spirit[2]—that Kavanagh registers in his poem may be traced to the aftermath of the Famine, to the deep psychological scars left by the endemic multiple trauma of death, disease, emigration, and despair, his title actually refers most immediately to the great sexual hunger suffered in the 1930s and '40s by bachelor farmers like Patrick Maguire, the central figure of "The Great Hunger." Thus, despite the obvious extent to which each poet engages with the same question that Tom Murphy asked as he worked on his play *Famine* in 1968—"Was I, in what I shall call my times, the mid-twentieth century, a student or a victim of the Famine?"(xi)—Kavanagh's themes remain more latent than active in Heaney's poem.

Hardly gratuitous, however, Heaney's oblique glance at Kavanagh's poem reflects the complex sense of literary kinship that Heaney feels toward his fellow Ulster poet.[3] "Kavanagh gave you permission to dwell without cultural anxiety among the usual landmarks of your life," Heaney acknowledged, recollecting specifically his first reading of "The Great Hunger" in 1962 ("Placeless Heaven" 9). In part, the kinship implicit in the echoing of "The Great Hunger" in "At a Potato Digging" is defined by the necessity that each poet perceives, and responds to in his individual way, of contesting the romanticized image of the rural Irish laborer preserved in a poem like Padraic Colum's "The Plougher," from his volume *Wild Earth* (1907): "the brute-tamer stands by the brutes, a head's breadth only above them" (*Poems* 80). In fact, it entails a virtually iconoclastic challenge to the conventional depiction of rural life in the Irish literary tradition.

Perhaps not surprisingly, a second "literary" dimension of "At a Potato Digging" involves Heaney's reworking, in the third section of his poem, details of the Famine culled from the major historical account available in the 1960s, Cecil Woodham-Smith's book (coincidentally sharing the title of Kavanagh's poem) *The Great Hunger*. Describing how in 1845 "The new potato, sound as stone, / putrefied when it had lain / three days in the long clay pit," how "Stinking potatoes fouled the land, / pits turned pus into filthy mounds," Heaney is clearly indebted to

Woodham-Smith's graphic account of the insidious nature of the potato blight:

> The soundness of the potato when first dug was responsible for bewildering contradictions. Optimists, delighted to witness the digging of what seemed a splendid crop, hastened to send off glowing accounts. . . .
>
> In almost every case, hope was short-lived. Within a few days the fine-looking tubers had become a stinking mass of corruption. . . .
>
> All specifics, all nostrums were useless. Whether ventilated, dessicated, salted, or gassed, the potatoes melted into a slimy, decaying mass; and pits, on being opened, were found to be filled with diseased potatoes. (43–44, 47)

Shortly, beginning with "The Tollund Man" in his volume *Wintering Out* (1972) and then in poem after poem in *North* (1975), Heaney would find in P. V. Glob's *The Bog People* "images and symbols adequate to our predicament" ("Feeling into Words" 56)—that predicament being the politically charged sectarian violence of contemporary Northern Ireland. His use of Woodham-Smith's book to recuperate the distant past similarly lends a more "learned, literate and conscious" and a less "lived, illiterate and unconscious" affect (or at least effect) to "At a Potato Digging."

Certainly the poem's self-conscious construction is intended expressly to provide "restoration of the culture to itself" through Heaney's "digging" into—his uncovering or discovering—the deep imprint that the Famine has made on the Irish psyche (the rural psyche specifically, but clearly with wider implications). "[W]here potato diggers are / you still smell the running sore," Heaney believes, finding even in the apparent obliviousness of latter-day potato diggers laboring atavistically in the field residual signs—or symbols—of a psychological, sociological, economic, and cultural continuum that both pre-dates and post-dates the famine of the late 1840s. For Heaney, the "higgledy line" of the potato diggers in the first section anticipates poetically but follows historically the "higgledy skeletons" of those who "scoured the land in 'forty-five, / wolfed the blighted root and died." Likewise, compared to "crows attacking crow-black fields" in the first section, the diggers evoke their ancestors' "faces chilled to a plucked bird," and the "Wicker creels" used to collect the potatoes recall the clay-walled "million wicker huts" where "beaks of famine snipped at guts."

Of course, the crucial image of the poem is that of the seemingly healthy potatoes at the end of section two, "live skulls, blind-eyed," that metamorphose into those "Live skulls, blind-eyed, balanced on higgledy skeletons" at the beginning of section three. Presenting with an utter lack of irony and to an unwonted extreme the notion that *we are what we eat*, Heaney inscribes a startlingly graphic identification of the Irish people with the crop that could as easily spell death and despair as health and prosperity. Ultimately, Heaney observes, his latter-day potato diggers reenact—unknowingly but significantly nonetheless—a ritual engagement with the land, with the rich "black / Mother" who in her fickleness is also "the bitch earth." Making "a seasonal altar of the sod"—that "faithless ground"—partaking of a secular communion of "Brown bread and tea" that ends with the crusts scattered and the tea spilled, they unwittingly create a tableau vivant of the "Millions [who] rotted" with the potatoes "in the long clay pit": "Dead-beat, they flop / Down in the ditch. . . ."

f

Yet, despite—or perhaps because of—such a studied verbal texture to the poem, an intricate warp and weft of motif and theme, Seamus Heaney himself has come to think of "At a Potato Digging" as anomalous within his body of poetry, choosing to omit it not only from *Selected Poems, 1966–1987* but also from the almost-comprehensive *Opened Ground: Poems, 1966–1996* (he had included it in *Poems: 1965–1975*). Perhaps to his mind the poem fails to strike the crucial balance between artifice and artificiality inherent in every form of symbolic art, as at least one influential critic, Edna Longley, has complained of how "a rather awkward metamorphosis changes potatoes as 'live skulls, blind-eyed' into the real thing" (142–43). Perhaps Heaney came to doubt the efficacy of the transparent rhetorical strategies of allusion and intertextual indebtedness. Perhaps, its lack of place specificity making it (especially in light of its literally "grounded" subject matter) such an uncharacteristic Heaney poem, "At a Potato Digging" fails most of all to satisfy the author's expectation, articulated in *The Place of Writing*, of how poets most persuasively engage with place. Deriving metaphors from "the old schoolbook definition" of *work*—"To work is to move a certain mass through a certain distance" (36)—and from Archimedes' claim that "he could move the world if he could find the right place to position his lever" (19), Heaney explains:

In the case of poetry, the distance moved through is that which separates the historically and topographically situated place from the written place, the mass moved is one of the writer's historical/biographical experience, and each becomes a factor of the other in the achieved work. The work of art, in other words, involves raising the historical record to a different power. (36)

Ironically, however, if devaluing "At a Potato Digging" on those interrelated grounds, Heaney may be overlooking the poem's remarkable affinity with the very aspect of Yeats's Ballylee poems that he so admires. For, uncharacteristic or not within Heaney's *oeuvre*, as a four-section poem with each section conspicuously employing a different poetic form, "At a Potato Digging" ultimately inscribes a sense of place in which, like Yeats's tower poems, "utterance and being are synonymous."

In his essay "Feeling into Words," Heaney worries about an overvaluing of form—of mere poetic "craft"—in poems: "Craft is the skill of making. It wins competitions in the *Irish Times* or the *New Statesman*" (47). Yet as Paul Fussell observes in his masterful book *Poetic Meter and Poetic Form*, "One of the foremost reasons for a poem's powers of endurance is its structural integrity, the sort of logical accommodation of statement to form, of elements to wholes," continuing:

> Although successful poems do not always inhabit a world of logic, their forms do; and just as the world of logic is constructed from immutable propositions, so those elements of poems which belong to that world partake of immutability. Like the forms of geometry or music, the forms of poetry . . . attach the art of poetry to a permanent world—that is, they effect this attachment if they are sufficiently logical, economical, and organic. (172)

While not flawlessly executed (occasionally, the demands of end rhyme thwart line integrity and result in awkward enjambment both within and between stanzas), the formal properties of "At a Potato Digging" still contribute substantially to the enduring quality of the poem.

For example, while seeming to record with documentary objectivity a latter-day potato digging, the opening section of the poem yet invites, by virtue of particular associations with its form, an almost subliminal awareness on the part of the reader of the somberly resonant implications of this annual task. As Fussell notes, part of the poet's "work" involves "knowing the prosodic conventions and . . . manipulating them so as to induce appropriate responses and illusions in an audience that knows them too" (176). Thus, written in so-called elegiac quatrains—stanzas of four iambic pentameter lines rhymed *abab*—the first section of Heaney's poem becomes intrinsically linked to at least two poems that lend the form its name: Thomas Gray's "Elegy Written in a Country Churchyard" and William Wordsworth's "Elegiac Stanzas Suggested by a Picture of Peele Castle, in a Storm, Painted by Sir George Beaumont." Writing in 1750, Gray established in the opening stanza of his poem the sobering tone and the ominous thematic weight that would become inevitably associated with the form:

> The curfew tolls the knell of parting day,
>   The lowing herd wind slowly o'er the lea,
> The ploughman homeward plods his weary way,
>   And leaves the world to darkness and to me. (37)

A little more than a half-century later, Wordsworth, lamenting the loss of his beloved brother, would write of the consequent loss of "steadfast peace":

> So once it would have been,—'tis no more;
> I have submitted to a new control:
> A power is gone, which nothing can restore;
> A deep distress hath humanised my Soul. (168)

Employing this same form, Heaney reinforces the section's thematic emphasis on how a common activity performed so "mindlessly" can have embedded in it the seeds of "darkness" and "deep distress."

The form of the second section of the poem likewise comments on its thematic content. Describing how "Good smells exude from crumbled earth" at a potato digging, this section seems to disregard the threat present in section one:

> The rough bark of humus erupts
> knots of potatoes (a clean birth)
> whose solid feel, whose wet inside
> promises taste of ground and root.

Containing this promise, however, in a recognizably deformed sonnet, Heaney not only questions but also truly undercuts the naïve optimism engendered by a healthy-looking potato harvest. Truncated to thirteen lines from the sonnet's standard fourteen lines (the lines too are truncated, most to eight syllables from the sonnet's conventional ten-syllable iambic pentameter impulse) and with only occasional rhyme, this "sonnet" anticipates by way of the "decomposition" of its form the revisiting of the horrors of the Great Hunger of the 1840s in the poem's third section.

In fact, exemplifying Fussell's principle that "separate and different shapes should embody separate and different things" (155), the third section of "At a Potato Digging," recording in graphic detail how

"Mouths tightened in" and "Hope rotted like marrow" in 1845, employs tightly compacted quatrains composed of off-rhymed couplets (*aabb*):

> Live skulls, blind-eyed, balanced on
> wild higgledy skeletons
> scoured the land in 'forty-five,
> wolfed the blighted root and died.

Featuring irregular line length, these stanzas seem as dubious—as inherently corrupt—as the blight-infected potatoes that so betrayed the Irish people in the 1840s. Appropriately, then, while returning writer and reader to the present, the fourth section of the poem adopts loose long measure quatrains (iambic tetrameter, *abab*) which yet come up a metrical foot short ("The rhythm deadens") of returning to the opening form. Having unearthed the true darkness that underlies a potato digging in the Irish context, Heaney could hardly justify restoring even the deceptive regularity of the iambic pentameter lines of the opening section.

In "The Makings of a Music," an essay comparing the "feeling into words" (as it were) of William Wordsworth and W. B. Yeats, Heaney observes of the latter: "In Yeats, the voice muscles its way over the obstacle course of the form and flexes like an animated vine on the trellis of its metric and rhyme scheme. We are aware of the finished poem as an impressive thing in itself but somehow more impressive because of a threshold of difficulties now overcome" (73–74). Perhaps more Wordsworthian himself—more inclined to author a verbal music of period and stanza that is "hypnotic, swimming with the current of its form rather than against it" (61)—Heaney has nonetheless flexed his voice in Yeatsian fashion in helping to break the great silence that had buried the Great Famine beneath the surface of Irish memory for more than a century. In effect bringing his readers *to* a potato digging in "At a Potato Digging" through what he has referred to as "the firmness and in-placeness and undislodgeableness of poetic form" (*Place of Writing* 32), Heaney truly brings into "being" "a place that was nowhere until it was a written place" (32).

Notes

   1. All quotations from "At a Potato Digging" refer to the version published in Seamus Heaney, *Death of a Naturalist* (New York: Oxford Univ. Press, 1966), 31–33.

   2. Playwright Tom Murphy catalogues such ills thus: "A hungry and demoralised people becomes silent. People emigrate in great numbers and leave spaces that cannot be filled. Intelligence becomes cunning. There is a poverty

of thought and expression. Womanhood becomes harsh. Love, tenderness, loyalty, generosity go out the door in the struggle for survival. Men fester in vicarious dreams of destruction. The natural exuberance and extravagance of youth is repressed." (xi)

3. For a detailed discussion of this kinship, see my essay "'At a Potato Digging': Seamus Heaney's *Great Hunger*," *The Canadian Journal of Irish Studies* 16.1 (July 1990): 48–58.

Works Cited

Colum, Padraic. *Poems*. New York: Macmillan, 1932.

Fussell, Paul. *Poetic Meter and Poetic Form*. New York: Random House, 1979.

Gray, Thomas. "Elegy Written in a Country Churchyard." *The Complete Poems of Thomas Gray*. Ed. H. W. Starr and J. R. Hendrickson. Oxford: Clarendon, 1966. 37–43.

Heaney, Seamus. "At a Potato Digging." *Death of a Naturalist*. 31–33.

---. *Death of a Naturalist*. New York: Oxford Univ. Press, 1966.

---. "Digging." *Death of a Naturalist*. 13–14.

---. "Feeling into Words." *Preoccupations*. 41–60.

---. "The Makings of a Music." *Preoccupations*. 61–78.

---. "The Placeless Heaven: Another Look at Kavanagh." *The Government of the Tongue: Selected Prose, 1978–1987*. New York: Farrar, 1989. 3–14.

---. *The Place of Writing*. Atlanta: Scholars, 1989.

---. *Preoccupations: Selected Prose 1968–1978*. New York: Farrar, 1980.

---. "The Sense of Place." *Preoccupations*. 131–49.

Kavanagh, Patrick. "The Great Hunger." *The Complete Poems*. Ed. Peter Kavanagh. Newbridge: Goldsmith, 1984. 79–104.

Longley, Edna. "'Inner Emigré' or 'Artful Voyeur'? Seamus Heaney's *North*." *Poetry in the Wars*. Newark: Univ. of Delaware Press, 1987. 140–69.

Murphy, Tom. Introduction. *Plays: One*. London: Methuen, 1992. ix–xxi.

O'Grady, Thomas. "'At a Potato Digging': Seamus Heaney's *Great Hunger*." *The Canadian Journal of Irish Studies* 16.1 (July 1990): 48–58.

Woodham-Smith, Cecil. *The Great Hunger: Ireland, 1845–1849*. New York: Harper, 1962.

Wordsworth, William. "Elegiac Stanzas Suggested by a Picture of Peele Castle, in a Storm, Painted by Sir George Beaumont." *The Essential Wordsworth*. Sel. and Intro. Seamus Heaney. New York: Ecco, 1988. 166–68.

Chapter Eight

Easing Integration:
The Impact of the Great Famine on the American South

DAVID T. GLEESON

Many Irish men and women who fled the Famine to migrate to the United States carried a psychological legacy with them. They were scarred by the horrific conditions they had experienced or witnessed in Ireland. A number of them blamed the British government for the disaster. Others felt it was the wrath of God, while many may have felt guilty about abandoning their homes and families.[1] This baggage they carried was exacerbated by the conditions many of them encountered upon reaching the New World. Whether they found the horrors of Grosse Île or life in a city slum, it is no wonder that Irish immigrants longed for home.[2] Those who came to the American South must have felt the pangs of dislocation even more than their compatriots farther north. Its climate and slavery—its "peculiar institution"—were particularly jarring. The arrival of these immigrants was equally jarring for many natives. The Famine Irish in the South created the same social problems they did in other parts of the United States. Many native southerners believed in the stereotype of the "drunken, riotous Paddy," and as the jails, poorhouses, and asylums grew close to the bursting point, the negative image of the Irish only increased. Some Irish already living and prospering in the region feared that their own acceptance would be threatened. One William Hill, for example, a Scots-Irish settler in Abbeville, South Carolina, wrote that he resented the "ignorant, unpolished, and uncivilized . . . rowdy class of Irish in this little town and neighborhood, mostly of the *Real Irish,* or papist stock." He worried that "*untravelled* [sic] Americans" thought that this "poor sample" of the Irish in America represented all Irish people.[3] Thus, when weighing the Famine experience it seems that it had an overwhelmingly negative impact on the position of all Irish in America.

However, upon closer inspection of the Irish experience in the American South, a different reality emerges. Here, the impact of the Famine ultimately aided rather than hindered Irish integration into the native society. Yes, the Irish in the South were cut from the same cloth as the Irish elsewhere. They did feel like exiles, and they did suffer as well as cause many problems in the urban South. Nevertheless, the Famine helped solidify the Irish community and make natives sympathetic to Irish woes. More important, both natives and immigrants began to see political parallels between their respective experiences. From this realization, both sides could find common ground and join together in struggling against overpowerful, centralized, distant, and bourgeois governments with values contrary to their own. To put it succinctly in the words of John Mitchel, a southern partisan and the greatest purveyor of the charge that the Famine was an act of British genocide, Ireland and the South had similar political problems and the only solution as Mitchel saw it for both places was "*Repeal of the Union.*"[4]

Who were the Irish in the South? The eleven states that became the Confederate States of America in 1861 contained only 10 percent of the Irish-born people in the United States. Only Louisiana had an Irish population higher than 2 percent of its total. These small figures hide the true significance of the Irish presence because the immigrants in the South settled primarily in towns. By concentrating their numbers, they became much more visible. New Orleans had a large Irish population. Although in other cities absolute Irish numbers were low, they made up large proportions of the population. For example, Memphis had only 4,159 Irish residents in 1860, but the Irish represented more than 22 percent of its white population. Savannah, similarly, had only 3,145 Irish in 1860, also representing more than 22 percent of its white population. New Orleans' 24,000 Irish, the largest enclave in the deep South, made up nearly 17 percent of that city's white population in 1860.[5] While the Irish in the South mostly labored, they worked in all occupations. They initiated ethnic societies, formed churches, and created vibrant Irish communities. They were a very visible and active minority in southern towns. One could not have visited a town in the Old South without noticing them. They were indeed strangers who had to integrate into southern society.[6]

The pre-Famine Irish already in the South helped their fellow strangers adjust. They actually used the trauma of the Famine to build an Irish political coalition across class lines. A number of pre-Famine Irish had prospered and formed elite Hibernian societies throughout the South.[7] These societies provided the political leadership for the quickly burgeoning Irish immigrant communities in southern towns. The leaders' negative reaction to the Famine and British rule in Ireland gave them credibility among their poorer fellow compatriots fleeing the Famine. Therefore, both in Irish and American political efforts, Irish immigrants displayed a remarkable unity. While the Famine itself still raged in Ireland, elite Irish formed and lead organizations in support of such nationalist groups as Young Ireland. More important for their cause, they were able raise money from the growing Famine-Irish population in the region. Excited at the prospect of revolution in Ireland, some leading Irish in New Orleans, for example, founded the new Irish League and Emmet Club to support an uprising against Britain in 1848. They raised more than one thousand pounds from all sections of their community to send to the leader of Young Ireland, William Smith O'Brien (Niehaus 151–52). In Mobile, the organizers of "The Friends of Ireland" believed that the European revolutions showed the way for the Irish in Ireland "to redeem their country from the evils of the British Union." With both Catholic and Protestant leadership, the new group raised money from Irish and native citizens to help Ireland gain "political independence and republican rights." They encouraged native Alabamians to help because "[t]he country of Washington owes a large debt of gratitude to Ireland." In Charleston some leading native-born citizens played prominent roles in the organizing of its "Association of the Friends of Irish Independence." The sixty-plus ward organizers for the association, however, were more likely to have names such as Hogan, Ryan, and O'Neill than surnames from among Carolina's first Irish families.[8]

In American politics the Famine Irish, like their immigrant predecessors, found a home in the Democratic Party. In New Orleans, the Irish-controlled uptown third-ward Democrats had been a force in the city's politics before the Famine. Here the old elite Irish attended St. Patrick's Church and used the votes of the new immigrants to become the leading force in the city's Democratic Party in the 1850s. Irish leadership and votes helped the Democrats take control of the usually Whig city in 1853 (Niehaus 80–81, 84–85). In predominantly Whig towns such as Natchez and Vicksburg, Mississippi, and

Nashville, Tennessee, the Irish formed the backbone of the Democratic vote.[9] In Memphis, the rapid growth of the Irish population gave local Democrats a voting bloc, much to the annoyance of local Whigs. In Savannah, the Irish were also solid Democrats. (Capers 108, 114; Shoemaker 343–45). Irish leaders in these cities gained positions on city councils on the backs of universal white male suffrage and the ever-increasing Famine-Irish vote. The Famine Irish gained too. Because the Democrats had control of federal patronage after 1845, they appointed all classes of Irish men to federal posts in cities throughout the South. They similarly provided Irish men with public jobs, particularly on the police force in Democratic-controlled cities.[10] During the nativist "Know-Nothing" challenge of the 1850s, all classes of Irish rallied to the Democratic party. This unity in the face of Know-Nothing opposition ultimately helped destroy the organized nativism in the South (D. Gleeson, *Irish* 107-20).

Irish immigrants benefited from uniting across class lines in southern politics to form an ethnic bloc. Of course, the Irish were still a minority in southern cities and could be seen as just the pawns of native-born political leaders. On some occasions they were exploited in this way, but voting as a bloc provided more positives than negatives. Public jobs were vital to many Famine immigrants' survival. For example, when ex-policeman Michael Gleeson of Charleston wrote to invite his father to join him there in 1857 rather than "perishing" in the North, he felt sure he could give the older man his own job because he knew that he could go "back to the police any time." With a Democrat mayor, who owed his position to Irish votes and who was a friend of the leading Hibernians in the city, Gleeson's confidence was well warranted. He had learned quickly the political ways of his more elevated predecessors.[11] Thus, the Famine gave the existing Irish leadership credibility among the new immigrants. The elite Irish had shown the way by integrating themselves into the American political scene, and they were right. Pre-Famine and Famine immigrants could unite in opposition to British rule in Ireland. Both groups, for the most part, could also unite under the banner of the welcoming Democratic Party. The whole Famine experience helped ethnicity trump class in the Irish communities of the Old South.

The added impact of the Famine on integration was the impression it made on native southerners who even before the catastrophe may not have had a very positive view of the Irish. As in the rest of the country, Irish stereotypes could stimulate "preadjustive behavior" among southerners, and "suggest to [them] what to expect of stereotype targets and incline them to respond in an appropriate way" (Knobel 103). One southern planter, for example, thought the Irish very similar to his slaves "and instanced their subserviency, their flattering, their lying, and pilfering, as traits common to the characters of both peoples" (a Mr. C[ouper], quoted in Scott 322). A southern woman complained that an "insolent" Irish woman working for her sister "refused to wash the children's clothes." This washerwoman "walked out" and called her employer "a *common* mean hearted *thief*," thus leaving a very unfavorable impression of her nationality.[12] Irish stereotypes could even influence children. On a trip to Europe, one southern woman's daughter "was sure she should not speak to one of them," that is, poor Irish children in steerage. After a few days, however, she weakened and went "on deck to look after her dirty little protégées."[13]

A more serious threat for Irish integration came from some southerners' fear of Irish participation in southern politics. Prominent Charlestonian Christopher Memminger felt that white workers, and foreign workers in particular, were "the only party from which danger to our institutions is to be apprehended among us." These workers who were increasingly replacing "negro mechanics . . . would soon raise the hue and cry against the Negro, and be hot abolitionists—and every one of those men would have a vote" (qtd. in Jordan 225). Upset at the militancy of Irish labor, many southern businessmen supported Memminger's view. For example, in Savannah, striking Irish longshoremen forced local merchants to try and "disperse altogether with this foreign aid, and employ slave labor in their stead" (qtd. in Siegel 227–28). After secession in 1860 and 1861, a number of prominent former unionists upset at the radical act of secession proposed disfranchising poor whites to prevent "revolution" (Siegel 221; Johnson 97–101). The perceived closeness between free blacks and Irish men also created fear for southern leaders. Many pro-slavery advocates saw free blacks as "fifth-column" abolitionists. The fact that Irish men and free blacks often lived in the same neighborhoods, worked the same jobs, and drank in the same "grog shops," persuaded some southerners that perhaps the Irish were also part of this fifth column. The occasional Irishman's proclamation of himself as an "abolitionist" only increased this fear.[14]

The Famine-induced influx it seems severely handicapped any Irish attempts to fit into the South. Yet, the Irish did survive and manage to form vibrant ethnic communities in the region. They did not curtail their involvement in southern politics, nor did scared natives succeed in any efforts to disfranchise the Irish.[15] Ironically, the Famine, which had initially exacerbated negative images of the Irish in the South and increased native fears, in the long term helped the Irish gain native acceptance. Many southerners were shocked by the news of the Famine in Ireland. They could not believe that one of the richest nations in the world, from which many of their ancestors had come, could allow this catastrophe to happen. They did what they could to help. In Sumter District, in rural South Carolina, for example, more than a hundred prominent men petitioned their General Assembly to send official aid to Ireland. They hoped that their "chivalrous State" would help alleviate "the condition of the peasantry" and the "despair [which] sits on the countenance of their stout hearts."[16] Unfortunately, the General Assembly did not support the petition because it was "the duty of every nation to support its own poor and to relieve the suffering of its people."[17] The Sumter petitioners were probably naive to expect state government aid for a foreign country, but these southerners had real fears for the fate of the Irish people.

Throughout the South, natives were concerned about the starving Irish. The relief effort in Mississippi was typical. On 17 February 1847, news of serious problems in Ireland hit the Magnolia state through the columns of the *Natchez Mississippi Free Trader*. The *Free Trader* appealed for ideas to help assuage the plight of "the starving Irish." That week, the people of Natchez answered its plea. They met on 20 February in the Mansion House hotel and responded positively to the mayor's suggestion that a committee be established to collect money for a relief ship to Ireland. At the meeting, prominent citizens heaped lavish praise on Ireland. One Samuel Cartwright told the attendees that "our free and happy land was watered by the blood of Ireland's sons— unless it had been thus watered[,] it in all probability never would have been free." He denied that the Irish were against "our Southern institutions," and he hoped that Natchez would see its contributions to Ireland as "paying a debt." A local planter, John B. Nevitt, asked his fellow citizens to give generously to help that "gem of the ocean . . . the green Isle of Erin." The meeting concluded with supportive messages from other towns in the locality.[18]

This initial committee expanded on 5 March into a regional committee to include the surrounding Adams County and Concordia Parish across the Mississippi River in Louisiana. On this occasion, the passionate speech making fell to prominent Mississippian Colonel F. L. Claiborne. Like his predecessors, he praised Ireland and its people, especially those who had come to the United States. By 17 March, the committee had collected more than $1,300, which included large contributions from local Protestant congregations. Later that year, the British ambassador to the United States thanked the people of Natchez for their altruism on behalf of the Irish people.[19]

Other Mississippi towns followed Natchez's lead. The citizens of Jackson met on 28 February "to consider the destitution of the peasantry of Ireland." Future governor and noted southern nationalist,

Albert Gallatin Brown, chaired the crowded meeting at which Mississippians extolled the virtues of the Irish and solicited aid to help them in their hour of need. The attendees appointed a committee of five to solicit contributions "from our citizens generally." The reporter was confident that his fellow "Jacksonians" would "confirm and strengthen [themselves] in their benevolent solicitude for suffering humanity." Within two weeks, they had collected $444.50 and sent it to New Orleans to purchase food. The committee was sure that at least another $100 "would be in by next mail" and more would come from collections taken up by the citizens of Woodville and Vicksburg.[20]

One of Mississippi's leading politicians took the campaign for the Irish to other states. Sergeant S. Prentiss, a recent victim of an Irish newspaper editor's vicious personal attacks, did not harbor bitterness toward the partisan's homeland or compatriots. On the contrary, during a visit to New Orleans in February 1847, the "Whig orator of the Old South," as his biographer described him, made "one of the greatest occasional speeches of his life." The nationally prominent Henry Clay and his fellow Whigs in the audience listened "spellbound" for an hour to Prentiss's "sublime" oratory. Prentiss stated that the Emerald Isle had "given to the world more than its share of genius." Ireland also had "been prolific in statesmen, warriors, and poets. Its brave and generous sons [had] fought successfully all battles but their own." He then described how "gaunt and ghastly famine [had] seized a nation with its struggling grasp," and he continued to prick the consciences of his listeners by emphasizing the horrors of an enemy "more cruel than the Turk, more tyrannical than the Russian." "Bread" could only stop famine, he declared. To ensure that contributions would be forthcoming, Prentiss concluded by telling his audience to return home and "look at your family, smiling, in rosy health, and then think of the pale, famine pinched cheeks of the poor children of Ireland." If they did that, he was sure they would "give according to [their] store, even as bountiful Providence was given to [them]—not grudgingly, but with an open hand" (Dickey 299–302).

This rhetoric, with descriptions such as "genius" and "brave and generous sons," from a politician whose party had a strained relationship with the Irish was remarkable. Only three years earlier, Henry Clay had lost Louisiana in the presidential election because a group of Irish New Orleanians had voted early and often for his opponent (Niehaus 80–81, 84–85; Holt 203). What a boost of confidence for Irish immigrants used to being described as drunken rowdy pauper criminals. This native southern effort on their country's behalf impressed large numbers of them. One P. Kennedy, for example, a railroad laborer working in southwestern Virginia in the 1850s, in a letter defended southern planters and complained about "Yankees" who went to Europe "to make money . . . complain about slavery and stir up English ladies," because Kennedy believed "the slave in Virginia is better fed and clothed than the poor Irish farmers." "[O]h, it would be well," he added, "for the Irish labourer if he was [sic] half as well fed and taken care off [sic] as the slaves [whose] master has an interest in the slave." P. Kennedy continued, "there may be a few bad masters, but compare the conduct of bad masters with the conduct of *Irish Land Lords* who will drive out [their] Tenant[s] on the road side to starve," and nobody, he thought, could justifiably condemn southern slavery.[21] According to Kennedy southern planters were far superior to Irish landlords.

Of course, the most articulate admirer of southern paternalism was John Mitchel. After his deportation in 1848, he contrasted it sharply with the callousness of the British government and Anglo-Irish landlords. As early as 1849, he had compared the plight of Irish peasants unfavorably with that of black slaves. His newspaper the *Southern Citizen,* founded in Knoxville, Tennessee, in 1857, thus had a strong pro-southern as well as a pro-Irish bent.[22] Although Irish people throughout America read the *Southern Citizen*, it remained the voice of the Irish in the South, with agents selling it in every southern town that had a large Irish populace.[23] Even Irish men in more remote parts of the region, who could not purchase the paper easily, received it from Irish friends.[24] Mitchel's paper undoubtedly impressed Irish men with sentiments such as Ulster migrant Robert McElderry of Virginia, who defended Mitchel's "intense hatred of the English government," because McElderry believed hatred was "a feeling which ought to pervade the breast of every Irishman." This loathing was justified because the British government despised "Ireland and the Irish with a perfect hatred." McElderry lamented the divisions between Catholics and Protestants, which kept the Irish as "abject slaves."[25] He did not, however, oppose slavery in the South. He felt that the image in Europe of "the slave driver cracking his whip and in every way one can imagine torturing human beings because they happen to be of a different color from their masters" was a false one. On the contrary, McElderry wrote, "if you only want to see a happy and contented lot of creatures, you should see a number of slaves after the days work is done and hear them play the banjo and see their dances."[26] McElderry's younger brother William echoed him by protesting that slaves "go about dressed in the very best . . . and sometimes make in a week 10 or 12 [dollars] and they have that to themselves." Although he had "seen some of them whipped," William believed that those who were had "deserved it."[27] The bitterness that Irish immigrants had toward the

British government, the Union, and Irish landlords and the contrast they saw between them and southern planters who allowed the Irish immigrants to live, work, worship, and vote in the South, blinded them to the horrors of southern slavery. They, like Mitchel, could paradoxically be strong advocates of Irish freedom while simultaneously supporting the enslavement of African Americans.

The Irish recognized that southerners had a different worldview from their northern compatriots. Southern propagandists, including the famous Virginia slavery apologist George Fitzhugh, supported slavery because, as historian Eugene Genovese suggests, they saw that: "Wherever capitalism has triumphed, the family has been undermined and all community has perished. Virtually alone the cash nexus rules the bourgeoisie world. The vehicle carrying the bourgeoisie to power has been the world market which it brought into being. Within the marketplace the strong crush the weak, the gifted rob the simple, and all are degraded in the process" (*World the Slaveholders Made* 231). Witnesses to the Irish Famine would have found it hard to disagree with this view. Indeed, Southerners such as Fitzhugh used Ireland's experience as a weapon in their fight against northern bourgeois capitalism. He saw capitalistic competition as a version of war that pitted the strong against the weak. In his 1854 work *Sociology for the South or the Failure of Free Society,* Fitzhugh used the imposition of free trade on Ireland by the British Parliament as a classic example of the exploitative nature of capitalism. He wrote:

> Free trade between England and Ireland furnishes the latter an excellent market for her beef and potatoes, in exchange for English manufactures. The labor employed in manufacturing pays much better than that engaged in rearing beeves and potatoes. . . . Again manufacturing requires and encourages skill and intelligence; grazing and farming none. But far the worst evils of this free trade remain to be told. Irish pursuits depressing education and refinement, England becomes a market for the wealth, the intellect, the talent, energy and enterprise of Ireland. All men possessing any of these advantages or qualities retreat to England to spend their incomes, to enter the church, the navy, or the army, to distinguish themselves as authors, to engage in mechanic or manufacturing pursuits. Thus is Ireland robbed of her very life's blood, and thus do our Northern States rob the Southern.

He feared that the "universal absenteeism" he saw in Ireland would also occur in the South (Wish 51).

Fitzhugh implied that slavery was good for all poor people. This position would not have impressed the mostly non-slaveholding poor

Irish, or indeed the majority of white southerners who also did not own slaves. He, however, backed away from this dangerous stance by stating, "We need never have white slaves in the South, because we have black ones. Our citizens," and here he did not distinguish between native and naturalized, "like those of Rome and Athens, are a privileged class." Fitzhugh went on to argue for education for poor whites so that the South would "soon be independent from the North" (Wish 94–95). These pro-welfare sentiments along with Fitzhugh's admiration for Roman Catholicism and his statement that southerners "abhor the doctrine of the 'Types of Mankind,'" would have made him acceptable to most Irish immigrants in the South and, indeed, the rest of the United States (Wish 93, 95; Genovese, *World the Slaveholders Made* 191–93).

While other Old South apologists were not as bothered in defending "[s]lavery in the abstract" they too criticized Britain's treatment of its own poor. They pointed out, for example, that "never did a slave starve in America," and that "[a]gents are always more unfeeling than owners whether placed over West Indian or American slaves or Irish tenants" (James Henry Hammond qtd. in Faust 172, 189, 196). Simultaneously, the southern partisans still believed in material progress, republican government, and for the most part, universal white male suffrage. Their problem was that they did not want these positive advances at the expense of community norms and relations. A more recent apologist for these Old South leaders summed them up thus: "Neither were they high Tory champions of an aristocratic regime on the continental European model. Community was their ideal–an informally hierarchical social organism in which all Southerners (including the Negro insofar as the survival of the community permitted) had a sense of investment and participation."[28] For many Irish immigrants in search of a new community, having seen their old one either personally or "transatlantically" sacrificed on the altar of evangelical and laissez faire individualism, this southern philosophy based on a paternalistic communalism was much easier to absorb than one that espoused an atomistic "every man for himself" ideal.

It could be argued, however, that Irish immigrants in the antebellum South were oblivious to this anticapitalist argument. Many did not have time did to keep up with the theories and propaganda of slavery, unless they read Mitchel's *Southern Citizen,* because they were too busy trying to make a living in their new world.[29] Nevertheless, there is some evidence that this "pre-capitalist" or "anticapitalist view" paternalist ideology did permeate down through southern society and into Irish communities. This permeation can be particularly observed among the minority of the Irish who managed to acquire slaves. Famine migrant Patrick Murphy, who immigrated to New Orleans and eventually settled near Natchez, Mississippi, managed to purchase some slaves in the 1850s. He had started his American life as a skilled artisan but became a contractor from which he acquired some wealth. He bought slaves as an investment and rented them out to local businesses. On one occasion, Murphy felt "sorry" for one "poor Neville" who had gotten into a fight with "Winston." He felt sorry for the bondsman because he knew he had to whip him for behaving "so stupidly." Murphy administered the whipping himself.[30] Punishment was a key element of being an efficient paternalistic slaveholder, but one had to see it as a burden more than a pleasure. There is a certain parental exacerbation in Murphy's tone, and he implies that he punished "poor Neville" for his own good, just as one would punish a child. Most native slave owners would have recognized a commonality of sentiment between themselves and this Irishman and would have seen the foreign Murphy more as a colleague than a stranger.[31]

Other Irish men recognized the more positive elements of southern paternalism from their own personal experience of the South. John McFarland, a County Tyrone native who had come to the South six years before the Famine, but like many Famine migrants arrived, as he put it, "a stranger and penniless youth," was grateful for southern paternalism. He survived and actually prospered in the South during the 1840s and 1850s. He had achieved material and personal success in large part because he "was taken by the hand by southerners, they have been kind to me."[32] John Mitchel was very impressed with the southern hospitality he encountered on an 1858 trip down the Mississippi River to New Orleans. On the journey, Mitchel noticed many "southern gentlemen" who were "men of refined and dignified manners, with that gentle tone of voice and courtesy of demeanor which are characteristic of the South, and which I attribute to the institution of slavery." During a stop in Natchez, he befriended Giles Hillyer, a former Know-Nothing candidate for Congress, and found the newspaper editor "an agreeable companion." Stunned to learn that Hillyer had been a member of the American Party, Mitchel contrasted his southern gentility with northern rudeness.[33] This "kindness" shown by southerners contrasted sharply with the Irish treatment at the hands of Irish landlords and their reception in the northern states. Irish journalist Dennis Corcoran of New Orleans expressed both contemporary and future Irish opinion in the Old South when, in 1843, he chastised Daniel O'Connell for condemning southern slaveholders. He was particularly concerned at O'Connell's attacks because he feared they would alienate "the slaveholders of the South—who received us among them with a liberality, and extended to us a hospitality which it is fair to presume would not be extended to us in the Eastern States, where prejudice against Irishmen and bigotry against their religion seem indigenous qualities."[34] Thus, both the Irish and native Southerners saw a great distinction between the social and economic values of the northern worldview and the southern one that, although based on slavery, seemed to be more "civilized" than the one North of the Mason-Dixon line.

Along with recognizing the common economic, social, and cultural dangers of a capitalist "new world," native southerners also saw political dangers.[35] Again, Ireland provided uncomfortable images of the future. In particular, many southerners saw the Famine as a warning with regard to their own relationship with a powerful central government. One Joseph Lesesne of Mobile, for example, wrote in 1847 complaining about the unfair economic burdens of the American Union on the South. He believed that the South was a colony of the commercial and industrial interest of the North. He stated that "the commercial privileges given by the Constitution to these people [northerners] has wholly deprived us of a mercantile middle class–and thus deprives us (I think) of the most certain means for the accumulation of wealth." He finished his argument hyperbolically to emphasize his point. He continued: "Instead of the condition of Ireland being that which we may *expect hereafter*, it is in fact that which we now suffer."[36] John C. Calhoun of South Carolina, who had once unequivocally stated, "I have ever taken pride in my Irish descent," his father having been born in County Donegal, was the South's greatest spokesman of the 1840s. He believed that Lesesne's nightmare scenario had not occurred yet, but he felt it was coming. He too believed in 1847 that the American Union would bring a "whole train of calamities" to the South. This disaster, he continued, "will be greater than ever befell a people. The condition of Ireland would be a state of bliss to ours."[37] This is a powerful statement especially when considering that Ireland was in the throes of "Black '47." Calhoun was arguing that the South was heading for colonial domination and perhaps famine. It is very likely that he made this statement purely for effect and it was never a real possibility. Nevertheless, the fact that this mature, conservative politician could come to such an extreme conclusion highlights the depth of the fear Ireland's plight created among native Southerners.

After Calhoun's death in 1850, the new generation of southern partisans also feared the parallels between Ireland and the South. United States Senator Jefferson Davis of Mississippi, the future president of the Confederate States of America, had written in 1849 that the American Union could only survive if "the independence and equality of its members should be preserved." Worried about the "Free

Soil" element in the North, which wanted to halt the expansion of slavery into the new U.S. territory acquired in the recent war with Mexico, he asked rhetorically: "Shall we [southerners] stand with folded arms until a sectional party with the unchecked power of a three-fourths majority holds sway over us? Shall we sink in the United States Congress to the *helpless condition* which Ireland occupies in the British Parliament?" (emphasis added). Inspired by this fear, Davis vigorously opposed efforts to turn the South into Ireland. After Abraham Lincoln's election victory in 1860, Davis decided that the only way to halt this disastrous scenario was for the South to secede from the American Union.[38]

Southerners, thus, were very aware of parallels between Ireland and their region. The Irish recognized them too. This common struggle against Unions was the key to Irish integration in the South. When the South eventually left the Union and formed its own Confederacy, most Irish in the South joined that cause. They had gained practical results from buying into southern values. John C. Calhoun took a lead role in supporting relief efforts for Ireland during the Famine and had also stood for the Democratic Party's statement declaring the United States "the land of liberty, and the asylum of the oppressed of every nation . . . and every attempt to abridge the present privilege of becoming citizens and the owners of soil among us, ought to be resisted." Irish societies and individuals thus often sought his advice and support for petitions on behalf of Irish immigrants in the United States.[39] Calhoun was not around to deal with the Know-Nothing threat of the mid-1850s, but other southern partisans took a lead role in the fight against nativism. Henry Wise of Virginia, for example, who George Fitzhugh dedicated his most famous book *Cannibals All! or Slaves without Masters* to in 1857, played a key role in defeating the spread of the Know-Nothings in the South. As the Democratic candidate for governor in 1855, he faced a serious challenge from Know-Nothing Thomas Flournoy. Wise managed to hold his party together, win the election, and halt "the 'serpent' [Know-Nothingism] . . . in his crawl southward" (Wish 99; Rice 67–75; Simpson 106–18).

Virginia's rejection of nativism on the state level influenced other southern states. Years after his victory, Wise recognized its importance by stating that Know-Nothingism was "the most impious and unprincipled affiliation by bad means, for bad ends." Expressing his feelings in terms that Irish southerners understood well, he believed that Americanism had at its core the Puritan "plans of Exeter Hall, in old England, acting on Williams Hall, in New England, for a hierarchical proscription of religions, for the demolition of some of the clearest standards of American liberty, and for a fanatical and sectional demolition of slavery" (qtd. in Rice 75). He was glad to have helped hinder its chances for success in the South. By linking the British evangelicalism expounded in London's "Exeter Hall" with its American version, which abolitionists explicated in "Williams Hall," Wise attacked two great Irish enemies. They saw the evangelical abolitionists in the North as kin to the ones in England who had prosleytised the famine as the "direct stroke of an all-wise Providence."[40] Just as the English "zealots" had destroyed their old homes, it seemed the American ones were out to repeat the performance in the South. The southern Irish, therefore, also rejoiced that the ardent state-rights southerner and secessionist Wise had stopped the spread of ideas that they agreed had been concocted in "Old England." They were ready to join him and other natives in the struggle for "southern independence" (Gleeson, "Irish" 263–75).

They became such supporters of the southern cause that they could not understand how the Irish in the North could fight to maintain a Union. Mitchel again was Irish southerners' most prominent spokesman. During the Civil War he wrote that those who thought "that the repeal of one union in Europe [the union between Great Britain and Ireland] depends on the enforcement of another union in America," were mistaken, and "our friends here [Confederates] do not well understand the process of reasoning which leads to [this] conclusion nor do I" (qtd. in Herndon 93). Southerners welcomed the local Irish support for their Confederate cause. When a former nemesis like Christopher Memminger of Charleston, who had once seriously questioned the loyalty of Irish Catholics to the South, recognized poor white men, including the Irish, as important members of the "peerage of white men," it became even clearer to the Irish that they had become a welcome part of southern society (qtd. in Jordan 225).

Famine migrant and slaveholder Patrick Murphy is a good example of this Irish integration. He kept a diary for most of his life, and it shows vividly that he felt deeply the dislocating pains of emigration. He regretted the South's dissolution of its bonds to the United States. Nevertheless, when news arrived of Union "Gun boats" with "10,000 men" ready to invade the Confederacy, he wrote in his diary that "I will go now where I am wanted . . . to help beat back the cursed Yankees."[41] This Famine migrant who often felt isolated in his new home now saw himself as member of this "peerage" of southern white men and was prepared to go and fight to maintain his membership of it. His Famine immigration experience had played a large role in transforming him from Irish stranger into Irish southerner. The Famine therefore had eased his and numerous other Irish migrants' integration into southern society. They were prepared to fight for their new home and risk everything to prove that they were an integrative part of the Old South. Their major motivation was that they did not want their southern future to turn into their Irish past. Despite all the problems and tragedy of the Famine, this motivation was its most important legacy to the Irish in the American South. Without it they could not have concluded their journey from stranger to southerner.

Notes

1. For the psychological and cultural impact of the Famine, see Lyons 4; Ó Gráda 194–225; Morash 40–55.

2. For the impact of the Famine on Irish immigrants, see Kinealy 297–341; K. Miller, *Emigrants* 280–344; K. Miller, "'Revenge for Skibbereen'" 180–95; K. Miller, "Class" 96–129.

3. William Hill to David Hill, 7 July 1859, William Hill Papers, Perkins Library, Duke University, Durham, North Carolina.

4. *Knoxville (Tenn.) Southern Citizen,* 18 March 1858. See also D. T. Gleeson, "Parallel Struggles" 97–116. Original emphasis.

5. Dodd and Dodd 2, 6, 14, 18, 26, 34, 38, 46, 50, 54, 58; DeBow 117; J. G. Kennedy xxix.

6. For the Irish experience in the South, see D. T. Gleeson, *Irish*; Niehaus; R. M. Miller 30–53; Clark 195–209; Shoemaker; and Thigpen.

7. For information on Hibernian Societies, see Minutes of the Charleston Hibernian Society, micro., South Carolina Historical Society, Charleston, South Carolina; James Black Diary, James Black Collection, D. 1725/18, Public Record Office of Northern Ireland (hereafter referred to as PRONI), Belfast, Northern Ireland; O'Hara; Niehaus 13.

8. *Charleston (S.C.) United States Catholic Miscellany,* 20 May, 8 July, 8 August 1848.

9. James 133–34; Shafer Goodstein 197; *Vicksburg (Miss.) Daily Whig,* 14 August 1855.

10. Niehaus 89; Shafer Goodstein 162; Shoemaker 359; *Eighth Census, 1860,* vol. 5 (Orleans Parish, LA).

11. Michael Gleeson to "father," 5 Sept. 1857, Correspondence, Diocese of Charleston Archives, Charleston, South Carolina; Gleeson, *The Irish in the South,* 118-119.

12. Octavia Smith to Richard H. Smith, 29 June 1839, Richard H. Smith and Family Papers, Louisiana and Lower Mississippi Valley Collections (hereafter referred to as LLMVC), Hill Memorial Library, Louisiana State University, Baton Rouge, Louisiana.

13. Marianne Edwards to "Maria," 17 June 1860, Marianne Edwards Papers, LLMVC.

14. Berlin 182–216, 231–32; Berlin and Gutman 1196; Olmsted 231.

15. In the mid-1850s in New Orleans nativist political violence did curtail Irish participation in elections but failed to eradicate the Irish vote. In fact, eventually the nativists campaigned for Irish votes. See Gleeson, *Irish* 114-18.

16. Petition of Citizens of Sumter District, General Assembly Papers, #2769, South Carolina Department of Archives and History, Columbia, South Carolina, (hereafter SCDAH).

17. Report of Committee on Finance and Banks on the Petition of Sundry Citizens of Sumter District, General Assembly Papers, #49, SCDAH.

18. *Natchez Mississippi Free Trader*, 17 February, 24 February 1847.

19. *Ibid.*, 10 and 17 March 1847.

20. *Jackson (Miss.) Southron*, 26 February, 5 March 1847.

21. P. Kennedy to Vere Foster, 19 March 1855, Foster of Glyde Papers, D3618/D/8/9, PRONI.

22. Mitchel 153–54; *Knoxville (Tenn.) Southern Citizen*, 21 January, 11 March 1858.

23. *Knoxville (Tenn.) Southern Citizen*, 4 February, 11 March 1858.

24. Patrick Murphy Diary, Patrick Murphy Collection, LLMVC.

25. R. McElderry, letter to Thomas McElderry, 31 July 1854. Robert McElderry Collection, T.2414/16, PRONI.

26. R. McElderry, letter to Thomas McElderry, 11 March 1852. Robert McElderry Collection, T2414/6, PRONI.

27. W. McElderry, letter to [Thomas McElderry], Dec. 1854? Robert McElderry Collection, T2414/8, PRONI.

28. M.E. Bradford, qtd. in Genovese, *Southern Tradition* 17–18. Genovese points out that the Old South paternalists could never reconcile their belief in progress, which capitalism drove, with their critique of the capitalist bourgeois world created by this progress. See in particular Genovese, *Slaveholders' Dilemma*.

29. There is a major debate on how much the paternalistic ideals of the large planters and their apologists filtered through southern society as a whole. See Oakes, esp. ix–xii, xv–xix.

30. Patrick Murphy Diary, Patrick Murphy Collection, LLMVC.

31. For discussion of punishment and paternalism in southern slavery, see Genovese, *Roll, Jordan, Roll* 67–68, 72–86.

32. John McFarland to "Emma," 9 October 1860, Blakemore (Lizzie McFarland) Collection, Mississippi Department of Archives and History, Jackson, Mississippi.

33. *Knoxville (Tenn.) Southern Citizen*, 11 March 1858. Hillyer was actually a transplanted northerner, but knowledge of this fact would have only reinforced Mitchel's favorable view of southern society.

34. Quoted in Ignatiev 18 and *Boston (Mass.) Liberator*, 24 June 1842.

35. Fitzhugh used terms such as: "We want no new world!" Qtd. in

Genovese, *World the Slaveholders Made* 234.

36. Jos. W. Lesesne to John C. Calhoun, 12 Sept. 1847, in *The Papers of John C. Calhoun*, vol. 24, ed. Clyde N. Wilson and Shirley Bright Cook (Columbia: University of South Carolina Press, 1998), 552-53.

37. John C. Calhoun to [Gilbert C. Rice] "Secretary of the Irish Emigrant Society," 13 Sept. 1841, John C. Calhoun to Chas. Jas. Faulkner, 1 Aug. 1847, in Calhoun 15:774, 24:481.

38. Jefferson Davis to Malcolm D. Haynes, 18 Aug. 1849, in Davis 4: 31-32; Cooper 277–324. For coverage of American sectional crisis in the late 1840s and early 1850s, see Sydnor 328–29 and McPherson 63–77.

39. John C. Calhoun to J. E. Scotland and others, 11 Aug. 1840, in Calhoun 15: 328-30. See also Calhoun, *Papers* 24: 59, 100, 113, 166; O'Sullivan, letter to John C. Calhoun, 1 March 1848.

40. Charles Trevelyan, qtd. in Gray, "Ideology" 93. Gray in another work points out that as the man in charge of the British government's purse strings, Assistant Secretary to the Treasury Trevelyan used a "blend of 'moderate' evangelical providentialism with an optimistic reading of Smithian economics [to give him] and his allies not only a resilient and intellectually satisfying paradigm through which to interpret the Irish catastrophe, but also a moralistic device for directing responsibility away from the state and its agents to the failings of the Irish as individuals and as a nation" (Gray, *Famine* 254). Trevelyan's "paradigm" contrasts sharply with George Fitzhugh's.

41. Patrick Murphy Diary, Patrick Murphy Collection, LLMVC.

Works Cited

Berlin, Ira. *Slaves Without Masters: The Free Negro in the Antebellum South.* New York: Pantheon, 1974.

Berlin, Ira, and Herbert Gutman. "Natives and Immigrants, Free Men and Slaves: Urban Workingmen in the Antebellum American South." *American Historical Review* 88 (December 1983): 1175-1200.

Boston (Mass.) Liberator, 24 June 1842.

Calhoun, John C. *The Papers of John C. Calhoun.* Ed. Clyde N. Wilson and Shirley Bright Cook. Columbia: Univ. of South Carolina Press, 1998.

Capers, Gerald M. *The Biography of a River Town, Memphis: Its Heroic Age.* Chapel Hill: U of North Carolina Press, 1939.

Charleston (S.C.) United States Catholic Miscellany, 20 May, 8 July, 8 August 1848.

Clark, Dennis. "The South's Irish Catholics: A Case of Cultural Confinement." *Catholics in the Old South: Essays on Church and Culture.* Ed. Randall M. Miller and John L. Wakelyn. Macon, GA: Mercer Univ. Press, 1983. 195–209.

Cooper, William J., Jr. *Jefferson Davis, American.* New York: Knopf,

2000.

Davis, Jefferson. *The Papers of Jefferson Davis.* Ed. Lynda Caswell Crist and others. Vol. 4. Baton Rouge: Louisiana State Univ. Press, 1983.

DeBow, J. D. B. ed. *Statistical View of the United States: A Compendium of the Seventh Census.* (Washington, D.C.: Govt. Ptr., 1854.

Dickey, Dallas C. *Sergeant S. Prentiss: Whig Orator of the Old South.* Baton Rouge: Louisiana State Univ. Press, 1945

Dodd, Donald B., and Wynelle S. Dodd. *Historical Statistics of the South, 1790–1970.* Tuscaloosa: Univ. of Alabama Press, 1973.

Eighth Census, 1860, vol. 5. Orleans Parish, LA.

Faust, Drew Gilpin, ed. *The Ideology of Slavery: Proslavery Thought in the Antebellum South, 1830–1860.* Baton Rouge: Louisiana State Univ. Press, 1981.

Genovese, Eugene D. *Roll, Jordan, Roll: The World The Slaves Made.* New York: Random, 1972.

---. *The Slaveholders' Dilemma: Freedom and Progress in Southern Conservative Thought, 1820–1860.* Columbia: Univ. of South Carolina Press, 1992.

---. *The Southern Tradition: The Achievement and Limitations of an American Conservatism.* Cambridge, Mass.: Harvard Univ. Press, 1994.

---. *The World the Slaveholders Made: Two Essays in Interpretation.* 1969. Middletown, Conn.: Wesleyan Univ. Press, 1988.

Gleeson, David T. *The Irish in the South, 1815-1877* (Chapel Hill, N.C.: Univ. of North Carolina Press, 2001).

---. "Parallel Struggles: Irish Republicanism in the American South, 1798–1877." *Éire-Ireland* 34 (Summer 1999): 97–116.

Gray, Peter. *Famine, Land and Politics: British Government and Irish Society, 1843–1850.* (Portland, Ore.: Irish Academic Press, 1999.

---. "Ideology and the Famine." *The Great Irish Famine.* Ed. Cathal Póirtéir. Cork: Mercier, 1995.

Herndon, Joseph M., Jr. *Celts, Catholics, and Copperheads: Ireland Views the American Civil War.* Columbus: Ohio State Univ. Press, 1968.

Holt, Michael F. *The Rise and Fall of the American Whig Party: Jacksonian Politics and the Onset of the Civil War.* New York: Oxford Univ. Press, 1999.

Ignatiev, Noel. *How the Irish Became White.* New York: Routledge, 1995.

Jackson (Miss.) Southron, 26 February, 5 March 1847.

James, D. Clayton. *Antebellum Natchez.* Baton Rouge: Louisiana State

Univ. Press, 1968.

Johnson, Michael P. *Toward a Patriarchal Republic: The Secession of Georgia.* Athens: Univ. of Georgia Press, 1977.

Jordan, Laylon P. "Schemes of Usefulness: Christopher Gustavus Memminger." *Intellectual Life in Antebellum Charleston.* Ed. Michael O'Brien and David Moltke-Hansen. Knoxville: Univ. of Tennessee Press, 1986.

Kennedy, Joseph G. *Population of the United States in 1860: Compiled from the Original Returns of the Eighth Census* (Washington, D.C.: Govt. Printing., 1864.

Kinealy, Christine. *This Great Calamity: The Irish Famine, 1845–52.* Boulder, Colo.: Rinehart, 1995.

Knobel, Dale T. *Paddy and the Republic: Ethnicity and Nationality in Antebellum America.* Middletown, Conn.: Wesleyan, 1986.

Knoxville (Tenn.) Southern Citizen, 21 January; 4 February; 11 March 1858; 18 March 1858.

Lesesne, Jos. W. Letter to John C. Calhoun. 12 September 1847. *The Papers of John C. Calhoun.* 24: 552–53, 481.

Lyons, F. S. L. *Ireland Since the Famine.* New York: Scribner,1971.

McPherson, James M. *Battle Cry of Freedom: The Civil War Era.* New York: Oxford Univ. Press, 1988.

Miller, Kerby. "Class, Culture, and Immigrant Group Identity in the United States: The Case of Irish-American Ethnicity." *Immigration Reconsidered: History, Sociology, and Politics.* Ed. Virginia Yans-McLaughlin. New York: Oxford Univ. Press, 1990. 96–129.

———. *Emigrants and Exiles: Ireland and the Irish Exodus to North America.* New York: Oxford Univ. Press, 1985.

———. "'Revenge for Skibbereen:' Irish Emigration and the Meaning of the Famine." *The Great Famine and The Irish Diaspora in America.* Ed. Arthur Gribben. Amherst: Univ. of Massachusetts Press, 1999. 180–95.

Miller, Randall M. "The Enemy Within: Some Effects of Foreign Immigrants on Antebellum Southern Cities." *Southern Studies* 24 (Spring 1985): 30–53.

Mitchel, John *Jail Journal.* Dublin, Ireland: Gill, 1921. Reprint.

Morash, Christopher. "Making Memories: The Literature of the Irish Famine." *The Irish World Wide,* vol. 6, *The Meaning of the Famine.* Ed. Patrick O'Sullivan. London: Leicester Univ. Press, 1997. 40–55.

Natchez Mississippi Free Trader. 17, 24 February 1847; 10, 17 March 1847.

Niehaus, Earl F. *The Irish in New Orleans, 1800–1860.* Baton Rouge: Louisiana State Univ. Press, 1956.

Ó Gráda, Cormac. *Black '47: Beyond the Great Famine in History,*

Economy, and Memory. Princeton: Princeton Univ. Press, 1999.

O'Hara, Arthur J. *Hibernian Society, Savannah, Georgia, 1812–1912: Story of a Century.* Savannah: Hibernian Soc. of Savannah, 1997. Reprint.

O'Sullivan, Patrick. Letter to John C. Calhoun. 1 March 1848. *The Papers of John C. Calhoun.* 25: 217–19.

Oakes, James. *The Ruling Race: A History of American Slaveholders.* 1982. New York: Norton, 1998.

Olmsted, Frederick L. *The Cotton Kingdom: A Traveler's Observations on Cotton and Slavery in the American States.* New York: Knopf, 1953. Reprint.

Patrick Murphy Diary, Patrick Murphy Collection, Louisiana and Lower Mississippi Valley Collections.

Rice, Phillip Morrison. "The Know-Nothing Party in Virginia, 1854–1851." *Virginia Magazine of History and Biography* 55 (Jan. 1947): 67–75.

Scott, John A. ed. *Journal of a Residence on a Georgia Plantation in 1838–1839.* Athens: Univ. of Georgia Press, 1984. Rpt.

Shafer Goodstein, Anita. *Nashville, 1790–1860: From Frontier to City.* Gainesville: University of Florida Press, 1982.

Shoemaker, Edward M. "Strangers and Citizens: The Irish Immigrant Community in Savannah, 1837–1861." Diss. Emory Univ., 1990.

Siegel, Fred. "Artisans and Immigrants in the Politics of Late Antebellum Georgia." *Civil War History* 27 (September 1981): 227–28.

Simpson, Craig M. *A Good Southerner: The Life of Henry A. Wise of Virginia.* Chapel Hill: Univ. of North Carolina Press, 1985.

Sydnor, Charles S. *The Development of Southern Sectionalism, 1819–1848.* Baton Rouge: Louisiana State Univ. Press, 1961.

Thigpen, Thomas Paul. "Aristocracy of the Heart: Catholic Lay Leadership in Savannah, Georgia, 1820–1870." Diss. Emory Univ., 1995.

Vicksburg (Miss.) Daily Whig, 14 August 1855.

Wish, Harvey, ed. *Antebellum Writings of George Fitzhugh and Hinton Rowan Helper.* New York: Capricorn, 1960.

Chapter Nine

Performing the Famine: A Look at Contemporary Irish Dramatists

JEROME JOSEPH DAY, O.S.B.

Since the late 1960s, the Irish stage has concerned itself with the causes, impact, and consequences of the Great Famine (1845–1852) more than ever. For more than a century, Irish dramatists paid scant attention to an event that has widely been seen as Ireland's worst catastrophe. Not until Tom Murphy's seminal *Famine* (1968) did Irish playwrights wrestle seriously with the 1840s crisis. Following Murphy, Tom MacIntyre's controversial and groundbreaking adaptation, *The Great Hunger* (1983), derived from Patrick Kavanagh's poem of the same name, introduced a highly physical and metaphorical approach to *hunger* in the Irish psyche and its social manifestations. Since then, at least eight other dramatists have explored dimensions of the Famine on the commercial stage, in theater-in-education programs, and on the amateur level. In their encounter, the stage and Famine studies have influenced each other. Theater has been challenged to depict and interpret a national cataclysm, and Famine studies have been challenged to explore history's effects on the present. First, this paper will examine the dramatic revolution initiated by Murphy in *Famine* and MacIntyre in *The Great Hunger*. Second, the paper will examine three relatively recent Famine plays: Brian Friel's *Translations*, Frank McGuinness's *Mary and Lizzie*, and John Banville's *The Broken Jug*.

This discussion will draw not only on the Famine experience, but also on several perspectives from critical and cultural theory. Michél Foucault emphasizes that ideas and attitudes can build up over time to become a field of discourse that shapes and conditions what any individual writer may produce (119–20). Likewise, he sees human knowledge as sedimented, one layer of understanding interpenetrating another, and thus requiring a kind of archeological process to excavate meaning. One of the sites of this archeology is the human body itself, which in its posture, positioning, and behavior gives silent evidence of this sedimentation of human knowledge (Foucault 83). Jürgen Habermas argues that social, even political change can occur when the public sphere, the social space where men and women go to interact as members of the *polis*, the community, or even the nation, sees the introduction of new topics and modes of communication (202–3). Claude Schumacher, addressing issues in the drama of the Shoah, or Holocaust, insists that not only must memory be transmitted through dramatic art, but that such art must also move the audience. Something more than mere representation—impossible when confronting the Shoah—must emerge on stage. Performance ought to help the audience approach the multiple layers of meaning of the event (Schumacher 4). Finally, Peggy Phelan finds that the use of the "phantasmatic," the mystical realm of ghosts, spectres, and spirits, becomes a way of expressing, distancing, and confronting the suffering and loss that come through trauma and death, as well as the frustration from failure to achieve interpersonal union in sexual, social, and spiritual terms (4–5, 16–17). Through the course of this discussion, these theoretical perspectives will help illustrate the significance of the Famine's representation on stage.

That Anglo-Irish Ascendancy and Irish Literary Revival dramatists would avoid the subject is no surprise. Building a national consciousness and striving for political independence generally requires a turn to the mythic and heroic, not the traumatic, especially when one's own class is implicated. Although the Famine is represented in oral tradition, ballads, and some prose work, its dramatic profile prior to the end of the 1960s was limited (McHugh 436). Four plays, however, do confront the catastrophe: *The Famine* (1886) by Hubert O'Grady (1841–1899), *The Countess Cathleen* (1892) by W. B. Yeats (1865–1939), *The Black Stranger* (1945) by Gerard Healy, and *Tenants at Will* (1947) by George Shiels. It was only little more than thirty years ago, however, that Irish audiences first saw the most agonizing and socially disruptive moment in their history staged in any detail.

I. Murphy: *Famine's* Ritual Confronts Trauma

In 1968, Tom Murphy's critically acclaimed *Famine* would change the trajectory of Irish drama. Increasingly, the Famine would become a subject for *dramatic* exploration. The Famine poses enormous challenges for theatrical forms. Its remote causes, proximate effects, sweeping scale, long duration, initial ravages, and prolonged consequences make it difficult to contain verbally and depict visually. Murphy employs ritual, traditionally used to tame chaos, enter the realm of death, and explore questions of eternal mystery. Murphy structures *Famine* through patterns of social ritual—a community wake, a relief meeting, courtship rituals, prayer, even lovemaking—that he successively destroys through disruption, blasphemy, death, and violence. In so doing, he invites his audience to experience something of the emotional confusion, socio-political impotence, and spiritual shock that so disabled Ireland in the long wake of the Famine. Fintan O'Toole writes that while the play dramatizes "the central event in 19th century history in Ireland," it is "all the time a play about the 20th century, about the spiritual and emotional famine of Murphy's own times" (112). Ritual, of course, functions in precisely this way, connecting the mundane "now" with the mythic "then" to create an eternal, super-charged "now." As Victor Turner suggests, this ritualizing process is especially crucial in moments of crisis and disruption (92). The play is rich in ritual structure, use of ritual in character development and, finally, ritualized language.

Murphy's *Famine* concerns the struggle of John Connor, powerless leader of the village of Glanconor in the West of Ireland, to cope with the starvation of his people. Despite numerous opportunities to respond with violence, O'Connor resists. Instead, he relies on law and morality, and their various cultural rituals and social structures, to prop up his collapsing world. He follows custom and hosts an expensive wake when his daughter dies. He holds a village council. He repeats conventional linguistic formulae. He relies on legal and ecclesiastical authority and their rituals of control. Thus he seals the fate of his community. Finally, however, he explodes, murdering his wife and son in an act of violence itself permeated by linguistic ritual in the formal cadences of Gaelic clan relationships.

II. MacIntyre: *The Great Hunger* of the Body

MacIntyre's 1983 play, *The Great Hunger,* likewise is heavily ritualistic as it explores the metaphoric potential of the performative body. A collaborative work between author, director, and actors, it is meant to evolve with each performance. The play, which premiered on 9 May 1983 on the Abbey Theatre's Peacock stage, compels leaps in understanding and connection, and therein lies its strength and weakness. Many Irish viewers were familiar with Patrick Kavanagh's famous 1942 poem of the same name. Once on stage, the play relies heavily on images and actions with personal and communal meanings. *The Great Hunger* offers a script, certainly, but it is a pared down, reorganized text of a poem that itself makes readers work. The play, adapted by MacIntyre and directed by

Patrick Mason with Tom Hickey in the role of Paddy Maguire, is a fluid, expressionistic panoply of the body in mime, ritual, and expressionistic movement. A landmark in Irish theater history, the play unquestionably confronts the Famine—yet does not deal with the 1845–1850 catastrophe, ignores the word *famine,* and omits overt discussion. Nothing explicit interferes with its treatment of Maguire, a frustrated, aging bachelor farmer from County Monaghan. Together with Murphy's *Famine,* however, *The Great Hunger* provides a critical step in contemporary dramatic appropriation of the Famine. Murphy uses ritual to explore the Famine and its consequences and to point to its metaphoric possibilities. MacIntyre, rooted in Kavanagh's poem, begins with the metaphors, using the performative body, often through ritual, to implicate Famine folklore, mythology, and history. For MacIntyre, the Famine is no further away than its cultural legacy—which he exposes in all of Maguire's frustrations. Irish social historians have shown that delayed marriages, matriarchal family structures, repressed sexuality, church dominance, and a grinding agricultural economy, all of which afflict Paddy Maguire, can be linked to consequences of the Famine (Lee 384).

The bachelor farmer's life is echoed in such elements as a potato field, a farm gate, a tabernacle, a green branch, and even a statue of an earth mother goddess, to whom a despairing Maguire renders homage. Matriarchy, the Church, and the constricted life of a farmer are introduced, while potato references in a work titled *The Great Hunger* immediately suggest the Famine. While the play's metaphors and images speak deeply to Irish experience, its elitism, coherence, and accessibility are troubling (Colgan 10). For defenders, however, the text is self-sufficient, comic. and imagistically connected (Nowlan 10). Murphy allows comic elements to emerge in *Famine* only to snuff them out. For example, a man talks to his wife in bed, but the audience soon realizes he is speaking with a corpse, and a romantic flirtation scene is played out amid dead bodies. But MacIntyre, having followed Kavanagh in distancing his work from the historical Famine, exploits the poem's comedy, counterpointing it with Maguire's self-imposed famine. In the published 1988 version of *The Great Hunger,* three scenes that have remained consistently important highlight the play's performative characteristics. These scenes include a dance of Maguire and his scarecrow-like friends, Maguire's masturbation (or bellows pumping), his frustrated feet-banging, his worship of the maternal idol, and a seductive procession of green branches. Moments of sensuality, clericalism, mysticism, homoeroticism, sexuality, and fecundity pervade the play in counterpoint to Maguire's own barren, hollow life.

How might one understand this succession of images, speech, and movement? Certainly, the play exposes vitiated aspects of Irish life, oppressed by spiritual Jansenism, disordered society, and relentless farm work. Vincent Hurley, discussing Kavanagh's poetic work and MacIntyre's adaptation, writes:

> *The Great Hunger* is a poem about stagnation, enervation and the slow, painful death of any hope of joy or fulfillment in the life of its central character, Patrick Maguire.... Rooted in quotidian reality, the play remains true to the spirit of the poem, conveying both its earthiness and its essentially tragic vision of the peasant life. (Kavanagh and MacIntyre 73, 77)

Sexual repression and an unhealthy obeisance to Church and family emasculate Maguire. Likewise, one can see *The Great Hunger* as an important theatrical experiment within the Irish tradition, an innovation designed to free the stage from dependence on speech at the expense of movement and image. Christopher Murray sees MacIntyre moving toward a ritualistic aesthetic, but more than this may be under way. MacIntyre

> is clearly an avant-garde playwright, and can therefore be assessed in the ritualistic tradition established by Artaud in the 1930s and developed by Beckett, Ionesco, and (to a certain extent) the later O'Casey. Theatre of Ritual seeks to recover for the present day the energy and connectedness of natural, primitive man. (56)

Murray challenges as simplistic the notion of "image" advanced by Hurley. MacIntyre's images "arrest but remain in isolation, discrete and arbitrary; indeed, the credo of improvisation to which the production style is committed necessitates this arbitrariness.... The critic ... demands coherence of form even where the subject in itself is fragmented" (Murray 56). *The Great Hunger* does maintain unifying connections among image, action, and dialogue to achieve a fluid harmony, particularly when seen in connection with the Famine. By its decentered focus, the play endeavors to demonstrate alternatives to Maguire's malaise. These alternatives, moreover, lie at the core of Kavanagh's poem; they are what Maguire should pursue. Una Agnew sees the "momentary brightness within the darkened narrative" of the poem as ephiphanic, and, in performance, the bodies of actors foreground such light (205–7). In any case, Murray's criticisms underline the challenge of achieving integrity and his observations regarding ritual establish a strong link between MacIntyre and Murphy.

At the heart of MacIntyre's work is the performative body, particularly the body of actor Tom Hickey, who plays Maguire. He sweats digging potatoes, hangs like a scarecrow, masturbates symbolically, nestles on the shoulder of a maternal effigy, vents rage and frustration by banging his feet, cavorts with green branches, recoils from women, roughhouses with male friends, and finally, gives his body up to clay. Postmodern theater and performance studies argue that the body is the subject of social discourse, and that, whatever its metaphysical possibilities, its materiality compels it to be understood in certain ways in each historical and cultural era. Philip Auslander writes, "In order to recover the possibility of seeing the performing body as an instrument of counterhegemonic artistic production, the history of the body in performance must be conceived as a part of the history of the body itself, a history understood as a study of how the body [has been represented]" (92–93). Against the image of the Irish peasant as hard-working, happy, and pious, fulfilled on his own land, an image that had its apotheosis in Eamon de Valera's famous 1943 radio broadcast extolling a utopian vision of rural Ireland, rises the body of Maguire (De Valera 146–50). And *body* it must be, for Maguire is neither conscious nor fluent enough to articulate his predicament. Here, the play's relationship to the Famine is important.

Historically, the body's appalling condition during the Famine repudiated attempts to repress it—and its latent political power—through official discourse. Hungry, emaciated, diseased, roaming the countryside in desperate search for food, left skeletal in a hovel to die, crowded into a county poorhouse, or tossed off a coffin ship, the human body provided its own defiant text. Mid-nineteenth century political and economic discourse, statistical analysis, landlord relief protests—none could make the "corporeal text" go away. Moreover, the Famine's legacy was significant (Brown 21–26). Antoinette Quinn makes a strong case for associating the poem with the Famine. Only a small leap is required to transform this Famine poem into a Famine play—and the body is at the center of the process.

Through *The Great Hunger's* reliance on the performative body, one is led to the way the body is understood in Ireland. The *corpus hibernicum* has a long history of repression. Foreign invasion, tribal collapse, plantation, dispossession, penal laws, military conflict, sectarian hostility, religious distortion, and cultural rigidity all played their part in shaping the Irish mind, which, in turn, has a profound impact on the Irish body. While cautioning against essentialism, Cheryl Herr asserts that most writers on Ireland suggest the Celtic consciousness is fraught with a "fatal divisiveness" and "emotional oscillation," as well as a strong sense of place and an obsession with death, along with "the current 'over-identity crisis'" (6–7). She adds that "Ireland has literally eroded, in the sphere of representations that constitute social identity, a comfortable sense of the body. . . . [There is] a reflexive and widespread resistance to *seeing* movement, to recognizing its necessity, and ultimately to sanctioning radical changes of posture" (13). This resistance, she argues, is manifested by excessive focus on celibacy, asceticism, resistance to touch, sexual repression, and even taboos on breastfeeding.

"Famine is a potent, anti-heroic national myth, stirring atavistic fears, rousing racial memories of extreme indignity and humiliation as well as impoverishment, suffering and death," writes Quinn (139). Kavanagh's poem assumes knowledge of the Famine background and consequently exploits it. In turn, MacIntyre's play exploits the poem's imagistic resources. Rural Ireland's social and economic conditions, as the poet Kavanagh saw, stemmed from the Famine. Afterward, as Quinn observes, "the economics of survival took precedence over all other considerations, and agricultural prosperity was achieved at the cost of self-expression and self-fulfillment. That cult and culture of the potato so savagely mocked in *The Great Hunger* had set in. The potato crop flourished but human lives were blighted" (139).

Like Murphy's *Famine* in 1968, MacIntyre's *The Great Hunger* in 1983 became a theatrical milestone. If Murphy appropriates the historical reality of the Famine and suggests links with a more contemporary Ireland, MacIntyre seizes its metaphorical possibilities. MacIntyre's use of ritual, and particularly his emphasis on the performative body, constitutes a major Irish theatrical innovation. The widespread popularity and critical attention these two plays attracted, coupled with increasing social, economic, and cultural self-confidence in Ireland, laid the groundwork for a significant rise in dramatic attention to the Famine. Ireland had entered what is now called the European Union in 1973 and began to receive massive infusions of capital. Urbanization, economic diversification, and educational opportunities were increasing. Television was widely available.

During the 1980s and 1990s, more plays dealing with the Famine were produced on the Irish stage than at any previous period. Taking their cues from Murphy and MacIntyre, playwrights and directors realized the Famine's dramatic potential. It becomes a prism through which audiences can refract and consider their own experience. While the quality of these works varies, they demonstrate confidence and sophistication in utilizing the Famine as historical subject and socio-political metaphor. These plays include Brian Friel's *Translations* (1980), Eoghan Harris's *Souper Sullivan* (1985), Frank McGuinness's *Mary and Lizzie* (1989), John Banville's *The Broken Jug* (1994), Joe O'Byrne's *The Last Potato* (1994), John McArdle's *Two Houses* (1996), and Jim Minogue's *Flight to Grosse Île* (1996). A brief examination of three of these works will expose the range of meanings the contemporary "Famine play" can bear. Friel's *Translations* uses the Famine as a shadowy, apocalyptic future toward which Gaelic civilization, already struggling with English rule and occupation, is moving. The very cultural dislocation represented by the renaming and mapping exercises of the Royal Engineers received its most powerful impetus from the linguistic disaster occasioned by the Famine. McGuinness's *Mary and Lizzie* employs the Famine phantasmatically, ironically and historically as part of the capitalist system critiqued by Friedrich Engels, with whom the two characters lived. Indeed, the Famine helps foreground the sisters, who, like women everywhere, find their stories often eliminated by a sexist history. Meanwhile, Banville's *The Broken Jug* sees the Famine as a silent presence, witnessing the inane trivialities of a courtroom farce, representative not only of the Ascendancy but also of the human capacity to ignore brutal realities. Friel, McGuinness, and Banville, the three dramatists to be considered, appropriate the Famine as metaphor and employ it as a key resource.

III. Friel: Famine as Metaphor in *Translations*

Friel's *Translations* (1980) was first performed at the Guildhall, Derry, by Field Day Theatre Company, 23 September 1980. An extraordinary text drawing upon the work of George Steiner in *After Babel: Aspects of Language and Translation* (1975), its audience can "hear" in English and Irish, although the script is entirely in English (Pine 7). The linguistic world and cultural perspective of the Irish-speakers of Ballybeg, a favorite setting for Friel, captures the audience, which at one level then hears its own language as something alien. *Translations* employs Famine imagery and references to depict the cultural trauma caused by the coming of English language and culture to Donegal, located in Ireland's northwest corner. Richard Pine writes,

> *Translations*, like *Philadelphia, Here I Come*, was both a hybrid and a defining moment in Irish theatre. . . . [It] occupies a place of similar importance in the development of Irish drama to that of *Philadelphia*, to the extent that it was a play which spoke publicly to Irish people about an experience which, in the case of the later play, was still resonant within the acoustic of racial memory. (182)

The play examines the limits of language and interrogates the way it constructs personal and communal identity through usage, past and present. In this sense, it is "more international than national, interglottal in its capacity to speak to other identities and the situations in which the collision of the public and private, the imperial and the local, time and Time, story and History, has occurred or may be happening today" (Pine 183). Ironically, a Famine perspective sharpens the universal importance Friel attaches to language. In Act I, Owen declares, "It's only a name. It's the same me, isn't it? Well, isn't it?" (Friel 408). A glib affirmative is the assumed answer, but by the play's end, the audience is not so sure.

In *Translations*, Ballybeg's Irish speakers confront a decision by the British government to map the country and standardize place names. The project will lead to a more just taxation, say the authorities. But each of the central characters understands the impending change differently: Manus, lame elder son of the hedge schoolmaster, sees military and cultural assault by imperialist colonizers; Owen, younger brother, sees adventure, employment, and opportunity; their father, Hugh, the sometime tipsy but always cultured master, sees a threat to embattled Gaelic and classical civilizations, yet an inevitable change to which villagers somehow must adapt; Maire, milkmaid and student, sees a stimulus to learn English to emigrate to America; Capt. Lancey, chief British officer, sees improvements to backward, and ungrateful, Ireland; and Lt. Yolland, consummate romantic and English Hibernophile, dimly sees his own complicity in a cultural dislocation that is the linguistic equivalent of Famine-era evictions.

Matters reach a crisis when Yolland, in love with Maire despite the linguistic divide, goes missing. The Donnelly twins may be the culprits, but Manus leaves Ballybeg abruptly, and thus draws suspicion on himself. His departure is due to Yolland's liaison with Maire, who had been Manus's intended, but she would not have him until he found work. Ironically, the offer of a schoolmaster's job arrives for Manus at precisely this moment. Meanwhile, the British camp is burned and Capt. Lancey threatens reprisals. Hugh shows how language bears the images that create and sustain a culture, but cites the danger of fossilizing images—in part, a commentary on the renewed Troubles in Northern Ireland, where sectarian and political violence has fed on language and images frozen and distorted in and by time. The play ends with Hugh, Ballybeg's schoolmaster, and Jimmy, the "Infant Prodigy," fluent in Greek and Latin, heroicizing their own less than glorious "part" in the Rising of 1798—shouldering pikes for a twenty-three-mile hike to a pub. Thereupon, the two old men "escape" into the world of myth. This same mythological world bedevils Friel's contemporary Ireland, particularly in the North.

How is *Translations* a "Famine play"? Friel links British cultural imperialism with the potato blight. Although the play is set in August 1831, fourteen years before the outbreak of the blight that led to the Great Famine, Ireland had been plagued by smaller, localized problems. Indeed, 1831 had seen a bad potato harvest and shortages. The blight becomes a metaphor for cultural attack in the form of the map project. Just as the audience knows that the Famine awaits Ballybeg, so too it knows that social upheaval waits to strike. Exacerbated by the Famine, Ireland's cultural trauma is due to a fatal conjunction of blight and imperialism.

Friel teases out references that deliberately echo the Famine. Maire, eager to escape poverty and farm work, shows off her hands: "Ooooh. The best harvest in living memory, they say; but I don't want to see another like it. . . . Look at the blisters" (Friel 388). Later, Jimmy, the aging prodigy, comments about a passage in Virgil's *Georgics:* "Listen to this, Manus. *'Nigra fere et presso pinguis sub vomere terra . . .'*" (Friel 392). Manus translates, "'Land that is black and rich beneath the pressure of the plough . . .'" (Friel 392). Jimmy interjects, "'And with *cui putre*—with crumbly soil—is in the main best for corn.' There you are! . . . 'From no other land will you see more wagons wending homeward behind slow bullocks.' Virgil! There!" adding, "Isn't that what I'm always telling you? Black soil for corn. *That's* what you should have in that upper field of yours—corn, not spuds" (Friel 392). The text suggests Ireland's agricultural wealth, while her peasants scratch for potatoes.

Maire notes that just over Cnoc na Mona, "the sweet smell [of blight] was everywhere" . . . "They say that's the way it snakes in, don't they? First the smell; and then one morning the stalks are all black and limp" (Friel 395). The infiltration of the English language, national schools, compulsory attendance, English-only instruction, a ban on Irish—all these insinuate themselves like the snake in Eden, to which Ballybeg is compared. Yet Maire maintains her confidence: "Sweet God, did the potatoes ever fail in Baile Beag? Well, did they ever—ever? Never! There was never blight here. Never. Never. But we're always sniffing about for it, aren't we?—looking for disaster" (Friel 395). Later, when Lt. Yolland's absence occasions a British army search, Doalty remarks, "They came to Barney Petey's field of corn—straight through it be God as if it was heather!" while Bridget adds, "Not a blade of it left standing" (Friel 434). As the search for Yolland becomes more desperate, the colonizer will become brutal. Captain Lancey threatens shooting livestock, evictions, cottage tumbling and, finally, complete clearance if Yolland is not found. This is a proleptic catalog of the coming Famine. Then, like a death sentence, the roll of villages changed by the mapping project is read, first in English, then Irish. The name change underlines the broader cultural changes taking place. When Maire announces, "Nellie Ruadh's baby died in the middle of the night," it portends not just the death of a child but also a whole culture (Friel 438). Likewise, Maire describes her last meeting with Yolland, and the English lieutenant's mistake accurately suggests where Baile Beag, not Ballybeg, is to be found—in the past. Maire says, "He left me home, Owen. And the last thing he said to me—he tried to speak in Irish—he said, 'I'll see you yesterday'—he meant to say 'I'll see you tomorrow'" (Friel 437). While the British camp erupts in flames, provoking only greater reprisal, Bridget sniffs the air: "The sweet smell! Smell it! It's the sweet smell! Jesus, it's the potato blight!" (Friel 441). What she smells, of course, are the burning tents of the British, but the British, their language, empire, and economy are connected to the blight inextricably.

Hugh, the schoolmaster, declares, "We [Irish] like to think we endure around truths immemorially posited" (Friel 418). But Friel interrogates such "truths," and Hugh himself suggests that they can only be passed along in language, which both conceals and reveals. Hugh declares, "Yes, it [Irish] is a rich language, Lieutenant, full of mythologies of fantasy and hope and self-deception—syntax opulent with tomorrows. It is our response to mud cabins and a diet of potatoes; our only method of replying to . . . inevitabilities" (Friel 418–19). "But remember that words are signals, counters. They are not immortal. And it can happen—to use an image you'll understand—it can happen that a civilization can be imprisoned in a linguistic contour which no longer matches the landscape of . . . fact" (Friel 419). This, of course, is one of Friel's classic concerns, the disjunction between language and the world, emotional and social, that language constructs and by which it is constructed. Famine chaos, which wrenched the linguistic life of Irish-speaking society, becomes an apt metaphor for such disjunction.

In the face of the onslaught of English, Hugh and Jimmy flee. Unlike Manus, Maire or Owen who have left or will leave Ballybeg physically, the master and his disciple escape into the mythic fantasy of 1798. Hugh recognizes the complexity of experience. He can read from the Name-Book, even though the list is painful to Irish ears. He can tell his son, "It is not the literal past, the 'facts' of history, that shape us, but images of the past embodied in language. . . . We must never cease renewing those images; because once we do, we fossilize. . . . Take care, Owen. To remember everything is a form of madness" (Friel 445). Friel's concern, while set within an Irish context, applies to such diverse situations as America's residual Cold War mentality, Britain's imperial memory, and Russia's Soviet heritage. Images and concepts grow old and stale but can resist change so that they distort an understanding of the present. For Friel, the Troubles in the North, where "Catholic nationalists" and "Protestant unionists" confront each other not only through political parties but also through a time-worn lexicon and iconography that fuel paramilitary groups and terrorists, illustrate the dangerous gulf between outdated images and concepts and actual reality. Hugh's self-knowledge is precisely that he knows his limits. He announces, "My friend, confusion is not an ignoble condition" (Friel 446). Even though he will be replaced by the national school and "Bartley Timlin, schoolmaster and bacon-curer," he can instruct Maire in . . . English (Friel 443). He announces, "Not today. Tomorrow, perhaps. After the funeral. We'll begin tomorrow. (*Ascending*) But don't expect too much. I will provide you with the available words and the available grammar. But will that help you to interpret between privacies? I have no idea. But it's all we have. I have no idea at all" (Friel 446). Hugh's own "privacy," within Gaelic and classical scholarship, exhibits the silencing pattern in *Famine* and *The Great Hunger* as traumatized characters repress pain.

The theoretical perspectives introduced at the beginning of this paper help explain the significance of Friel's play. Hugh and *Translations* generally indicate how Habermas's public sphere, the social space where public concerns are contested and actions determined, is enriched by considering the complexities of language itself. Foucault's notion of discursive layering becomes apparent even in the speech of individuals; Lt. Yolland's romantic vision of Ireland, for example, is intertwined with his destructive colonial activities. Meanwhile, Schumacher's concept of memory and its performance is illustrated in the play's consistent reworking of tradition—the classics, the Gaelic order, and '98—into patterns of confrontation and escape each designed to support personal, communal, or cultural survival. Phelan's notion of the phantasmatic is underlined by the play's reliance on an inner struggle between the evanesence of language and frustrated desires for physical union, sexual and social, political and personal. Neither Manus and Maire nor Yolland and Maire can achieve union. Indeed, only by escaping Ballybeg, physically or psychically, is such union possible.

IV. McGuinness: *Mary and Lizzie* and the Marginalized

If Friel is interested in the Famine and the tensions between local culture, linguistic shift, and universal values, McGuinness carries the Famine to Britain to examine its connections to imperialism, industrialization, and worker exploitation. McGuinness's *Mary and Lizzie*, first performed by the Royal Shakespeare Company in the Pit at the Barbican Theatre, London, on 27 September 1989, employs the Famine as a rural manifestation of colonial policy run amok, the Irish consequence of worldwide worker exploitation and the symbolic depiction of the cost of bloodless rationalism over human emotion. The underworld, Famine specters, industrial sweat shops, drawing room tea-and-strawberry parties, and Soviet prison camps help McGuinness play with sexuality, time, and identity. This same process occurs in *Observe the Sons of Ulster Marching to the Somme* (1985) and *Carthaginians* (1988), as characters fade in and out, and the lines between the historical and the mystical blur.

The title characters, Mary and Lizzie Burns, are Irishwomen largely lost to history but for their relationship with Friedrich Engels (1820–1895), the

German communist theorist and collaborator with Karl Marx (1818–1883). Engels lived in Britain from 1842 to 1844, and took the two women under his roof (Ilyichov 34–47). The historical Famine had not yet begun, yet the conditions that caused it are well established. The Irish sisters are depicted alternately as his whores, dominatrices, lovers, companions, and servants, but McGuinness carefully crafts the play as *their* search, not Engels's. Eamonn Jordan sees *Mary and Lizzie* as "one of McGuinness'[s] most complicated and accomplished" works, one in which "time is multiple and accumulative" and "the stability of space is dissolved by movements in time and is distorted by the devices of carnival" (124). He adds, "By setting the play in an era prior to famine Ireland, McGuinness is provided not only with the possibility of anticipating the famine but also with the opportunity to deconstruct the specific mythology of deprivation which has grown up about the event," targeting not "some freak of nature" but "something which was derived from the social and political dynamic of a [colonizing, capitalist and imperialist] nation" (132).

Driven from their home by difficult conditions, the two sisters travel to Manchester, heart of a burgeoning Industrial Revolution. Having lost their mother in childbirth, the sisters search for their father. In McGuinness's highly expressionistic play, narrative is less important than image. The plot is relatively straightforward. In England, the girls discover their father's plight, meet Engels, show him about, move in with him and then spend an evening with Karl and Jenny Marx, whom Engels underwrites. At the Marx home, the girls engage in sex with Engels, while he and Marx try to discuss political economy. They argue with Jenny, who loathes their lower-class status. The scene then shifts to a Soviet work camp, where Mary and Lizzie hear a chorus of women speak of life's hardness and love's possibilities. Their mother, whom the audience first encounters in a similar apparition spoken in the Irish language, reappears and the scene concludes with a paean to human love.

If plot is straightforward, form is a different matter. Jordan writes that *Mary and Lizzie* finds its power in its "the ability of . . . [its] fantastic form to suggest a simultaneity of theme, whereby it appears as if each scene not only mirrors the other, but that there is a layering process that ensures that each scene is superimposed upon the other" (124). Scene, action, and phrase counterpoint. The third scene with the Black Mass and apostate priest, whose mother seeks to procure women to seduce him into contrition and submission to Rome, exposes vampirism in tribal religion. When Mary and Lizzie turn the tables, threatening to eat the priest, they reveal not only the folly of such sectarianism but also the human desire for love and unity—in this case with their own deceased mother. In Scene 7, immediately after the girls flee Ireland, meet Queen Victoria, hear her diffidence about imperial burdens, and observe Marx and Engels cuddle in bed with their philosophies and fantasies, McGuinness depicts the brutal struggle of the worker to survive. Half-naked, bronzed by grime and pummeled by industrial noise, their father fights to control his shaking hands, the "tools of my trade" before they "lead me to the workhouse" (McGuinness 30). With his daughters at his side, he laments the unending cycle of labor:

> Press. Press. Watch the wheel, the rope's slackening. Press, girl, press. Watch the room. For warmth, for wet. If the thread snaps, the machine stops. Never let the machine stop. Never let the hand stop. Press, woman, press. . . . Man's body's woman's work. Sore eyes, sore hand, sore work, sore body. I want to work, I want to die. I need to wash the dirt off myself. I need to die. (McGuinness 31)

Scene 8's fellatio, their sexual encounter with Engels in the Marx home, reveals less about the girls' desire for Engels than it does about the distance between abstract thought and human desire.

Scene 4, "The Feast of Famine," is the play's most powerful. Having entered the underworld, the girls encounter their mother. She is attended by six women in "*elaborate, jewelled costume* . . . [and they are carrying] *six covered gold platters*"—they are women who died in childbirth (McGuinness 14). A tough-talking, clear-eyed realist whose maternal instincts dried up long ago, Mrs. Burns is tired of life's demands and pretense. "It does funny things to a woman, birth," she tells them. "You choose your time to live and die. When you arrived, I chose to go. I let you live. I gave you my life. Don't bother thanking me. I wanted out of this world. Heaven's great, girls, best of everything. Are yous married yet?" (McGuinness 14–15). When they tell her they are not, she advises, "Don't. And don't have children. They kill you" (McGuinness 15). She advises her daughters to leave Ireland, for her attendants—"the girls are a bit on the gloomy side, they know what they're talking about"—will provide a litany of future woes: famine, death, disease, exile, hunger, and fever (McGuinness 15). The mother and the attendants proceed to describe a "feast of famine" that will engulf Ireland, through another ritualized, litanic presentation of symbolic objects on the platters: a stone, straw, book, rags, spoon, and bone. Various voices sing:

> This spoon wants a mouth to shout,
> Throw me in the pot, throw me in the pot.
> ...
> When it's dead, boil its head
> Make it into soup and bread.

...
Bread of bone and bread of rags,
Eat the dead of starving hags.
...
Do this all of you in memory
Of the race hunger freed.
Do this all of you in memory
Of the race that ate its seed.
Do this all of you in memory
Of the race that died in need. (McGuinness 16–17)

Their chant is a chilling explication of the Famine and its effects.
Everything is reduced to the question of survival; the "pot" is all that
matters. The chant's sing-song, iambic rhythm recontextualizes the horror
of the Famine into the broader futility of life—which only human love,
consciously chosen, can resist. The women's incantation also echoes the
Catholic Mass and, perversely, the Black Mass. Ironically, of course, the
Famine triggered massive emigration, slashed marriage and childbirth
rates, and renewed calls for the repeal of the 1800 Act of Union with
Britain. That this incantation occurs while a pregnant girl mixes a cauldron
with a bayonet imagistically suggests phallic oppression, the Fates, the
three weird sisters of *Macbeth,* and Jonathan Swift, whose famous satire, *A
Modest Proposal* (1729), lampoons British government policy in Ireland
by suggesting that Irish babies be eaten as a solution to overpopulation.
The girl in the scene is pregnant by a British soldier, who abandoned her
and whose comrades gave her the bayonet, presumably to kill herself or
abort. The scene is echoed later when Queen Victoria discusses the
burdens of empire, and Engels and Marx consider capitalism, socialism,
and class divisions. British industrialism was fueled in large part by Irish
labor, seen as uncouth but cheap, completing the link between the Famine
past and the industrial and political future of *Mary and Lizzie.*
Imagistically, McGuinness has charted a course for the twentieth century.
    The entrance of a dancing pig confirms all these connections: "In
Ireland I am called the gentleman who pays the rent. And so I am well
treated. I'm not for eating, I'm for exporting. Have you heard of
landlords? Well, I line their pockets." Gentleman Pig composes his song
about "the most distressing country that ever has been seen" and the fate of
some Irish "we shall call the family Green." The ballad details how the
family survives on potatoes, buttermilk, and fish, while "the rest of what
they grew made the landlord's dainty dish." The Greens overpopulated,
"the Good Lord sent a plague," and "Died a lovely little family, they all
had turned quite green" (McGuinness 18). The final verses underscore

McGuinness's view of the Famine's place in the wider Western economic system and the disdain for the Irish as the "other." For his efforts, Gentleman Pig's throat is slit by the pregnant girl, but he manages to squeal and scamper off stage. Ironically, the pig's parody of capitalism and colonialism has its mirror in the attitude of Marx and Engels toward the Irish in Scene 8. "You're dangerous, a rotting mass, sitting there, passive, the lowest of the low," sneers Marx, "you might have your uses, you could be swept into life, but in your condition you're part and parcel of the old regime" (McGuinness 41). Engels, in fact, described the Irish as drunken, unstable, and dissolute in *The Condition of the Working Class in England* (1845). Mary tells Engels, "You fear us. So you'll remove us. The breastbeaters would save our souls for the sake of their own salvation. How will you save us? Change the world, eh? Change us. Change yourself first" (McGuinness 42). The key to survival and happiness, for McGuinness, lies in the individual, personal decision to love and the recognition that such a human choice fashions the world. Indeed, "God didn't make the earth. We sung it. He heard us and joined in. We did it together, creation," declares Mother Burns, who then joins Mary and Lizzie in singing, "No rest have I, nor liberty, / For love is lord of all" (McGuinness 48–49).

Thematically and structurally, the play struggles to establish final confidence in the victory of human love. McGuinness simply asserts such a victory; he fails to probe it dramatically. Yet it is an assertion of the fundamentally human in the face of the ideological and tribal. McGuinness yokes together the phantasmatic (figures from the otherworldly realm of the dead, such as the priest and his mother, dancing women and Mother Burns), the feminine (Mary and Lizzie), and the Famine (conditions of hunger and disease in Ireland, their father's emigration and work in Britain) to explore dimensions of Irish reality silenced by dominant ideologies. The use of the Famine as both a symbol of human greed and as a model for the interconnections of modern social forces—imperialism, colonialism, capitalism, industrialism, sexism, and socialism—marks an important theatrical appropriation and recontextualization.

V. Banville: Tragicomedy in *The Broken Jug*

If McGuinness's characters thrust the Famine before the audience, many of those populating *The Broken Jug* (1994) are blissfully unaware of it. Yet Banville deliberately transposed a comic blank verse play, *Der Zerbrochene Krug* (1807) by Heinrich von Kleist (1777–1811) from its original setting in Holland to Ireland, the village of Ballybog (a double pun, meaning "town in the bog" and spoofing Friel's Ballybeg, or "little town") in the West in August of 1846. In so doing, the play, which is the first *comic* theatrical depiction of the calamity, and the Famine comment on each other. *The Broken Jug*, which opened on 1 June 1994 on the Abbey Theatre's Peacock stage under the direction of Ben Barnes, received wide critical acclaim. Banville said he was attracted to Kleist because of the German's ability to craft a comedy that foregrounds "the absolute hysteria of his character and his time" (Clarke B10). "The kind of hectic quality and the frenzy of *The Broken Jug* seemed to me to suit the Ireland of that particular time when a catastrophe was taking place . . . ," said Banville (Clarke B10). *The Broken Jug* scores the human capacity to miss the point—and underlines official failure.

With frenzied characters and rapid dialogue, reminiscent of Restoration comedies, the play centers on the corrupt but endearing Judge Adam, whose dangerous liaison with Eve Reck is complicated when he must try a case involving her mother, the Widow Reck. She believes a break-in has led to the destruction of her jug, a family heirloom, and, by the way, an attempt on her daughter's virtue. Robert Temple, a soldier, is dismayed to find himself the prime suspect. Consequently, Temple, Eve's most ardent suitor, is plagued by doubts about her fidelity. Besmirched virtue, outraged honor, and forgotten lies fuel a comedy in which Judge Adam "misremembers." Worse, the case arises just as Sir Walter Peel arrives to inspect Judge Adam, whose clerk, Lynch, delights in exposing his hapless boss.

The play employs and exploits Famine connections. Early on, Judge Adam hears a denunciation of a profiteering magistrate. "Who starved? We have no hunger around here. / Our folk are fit as fiddles, and well-fed. / We have no hunger here" (Banville 19). Maggie, Adam's serving girl, and Ball, Peel's cockney servant, both see what the upper class cannot. "No hunger! Jesus!" cries Maggie in an aside, while Ball adds, "I must have been imagining it then; / I swore I saw them dying in the streets" (Banville 19). Judge Adam self-righteously rejects this view. "I tell you, stuff and nonsense! Lies, all lies! / It's everywhere the same; these cunning brutes / Put on a show whenever strangers come; / All sham, and nothing more" (Banville 19). Ball, an English outsider, is more observant and analytical than the magistrate, who represents an Ascendancy landlord class largely blind to its own social and moral responsibilities before and during the Famine. Adam then demands breakfast for Sir Walter—and Banville emphasizes table fare. Maggie tells the judge, for example, that if his tenants "got a sniff" of the black pudding he purchased, "there'd be a riot in the town" (Banville 22). The audience is reminded that justice was largely in the hands of landlords, and that food supplies existed beyond the reach of the poor, supplies controlled often by Catholic co-religionists. Banville reads social dynamics carefully. Judge Adam, in Scene 4, tells Lynch that he "dreamt last night that I was both judge and judged / . . .

And casually condemned myself to death. / . . . I'm telling you, I woke up in a sweat" (Banville 25). The symptoms the magistrate manifests due to his bad conscience mirror those of starvation and famine fever. Irony, of course, abounds in Adam's anxiety and self-interest. Moreover, he is blind to his own complicity in the exploitation of starving tenants; his lack of vision is self-protection. "Those people, there—they look like skeletons," says Sir Walter, to which the judge responds, "What people, where? I don't see anyone" (Banville 26). Ball replies laconically, "A very handy sort of blindness" (Banville 26). The judge's lands are divided in ways that help lead to excessive reliance on the potato, but he hardly notices that people live on a single crop. "Potatoes! Ah, potatoes. Yes. The spuds" (Banville 27). And, similarly, he sees relief work as a sychophant's means to credit for the inspector's journey. But even Sir Walter sees the truth. "We saw them working, if you'd call it that: / A line of scarecrows, scrabbling in the clay / And eating grass, and roots that they dug up" (Banville 27). On one level, this inability to see is amusing. But likewise this failure of vision caused the Famine: land distribution, excessive reliance on a single crop, relief needs, and Irish social justice were all invisible to the power elites of the time. As a result of a refusal to see and act, blight on the potato became famine for a nation. And the living specters passing the window underline its tragedy and provide, as Phelan might suggest, phantasmatic commentary, silent but eloquent. Historically, Irish peasant were quite real, but government policy pretended they were invisible.

Sir Walter's remit is to see that the law—British-controlled law—is upheld, "That laws shall be fairly administered, / Transgressors punished, and the realm protected" (Banville 28). This lets Judge Adam catalog his troubles, ranging from lazy peasants to greedy townsfolk to litigious landlords. His self-defense, in fact, becomes an indictment of the exploitative nature of colonialism. Moreover, Banville paints him as typically divided, appropriating native Irish culture for rhetorical purposes when it suits him—the Brehon laws, the Firbolgs, the Tuatha Dé Danaan, and William of Orange. Even Sir Walter's seeming beneficence is shown to be deficient. The laws he wants to be just come from a foreign parliament that excludes most of the Irish. Sir Walter discovers just how complex Ireland can be when the Recks, Protestant planters, and the Temples, dispossessed Catholic gentry, each with ironic names, plead their cases. "Dear God, more history! . . . / Dear Lord, my head! / This godforsaken place will drive me mad," cries the inspector (Banville 47–48).

Stage directions play an important role in *The Broken Jug*. Windows and open doors—liminal spaces marking the borders between prosperity and famine, between gentry and peasantry, between the living and the dead—reveal the catastrophe. Ball informs the judge during the session in Scene 5 of Act I that fifty plaintiffs are at the door, but Adam dismisses them as mere "scroungers back again" (Banville 29). Ball, predictably, sees through Adam's excuses that it is all an act and observes, "They faint convincingly, I'll say that for them: / That young one with the baby just went down" (Banville 30). Act II opens with another table scene. Court officials and their attendants are eating, while through the window, the faces of the starving continue to appear. Judge Adam, in dumbshow, keeps trying to shoo them away.

Central to comedy is exposure, and *The Broken Jug* reveals the extent to which the colonial system was complicit in masking and denying the realities of Famine Ireland. But, because the play is Banville's adaptation of Kleist, whom he wanted to bring to the Irish stage, the human realities of subterfuge and hypocrisy arise. "I wanted people to get the point of Kleist," says Banville, "which was not that he was saying 'isn't life quirky, funny and wonderful?' but 'isn't life appalling and appallingly funny?' So while you have all of these people arguing over a broken jug or maybe this young girl's virtue, it is pretty trivial to what is happening around them" (Clarke B10). The play is set in Famine Ireland, "because I wanted it to be accessible, familiar, to Irish audiences. The Famine is the most important event in modern Irish history. I like the idea of having [almost] everyone in the play busy ignoring the fact that there's a famine going on" (Battersby 10). Theatrical space and dramatic performance become what Habermas would recognize as a public sphere. Banville's satire exposes the local, that is, the failure of British policy during the Famine, and depicts the universal, the folly of human deceit and self-delusion as seen in the judge's peccadilloes. Banville's play reveals both the amusing and the lamentable in the fact that Judge Adam is *not* evil—only blind.

To conclude with reference to the critical theorists, the Famine in some ways offers the ultimate in postmodern challenges, as it resists any comprehensive metanarrative. It turns to the situated and the local to tell its story, and it tells it best in the voices of its victims, its perpetrators, and its children. In Murphy, ritual action focuses on the body and its needs and turns in on itself to show the dual character of ritual: mythic past, eternal present. Yet at the same time, Murphy's *Famine*—perhaps the most significant of all "Famine plays"—resolutely destroys the rituals by which its narrative and structure proceed. Meetings end in dispute and hostility. Prayers end in blasphemy. Courtship and lovemaking end in confrontations with death. In MacIntyre's *The Great Hunger,* the performative and the metaphoric again turn to the body—and the soul—to map possibility and frustration. In Friel's *Translations,* the elusive character of language is explored in both its expressive and constituting dimensions, and thus demonstrates the depth of the Famine tragedy. By delivering the coup de grace to the Irish language, it changed forever who the Irish people were. In a sense, language is the mother of all discourse, and its change, as Foucault might suggest, is tectonic. The discourse, no less than the cartography and topography, is altered forever, and one's public sphere becomes unrecognizable. Conversely, however, by recognizing such a phenomenon, one begins to rediscover that sphere. In McGuinness's *Mary and Lizzie*, the public sphere widens. The Famine's links to class and gender oppression are clearly visible. He excavates, in a Foucauldian sense, the discourse on its causes and effects and, finally, recovers repressed bodies and silenced memories of women and workers, as Phelan and Schumacher suggest, through "true" but "phantasmatic" performances. Finally, in Banville's *The Broken Jug*, the Famine emerges as a silent, spectral presence—through an emphasis on the body, as Foucault, Schumacher, and Phelan all suggest—to condemn human folly. Through the starving, already nearly phantasmatic, at the window, Banville reminds his audience that the public sphere is not simply what those *in power* see or want seen. This is precisely the point Habermas makes in charting the expansion of the public sphere. Ironically, however, the folly Banville depicts can be amusing, in a restricted sense, when pointed out by subalterns who see through the pretense—and thus add yet another layer to Famine discourse, as Foucault's archeological approach to discourse suggests. In some sense, all these plays—and the others to which reference has been made, acknowledge the burden of witnessing, as Schumacher urges. "There is no model," he argues, "of representing the unrepresentable," but one can move beyond mere knowledge to "stimulate the imagination" and leave the audience "disturbed," "perplexed," and "stunned [into] silence" (Schumacher 8). The Famine confronts dramatists with a challenge that is analogous, though not identical, to the Shoah.

The would-be Famine drama faces three critical problems. First, it must give voice to the silent millions who died or fled, and to make that voice ring true from a legitimate perspective. Second, that voice must be staged in a compelling, though not necessarily realistic, performance. Indeed, approaches moving beyond realism—as shown by the success of Murphy, MacIntyre, and others—may be the most effective strategies. Third, the voice-in-performance must speak meaningfully of the Famine to contemporary audiences. The play, through the clarity of its theme and the aesthetic character of its dynamic form—movement, language, and images—must represent what is, on one level, unrepresentable. The five plays considered here—*Famine* by Tom Murphy, *The Great Hunger* by Tom MacIntyre, *Translations* by Brian Friel, *Mary and Lizzie* by Frank McGuinness, and *The Broken Jug* by John Banville—endeavor to undertake this representational challenge through speech, silence, and movement, with considerable success. In a paradoxical way, the emergence of this drama continues, in new voices for different ears, the silence and the lament of *an Gorta Mór*—in its own way as creative and as necessary as the keening of long ago.

Tom Murphy asks himself, in his introduction to *Famine*, "Was I, in what I shall call my times, the mid-twentieth century, a student or a victim of the Famine? It was that thought/feeling, I believe, that made me want to write the play, the need to write about the moody self and my times (xi). Increasingly, Irish writers are finding *An Gorta Mor,* their greatest national disaster, holds the potential to become one of their richest cultural resources.

Works Cited

Agnew, Sister Una. *The Mystical Imagination of Patrick Kavanagh.* Dublin: Columba, 1998.

Auslander, Philip. *From Acting to Performance: Essays in Modernism and Postmodernism.* London: Routledge, 1997.

Banville, John. *The Broken Jug.* Loughcrew, Oldcastle, County Meath: Gallery, 1994.

Battersby, Eileen. "Comedy in a Time of Famine," *The Irish Times* (Dublin), 24 May 1994: 10.

Brown, Terence. *Ireland: A Social and Cultural History: 1922–1985.* London: Fontana, HarperCollins, 1985.

Clarke, Jocelyn. "A Man Who Finds Life Appallingly Funny," *The Sunday Tribune* (Dublin), 29 May 1994: B10.

Colgan, Gerry. Review of *The Great Hunger. The Irish Times,* Tuesday, 10 May 1983: 10.

De Valera, Eamon. Saint Patrick's Day speech, 17 March 1943. *Great Irish Voices: Over 400 Years of Irish Oratory.* Ed. Gerard Reid. Dublin: Irish Academic Press, 1999. 146–50.

Foucault, Michél. "What Is an Author." *The Foucault Reader: An Introduction to Foucault's Thought.* Ed. Paul Rabinow. London: Penguin, 1991. 101–20.

Friel, Brian. *Translations. Plays: 1.* London: Faber, 1996.

Habermas, Jürgen. *The Structural Transformation of the Public Sphere.* Cambridge, England: Polity, 1996.

Harris, Eoghan. *Souper Sullivan: A Play about Irish Protestants.* Unpublished ms., 1984.

Healy, Gerald. *The Black Stranger.* Dublin: Duffy, 1950.

Herr, Cheryl. 'The Erotics of Irishness." *Critical Inquiry* XVII.1 (Autumn 1990): 1–34.

Ilyichov, L. F., et al. (Institute of Marxism-Leninism of the Communist Party of the Soviet Union,Central Committee). *Frederick Engels: A Biography*. Trans. Victor Schneierson. Moscow: Progress, 1974.

Jordan, Eamonn. *The Feast of Famine: The Plays of Frank McGuinness*. Berne, Switzerland: Peter Lang, 1997.

Kavanagh, Patrick, and Tom MacIntyre. *The Great Hunger: Poem into Play*. Gigginstown, Mullingar, County Westmeath: Lilliput, 1988.

McArdle, John. *Two Houses*. Dublin: TEAM Educational Theatre, 1996.

McGuinness, Frank. *Mary and Lizzie*. London: Faber, 1989.

McHugh, Roger J. "The Famine in Irish Oral Tradition." *The Great Famine: Studies in Irish History 1845–52*. Ed. R. Dudley Edwards and T. Desmond Williams. Dublin: Browne and Nolan, 1962.

Minogue, Jim. *Flight to Grosse Ile*. Unpublished ms., 1996.

Murphy, Tom. *Plays: 1*. London: Methuen, Reed, 1997.

Murray, Christopher. Review of *The Great Hunger: Poem into Play*. *Theatre Ireland* XVI (September–November 1988): 56.

Nowlan, David. "Should Critics Read Scripts" in "Prompts." *The Irish Times,* Friday, 27 May 1983: 10.

O'Byrne, Joe. *The Last Potato*. Dublin: Passion Machine, 1994. (Copyrighted, but unpublished.)

O'Grady, Hubert. *The Famine* (1886). *The Journal of Irish Literature* XIV.1 (January 1985): 25–49.

O'Toole, Fintan. *Tom Murphy: The Politics of Magic*. Dublin: New Island, 1994.

Phelan, Peggy. *Mourning Sex: Performing Public Memories*. London: Routledge, 1997.

Pine, Richard. *The Diviner: The Art of Brian Friel*. Dublin: U College Dublin P, 1999. (Rev. ed. of *Brian Friel and Ireland's Drama*. London: Routledge, 1990.)

Quinn, Antoinette. *Patrick Kavanagh: Born-Again Romantic*. Dublin: Gill and Macmillan, 1991.

Schumacher, Claude, ed. *Staging the Holocaust: The Shoah in Drama and Performance*. Cambridge, England: Cambridge Univ. Press, 1998.

Turner, Victor. *From Ritual to Theatre: The Human Seriousness of Play*. New York: PAJ, 1982.

Yeats, W. B. *The Collected Plays*. London: Macmillan, 1966.

Chapter Ten

The Great Hunger:
Act of God or Acts of Man?[1]

WILLIAM B. ROGERS

Many historians believe that the Great Hunger is the defining event in Irish history. This claim, like most every aspect of the Famine (including the years of the Famine, the number of dead, its lasting impact, how it should be remembered, and even its name), is debatable, but there can be no doubt that the Famine had profound effects on Ireland, Britain, and the United States. Another significant question surrounding the Famine is whether it should be considered an example of government-supported genocide. The Famine has been included in the New Jersey State curriculum on genocide and the Holocaust, both because some see a clear record of government complicity in this tragedy and because of the political power of Irish Americans in New Jersey. Similarly, the Center for Holocaust Studies at Drew University has expanded its areas of concern to include genocide studies, and the Caspersen School of Graduate Studies in 1999 added a certificate program in Holocaust and genocide studies that includes coursework on the Famine. While the label of genocide is more and more being used in relation to the Famine, unlike in the Armenian genocide, there is relatively little ongoing debate in academic circles (particularly in Ireland or Britain) about whether the Famine should be considered an act of genocide or simply the unfortunate confluence of demographic, economic, political, and natural forces. In other words, was it an act of God or the acts of humans that resulted in this catastrophe?

I decided to explore this vital issue by examining the current definitions of genocide in order to better illuminate whether the causes of the Famine, the policies and response by the British government, and the actions of

Irish landlords should lead us to classify the Great Hunger as a genocidal event. The purpose was to develop an assessment that goes beyond a mere polemic. The discussion of the Famine as genocide has occurred much more in what might be considered the popular press and Irish emigrant social/cultural organizations, mainly in America.[2] Scholars have been less eager to take on this issue, especially in Ireland and Britain. The reaction to Prime Minister Tony Blair's apology for the conduct of the British government during the Great Hunger demonstrates that many in Britain and Ireland are not willing to come to grips with the implications of the Famine. It is clear that some in Ireland, America, and England seek to minimize what might be considered the genocidal aspects of the Famine for current political gain. Others may accentuate these genocidal components for similar reasons.[3]

It seemed an investigation of this question utilizing current definitions of genocide and comparative options should prove fruitful in engaging the profound question of whether this horrible event can be properly classified as genocide as defined since World War II.[4] By applying the current definitions of genocide to the Famine, it might be possible get beyond both Irish-American hyperbole against "the bloody Brits" and scholarly reluctance even to consider the possibility of genocide in this historical instance. These definitions can offer a logical, legal, and widely agreed upon basis for evaluating the events of the Famine. Further, examination of other purported genocides-in Cambodia and Armenia, the Holocaust, the Chinese famine of the late 1950s, Stalin's treatment of the peasants in the 1930s-provides some real world events for both testing the validity of the idea of the Famine as genocide and the usefulness of the current definitions of genocide.

Thus, when it came time to organize a graduate-level class on the Great Hunger for the spring 2000 semester, I determined to make the genocide debate one of the key questions for the class. With a renewed focus on the Famine during the last decade or so, coupled with ever-increasing interest in all facets of genocide (history, literature, prevention, remembrance), it seemed like an effective teaching tool (see for example, Riemer; Balakian).

At the first class meeting I outlined my expectations and hopes for the class and encouraged the students to keep the issue of genocide in mind as they read the books for the course in the process of doing their research. Two of the fourteen students were teachers, with the rest coming from a wide variety of professional occupations. Eleven of the fourteen were Irish Americans by birth and two by marriage. Most had some vague notion about the Famine, but all confessed to be more or less ignorant about the details of what occurred. This is an interesting example of one theory of how we develop ideas about history-that we absorb from family, friends, and society a story about an event that may or may not have much relationship to reality. Several were honest enough to admit that they felt the Famine was the fault of the English, but without being sure why.

In the course readings, we started with Cecil Woodham-Smith's *The Great Hunger,* and almost immediately two students began to complain about the "whitewashing" of the Famine by historians. For example, Woodham-Smith ended her book with Queen Victoria's visit in 1849. Since starvation and disease continued to be widespread until at least 1852, and foreclosures, shortened life spans, and mass emigration continued for years afterward, these students felt that even Woodham-Smith had not told the full story. They saw the Famine as genocide-massive amounts of food were exported from Ireland while people starved, landlords were allowed to evict freely, the relief projects required sick and dying people to work for assistance, and so on-and wondered why others didn't. Most of the rest of the class seemed reluctant to move so precipitously to a conclusion on one of the central foci of the course.

I recount this as evidence of what I believe to be the general attitude of many Americans toward the Great Hunger-ignorance of the details, uncertainty about its historical significance, feelings of blame toward the British government and people, and among some, a nearly palpable rage that no one seems to notice the enormity of the crime committed against the Irish by Britain. Attitudes among the Irish are another matter-several of my students tried to get Irish friends (one who had lived in Ireland for two years spent a week there during the course) to talk about it, and interestingly, they met with no interest at all, and in some cases, actual antipathy to the subject. One of the many fascinations about the Famine is that Irish Americans seem so much more upset and willing to discuss and debate it, even 150 years later, than do native Irish. That, however, is the subject of another paper. In order to broaden the students' engagement with the Famine, we included a variety of readings, films, and even music.[5]

How does one go about bringing a charge of genocide against a nation for something that happened 150 years ago, when the term didn't even exist? (Although it is interesting that Michael Davitt referred to what happened to the Irish as a holocaust, small h.) As Christine Kinealy has said, "Even compared with contemporary famines, the Irish Famine was the most lethal in modern history. Also unlike today's famines the Irish Famine occurred within jurisdiction of, and a stone's throw away from, the capital of the richest empire in the world" (Gribben 247).

Clearly, by pursuing this investigation, we are open to the charge of being ahistorical by placing modern expectations on past human actions. However, a historian can only try to proceed as Thomas Gallagher stated in the Prologue to *Paddy's Lament:*

And so I determined to bring the evidence into the glaring light as best I could. I would speak for the victim, comment on his behalf, and describe the suffering he endured. I would try to avoid the role of propagandist and cling to the record. Let the eyewitness reports and corroborated fact and figures speak for themselves, and if they amount to an indictment, so be it. In light of what my research uncovered, I could do no less.

The question of what contemporaries thought of the events in Ireland at the time will be explored later, but to begin the discussion I want to start with twentieth-century definitions of genocide. Therefore, listed below are definitions from six sources:

1. The definitional article included in the United Nations Genocide Convention, 1948, stipulates in Article II:

> In the present Convention, genocide means any of the following acts committed with intent to destroy, in whole or in part, a national, ethnic, racial or religious group, as such:
> (a) Killing members of the group; (b) Causing serious bodily or mental harm to members of the group; (c) Deliberately inflicting on the group conditions of life calculated to bring about its physical destruction in whole or in part; (d) Imposing measures intended to prevent births within the group; (e) Forcibly transferring children of the group to another group.[6]

2. The definition of *genocide* by Rafael Lemkin, whose influence played a key role in the term's incorporation into the Geneva conventions, is:

> Generally speaking, genocide does not necessarily mean the immediate destruction of a nation, except when accomplished by mass killings of all members of a nation. It is intended rather to signify a coordinated plan of different actions aiming at the destruction of essential foundations of the life of national groups, with the aim of annihilating the groups themselves. The objectives of such a plan would be the disintegration of the political and social institutions, of culture, language, national feelings, religion, and the economic existence of national groups, and the destruction of the personal security, liberty, health, dignity, and even the lives of the individual belonging to such groups. Genocide is directed against the national group as an entity, and the actions involved are directed against individuals, not in their individual capacity but as members of a national group.

3. Helen Fein, a leading scholar of genocide, has developed the following definition, "Genocide is sustained purposeful action by a

perpetrator to physically destroy a collectivity directly or through interdiction of the biological and social reproduction of group members."(96)

4. Richard L. Rubenstein, in *The Age of Triage: Fear and Hope in an Overcrowded World* states, "a government is as responsible for a genocidal policy when its officials accept mass death as a necessary cost of implementing their policies as when they pursue genocide as an end in itself."

5. Israel Charny, in an attempt to more broadly define genocide, formulated what he calls a "generic definition of genocide:" "Genocide in the generic sense is the mass killing of substantial numbers of human beings . . . under conditions of the essential defenselessness and helplessness of the victims." (75) He also argues, "Genocide that is undertaken or even allowed in the course of or incidental to the purposes of achieving a goal of colonization or development of a territory belonging to an indigenous people, or any other consolidation of political or economic power though mass killing of those perceived to be standing in the way." (80)

6. According to *The Oxford English Dictionary,* genocide is "[t]he deliberate and systematic extermination of an ethnic or national group"[7]

While containing a variety of criteria for determining genocide, some commonalities exist among these definitions. The actions must first, be that of a government deliberately undertaken; second, aimed a "group" of people, not for actions but for membership in that group; third, result in large numbers of intentional, planned deaths; and fourth, attack that which makes the "group" distinct-religion, culture, music, language, and so on. A critical element is the presence of an "intent to destroy," which can be either "in whole or in part," groups defined in terms of nationality, ethnicity, race, or religion.

These definitions of genocide have come to encompass additional groups of people and have been applied to situations occurring both before and after the Holocaust, including the Famine. It is worth noting that the term *holocaust* has been appropriated to refer to one specific example of genocide. One of the first to take this approach to the Famine was Thomas Gallagher in *Paddy's Lament* (xiv).

According to historian Dennis Clark, the Irish Famine was "the culmination of generations of neglect, misrule and repression. It was an epic of English colonial cruelty and inadequacy. For the landless cabin dwellers it meant emigration or extinction" (7). A former theologian at Drew-who does not have Irish ancestry-told me that in his opinion there have been three genocides in Irish history: that perpetuated by Cromwell and his troops in the 1600s, the famine of 1740-41, and the Great Hunger. Perhaps historian Christine Kinealy, author of *This Great Calamity* and *A Death-Dealing Famine: The Great Hunger in Ireland,* has produced the best works on the moral implications linked to the Irish Famine. She asserts, "Despite the overwhelming evidence of prolonged distress caused by successive years of potato blight, the underlying philosophy of the relief efforts was that they should be kept to a minimalist level; in fact they actually decreased as the Famine progressed" (*Death-Dealing Famine* 17). These indictments maintain that the actions of the British during this period were aimed at changing Irish society. This is why Rubenstein's and Charny's definitions seem to resonate with the case of the Great Hunger. A series of theories about society, economics, and human beings-and the policies implemented in the name of these beliefs-led to the disaster. Please note, however, that Helen Fein's definition calls for the intentional and systematic mass killing of members of a group.

The role of laissez-faire economics in the Famine is well documented. Suffice it to say that many of the key actors in the British government were devoted disciples of this theory and sought to use it as guidance in policy formulation. In terms of natural disasters such as the destruction of the potato crop, laissez-faire theory simply postulated that it was not for the government to provide relief and assistance to its citizens. Equally as important, this theory held that any government interference with the trading of goods would be harmful to the stability of the British economy. For the Whig Party, which controlled the relief efforts throughout most of the Famine, any interference would be disastrous. Unlike his predecessor, Robert Peel, Prime Minister Lord John Russell made clear his view on treating the Famine. "It must be thoroughly understood that we cannot feed the people. . . . We can at best keep down prices where there is no regular market to prevent established dealers from raising prices much beyond the fair price with ordinary profits" (Ranelagh 3).

This non-interventionist attitude toward treating the worsening economic situation would only mean further suffering, as "preventing mass mortality was simply impossible. Even attempting to do so was wrong, since it would bankrupt Irish landlords, and the ensuing demoralization would destroy 'industry' and 'self-dependence' and ultimately put a stop to economic activity" (Ó Gráda 82). Clearly, the top leaders of the British government were more concerned with the long-term economic effects of interfering with the economy than with the short-term human elements affiliated with the Famine.

Since Ireland was a part of the United Kingdom, and was in fact joined to Britain by the Act of Union in 1800, it should have enjoyed the same welfare benefits and "human rights" as existed in Britain at the time. The Agricultural Revolution that so changed the English economy and society-consolidating and enclosing the land, throwing tenants off the land and into the growing cities-did come to Ireland, but with specifically Irish circumstances. What differed in Ireland was the structure of land holding. Landlords had taken over the small farms, and there were tenant farmers. But there were few cities with factories for the displaced. Most of the capital resulting from any agricultural surplus was diverted back to England by the large number of absentee landlords who chose to live there. As Woodham-Smith asserts, "rents were spent in England or on the continent. In 1842, it was estimated that 6,000,000 pounds of rent were being remitted outside of Ireland" (21).

With nowhere to go, and no industrial workforce to join, the Irish peasant could only hope to be allowed to divide the land into smaller and smaller parcels as the size of his family increased and each new generation came of age. This benefitted the landlord because he could now collect more rent for the same land, much like renting an entire house versus dividing it up into one-room apartments (Woodham-Smith 22). The potato made this all possible, temporarily. The result, however, was a variation on feudalism, where Irish peasants were tied to the land simply because they had no other alternative except emigration. Landlords, on the other hand, had preeminent power and control. John Stuart Mill realized this when he wrote, "in Ireland alone, the whole agricultural population can be evicted by the mere will of the landlord" (Woodham-Smith 24). There was little capital and no workforce for industrialization. Many landlords drained their holdings of value to support their lifestyles and had little or no sense of responsibility toward them or their tenants. They simply collected the rents and spent the money elsewhere. Or, as a student in my class argued; "The serfdom of the Middle Ages had been replaced with the serfdom of leasing."

By the harvest of 1846, even after it became clear the blight had destroyed a second potato crop, Charles Trevelyan (Assistant Secretary of the Treasury and the official in charge of relief to the Irish during the Famine under the Russell Administration) and the British government refused to change their policy. The policy did change at the beginning of 1847, because the public works mode of relief had failed so miserably, but the essential underlying philosophy had not changed. In fact, Trevelyan became more entrenched in his belief in the laws of supply and demand. Woodham-Smith writes:

The Government had now accepted the fact that a second failure of the potato was about to occur, and Trevelyan . . . was determined to pursue a new policy. . . . (He) had decided that, in the second failure there was to be no Government importation of food from abroad and no interference whatsoever with the laws of supply and demand; whatever might be done by starting public works and paying wages, the provision of food for Ireland was to be left entirely to private enterprise and private traders. (91)

The most problematic part of Trevelyan's failure to act is that he knew from his Relief Commissioner, Sir Randolph Routh, that more relief was needed from the British authorities. Routh pressed Trevelyan to change his policies and to import food to the western counties of Ireland that had been hit the hardest by the Famine. "You cannot answer the cry of want by a quotation of political economy," he wrote Trevelyan during the first phase of the second failure (Woodham-Smith 91). But resolute faith in laissez-faire allowed Trevelyan and his followers to continue a policy of minimum intervention. He believed that if food depots were still operating when the Irish people discovered that the second failure was even more widespread than the first, they would "expect to be fed." He wrote to Routh, "The only way to prevent the people from becoming habitually dependent on Government is to bring the (depots) to a close. The uncertainty about the new crop only makes it more necessary" (Woodham-Smith 89). To many, this would seem the time to keep food depots in operation and to increase their role. The approach of the British government fitted in with prevailing ideological attitudes of the time-that poverty was the fault of the individual and that relief had to be kept to a minimum (Ó Gráda 6; Kinealy, *Death-Dealing Famine* 1-16).

This was an extremely harsh view in light of the horrid conditions in Ireland where the people had almost no resources to draw upon. A question remains, though. Why did Routh and others not push harder in opposition to Trevelyan? Even though they knew the real conditions in Ireland, they shrank from publicly opposing the government. Routh, for example, was too entrenched in the system and, essentially, was a civil servant just like Trevelyan. The "training of a lifetime forbade it." Woodham-Smith writes of Routh's failure to take more assertive action, "He tried therefore to convince himself that Trevelyan's policy was just and wise" (89). The "old-boy network" remained intact while the Irish starved to death.

A related feature of British policy was their expectation that the Irish would work in order to receive relief in the belief that nothing should be given away lest the people take advantage of the government. Thus, relief projects were created in an attempt to provide cash to the Irish poor. Using these funds, they would be able to buy food at market prices and the capitalist system would prevail with everyone benefiting. The British "were convinced that, once wages were being paid on the new large-scale public works, and the people had money to spend, then food would be attracted to Ireland. The field was to be left strictly to private enterprise." Woodham-Smith attributes the failure of this thinking to the fact that "the population (in Ireland) lived so exclusively on the potato that no trade in any other description of food existed" (107). Although there was a significant trade in corn, often grown by poor people as a cash crop and exported to Britain, the poor Irish were unfamiliar with this food as a staple. Furthermore, they needed it to pay their rents and there was no developed import network. Thus, Trevelyan's philosophy did not work because the conditions in Ireland did not fit the British model. There was no available food, little trade in food, and almost no capital to invest in any food trade other than the potato. The public works only served to increase the suffering as half-starved, half-naked people worked in outdoor conditions (Gallagher 92).

The too-low wages did not help much because the price of the food that was available for purchase was too high. Trevelyan tried to force the reality in Ireland to respond to an untried (and sometimes conveniently forgotten) theoretical model (i.e., the Corn Laws, intervention in China [Kinealy, *Death-Dealing Famine* 8]), and as a result caused the Irish to suffer significantly more than necessary. His failure to look at the situation objectively allowed him to continue to pursue such a rigid and unyielding philosophy. Rubenstein argues that a "government is responsible for a genocidal policy when its officials accept mass death as a necessary cost of implementing their policies." This would clearly seem to be the case with Trevelyan and the British government with respect to the Famine. As John Mitchell noted:

> In the first year of the famine, then, we find that the measures proposed by the English government, were, first, repeal of the Corn Laws, which depreciated Ireland's only article of export; second, a new Coercion Law, to torment and transport the people; and third, a grant of 100,000 to certain clerks or commissioners, chiefly for their own profit, and from which the starving people derived no benefit whatever. Yet, Ireland was taunted with this grant, as if it were alms granted to her. Double the sum (200,000) was, in the same Session, appropriated for Battersea Park, a suburban place of recreation much resorted to by Londoners. (Keneally 115)

It is reasonable to ask whether the British government could have done better. Christine Kinealy argues that it did do better, when in the summer of 1847 soup kitchens daily fed 3 million people, without any proof of destitution. This short-term experience demonstrates that with the proper will, the mass starvation could have been alleviated (*Death-Dealing Famine* 9). Similarly, Ó Gráda makes a compelling case that if the British government had subsidized emigration, the deaths from disease, starvation, and the horrifying sea voyages could have been greatly reduced (121).

As one examines the charge of genocide against the British government, there are four main areas in addition to the above discussion of relief efforts that need to be explored further to come to a reasonable determination. These are: the destruction of Irish culture; the exportation of food during the Famine; the evictions undertaken and the resulting emigration; and, possibly most crucial, the racist attitudes that allowed the Famine to occur in the first place. Keep in mind Lemkin's definition of genocide, wherein destruction of culture is one of the components of genocidal activity.

Clearly, the Famine destroyed much of Irish culture and nearly destroyed much more. "It didn't matter who was related to you, your friend was whoever would give you a bite to put in your mouth," recalled an old woman in a handwritten memoir. "Sport and pastimes disappeared. Poetry, music, and dancing stopped. They lost and forgot them all. . . . The Famine killed everything" (Kinealy, *Death-Dealing Famine*, 155). As various scholars have noted, everything changed after the Famine, and if it hadn't been for middle- and upper-class Protestant and foreign travelers and scholars taking copious notes about music and folklore, much of what does remain would have been lost forever. Of course, we have no idea how much was lost, but certainly the Irish language came perilously close to extinction, and much folklore and music was lost. Despite the claims of such revisionists as Roy Foster, who argue that these changes were happening anyway and the Famine only accelerated the process, the fact remains that the Famine nearly depopulated the west of Ireland, where the majority of Irish speakers lived. The same holds true for the loss of much music, dance, and other aspects of Irish culture.[8]

In assessing the responsibility of the British in exacerbating the Famine, it is necessary to look at one of the most controversial facts with regard to the economic policies of Britain. While the potato crop was failing, the country was still exporting a great deal of food to its neighbors. According to Cecil Woodham-Smith, "[N]o issue has provoked so much anger . . . between the two countries (England and Ireland) as the indisputable fact that huge quantities of food were exported from Ireland to England throughout the period when the people of Ireland were dying of starvation" (75). Some historians, such as Cormac Ó Gráda, Christine Kinealy, Thomas Gallagher, and others, contend that the amount of food produced in Ireland during the Famine could have fed a country with a larger population.

According to Gallagher (of whom it must be said that some doubt his validity as a historical source because of his passionate indictment of the British government):

> It must be remembered that there was still enough wheat, oats, barley, butter, eggs, beef, pork, and lamb in Ireland, even in this famine year of 1847, to feed for a year four times as many people as were leaving the country. But all this produce was still being sent to Liverpool on the very same ships that carried the emigrants, whom the English lawmakers claimed could not be fed, were redundant in their native land, and therefore had to go somewhere else. (148-49; Kinealy, *Death-Dealing Famine* 79-81)

Unlike other famines in Ireland, such as the famine in 1782-83, the ports of the country remained open, prices remained relatively high, and the viewpoints of the distressed people were not taken into account.

Besides these grain crops, various types of livestock continued to be exported to Britain during this time, supplies which could have been distributed in large quantities to feed the distressed. Firsthand accounts document the departure of ships full of foodstuffs: ". . . several ships laden with maize, including the *Sun* from New York with 116,034 bushels on board, made stops in Cork in February and March without landing any of their cargoes" (Ó Gráda 123). Although the debate continues over whether the total number of imports brought into Ireland outnumbered the exports during the Famine years, the image of food supplies sitting in front of a starving population has provided a damning portrait of the British relief effort. Again, might not these events constitute genocide as defined by Rubenstein and Charny?

Along with the picture of armed troops guarding the shipments of food out of Ireland during the Famine years, the other lasting image of the period is that of the destitute family standing sadly by as their hovel is pushed to the ground by the landlord's men-often with military personnel present to ensure order is preserved.

Throughout the Famine, thousands of tenants fell in arrears of rent and were evicted from their homes. As the Famine continued, many landlords came to the decision, sometimes reluctantly, that their own survival depended on removing from their land the "surplus" Irish. This trend accelerated as the peasants ran out of pigs, sheep and other ways of paying their rents. "A tenant farmer, no matter what the Famine had done or was doing to preclude his ability to pay the rent, was subject to eviction by reason of his failure to pay it" (Gallagher 45).

Josephine Butler, an Englishwoman who witnessed ejections, wrote:

Sick and aged, little children, and women with child were alike thrust forth into the snows of winter. . . . And to prevent their return their cabins were leveled to the ground . . . the few remaining tenants were forbidden to receive the outcasts-the majority rendered penniless by the famine, wandered aimlessly about the roads or bogs till they found refuge in the workhouse or the grave (Costigan 181).

Additionally, the overall record of the Irish landlords is a poor one, since many chose to evict their starving tenants instead of providing relief for them. "In consequence, they (the landlord class) cared little about what went on in their estates so long as they yielded the maximum money income" (Green 265). As one Irishman put it,

The landlords discovered that the best plan would be to get completely rid of those who were so heavy a burden upon them, by shipping them to America; at the same time publishing to the world, as an act of brotherly love and kindness, a deal of crafty, calculating selfishness-for the expense of transporting each individual was less than the cost of a year's support in a workhouse (Whyte 11).

During the Famine, many pieces of legislation were designed to remove the Irish from their land holdings. One such law, known as the Gregory Clause (Gregory was an Irish landlord), is a prime example. "The most notorious section of the 1847 Amendment Act was the 'Gregory' or 'Quarter of an Acre Clause,' which stated that any occupier of more than a quarter of an acre of land could not be deemed destitute and therefore was ineligible to receive relief paid for by the poor rates" (Kinealy, *This Great Calamity* 181). In several situations, the actions of the Irish landlords were such that they were able to secure British support in removing tenants from the land. According to James Donnelly, "I would draw the following broad conclusion: at a fairly early point of the Great Famine the government's abject failure to stop or even slow down the clearances (evictions) contributed in a major way to enshrining the idea of English state-sponsored genocide in the Irish popular mind" (170-71). For the victims of the evictions, it was just another obstacle that these people had to deal with in the worsening Famine years. "Mass evictions . . . will forever be associated with the Irish Famine. It has been estimated that, excluding peaceable surrenders, over a quarter of a million people were evicted between 1849 and 1854. The total number of people who had to leave their holdings in the period is likely to be around half a million and 200,000 small holdings were obliterated" (Póirtéir 229).

The conditions the evicted Irish were forced to travel under were horrifying and have been well documented. Some have argued the phrase *coffin ships* is an exaggeration since most did live to see the New World. But when one takes into account the mortality of the immigrants-far higher than native-born Americans or earlier immigrants-then the term retains its relevance (Kinealy, *Death-Dealing Famine* 2).

As just one example, Gallagher writes, "Like some species of animal whose value was far below that of cattle, pigs, and sheep, the Irish were ferried to Liverpool, standing room only on the upper deck, where they were subjected to dreadful exposure during the thirty- to thirty-six-hour crossing. Sometimes as many as a thousand emigrants, with a full cargo of pigs between decks, were taken aboard steamers weighing only eight hundred tons" (Gallagher 149).

Note that the Lemkin definition of genocide includes the disintegration of social institutions, which forced migration/emigration would surely accomplish. The central question of this exercise may be whether the exportation of food, the mass evictions, and the horrible conditions the emigrating Irish suffered should be seen as unfortunate side effects of a natural disaster or as the result of human decision and agency.

Much has been made of "comparative" genocides, that is, questions such as, which was worse, the slave trade or the Holocaust? In our class, several students made presentations comparing the Famine to the Armenian genocide and the Chinese famine of the 1950s. While instructive to the student, this exercise may well be an irrelevant debate for the victims of these tragedies. However, at least one eyewitness had this to say about the conditions the Irish traveled under: "One member of the House of Commons stated before his colleagues that a navy captain who had been engaged in suppressing the slave trade off Africa had declared that 'the condition of many Irish emigrant vessels which he had seen . . . begged all descriptions of the state of the captured slave ships'" (Gallagher 206). Gallagher argues that

> more was in fact done by the British to eliminate the inhumanity of the African slave trade than ever was done to alleviate the suffering of the Irish, who as tax-paying British subjects, with representatives in Parliament, were entitled to the same treatment as any Englishman living in England. Instead they were made to live under conditions aboard ship far worse than those suffered by African slaves. (207)

As Woodham-Smith notes, "The worst ships were those that brought emigrants sent out by their landlords, and of all the sufferings endured during the Famine none aroused such savage resentment, or left behind such hatred, as the landlord emigration" (227). Prominently featured in the PBS documentary, *The Irish in America*, was landlord Dennis Mahon, who evicted a large number of his tenants and was subsequently assassinated when word got back to Ireland that so many had died on the sea voyage.

A primary criticism of the British government and nation during the Famine revolves around the contention that the British viewed the Irish race as an inferior group of people and that it was this racist attitude that made the Famine possible. While some of the economic practices affiliated with this viewpoint have already been examined, it is necessary to summarize how the British government viewed the Irish as a whole population. In other realms, such as that of the popular press, the Irish were commonly degraded and portrayed as having subhuman characteristics. Popular cartoons, such as "The Irish Frankenstein" and "The Irish Tempest," illustrate how many British saw the Irish as savages who roamed the countryside.

These racist views were "reinforced by other cartoons, such as those that appeared in *Punch,* which gave Irish men apelike features. It refused to take into account-possibly intentionally-the fact that, during the course of the nineteenth century, the Irish in Britain were, in reality, a diverse group and a sizable proportion of them were distributed in higher echelons of the social and economic hierarchy" (Kinealy, *This Great Calamity* 329). When one considers the fact that many of the Irish were different in their customs, dress, language, literature, and religion, along with the widespread assumption that the Irish presented a threat to the working classes of Britain it is clear that the Irish were combating an unpopular public image when the Famine first commenced in 1845.

Obviously, negative British attitudes towards the Irish were not a recent development. Nassau Senior, an economics professor at Oxford University, remarked to a colleague that the Famine "would not kill more than one million people, and that would scarcely be enough to do any good" (Gallagher 85). As late as the 1860s, the Irish people were often compared to apes and chimpanzees, which linked them to other savage civilizations present in the world. Upon his return from the United States in 1881, British historian Edward Freeman commented, "This would be a grand land if only every Irishman would kill a Negro, and be hanged for it. I find this sentiment generally approved-sometimes with the qualification that they want Irish and Negroes for servants, not being able to get any other" (Curtis 81).

More than any other, the magazine *Punch* hammered away at the Irish, even during the worst parts of the Famine. "Almost weekly *Punch* published cartoons portraying the Irishman as a dumb brute, a lazy lout, a liar, or a filthy beggar who spent whatever money he collected on weapons with which to assassinate the British" (Gallagher 70-71). Religious intolerance also played a key role, as Protestant theologians claimed that Roman Catholicism, better known in England as "popery," was the true cause of the potato blight. "The prolonged and seemingly ineradicable presence of Catholicism in Ireland, coupled with England's guilt in allowing it to perpetuate itself, had brought on God's punishment" (Gallagher 84; cf. Nagatus 49; Kinealy, *Death-Dealing Famine* 15).

Possibly most distressing is that even many British intellectuals were critical of the Irish. Costigan relates the story that after Alfred Nobel invented dynamite, Alfred Tennyson, the nation's poet laureate, called the Irish "furious fools" who "live in a horrible island and have no history of their own worth the least notice," and recommended the following course of action: "Could not anyone blow up that horrible island with dynamite and carry it off in pieces-a long way off?" (186-87).

Trevelyan did not invest the effort to tour rural Ireland and see with his own eyes the degradation he discussed with such glib simplicity and lofty detachment. William Bennett, another Englishman, strongly disagreed with Trevelyan's attributing the Famine to God. The west of Ireland, he said,

> exhibited a people not in the center of Africa, . . . but some millions of our own Christian nation at home . . . living in a state and condition low and degraded to a degree unheard of before in any civilized community; drive periodically to the borders of starvation; and now reduced by a national calamity to an exigency which all the efforts of benevolence can only mitigate, not control; and under which thousands are not merely pining away in misery and wretchedness, but are dying like cattle off the face of the earth, from want and its kindred horrors! Is this to be regarded in the light of a Divine dispensation and punishment? Before we can safely arrive at such a conclusion, we must be satisfied that human agency and legislation, individual oppressions, and social relationships, have had no hand in it. (Gallagher 138)

With some government assistance and funding, regulated emigration could have lowered the mortality rate in Ireland during the Famine years. Instead, the government did not follow this course of action and relied on an individual effort. "Recent calculations imply that no more than 3 or 4 per cent had their passages paid by landlords or government, though others were subsidized by charity and rent rebates" (Ó Gráda 104). As Foster notes, "the general reaction of the British government was a negligent one, with its two stark choices: emigration or death. The result was a selective depopulation and the export of memories of horror and hatred around the world" (167). It was this neglect that has helped make the Irish Famine one of the most controversial peacetime disasters in modern history.

The reaction of the British government in response to the food problem in Ireland will continue to be debated. While there were certainly differing views on how to deal with the Famine during its later years, the British authorities made a wholly inadequate effort to combat the economic, political, and social problems of the blight. The fact that the British government had declared that the Famine was over in 1848 illustrates the notion that its authorities never fully understood or acknowledged how they were hurting the Irish. Their commitment to economic and political philosophies that failed to take into account the full ramifications of the potato failure was flawed from the start. As Clark writes: "The British government's insistence on 'the absolute rights of landlords' to evict farmers and their families so they could raise cattle and sheep, was a process as close to 'ethnic cleansing' as any Balkan war ever enacted" (9).

In summary, does comparing the definitions of genocide against the evidence indict the British government of committing genocide against the Irish during the Famine of 1846-52? As a good academic, I am forced to answer both yes and no, for a variety of reasons. In support of the concept of the Famine as genocide:

· The British had put into place a system of laws over time that deprived the Irish of much of their land, language, trade, education, role in government and free practice of religion.
· Longstanding British racism against the Irish people dehumanized, debased, and helped pauperize the Irish, making the failure to somehow relieve their suffering acceptable to the British public and government.
· The right of landlords to evict Irish families during the Famine regardless of circumstances was upheld by the British government.
· Significant quantities of food were exported from Ireland during the Famine, justified under the doctrine of laissez-faire and with the active support of the British government.
· Much of Irish culture was lost, including a significant majority of all Irish speakers.
· The British could have done more to alleviate the suffering of the Irish, as demonstrated by Kinealy, Ó Gráda, and others. (New Jersey Great Irish Famine Curriculum; Genocide Section)

Yet there is another side. Just as there were "righteous Gentiles" who helped Jews at the risk of their own lives during World War II, so too were there thousands of British people and many Irish landlords who worked to alleviate the suffering of the Irish. These efforts could be as small as sending a few pence to a relief collection or as large as volunteering to work in a heavily afflicted area. The death rate among doctors and other relief workers was incredibly high, without hope of reward. The Quakers are still famous in Ireland for their help during the Famine (Woodham-Smith 157-59, Póirtéir, 224-225). Even the "hated" British government made some attempts-roughly 10 million pounds were spent on relief, clearly not a trivial sum, although it was mostly in the form of loans. Some landlords, such as William Smith O'Brien, stuck by their tenants or went bankrupt in trying to save them, even though most took the opportunity to clear the land. Again, just as many Americans engaged in efforts to save and improve the conditions of American Indians at the same time General Phil Sheridan was declaring that the only good Indian was a dead Indian, so too were there highly placed members of the British ruling elite working to aid the Irish.

In 1849 Edward Twisleton, an Englishman and the Irish Poor Law Commissioner, resigned to protest lack of aid from Britain. The Earl of Clarendon, Lord Lieutenant of Ireland, told British Prime Minister Lord John Russell the same day, "He (Twisleton) thinks that the destitution here [in Ireland] is so horrible, and the indifference of the House of Commons is so manifest, that he is an unfit agent for a policy that must be one of extermination." In regard to his anger at the lack of support provided to the Famine by the House of Commons, the Earl of Clarendon made his feelings known to Prime Minister Russell. "I do not think there is another legislature in Europe that would disregard such suffering as now exists in the west of Ireland, or coldly persist in a policy of extermination" (Woodham-Smith 380-381). However, politicians like the Earl of Clarendon were in the minority. More crucially, these efforts by leaders, religious groups, and common citizens were obviously not nearly sufficient to stop the suffering and dying.

So in the end, what do graduate students say about the Great Hunger and genocide? In my class, the final vote was 9 to 5 in favor of indicting the British government for genocide. This may say something about the impact of studying a horrible human experience for months on end as well as developing the view that since the Famine didn't have to happen, someone *must* be to blame. In addition, the mode of the course may have contributed to the students' passionate feelings about the Famine and the British government's role in it. Beyond the endless recitation of statistics in Woodham-Smith, Ó Gráda, and Kinealy, which can become mind-numbing over time, the class read Sean Kenny's novel and Seamus Heaney's poetry, and viewed the films *The Hanging Gale* and *An Gorta Mor*, both of which are powerful pieces. The class also read contemporary accounts of the Famine and looked at the extant illustrations available on various Web sites. While helping to make the dry facts of history come alive, the use of art, film, and literature in the study of history is always tricky-it has the power to make a student's engagement with the material almost too "personal." Further, each week a student made a presentation in greater detail on some aspect of the Famine. Thus, week after week the class heard about the coffin ships, the poorhouses, the relief projects, the epidemiology of the diseases of the Famine and the stages of starvation, the demographic impact of the death toll and the massive emigration, the destruction and disruption to Irish culture (dancing, for example, or the loss of the traditional wake), and the conditions the new emigrants lived under in America. It is nearly impossible to remain unaffected by more than three months of intensive study of such a tragic event.

Yet, interestingly, the five who voted against indicting the British government clearly felt troubled about doing so, as did some in the assent. What was the deciding evidence in the minds of these students? Although many reasons were given, those most often mentioned included the export of massive amounts of food, the dispassionate assessment of the suffering of the Irish by Trevelyan and other British officials and commentators, and, interestingly, the indictments made by Irish and British officials such as Randolph Routh, Lord Clarendon, Edward Twisleton, Maria Edgeworth, William Bennett, Daniel O'Connell, and others. If contemporaries of the major players in the Famine could see the devastation and suffering underway, then my class was not inclined to excuse Russell or Dennis Mahon or Trevelyan. Most of the students did not expect miracles from the British government, yet the successful relief program of 1846 and the soup kitchens of 1847 convinced them that the politicians and policy makers could have done more if they had had the political and moral will to do so. Ó Gráda frequently cites economist Amartya Sen's contention that, "given good will, preventing famine mortality in the less developed world is easy or elementary" (Ó Gráda 9). While he recognizes that Britain of the 1840s did not have all the resources of the modern developed world, he still agrees with historian John Post's argument that "the success or failure of public welfare and relief measures more than any other variable influenced the relative severity of the national mortality peaks" (Ó Gráda 9). Thus, if there is a villain to the Famine story, my class believed it to be Charles Trevelyan, as he personified both blind loyalty to laissez-faire economics and blind prejudice against the peasant Irish. I'm sure they would indict him as a criminal, which, ironically, he would be incapable of comprehending.

As further proof of the complexity of this issue, Cormac Ó Gráda, whose work forms a good deal of the evidence for the argument presented here, is extremely reluctant to use the term genocide. He believes that "not even the most bigoted and racist commentators of the day sought the extermination of the Irish" (10). He also argues that claims of genocide underestimate or ignore the enormous logistical problems facing relief agencies. He states, "A charge of doctrinaire neglect is easier to sustain than one of genocide" (10). Yet we have seen how some definitions of genocide can include what Ó Gráda is labeling "doctrinaire neglect." He cites as support a piece in the *Washington Post* by Timothy Guinnane entitled "Ireland's Famine wasn't Genocide." Guinnane makes the case that the inclusion of the Famine in school genocide curriculums is due solely to the ideological imperatives of a small group of Irish-American leaders. But, even Guinnane admits significant culpability on the part of the British government. For example, he states, "Official efforts to combat starvation were tardy and half-hearted. The British government insisted the famine be treated as an Irish problem with Irish solutions. Given the magnitude of the crisis, this demand was madness" and "Few doubt that a more energetic relief effort was possible and would have saved many thousands of lives. There is also little doubt that had the crop failure struck a part of England, the government would have reacted quite differently. But does the government's inadequate response to the famine constitute genocide?" (A19) Of course, that is the question I have been attempting to deal with in this paper. He closes by claiming, "To call the famine genocide cheapens the memories of both the famine's victims and the victims of real genocides" (A19). Clearly, despite his own indictment of the British government's actions as both "madness" and "costing thousands of lives," Guinnane's attitude is counter to Israel Charny's injunction to scholars "to be faithful to the commonsense meaning of loss of human lives so that we do not exclude in arbitrary, cynical, or intellectual elitist ways the deaths of any group of our fellow human beings from our definitions of genocide" (75), although he is more in agreement with Fein's definition of genocide.

The students' discussion led me to the conclusion that most of the definitions of genocide, and particularly the UN convention, were written in response to a singular event-the Holocaust. In the Armenian genocide, as in the slave trade, the devastation of Native Americans and of aborigines in Australia, there were some opposing forces within the dominant society. In none of these other examples did the government actually formulate a precise plan, devoting scarce resources in time of a life and death national struggle to the extermination of various relatively harmless groups in society. The Germans institutionalized murder, and although the other examples all had state complicity, there were stronger or weaker countervailing forces working against the state's goals. Thus, I conclude that it is the definition of genocide that is at fault-nothing but a Holocaust-like state-planned, supported, and implemented destruction and mass murder of a group or groups will ever be considered genocide by most historians. Just as we find criminals guilty of first-degree murder, second-degree murder, or manslaughter in various degrees-depending on the depravity of the act-so we should have varying levels of genocide. In that context, I would contend that Great Britain is clearly guilty of second- or third-degree genocide (or what may be more rightly called passive genocide), but not guilty of genocide as defined in the United Nations convention.[8]

To close, a quote from Woodham-Smith:

> It is not characteristic of the English to behave as they have behaved in Ireland; as a nation, the English have proved themselves to be capable of generosity, tolerance and magnanimity, but not where Ireland is concerned. As Sydney Smith, the celebrated writer and wit wrote: "The moment the very name of Ireland is mentioned, the English seem to bid adieu to common feeling, common prudence and common sense, and to act with the barbarity of tyrants and the fatuity of idiots." (411)

Notes

I want to thank the members of the class for their insights as I formulated this paper. Special thanks go to Daniel O'Kane, Peter Conlon, Helena Swanicke, James Smith and Karen McNamara.

1. I chose the title Acts of Man for its aural impact rather than out of any antipathy to gender neutral language. However, it is true that the key decision makers in the Great Hunger were men. Of course, many thousands of women played important roles in the relief efforts, but it was the male political leadership of Great Britain that made the crucial policy decisions.

2. See, for example, James Mullin and others at the Irish Famine Genocide Committee Web page, and the New Jersey Great Irish Famine Curriculum Web page, and some of the entries in Hayden:

<http://www.ifgc.org/firstpage.htm>

<http://www.nde.state.ne.us/SS/irish/irish_pf.html>

3. For an excellent discussion of the various ideological approaches to the Famine, see Kinealy, *Death-Dealing Famine* chapter 1.

4. This approach was suggested by two legal opinions on the Irish Famine Genocide Committee web site; Charles E. Rice and Francis A. Boyle both wrote brief opinions that conclude the Famine was genocide under the United Nations definitions. The NJ Great Irish Famine Curriculum section on genocide also follows this line of argument.

5. Texts included Woodham-Smith, *Great Hunger;* Hayden, *Irish Hunger;* Kenny, *The Hungry Earth;* Ó Gráda, *Black '47;* Gribben, *Great Famine;* and Kinealy, *Death-Dealing Famine.* Films included *The Hanging Gale* and episode one, *An Gorta Mor,* from the PBS series *The Irish in America.*

6. http://www.preventgenocide.org/law/gencon/english.htm

7. Oxford Educational Dictionary (OED), 2001, http://dictionary.oed.com/cgi/entry/00093704. The OED cites Lemkin as the first to use the word: "1944 R. LEMKIN *Axis Rule in Occupied Europe* ix. 79 By 'genocide' we mean the destruction of a nation or of an ethnic group."

8. Ó Hallmhuráin, *The Great Famine;* Dhomhnaill, *Ghostly Alhambra;* Lacey, *The People Lost and Forgot.*

Works Cited

Andreopoulos, George. ed., *Genocide: Conceptual and Historical Dimensions*, Philadelphia: Univ. of Pennsylvania Press, 1997
Balakian, Peter. *Black Dog of Fate.* New York: Basic Books, 1997
Charny, Israel. *Toward a Generic Definition of Genocide.* Andreopoulous, pp. 64-93
Clark, Dennis. "The Great Irish Famine: Worse Than Genocide?" *Irish Edition*, July, August, and September 1993, qtd. in New Jersey Great Irish Famine Curriculum,
<http://www.nde.state.ne.us/SS/irish/unit_6.html>
Costigan, Giovanni. *A History of Modern Ireland.* New York: Bobbs Merrill, 1969
Curtis, L. P. *Anglo-Saxons and Celts: A study of anti-Irish Prejudice in Victorian England.* Bridgeport: University of Bridgeport Press, 1984
Dhomhnaill, Nuala Ní. *A Ghostly Alhambra,* Hayden, pp. 68-78
Donnelly, James S., Jr. "Mass Eviction and the Irish Famine: The Clearances Revisited." Póirtéir, pp.155-173
Fein, Helen. *Genocide, Terror, Life Integrity, and War Crimes: The Case for Discrimination*, Andreopoulos, pp. 95-107
Foster, R. F. *The Oxford History of Ireland.* Oxford: Oxford University Press, 1989
Gallagher, Thomas. *Paddy's Lament.* New York: Harvest, 1987
Green, E.R.R. *The Great Famine.* Moody and Martin, pp. 263-274
Gribben, Arthur, ed. *The Great Famine and the Irish Diaspora in America.* Boston: University of Massachusetts Press, 1999
Guinnane, Timothy. "Ireland's Famine Wasn't Genocide." *Washington Post*, September 17, 1997, A19
Hayden, Tom, ed. *Irish Hunger.* Boulder, Colo.: Roberts Rhinehart, 1997.
Keneally, Thomas. *The Great Shame.* New York: Doubleday, 1999
Kenny, Sean. *The Hungry Earth.* Boulder, Colo.: Roberts Rhinehart, 1995
Kinealy, Christine. *A Death-Dealing Famine: The Great Hunger in Ireland.* London: Pluto, 1997
---. *This Great Calamity.* Boulder: Roberts Rhinehart, 1995
Lacey, Brian. *The People Lost and Forgot.* Hayden, pp.79-92.
Lemkin, Rafael. "Beyond the 1984 Convention-Emerging Principles of Genocide in Customary International Law." *Maryland Journal of International Law and Trade* 17.2 (Fall 1993): 193-226.
<http://preventgenocide.org/lemkin/freeworld 1945.htm>.

Moody, T.W. and Martin, F.X. eds. *The Course of Irish History.* Boulder, Colo.: Roberts Rhinehart, 1995

Nagatus. *The Connections between Famine Pestilence, and the Great Apostacy,* Halliday Pamphlet. Vol. 1. 1847. Dublin: 1990.

New Jersey Great Irish Famine Curriculum, November 1998, <http://www.nde.state.ne.us/SS/irish/irish_pf.html>

Ó Gráda. *Black '47.* Princeton: Princeton Univ. Press, 1999

Ó Hallmhuráin, Gearoid. *The Great Famine: A Catalyst in Irish Traditional Music Making.* Gribben, pp. 104-132.

Oxford Educational Dictionary. 2001. http://dictionary.oed.com/cgi/entry/00093704.

Póirtéir, Cathal, ed. *The Great Irish Famine.* Dublin, Ireland: Mercier Press, 1995.

—. *Folk Memory and the Famine,* Póirtéir, pp. 219-232

Ranelagh. *A Short History of Ireland.* Cambridge: Cambridge Univ. Press, 1994.

Riemer, Neal, ed. *Protection Against Genocide.* Westport, Conn.: Praeger, 2000

Rubenstein, Richard L. *The Age of Triage: Fear and Hope in an Overcrowded World.* New York: Beacon Press, 1984

Whyte, Robert. *The Ocean Plague, or, A Voyage to Quebec in an Irish Emigrant Vessel.* Boston: 1848. Irish-American Book Co. 1997

Woodham-Smith, Cecil. *The Great Hunger.* London: Penguin, 1962

Chapter Eleven

"I will sone be home":
Margaret Maher, Emily Dickinson, and an Irish Trunk Full of Poems

CONNIE ANN KIRK

One positive outcome the Great Hunger did provide for later generations was the amazing legacy of Famine survivors. Whether they emigrated to the United States or elsewhere to begin life anew or "stayed behind" to rebuild their lives after the plight, the lasting effects of their suffering, strength, and talents will continue to be felt for generations to come. With the Famine coming under a more critical historical eye in recent years, perhaps it is time to do more of the hard digging that is necessary to uncover the stories of these survivors so that they do not rot away rather than yield a bounty of knowledge for their descendants and the world at large.

Some of the stories are quiet acts of strength in keeping a family alive and together. Others tell of major contributions to the industries, politics, or commerce of nations. Still others involve working hard to improve the quality of life that would hopefully prevent the same thing from happening to their children.

If we dig deep and follow where the roots of these stories go, we are apt to find survivors crossing paths and making history with other people in the world in intriguing and fascinating ways that we may not have expected. It is one of these stories that this article will attempt to describe.

Margaret Maher (1841–1924) was born near the Hill of the Women (*Sliabh-na-mBan*) in Kilusty, Parish Kiltinan, County Tipperary (Murray 706). She survived *An Gorta Mor* and emigrated to the United States with her parents and three siblings in the mid-1850s, probably to improve the economic conditions of the family by seeking out the work for women that was reported to be found near railroad construction in western Massachusetts (706).

After early employment with the Boltwood family as a domestic worker for several years, Maher was hired as maid-of-all-work by Edward Dickinson of Amherst, Massachusetts, father of the then-unknown poet, Emily Dickinson. Though the job was intended to be a short step toward a dream move to California (707), Maher's employment at the Dickinson Homestead would last thirty years, through the deaths of not only Edward but also his wife and both daughters, Emily and Lavinia (Leyda lxi).

During her time of service, Margaret Maher, or Maggie, as the Dickinsons called her, personally contributed to the poetic legacy of Emily Dickinson. She did this in at least three important ways. First, as the artist and scholar, Aife Murray, notes in her foundational article, "Miss Margaret's Emily Dickinson," Maher sustained and protected the poet both physically and emotionally as she lived and wrote. Second, Maher was quite possibly instrumental in preserving the poems by keeping them in her own trunk (presumably in addition to those said to be found in the poet's bureau drawer) and then actively contributed toward moving them to publication after the poet's death. She also claimed to have rescued and preserved the only authenticated photograph of Dickinson that exists to this day. Last, through her close relationship with the poet during Dickinson's seclusion in the Homestead, Maher had a direct effect on developing Dickinson's empathy for people different from herself, particularly the Irish immigrants who had moved into the country in large numbers after the Famine.

These two very different women, one a working-class Irish immigrant, the other a prominent lawyer's daughter descended from Puritan-English stock, managed to bridge gaps of class and race that nations have yet to do by apparently influencing one another in a unique and productive way within the domestic sphere. A close look at the correspondence between the two women, as well as letters by Dickinson that refer to Maher and members of Maher's family, combined with firsthand accounts by family and friends, contribute insights into this complex and fascinating relationship.

Aife Murray summarizes Maher's contribution to the poet through their working relationship by saying that "Dickinson's 'voice,' in a sense, had depended on Maher's 'silence'" ("Miss" 698). Emily's mother, Emily Norcross Dickinson, had been sickly since Lavinia's childhood, and the task of cooking and cleaning had fallen on the sisters in earlier days. After a succession of hired domestic help, including one employee of several years, another Margaret, Margaret O'Brien, the steady hand of Margaret Maher must have come as welcome relief to Emily, who disliked housework and found it taxing on her writing time.

Maher's contribution of silence is valid in the figurative sense that Aife Murray illuminates. Dickinson was allowed to craft her poems while Maher assumed the underappreciated occupation of maid-of-all-work with its voice and history that gets washed away with the dirt in cleaned houses. Maher was also a talented nurse and became the principal healer of the household, as well as of the household of Austin Dickinson, Emily's brother, with its young children next door at the Evergreens (720). Ironic as it might seem, however, Maher did have an important voice that went beyond dominating domestic affairs with such competence and directness as to create a formidable reputation in the neighborhood. Importantly, Maher's strong domestic voice enabled Dickinson to enjoy a public silence.

Dickinson maintained her work as family baker, even after Margaret's employ, and often wrote about working together with her in the kitchen. A few months after Margaret's arrival, Dickinson made the conscious choice of self-imposed exile within her father's house. She saw no strangers, other than possibly children from the neighborhood, and never left the grounds of the Homestead for the last seventeen years of her life. Maher effectively turned away prospective visitors with gifts of baked goods and flowers and otherwise protected the poet's fierce desire for privacy.

Emotional support was also part of the job over time, and it was probably during this phase in their relationship that Dickinson came to trust Maher more and more with certain aspects of her work. In one example of this, Maher's silence turned quite literal. The circle of those who knew of Dickinson's writing habit seems to widen with each year of ongoing research, but it still appears that the large volume of her poems, nearly 2,000 in all, came as a surprise to almost everyone who knew her. Though there may be questions surrounding her claim, according to Maher, Dickinson asked her to store the poems in the trunk she'd used to emigrate from Ireland (Murray 726). The fact that Maher was willing to protect the poet from outsiders at a time when she craved solitude makes this conspiracy between the two women of hiding the poems plausible. Maher had taken on the role of protector of the poet's sensibilities and desires, and a unique trust of a non-Dickinson by a Dickinson seemed to build out of that. In fact, Margaret Maher is one of the witnesses at Emily Dickinson's will (Leyda 2,237)

One of Dickinson's deathbed requests to her sister Vinnie (Lavinia) was that she burn her correspondence (Murray 726). Vinnie carried out her sister's wishes, burning most of the letters that Dickinson had received and saved over her lifetime. One of Emily's last requests to Margaret was that *she* burn the poems (Bianchi 60), probably because she knew where all of them were stored in the Homestead, and probably because Dickinson trusted her to carry out this act in secret. Maher had a difficult decision. Should she honor the deathbed request of her mistress, a woman she'd nourished and protected from the outside world, or should she value the *poetry* over those wishes, for whatever gift *it* could offer to the world. As Aife Murray points out:

> Not only did she come from a culture that considers the poet the most important member of society, but the Maher (or Meagher) family had provided poets and scholars to South Tipperary for hundreds of years. . . . Maher's literary sensibility, shaped in County Tipperary and reinforced at the Homestead, made preserving Dickinson's poems a difficult but inevitable choice. (727)

In the end, Margaret Maher chose the poetry over the poet's wishes, a choice that arguably shows her value of that which *sustains*. When one has survived hunger in her homeland and attended deathbeds in her new country as a nurse, it might be argued that she realized, either consciously or not, that poetry has the power to sustain and outlive generations. Perhaps while baking bread together during long days at the Homestead, Dickinson understood Maher's feelings about her poems and trusted her to make the right decision regarding them after her death. Perhaps Maher considered the poems as she did Dickinson's bread and flowers, as gifts that could be given to callers whom her mistress refused to see in person. Perhaps she saw her role with the poems as she did with these other handmade items—to be the agent of Emily's gifts to the world. In any case, Margaret Maher, "torn by her own conflicting loyalties" (Bianchi 60) retrieved the poems, along with those found by Lavinia in her bureau drawer, and later worked in domestic service for their first editor, Mabel Loomis Todd, to help move them toward publication.

It was at this time as well that she produced a daguerreotype of Emily as a girl, which she had saved after the family had discarded it (Murray 728). The daguerreotype, though altered by Vinnie, who still disliked it, was used in an early publication of the poems. Despite several other discoveries, it is still the only authenticated photographic image of the poet in existence.

Perhaps the closest glimpse we can achieve into the relationship between these two women is by examining surviving correspondence. Aife Murray recounts much of Maher's own sensibilities through her letters to her former employers, the Boltwoods, which include references to her employment with the Dickinsons. Murray, does not, however, discuss at length correspondence we might have between Maher and Dickinson themselves. Likewise, in taking Margaret's viewpoint in her article, Murray does not dwell on Dickinson's frequent references to Margaret in her correspondence with others. In giving back the long lost voice of Margaret Maher, Aife Murray ought not be charged with omission for toning down Dickinson's well-known, powerful voice in her exploration. However, Dickinson lived in the same house with Maher, too, not just the other way around, and she can tell us about the woman and their relationship if we look for this kind of evidence in her writing.

References to her maid occur over fifty times in Dickinson's surviving correspondence (MacKenzie 451). The references are handily and readily made. It is clear her correspondents knew who "Maggie" was and did not need any explanation about her relationship with the poet. A look at the hard physical labor of Margaret's working day in a nineteenth century well-to-do household can be seen from her observant mistress's point of view, simply by looking at verbs Dickinson uses to describe some of Maggie's activities: "Maggie dragged" (L337); "Maggie is ironing" (L340); "Maggie is helping her" (L375); "Maggie pulled it out" (L390); "Maggie is cleaning" (L412); "Maggie is making" (L727); "Maggie gave her Hens" (L682); "Maggie is getting" (L727); "Maggie stood" (L337); "Maggie is ill" (L409). The labor Margaret exerted for her good wages at the Dickinsons' often lasted into the night.

Edward Dickinson was not only a successful lawyer in Amherst, but he was also a former Congressman and treasurer of Amherst College, which his ancestors had helped to found (Sewall xxv–xviii). Murray relates that the volume of work in a house the size of the Dickinsons, who had many visitors and social obligations because of their prominence in the community, was tremendous. In addition, the conditions of maintaining a clean house and cooking food for the table in nineteenth-century New England was formidable. Fires had to be tended in most rooms, which meant stoking and cleaning, then cleaning the residue and soot they created. Chamberpots needed dumping in the outhouses each morning. Lamps used homemade candles and whale oil, which meant that they also needed to be cleaned daily and maintained. Cooking was done from scratch, and meals were served on a regular schedule and in a timely manner. Often, Maher also prepared meals for Austin's family in the Evergreens. Dressmakers were regularly employed for new clothing, but laundering and mending were performed at home (714–719).

Dickinson neighbor, MacGregor Jenkins, recounts childhood memories of playing with Martha Dickinson, Emily's niece next door, and the influence Margaret had over the household where the children used to visit and beg for cookies and gingerbread treats. He describes Margaret's relationship with the neighborhood children as "tempestuous" (27), since she was inclined to save the freshly baked goods for the family's purposes, while Emily was inclined to dispense them randomly to the children at whim. Though he says she was a "formidable garrison" (29), he remembers her fondly, saying that "[n]o woman in the world but Maggie could have been found in such a household" (27). He claims that she was very Dickinsonian in character and drive, that she shared their "rugged independence of thought and action" (28). Jenkins, looking back, regarded Margaret's role at the Homestead as "guardian and dictator in the home of genius" (28). While he sometimes feared her as he would a thunderstorm as a child, he says, "Next to Miss Emily, Maggie was beloved . . . we loved her because we knew she loved Miss Emily and she loved us too" (29).

Other clues to Margaret's character and particularly the fact that her opinions were apparently known and discussed with Emily, that she was part of conversations, are apparent with another look at phrases from Dickinson's letters. Phrases such as "Maggie preferred" (L388); "Maggie prized" (L794); "was sitting by" (L610); "Maggie was charmed" (L693) show a present, observant Dickinson taking note of Maher's actions and feelings on the subjects of the day. Perhaps the most cherished of Maher's opinions embraced by Emily was her decision not to join her brother, who had gone mining in California, when he sent for her. By this time, Maher was actively engaged in helping establish Kelley Square, the Irish neighborhood in Amherst (Murray 708). Dickinson writes, "Maggie preferred her home . . . so with a few spring touches, nature remains unchanged" (L388). Immediately after this statement, she adds this poem:

> The most triumphant bird
> I ever knew or met
> Embarked upon a twig to-day—
> And till dominion set
> I perish to behold

So competent a sight—
And sang for nothing scrutable
But impudent delight.
Retired and resumed
His transitive estate;
To what delicious accident
Does finest glory fit!(L388)

The poem is about a "triumphant bird" perching on a branch and singing for the joy of it. Instead of flying off afterward as one might expect, it stays right where it is. The speaker, who has been watching, delights in the glory of beholding the "accident" of the bird's choice. The editor of Dickinson's letters, Thomas Johnson, notes that this poetic flourish at the end of the letter may indicate that Emily is relieved that the "faithful Maggie" (Dickinson 505) would not be leaving the household.

Still other phrases from the numerous references to Margaret in Dickinson's letters represent an increasing closeness between the two women living and working in the same house, sharing the trials and tribulations of everyday life as well as the tragedies that befall both of them in their family relationships: "I whispered to Maggie" (L610); "Maggie will write" (L401); "Maggie remembers you" (L525); "Maggie so extols it" (L737); "Maggie gives her love" (L1034); "Maggie's brother is killed . . . Maggie wants to die" (L670).

In Letter #610, Dickinson tells the story of Margaret sitting by Mrs. Dickinson's bedside when Emily and Vinnie were awakened by firebells from town and bright light outside the windows. Vinnie tells Emily that it is only the Fourth of July fireworks. They go to their sleeping mother's room, and when Vinnie leaves for a moment, Emily whispers to Maggie, asking her what was going on. Maggie tells her that it is the Stebbins's barn, on fire. Vinnie had wanted to protect Emily, but Emily went to Maggie for the truth, and together they did not let on to Vinnie that Emily now knew it. The scarcity of surviving correspondence directly addressed between the two women is meaningful and brings up several possible causes: (1) Daughters of prominent New England lawyers who had the education and leisure to write letters didn't write to their father's Irish employees who did not. (2) Maher didn't keep or share more of her private notes or letters from the poet. (3) In the seventeen years they knew each other, Maher wasn't away enough to require a letter; but distance didn't stop Dickinson from writing letters—she sent the bulk of her correspondence right next door to "Sister Sue" (her sister-in-law) at the Evergreens. (4) Their exchange was primarily verbal and private, based on Maher's proximity in the domestic sphere and *availability* to the poet. This latter reason supports an argument of emotional attachment and shared confidences.

Whatever the reason, to this day there is only one known surviving letter from Dickinson to Maher and a single response to this letter from Maher to Dickinson. Interestingly, the subject of the correspondence is health, a subject not so foreign from the times in which they lived, with famine, diseases including the prevalent consumption, and death influencing their lives. They are notes, really. Margaret was ill with typhoid fever and had gone to Kelley Square, the area in town where her immigrant relatives settled and developed a cohesive Irish neighborhood that she helped to establish financially. In September 1882, Dickinson writes:

> The missing Maggie is much mourned, and I am going out for "black" to the nearest store. All are very naughty, and I am the naughtiest of all.
> The pussies dine on sherry now, and humming-bird cutlets. The invalid hen took dinner with me, but a hen like Dr T[aylor's] horse soon drove her away. I am very busy picking up stems and stamens as the hollyhocks leave their clothes around. What shall I send my weary Maggie? Pillows or fresh brooks?
> Her Grieved Mistress. (Leyda 2, 378)

Here is Margaret's reply: "Some times I think I don't be Sick at all and the Next time I am sick again give my love to Mother and tell her I miss her and I will sone be home to her how is the colds I hope ye are better" (Leyda 2, 378).

This exchange is intimate and caring, almost as one between a daughter and a mother. When first read, Maher sounds much older than Dickinson and both seem, perhaps, to be in early adulthood. In fact, they were both middle-aged; Margaret was in her early forties and had already given up her earlier dream of moving to California. Like Dickinson, she never married but worked hard at her trade all her life. By contrast, Dickinson, with the childlike voice, was older, a fifty-two-year-old woman who was living in the house where she was born, and by this time never went out, so her comment about going out to the store is problematic.

The exchange reads as one between two women who normally don't need to write to communicate. Dickinson's note is typically clever—the alliteration with *missing Maggie much mourned* sounds almost like a headline—this is the real news of her letter. She jokes about how the house is falling apart without Maggie there to take care of it, and how she must dine alone, except for the misbehaving chickens. There is a distancing and a playfulness in referring to the addressee in the third person. The distancing might be one of uneasiness in writing to a domestic worker, or it might be a stance that seemed appropriate to her to cover uneasiness in writing when they normally chat together so closely. Most likely, however, the stance is a defensive tone on the part of the "naughtiest of all" who is left at home. Dickinson's tone is like a child's apologizing to a parent for misbehaving while she is out. Describing herself in this way suggests that she is not doing her part as housekeeper in Margaret's absence. If Dickinson is not keeping house to make up for Maher's work, then she is probably tending to her plants in her conservatory ("picking up stems and stamens")—and writing. We get the impression that Dickinson's "naughtiness" would not surprise Maher in the least. The letter closes with a question of what to send her exhausted and ill friend, "pillows or fresh brooks." She doesn't know whether rest or cool water or a diversion is the answer; one wonders if fresh brooks is not a pun on fresh books.

Margaret's note, by contrast, forgoes a salutation and gets down to the business of informing Emily of the instability of her condition and then quickly moves to concern for Emily's ill mother, with whom she seems to have a special bond. It's interesting that though she is among her own people at nearby Kelley Square when she writes the note to Dickinson, she speaks of coming home soon to the Homestead. Though she may be saying that for Emily's sake, it must be noted that, for immigrants, as well as domestic workers, the concept of having two homes is borne of necessity. Her note ends with concern over Emily, and presumably her sister Vinnie, and their colds. This is undoubtedly one of the rare times when the roles of nurse and patient are reversed in their relationship—and Margaret reverts to her more comfortable role as caretaker of the Dickinson's lesser colds in her note while recuperating herself from the far more serious typhoid. Also characteristic of one who lives life thinking of others before herself, she diminishes her importance and identity at the end of the note by not signing it.

The intimacy of the notes suggests anything but a lack of respect and affection for her Irish maid, Margaret Maher, on the part of her mistress. This level of warmth toward the Irish did not always appear to exist in Dickinson, however, as a correspondence with her brother, Austin, many years earlier, suggests. Years before Margaret Maher's employment with them, the Dickinsons, though educated, manifested many of the well-known sentiments of established Anglo-Americans in New England at the time when Irish immigrants began arriving in Boston in large numbers. In 1851, Emily's brother, Austin, a recent graduate of Amherst College, had taken a job at the Endicott School in

Northern Boston teaching young Famine immigrant boys. Their uncle, Loring Norcross, served on the school committee (Dickinson 112). Austin would, like his father, later become a lawyer, and his family believed that his talent at teaching was dubious at best. At home in Amherst, his twenty-one-year-old sister missed him terribly and wrote him frequently. Anyone or anything that kept her dear Austin from returning was written about as a threat to her happiness. On June 15, 1851, she wrote: "We are quite alarmed for the *boys*, hope you wont *kill*, or *pack away* any of em . . . Father remarks quite briefly that he 'thinks they have found their master,' mother bites her lips, and fears you 'will be *rash* with them' and Vinnie and I say masses for poor Irish boys souls" (L43). After this jovial indictment of her brother's teaching abilities, Dickinson adds this statement, "So far as *I* am concerned I should like to have you kill some—there are so many now, there is no room for the Americans" (L 43). Aife Murray writes that later on in the 1850s Austin was an influential leader in Amherst's Know-Nothing or Native American Party, a group known to be anti-Catholic and anti-immigrant (705). Recently found documents attributed to Southern relatives also accuse Austin Dickinson of paying $500 for an Irish replacement to serve in his place in the Union Army in the Civil War (Smith). Class and cultural biases rampant at the time in New England apparently did not pass over the Dickinson household.

Many years later, with maturity and life experience, but also perhaps from the direct influence of Famine immigrant Margaret Maher and the other Irish workers on the Homestead grounds, Dickinson appears to exhibit more compassion for the Irish and their troubles. This is evident in Dickinson's letters to other correspondents. A year after she alludes to the hangings of the "heinous" Mollie Maguires in Pennsylvania in 1879, she writes a letter in the autumn of 1880, asking her cousins to send Margaret a note to help her mourn the death of her brother in a coal mine in Pennsylvania: "Maggie's brother is killed in the mine, and Maggie wants to die, but Death goes far around to those that want to see him. If the little cousins would give her a note—she does not know I ask it—I think it would help her begin, that bleeding beginning that every mourner knows" (L670).

In early December, 1882, she writes of sending a fruit basket to "a dying Irish Girl in our neighborhood—" saying, "Those that die seem near me because I lose my own" (L790). She writes of Maher's niece: "Little Irish Maggie went to sleep this morning at six o'clock, just the time grandpa rises, and will rest in the grass at Northampton tomorrow. She has had a hard sickness, but her awkward little life is saved and gallant now. Our Maggie is helping her mother put her in the cradle." (L375).

Sharing tragedies of Margaret Maher's family helped humanize the Irish for Dickinson as she was able to relate their various troubles to her own. Certainly one might suspect that a thoughtful writer would come to this more humane understanding on her own, yet Dickinson rarely had contact with people and had not attended church for decades. While she knew people involved in suffrage and abolitionist movements, she was not an outward social activist herself. Yet, descendants of Thomas Kelley claim that Emily was not conscious of or standoffish about class distinction as were Austin and her parents. According to the Kelley relatives, she treated everyone equally, regardless of social standing (Murray 723).

A final act that is also a testament to these women's relationship as well as to Dickinson's feelings about the other Irish workers at her home is evidenced by her funeral procession. Dickinson broke a Protestant taboo when she requested that Irish-Catholic Tom Kelley and five other Irish workmen from the Homestead grounds—Dennis Scannell, Stephen Sullivan, Patrick Ward, Daniel Moynihan, and Dennis Cushman—serve as the pallbearers at her funeral (Sewall 610). This gesture of a woman from Amherst's most visible and notable family was perhaps her most public statement of appreciation and honor of the lives and work of the Irish immigrants who tended to her family.

Assuming that Margaret Maher and her family would not have emigrated to the United States were it not for hardships brought to them by the Famine, it seems safe to say that the legacy of *An Gorta Mor*, in this one survivor's story, was a profound effect on American letters. It seems incredible that quite possibly a large portion of Emily Dickinson's body of work would have burned (if it had even been written in the first place) were it not for the independent decision of an Irish-immigrant maid. It also seems incredible that these poems, many of which were written on fine Irish linen stationery, rested safely and secretly inside an Irish immigrant's trunk for years. One can only wonder what other stories are out there, what further investigative research will turn up about Famine survivors and their influence. Perhaps it is no accident that the Renaissance period of American literature in the mid-nineteenth century occurred at the same time as the influx of Irish Famine immigrants into the country. It is time to uncover buried voices.

Works Cited

Bianchi, Martha Dickinson. *Emily Dickinson: Face to Face.*
   Cambridge: Riverside, 1932.

Dickinson, Emily. *The Letters of Emily Dickinson*. Ed. Thomas
   Johnson. Cambridge: Harvard Univ. Press, 1955. (Letter numbers are
   designated L within the text of the essay.)
Jenkins, MacGregor. *Emily Dickinson: Friend and Neighbor*. Boston:
   Little, Brown, 1930.
Leyda, Jay. *The Years and Hours of Emily Dickinson*. 2 vols. New
   Haven: Yale Univ. Press, 1960.
MacKenzie, Cynthia. *Concordance to the Letters of Emily Dickinson*.
   Boulder, Colo.: Colorado Univ. Press, 1999.
Murray, Aife. "Miss Margaret's Emily Dickinson." *Signs: Journal of
   Women in Culture and Society* 24.3 (Spring 1999): 697–732.
Sewall, Richard B. *The Life of Emily Dickinson*. 2 vols. New York:
   Farrar, 1974.
Smith, Martha Nell, Ellen Louise Hart, and Marta Werner, eds.
   "Archives in the Classroom: Civil War." *Dickinson Electronic
   Archives*. Institute for Advanced Technology in the Humanities
   (IATH), University of Virginia. 27 November 2000.
   http://jefferson.village.virginia.edu./dickinson/classroom/civilwar/cw
   dex.htm

PART THREE: COMMEMORATION

Chapter Twelve

Famine Commemorations: Visual Dialogues, Visual Silences

KATHLEEN O'BRIEN

The one hundred and fiftieth anniversary of the Irish Famine stimulated a dramatic expansion in academic research as well as construction plans for commemorative monuments in diverse communities in Ireland and in countries that experienced large influxes of Irish arrivals in the wake of the Famine years, which peaked in the late 1840s. The recent surge of interest in the Famine has coincided with complex debates about cultural production generated around fiftieth-anniversary commemorations of World War II, including remembrances of the Holocaust in Europe, the atomic bombs dropped on Japan, and other episodes of large-scale human decimation. Areas of academic and popular interest, such as cultural studies and visual art programs that developed and expanded in the post-war era, have been instrumental in raising public awareness and participation in the development of imagery employed in public spaces, including critical reviews of nineteenth- and early twentieth-century commemorative practices. Hence, efforts to commemorate seemingly unrelated events like Irish deaths in the late 1840s and Jewish deaths in the early 1940s have intersected in heated cross-cultural dialogues about appropriate representation in commemorative discourse surrounding episodes of violent trauma. In addition, anniversaries of such events can emphasize some of the diverse cultural concerns that have shifted across time and physical distance among groups of different ages, cultural affiliations, and other social alliances. While representation of personal and collective memory is central to commemorative efforts, choices of how those experiences should be visualized have also come to be affected by concerns about how such imagery may impact the lives of diverse populations who will live in the shadows of these visual expressions of cultural identity. Though perhaps less visible to the public in those efforts, trends of thought that inform artistic production are highly instrumental in these determinations. Thus, it is from my vantage point as an artist that I began research on representations of the Famine in Quebec and Ireland in 1996. This paper will address some of the similarities and differences among early Famine commemorations and the diverse contexts in which they have been constructed and perceived in Irish and North American communities. The focus will be the small island of Grosse Île, Quebec, and Ireland's west Cork community of Skibbereen, two sites that experienced extreme destitution during the Famine. In each place, several commemorative attempts have been made that bear multiple and conflicted meanings on local and diasporic levels. Analysis of the contexts in which these sites have functioned is important to the consideration of how the recent surge of commemoratives may affect future understandings of the Famine. The paper will conclude with a brief discussion of two outdoor sculptural installations I created in Ireland that address issues raised in part by my examination of these two sites in Quebec and Ireland.

The coincidence of the commemorative efforts created around the fiftieth anniversary of World War II in 1995 and preparations for the Famine anniversary created a context that emphasized similarities and differences between intent and effect of government policies in the different contexts of Holocaust and Famine; it also highlighted difficult issues regarding collective silence and violence. In addition, the coincidence raised challenges to notions of complex roles played by "memory" in commemorative processes. Unlike survivors of World War II, no one alive today has personal memory of the Famine experience. As Chris Morash has noted, what is "remembered" is imagined primarily from text-based narratives (3), while the potency of retold tales and local visual reminders have become fragmented or disappeared in many cases. At the same time, informal exchange generated around the surge of research and commemorations often reveals that "the Famine was never mentioned" in many families, communities, or formal studies of history and literature, particularly in North American contexts. Thus, significant factors in the recent growth of Famine interest may involve a need to "remember" for some participants, but among others, constructions of new "memory" has developed since previous to the recent focus, they had little or no interest in or knowledge about the Famine. For still others, the sentiments of the supermarket owner in Nuala O'Faolain's novel, *My Dream of You,* represent another kind of "memory": the "owner wouldn't let the Famine Commemoration committee put up a plaque there. All that kind of stuff is best forgotten, he'd said to Miss Leech. I have to pay the schoolkids a man's wage now to do a bit of work around the place, Ireland's doing so well" (111).

Another contrast in the current commemorative debates is that while the human and cultural devastations of World War II are usually assumed to be embedded in the politics of war, the Famine has been subject to a variety of attempts over the years to depoliticize, repoliticize, or otherwise reframe its context with emphasis on, or distance from, its associations with political violence. The reconstruction of Famine memory at fifty-year intervals has been influenced by the recurring conjunction of its anniversaries with commemorations of the Irish rebellions of 1798 and 1848,[1] two brief but intense episodes with far-reaching consequences that continue to reconfigure Famine memory against a variety of violent conflicts. The celebratory events in Ireland during the 1898 centennial of the 1798 rebellion utilized the still-potent memory of Famine experience, coupled with the abortive Young Ireland uprising in 1848, to spur renewed efforts to increase Irish independence from Britain by violent means, if necessary (Owens 103–17). By contrast, in the years just after World War II, the magnitude of horror surrounding the concentration camp discoveries seemed to overshadow the marking of a century of Famine memory. Ireland's pre-war links with German nationalism and the Free State's neutrality during the "Emergency" further complicated a return to an 1898 interpretation of the Famine in the context of the newly formed Republic of Ireland and its nation-building attempts in 1948. At the third fifty-year mark, however, extensive efforts around the world to reflect on the cultural aftermath of devastation in World War II seem to have enabled and perhaps stimulated new debates on the Famine. In contrast with challenging post-war rebuilding imperatives of a partitioned Ireland and other countries in its diaspora in the 1940s, many recent Famine commemorations have emphasized particularly personal aspects experienced locally in the Famine years; these choices also reflect the current international discourse on representations of cultural identity and human violence.

Despite an often cited "silence" surrounding the Famine until recently, certain geographical locations have long been revered as potent sites in Famine narratives. Contradictorily, the isolation of sites like Grosse Île and Skibbereen may have contributed to the scale of death experienced there, but visual images associated with them have been important "silent" aspects of their ongoing central positions in that discourse. One of the first and most potently charged sites to be marked with an official commemoration of the Famine was the remote island of Grosse Île, Quebec. The narrow three-mile-long island is almost five miles out in the St. Lawrence River some forty-five miles north of Québec City in the mostly French-speaking and historically Catholic Canadian province of Quebec. Despite this isolated geography, impulses to create visual remembrances of the thousands of Irish buried on Grosse Île have been initiated intermittently. From 1832 to 1937, the island functioned as a main port of entry to North America; prior to 1848, many emigrants lacking higher fares to other locations and sick passengers onboard overloaded ships that were refused entry into United States ports came through Grosse Île (MacKay 295–96). Combined with the drama of its devastating immigration season in 1847, the island's history has given it a central voice in Famine narratives. Yet in some ways, its contemporary isolation is important to the understanding of its potency as a site of cultural analysis. Its distance from Ireland and its isolation from larger cities better known today for large Irish immigrant communities is a poignant reminder that on the local and diasporic levels, isolating "silences" surrounding Famine memory are powerful influences in its dialogues, not vacant absences from them.

Controversies surrounding Grosse Île have taken different forms over the years; several commemorative efforts have been realized, but these have resisted rather than reached resolution of the Famine's effect on the cultural landscape of Quebec. A study of this small island is important for several reasons: (1) as a single location, Grosse Île is the site of perhaps the most dramatic episode of the Famine exodus; (2) it offers a tantalizing suggestion of the camouflaged magnitude of the Irish influence in Quebec and, correspondingly, Quebec's place in the Irish diaspora; (3) it embodies many complexities and multiple messages that speak to the difficulties of commemorating deeply problematic aspects of the Famine; (4) currently under extensive government-sponsored refurbishment, it is a site in flux just as the Famine is in the process of being redefined for successive generations; (5) its history is complex and not uniquely linked only to Irish immigrants; and (6) it provides a point from which to examine implications of a broad trajectory of visual representations of the Famine that continue to be generated in many similarly "isolated" locations.

Before taking a closer look at the voices and silences visualized on Grosse Île, it should be noted that, in the broader context around

Famine commemorations, large heroic figures, flags, and other iconographic symbols of warfare and national identity employed in monument construction across Europe and North America during the nineteenth and twentieth centuries have become increasingly problematic public images in contemporary cultural spaces. These emblems have experienced shifts in meaning or lost significance altogether as new residents, including emigrants from the "defeated" countries, have formed vital communities within the "victor's" landscapes. In other cases, the mobility of contemporary populations may simply negate the requisite common language, cultural beliefs, and attachment to local community for a continuity of "monumental" meaning to be sustained. In addition, emblems of "universal" celebration of war or political oratory have also come to be critically reread as dangerous reminders of attempts to employ public spaces to silence diverse political and cultural voices. Hence, as increasing attempts are made to circumvent linguistic barriers in global venues like the Internet, media news, and advertising where received meanings of those images are more difficult to predict, one potent function of visual representation is underscored—the simultaneous ability to amplify and simplify complex and contradictory messages. It is useful, therefore, to consider the implications of text panels on monuments as visual representations in themselves that can amplify, neutralize, or contrast with the texts they purport to convey.

In the context of Famine commemorations, much recent debate over visual representation has taken place at local, academic, and governmental levels across the diaspora. While Celtic cross motifs have been utilized in some early and recent sites, in other cases, that emblem has been considered but another chosen to offset associated political ideologies.[2] In still other instances, like the Philadelphia and Dublin experience, figurative depictions have raised questions about the desirability of tattered and emaciated Famine bodies suggestive of the debilitating stereotypes of poverty and disease that haunted Irish immigrants into the twentieth century. When the visual representations of Famine prove more complex than anticipated, discussions can involve new understandings of visual cultural production in which discomfort with meta-narrative has reconfigured the reception and meaning of commemorative imagery designed for public spaces. Increasingly, works like the Vietnam Veterans Memorial in Washington, and diverse Holocaust commemoratives have shifted focus away from a nineteenth-century emphasis on a collective "national" voice resounding with triumphant resolution. Instead, these images tap the power of unresolved strife latent in individual experiences, anonymous contributions, and personal introspections in the aftermaths of such large-scale conflicts as war and famine. One Famine work that functions on such a level is located across the road from the site of the former Ennistymon workhouse in Co. Clare. This work features fragmented images based on a letter written at the depth of the Famine about a local four-year-old boy turned away from the workhouse. The large solid metal rectangles at oblique angles at the open field's edge form poetic allusions to the workhouse doors and charge the viewers' imaginations through the use of small images, cryptic texts, and poignant emptiness rather than through monumental forms and nationalist rhetoric.

Contemporary artists have begun to expand Famine-related imagery, but the Celtic cross continues to be a recurring one in discussions of Famine representation. It is a deceptively simple design with complex histories. Visually linked to the high crosses of Ireland, it has been conceptually reconfigured not only into Famine commemorations but also into Irish nationalist monuments in many Irish towns and communities elsewhere; it is emblematic of the split and multiple messages in which Famine discourse has jostled turbulently. The 1909 Celtic cross monument on Grosse Île is a significant crossroads in that discourse. Though the cross was not the island's first Famine commemoration, it continues to be the most reproduced symbol of the island's history; yet, paradoxically, this image also functions as a visual icon of competing voices and silences not only in this isolated geographic location but also in much of the Famine's representation.

To spotlight some of these silences, reference to other events in Grosse Île's history is needed. Chosen for its isolation, a quarantine station was opened on Grosse Île in May 1832, in response to the large numbers of people fleeing the cholera epidemic in Europe. The Irish were the largest immigrant group recorded at the station that year. Also, news of arrivals at Grosse Île printed in the *Quebec Mercury* indicates that the first vessel known to arrive at the station with passengers suffering from cholera was the *Carricks* from Dublin. In that initial crisis, records of health boards along routes from Grosse Île to inland communities vary dramatically, but estimates indicate that six to nine thousand people died on ships, in quarantine at Grosse Île, or in communities along the St. Lawrence River (MacKay 136–46). The arrival of the Irish in 1847 was the only period in the station's 105-year history that surpassed the massive scope of that first year's events. In less than six months in 1847, Grosse Île became the site of probably the largest mass grave of the Famine era, though large numbers of deaths also occurred in Montréal and in many smaller towns along the St. Lawrence, as well as in several sites in Ireland. Hence, the Irish are prominent in the two most critical years of the Quarantine Station's history. Ironically, as the *Carricks* was carrying passengers from Sligo to Quebec in 1847, the ship was wrecked off the eastern tip of Quebec; the bell from the ship and a Celtic cross mark that event on the shore near the Quebec community of Cap-des-Rosiers in the Parc national mémorial Forillon, but no mention is made there of the *Carricks'* notorious 1832 history at the Grosse Île Quarantine Station. Only two indirect commemorative efforts have been made so far at Grosse Île to note the 1832 epidemic: the name of nearby "Bay of Cholera" and a small bronze plaque placed by the Canadian government about twenty years ago that simply states that the station was opened to prevent the introduction of cholera from Europe.[3] Following the placement of this modest plaque, however, its opaquely neutral language sparked responses from diverse communities, a reflection of the island's complex histories. For instance, on the island there was a small but long-standing mostly French-speaking Catholic community, itself fragmented and displaced to towns along the river by the Quarantine Station's closure in 1937. After this date, the Canadian and U.S. governments conducted biological research on the island; public access was highly restricted until it was closed off completely in 1947. Of the dozens of remaining buildings, only the island's oldest structure, the small wooden lazaretto at the east end, presents any physical remains of the quickly constructed hospitals built in 1847. Thus, the pre-Famine history and post-Famine physical environment complicate the site beyond simply a memorial for the Famine dead. This visual diversity also provides continual challenge for the insertion of different perspectives into the ongoing refurbishment of the island as a historic site.

Commemorative sites are provocative crossroads for the construction of cultural identity. While visual representations of those identities may attempt to fix islands of meaning against the currents of time, the interpretation of those images is not stable. Since 1996, Grosse Île has been under an extensive refurbishment plan by Parks Canada. As a site of many layered histories, the Grosse Île project is fertile ground from which to investigate how cultural identities in successive generations have framed their pasts within diverse contemporary agendas.

The first Famine monument at Grosse Île was put up in 1852 by Dr. George Douglas, Superintendent of the Quarantine Station from 1832 to 1864. On one side, Dr. Douglas lists the names and the home regions of his colleagues, the doctors who died working on Grosse Île in 1847; on another side, he remembers "the mortal remains of 5424 persons who fleeing from pestilence and Famine in Ireland in the year 1847 found in America but a grave." This specific number of burials includes Douglas's own daily records in which cryptic entries like "112" are listed in the record of burials made each day (Gallagher 173). The lists are stoic resonances of the seismic nature of the six-month emigration season on the tiny island that year, but even the sporadic entry dates suggest their incompleteness. Also, though the very size of such numbers under the circumstances destabilizes their precision, the starkness of this specific number incised in stone offers a tangible grasp on the vagueness and anonymity of the undulating gravesite beyond (see Fig. 12.1). Despite research that suggests that many thousands more died here than indicated by this number (MacKay 290–93, Quigley 36), the voice monumentalized in this visual form is a striking example of an attempt to put a finite containment on the chaotic trauma of that summer. Nonetheless, its numerical solidity enshrines this visual text as a significant contradiction that continues to persist in many accounts of the Famine: the number itself acts to contain the scope of the disaster that befell the people it seeks to "remember"; it also inadvertently amplifies governmental attempts to obscure the human aspects of suffering through the namelessness of statistical accounts.

FIG. 12.1. DOUGLAS MONUMENT WITH WHITE CROSSES
ON MASS GRAVES

Adjacent to the Douglas marble is the much larger memorial constructed in 1998; it does not cite Douglas's number directly (and indeed includes names of the known dead buried on the island from all years) but in its own way, the long detailed lists of names featured in its display reiterate even more strongly the need for specificity in resistance to the vast extent of the tragedy. However, most of the names come from Douglas's records, thus silently supporting his accounts; the limited number of blank spaces reserved on the glass wall acknowledges the discrepancies but still seeks to contain the unresolved and controversial scope of disaster at the site (see Gauthier).

The small Douglas marble is among the first formal Famine commemorations anywhere, although the Church of Ireland in Skibbereen has two memorials that may predate Douglas's: one to its minister on the church interior and another detached stone engraving outside. The language on the stones in the back churchyard carries a very different message from the markers on Grosse Île. It reads: "erected in 1847–8 by British munificence anxious to turn the awful visitation of God in the destruction of the potato crop in the autumn of 1846 into a lasting benefit to their Irish subjects who survived." In both locations, the commemorative sponsors stressed certain interests in the tragedy while remaining silent about others. Both written texts prioritize specific local events and people. These early stone texts are themselves constructed as visual monuments. Unlike many later commemoratives, no additional visual imagery is employed for emphasis or monumental positioning. While the reasons for text alone on these early markers is unrecorded, the prominence of imagery with text in later commemoratives is made all the more provocative by contrast.

Behind the Douglas marble, the white crosses on the mass grave site visually suggest individual graves, perhaps somehow marked since the time of burial. Such is not the case, however. The crosses were placed there in the early 1980s by Freddie Masson, a longtime Parks Canada employee whose family lived and worked on Grosse Île for generations. His family's long-standing connection to the island yields yet another viewpoint; his poetic memories of Grosse Île appear in the 1981 memoir *Grand mamon raconte La Grosse Île* published by Masson's aunt, Jeannette Vekeman Masson. Here, her family anecdotes about the Famine and subsequent commemorative pilgrimages are nestled into affectionate accounts of daily childhood life on the isolated island from the mid-1860s onward. In the undulating rows of earth made uneven by the passage of time in the mass grave site, the punctuating white wooden crosses resemble military burial places like Vimy Ridge, a World War I French battleground where many Canadian soldiers died, an image refreshed across Canada in 1995 during televised ceremonies of the fiftieth anniversary of the end of World War II. For other visitors, this site can evoke the images of Arlington Cemetery made familiar to TV viewers at the funeral of John Kennedy. Since his assassination, that image has often been used in portrayals of him as a kind of contemporary Irish folk hero, again despite many other conflicting aspects of his life. In the early 1980s, however, for the few mostly local participants in commemorative events on Grosse Île, these conflated images of war, politics, and hunger echoed with silent but potent contemporary overtones in the media coverage of the hunger strikes by Bobby Sands and other prisoners jailed in Northern Ireland. On contemporary murals in Northern Ireland, images of similar white crosses, Celtic crosses, and references to the dead at Grosse Île are redirected toward the hunger strikers and violence of that period. Thus, the solitude of the white crosses on Grosse Île's Famine graves belies fragmented and contradictory local meanings in visual discourse across the Irish diaspora (Rolston 60).

FIG. 12.2. CELTIC CROSS AND TEXT PANELS, GROSSE ÎLE

The large stone Celtic cross monument was erected on Grosse Île in 1909 on the island's highest point [see Fig. 12.2]. The selection of a prominent hilltop location is a tradition associated with ceremonial sites of Gaelic chieftains; this position thus suggests a dramatic contrast between the destitution of the Famine and the pre-British strength of Gaelic Ireland. Until the island's recent refurbishment, photographs of this monument's dedication ceremonies were the main images of Grosse Île in circulation after the Quarantine Station closure. The stone Celtic cross design visually relates to centuries-old standing stone crosses throughout the Irish landscape. In popular legends, the design blends the Christian cross with the circle, a reference to the ring forts of pre-Christian culture also evidenced in the Irish terrain. Hence, the cross on Grosse Île links the Famine with Catholicism but with a distinctively Irish version. Sighle Bhreathnach-Lynch, curator of the Irish collection at the National Gallery of Ireland, has described the Celtic cross in early twentieth-century Irish nationalist representation: "The early Irish symbol of a cross with a Gaelic inscription can also be interpreted as a declaration of the increasing desire by Irish society to establish a distinctive 'Irish Ireland' identity, one firmly linked to Catholicism and to an ancient and noble pre-conquest past, with its single Gaelic tradition, culture and language" (124). Such intention surely motivated the Grosse Île design, but a more complex reading of it is needed.

The monument was designed by Jeremiah Gallagher, an Irish nationalist born near Macroom (about 30 miles from Skibbereen) who emigrated to Quebec in the late 1850s. Gallagher was president of the Quebec A.O.H. chapter and instrumental in raising the funds for it. Since Madame Masson's 1981 memoir, Gallagher's granddaughter Marianna O'Gallagher has published several books related to the history of the Irish in the region (some in collaboration with members of the Masson family mentioned earlier). In her first book, *Gateway to Grosse Île*, she notes that plans for the Grosse Île monument began in 1897, during the fiftieth anniversary visit to Grosse Île's mass grave (83). During that same period, plans were underway in Ireland for the centennial of the 1798 rebellion. Conflation of the Famine with political struggle thus gained new thrusts in Ireland and North America. The monument's dedication date on Grosse Île was the Feast of the Assumption, a Catholic holiday celebrating the Virgin Mary's assumption into heaven without experiencing human death. In 1898, that same date had also been symbolically selected as Wolfe Tone Day in Dublin, the largest public celebration of the 1798 centennial (Owens 103–17). In the Catholic countryside of Quebec, the Assumption was a popular late summer holiday before early winter encroached into the northern climate. The souvenir program for the 1909 event refers to the cross as "the national memorial monument" and its dedication as the "fruit of the patriotic movement" and the "culmination of a national duty" (Jordan 11). Notably, the specific "nation" was not defined. Since participants included many representatives of the Catholic clergy and government officials from Canada, Quebec, Ireland, and the United States, such terminology emphasizes abstract commonalties while remaining silent about diverse differences such as religious frictions, linguistic barriers, and other unforgotten disputes like the Fenian raids launched into Canada in the 1860s from U.S. towns along the Quebec and New Brunswick borders. Nevertheless, the prominence of the

Quebec flag in pictures of the day highlights the local fervor of the large crowd in attendance, while the lengthy list of speakers emphasizes the participation of French Canadian Catholic clergy and a wide range of political figures.

Four text panels on the monument's base, however, echo with different messages to different viewers. One lists names of the clergy, almost all noted as Catholic, who attended the sick and dying on Grosse Île in 1847–1848, and prominently frames "the Ancient Order of Hibernians in America" as the sponsors and the "Feast of the Assumption 1909" as the dedication date. The text of this panel is in English only and characterizes this Famine monument as clearly Catholic. Thus, Famine-era links between Irish Catholic immigrants and inhabitants of the surrounding Catholic French-speaking regions are made, but shifting linguistic allegiances among the mostly English-speaking Irish Canadians in the intervening years can also be read through this panel's language. The other three panels at first appear to be translations in Irish, French, and English of a tribute to the dead buried on Grosse Île. By describing the dead as those who "suffered hunger and exile" in order "to preserve their faith," the monument does not recognize that Protestants are also buried here and is instead imbued with overtones more resonant with the political struggles and cultural identities in turn-of-the-century Ireland. In addition, the visual suggestion of translation is deceptive.

Although the text in French and English is similar, the reference to *le prêtre Canadien* on the French panel prioritizes the French Canadian Catholic priests, not their English-speaking Anglican counterparts; no such distinction is made on the English panel. For the French-speaking employees and their families who, as the island's residents, would probably be the most frequent visitors to the monument, Catholic links are again strengthened in the almost completely absent mention of Irish and Canadian Protestants' roles during the Famine. Thus, an ambivalent and shifting allegiance can be seen through comparisons of the choices of word phrases and languages in spite of the sentiments stated on the individual panels alone.

By contrast, the words of the Irish panel would have been readable by only a few visitors to this island by 1909 since Irish immigration to Quebec had diminished dramatically since the Famine era. The Irish panel, however, is not visually meaningless and, indeed, it functions on a very different political terrain from its French and English companions. After the initial announcement in the 1980s that Grosse Île would become a Canadian historic site, an image of this panel was used in a postcard campaign by Action Grosse Île, an Irish-Canadian group, in an effort to refocus more attention toward the history of the Irish on the island at a time when the Canadian government began official recognition of the island's significance to Canadian history. The following translation of the Irish text was also offered on that card: "Thousands of the children of the Gael were lost on this island while fleeing from tyrannical laws and an artificial Famine in the years 1847–48. This stone was erected to their memory and in honour of them by the Gaels of America. God save Ireland!" Though the translation resonates with the language of Irish independence movements of the early twentieth century and its Irish text would have been unreadable by most Canadian recipients of the postcard in the last decades of the twentieth century, the visual image of the Irish language had a contemporary cultural resonance in Canada at that time. In this period, one marked by contested cultural identities pivoting around issues of language, the card could have been a reminder to French Canadians that without diligence, a language can be quickly lost. However, the card was circulated in Ireland but issued mainly as a plea to the mostly English-speaking Irish-Canadian population that the once burgeoning Irish contribution to the development of Canada was facing its own marginality in the multicultural context stressed in the newly refocused attention to this long-neglected island.

II.

Similar to Grosse Île in some respects, Skibbereen is another site with a central voice in Famine narratives due to the large number of deaths there during the late 1840s but also because of the lasting images created of that region by drawings in publications such as *The London Illustrated News*. In sharp contrast to those Famine sketches of raggedly dressed emaciated mothers, starving animals, and densely crowded villages, a large monument dated 1904 stands in Skibbereen town center; it is not a Famine commemoration but features a remarkably robust but pensive female figure—the Maid of Erin, an Irish counterpart to Marianne, the French figure of *Liberté*. Unlike the French figure, whose passion is shown in her torn flowing garments, Erin is not leading her sons in the charge but is paused here in thought and fatigue. She leans her large hand heavily on a Celtic cross as a crutchlike support, her fingers almost drumming with impatience.

This imposing image, a daily reminder in the town center, refuses the destitution of emaciated Famine bodies, but in contrast with her visual presence, harnesses the invisible but hardly forgotten memory of those Famine images toward support of a new agenda. Like the Grosse Île monument, the text panels on the four-sided base link with the image above them to dress the monument in multiple layers of meaning. Here the solitary dates inscribed one to a panel—1798, 1803, 1848, and 1867—need no text to invoke the bitter memory of four Irish rebellions;

visually linked just above eye level, the dates literally form the base of unfinished business upon which the strong body of Erin awaits further action. The monument's location in town center acts as a constantly visible reminder that the debilitation of the Famine era can be rejected but also maneuvered into the position of a nationalist weapon; this cross is ready for its transition from crutch to weapon. This echoing dialogue of Celtic crosses would find a new voice on Grosse Île five years later but with distinctly local implications in the shifting cultural politics of Irish immigrants in the terrain of quickly changing development in post-Famine Quebec [see Fig. 12.3].

FIG. 12.3. MAID OF ERIN, SKIBBEREEN

In 1995, through the town of Skibbereen, a series of Famine sites were designated, creating an imaginary pathway woven into the visual array of the late twentieth century, in some ways similar to developments of commemoratives in the Grosse Île context decades earlier. The Sculptors' Society of Ireland hosted twelve temporary sculpture installations in Skibbereen, mostly ephemeral constructions now dissolved into local memory, though a few personal photographs recorded the occasion. In addition, the Irish Famine Commemoration of Skibbereen designated several sites along a walking tour called "The Skibbereen Trail," which starts in the square where the Maid of Erin monument is located. Available in nearby bookstores, the guidebook, however, marks the square with local stories of children presumed dead but miraculously revived before untimely burials during the Famine years; the stories bear curious parallels to the feast of the Assumption but without the official Catholic attachment. No mention is made of the nationalism resuscitated in the looming image of the nearby ponderous Maid of Erin monument, thus suggesting that even imposing icons are subject to silent treatment.

The Famine is not stripped of its political associations on the Skibbereen Trail, however. The second site marked on the Trail is the house of apothecary Jeremiah Crowley. Here *The Skibbereen Walking Tour* notes: "in 1856 he, O'Donovan Rossa, and others founded the Phoenix National Literary Society. Out of this society later developed the Fenian Movement" (7). At another marked site is a portrait of Jeremiah O'Donovan Rossa whose prominent Skibbereen family was drawn into poverty during the Famine. The portrait marks the building where he worked for his cousin's husband after the death of his father and the family's subsequent eviction and emigration to the United States. The site is titled "O'Donovan Rossa's—Emigration a Solution?" It is not clear that the Grosse Île cross designer Jeremiah Gallagher was affiliated with Rossa and his colleagues, but it was during this period in the late 1850s that the nationalist Macroom native also emigrated to Quebec (O'Gallagher 98). While the text at the Grosse Île site deplores Famine emigration as an "exile," it raises no question about the effects of that exodus on those who remained in Ireland. The 1995 questioning title noted on this now prosperous corner in Skibbereen town center seems to look simultaneously back at the Famine and forward to Ireland's current prosperity to raise its own set of local issues.

III.

By the closing years of the twentieth century, a critical review of cultural and aesthetic dimensions had grown around the array of allegorical and nationalist monuments constructed across European and North American landscapes during the last two centuries. Contemporary public commemoratives of any kind must confront those practices of utilizing public space in their attempts to address diverse current concerns and to anticipate those of future participants in the spaces. Contemporary visualizations of the Famine function in this dilemma but differ in several respects from earlier commemorative projects that attempted to speak collectively from one universal or national viewpoint. Recent Famine projects have often focused on a particular poignant local episode and are supported by individuals with personal investments in the fabric of that community. The Hyde Park Barricks in Sydney, Australia, for instance, spotlights the shiploads of single and widowed Irish women sent there in 1848. From trees around this recently commemorated space, electronically recorded women's voices speak the fragments of information known about each woman and highlight the invisibility of such information in official histories. Some commemorative endeavors have faced disinterest because no locally compelling episode can be attached to the overwhelmingly large disaster narrative. As suggested by Nuala O'Faolain's fictional supermarket owner, other efforts have faced resistance because such episodes linger all too uneasily among descendants of families who did survive the Famine calamities, perhaps through actions for which public reminders would be anything but redemptive. It would seem that while a fifty-year distance may stimulate "memory" in some ways, one hundred and fifty years may not yet be "past" enough for other aspects of the Famine.

Though there have been many new monuments constructed to remember the Famine dead and its survivors, many other contemporary representations of the Famine have been designed for display in public spaces but not as permanent monumental structures. The four large installations I have constructed in Ireland since 1996 are contemporary attempts to personalize a site or event through acknowledgment of the invisible dramas enacted in the anonymous individual lives out of which came the statistics, death tolls, and mass migrations. The installations cannot tell the personal stories tangential to or hidden by the large narratives, but they attempt to stimulate thought that those stories matter and can become imaginable when differently structured questions are asked.

The first of the series of installations was titled *La langue d'eau: In the Wake of Grosse Île* and was completed in Clondalkin, Co. Dublin, in 1996 (see Fig. 12.4). The floating structure was constructed with thousands of medical tongue depressors and wooden freight palettes in recognition of the diseases spread by inadequate medical practices and facilities for the emigrating people who came through the Grosse Île Quarantine Station in its two crisis years. Anchored near an island in the Camac River at Carbury Water Gardens, the work contained debris of red stone from the shores of the St. Lawrence River to mark it as a sort of ghost ship in homage to the *Carricks* and its passengers to Quebec between 1832 and its demise in 1847. Ephemeral paper copies of the records of passengers who arrived at Grosse Ile's Quarantine Station in 1832 and 1847–1848 were scattered along the edges of the

Camac site for visitors to read or ignore. The small white crosses on the structure and floating in the water around it clearly referenced the Grosse Île graves and the unknown numbers of Irish people still unaccounted for. The tattered structure also refers to the poignant state of disrepair of Grosse Île's oldest structure—the derelict wooden

FIG. 12.4. KAT O'BRIEN, *LA LANGUE D'EAU:*
IN THE WAKE OF GROSSE ÎLE (DETAILS)

lazaretto—before its recent controversial brightly colored restoration. Begun just as my work in Co. Dublin was finished, that refurbishment turned back the lazaretto's visible age to its supposed appearance at the Quarantine Station's closure in 1937. Ironically, the sense of the structure as a Famine "witness" is now preserved only through postcards and photographs taken before the renewed efforts to highlight the island's histories began. The floating structure was a kind of fading blueprint of that moment. Another "silence" in the floating structure lay in the dual language of the title, an allusion to the Irish women who did not die at Grosse Île but statistically "disappeared" through their marriages into French families of Quebec. While many contemporary Quebec names like Françoise Sullivan and Kathleen Leduc press the visibility of this history, transitions of many other Irish women into French-speaking families are visible only in the pages of archived records. Like the lore around the appearance of ghost ships, this installation was a temporary work left to the dismantlement of weather and time.

A second outdoor work was commissioned by Sculpture in Woodland in 1996 for long-term display in its sculpture park in the Devil's Glen, Co. Wicklow. This work is constructed mainly of discarded tree parts reclaimed from a nearby logging site. It consists of seven wooden shrines positioned in isolated locations on the hillside above a path through the Devil's Glen in a trench locally believed to be an abandoned "Famine road" project.

The work was conceived as a commemoration to seven generations of women born after the Famine; the number is utilized in reference to the two Irish words, *seachtar* meaning "seven people" and *seachtair* meaning "outside, without, beyond." Most people living today are removed from the Famine by four generations; their marginal "memories" of that period are stretched to the edge of retaining or releasing the fragile threads of translated experiences from the three generations before them for the three that will follow. The "memory" enshrined here is a series of figures constructed of logged timber, distorted and discarded bits, left behind after the surrounding land clearance has been long silent. The small suspended figure (see Figs. 5 and 6) in the fourth and middle position of the *Na Seacht Scrínte* series is composed of two parts. The upper torso is part of a root system partially burned as refuse at an adjacent site where timber was cut and cleared for replanting. The lower part of the torso is a piece of a Quebec sugar maple tree, cut after the sap was tapped for syrup; it was a gift to the project from Sylvie Gauthier, a Montréal descendant of Sarah Brady Gauthier, born in Co. Monaghan in 1835 and buried in an unmarked site in Montréal's Notre-Dame-des-Neiges Cemetery.

FIGS 12.5. KAT O'BRIEN, *NA SEACHT SCRÍNTE (THE SEVEN SHRINES)*,
CO. WICKLOW (DETAILS)

FIG.12. 6. KAT O'BRIEN, *NA SEACHT SCRÍNTE (THE SEVEN SHRINES)*,
CO. WICKLOW (DETAILS)

Despite these intentions, however, the location of the "shrines" in this sculpture park in the Wicklow Mountains invokes another history, that of Irish rebels hiding in these mountains after the 1798 rebellion. While neither the Sculpture in Woodland project nor the abandoned trench above the pathway are intentionally linked to this history, the placement of the haunting disfigured shapes in this place again triggered connections between the Famine and violent rebellion for local residents who discovered them on quiet walks through this familiar woodland. Though the work is commissioned as a "permanent" sculpture series, the wooden structures will inevitably weather in unpredictable ways and become subject to reinterpretation as the quiet and dense vegetation of the woodland is altered by the encroaching effects of nearby urbanization.

As these installations join related monuments constructed in other locations and in other eras, the fabric of commemorative impulses that purport to fix memories of the past will continue to be empowered and challenged by contemporary concerns linked to it. In the recent surge to impart meaning to the massive scale of death and displacement wrought by the Famine, a shift in the visual representation of it is taking place. Abstract and monumental expressions like the Celtic cross attempt to register a solidarity and a fixed ideology that is contradicted by its histories of appropriation for diverse purposes, by the experiences of those who have lived in the shadows of those ideologies, and by troubled reinterpretations of successive generations who are blocked by rather than engaged with the intentions behind the icons. The diversity obscured by such icons of "unity" can in time become the noise that denies their intended meanings. In recognition of such twisting paths, many contemporary interpretations stress the local, the personal, and the ephemeral aspects of memory rather than trying to seek resolution on a grand scale. If public memory of atrocity is to have a constructive impact on future participants in such sites, attempts can be made to situate diverse experiences, not as voices to be silenced but as inflections to be reconsidered. As an artist in an era suspicious of meta-narratives and monumental icons, many questions that sent me out of the studio and into the landscapes of Quebec and Ireland in 1996 remain open: Why is the Famine compelling now? What are we actually remembering and what are we striving to forget? Who are we talking to and what will be understood of our commemorative impulses in years to come?

All photos by K. O'Brien

Notes

1. Government efforts, like the oral histories collected by the Irish Folklore Commission, were notable attempts to mark the passage of the Famine generation but they did not constitute large diasporic-wide recognitions generated at the other fifty-year anniversary periods.

2. Commemorative works at Clones (Co. Monaghan), Melbourne (Australia), and the 1998 commemoration at Grosse Île utilize the motif in flat pathway design, while a series of sites like those in New Brunswick (Moncton, Partridge Island and Middle Island) and Quebec (Cap-des-Rosiers and Québec City) have employed erect standing Celtic crosses. At other sites, including Montréal, Buffalo (NY), and Sydney (Australia), representations of particular local significance have won preference.

3. The English section of the dual-language text panel reads:

GROSSE-ILE QUARANTINE STATION • In 1832 a quarantine ground was established here on Grosse Île in an attempt to prevent the introduction of cholera from Europe. The station's medical staff and quarantine facilities proved inadequate in the face of the cholera and typhus which periodically accompanied immigrant ships; consequently, epidemics spread through the Canadas on a number of occasions in the mid-19th century. Originally designed as a temporary establishment under a military commandant, the station was later operated as a regular service by the Canadian government until superseded in 1937 by new facilities at Québec. HISTORIC SITES AND MONUMENTS BOARD OF CANADA

Works Cited

Bhreathnach-Lynch, Sighle. "The Art of Albert G. Power, 1881–1945: A Sculptural Legacy of Irish Ireland." Kennedy and Gillespie 124.

Campbell, Stephen J. *The Great Irish Famine: Words and Images From the Famine Museum, Strokestown Park, County Roscommon.* Strokestown: Famine Museum, 1994.

Canadian Heritage (Parks Canada). *Instructions to Bidders: Project to Create a Memorial at the Site Grosse Île and Irish Memorial National Historic Site.* Ottawa: Gvt. of Canada, 1997.

Cleary, Pat, and Philip O'Regan, eds. *Dear Old Skibbereen: Guide to Famine Sites Included.* Skibbereen, 1995.

Crawford, E. Margaret, ed. *The Hungary Stream: Essays on Emigration and Famine.* Inst. of Irish Studies and Queens U Belfast, 1995.

Crysler, Julie. "Beyond the Grave." *Azure: Design, Architecture, and Art* (September/October 1998): 24.

Daly, Eamon ed. "Famine Commemoration." *Newsletter.* Dublin: Sculptors' Soc. of Ireland (January 1998): 24–32.

Donnelly, J. S. Jr. "The Great Famine and Its Interpreters Old and New." *History Ireland* (Autumn 1993): 27-33.

Edwards, R. D., and T.D. Williams. *The Great Famine: Studies in Irish History.* New York: New York Univ. Press, 1957.

Environment Canada Parks Service. *Public Consultation: Grosse Île National Historic Site Proposed Development Concept.* Ottawa: Environment Canada, 1992.

Gauthier, Sylvie. "Le Mémorial: An Irish Memorial at Grosse Île in Québec." *Ireland's Great Hunger: Silence, Memory, and Commemoration.* Ed. D. Valone and C. Kinealy. Lanham, Md.: University Press of America, 2002.

Grace, Robert. *The Irish In Québec: An Introduction to the Historiography.* Ste-Foy, Quebec: Institut québécois de recherche sur la culture, 1997.

Hall, Stuart. "The Local and the Global: Globalisation and Ethnicity." *Culture Globalisation and the World-System: Contemporary Conditions for the Representation of Identity.* Minneapolis: Univ. of Minneapolis Press, 1997: 19-39.

Hall, Stuart, and David Held, eds. "Citizens and Citizenship." *New Times: The Changing Face of Politics in the 1990s.* London: Lawrence and Wishart, 1989: 174-88.

Irish Famine Commemoration (Skibbereen) Ltd. *The Skibbereen Trail: An Historical Walking Tour.* Skibbereen, 1996.

Jordan, J. A. *The Grosse-Isle Tragedy and the Monument to the Irish Fever Victims 1847.* Québec: Telegraph, 1909.

Kelleher, Margaret. *The Feminization of Famine: Expressions of the Inexpressible?* Cork: Cork UP, 1997.

Kennedy, Brian P., and Raymond Gillespie, eds. *Ireland: Art into History.* Dublin: Town House, 1994.

Kinealy, Christine. *This Great Calamity.* Dublin: Gill and Macmillan, 1994.

Leerssen, Joep. *Remembrance and Imagination: Patterns in the Historical and Literary Representation of Ireland in the Nineteenth Century.* Cork: Cork UP, 1997.

Lloyd, David. *Ireland after History.* Cork: Cork Univ. Press, 1999.

MacKay, Donald. *Flight From Famine: The Coming of the Irish to Canada.* Toronto: McClelland and Stewart, 1992.

Masson, Jeannette Vekeman. *Grand-maman raconte La Grosse Île.* Montmagny, Québec: Les Éditions La Liberté, 1981.

Morash, Chris. *Writing the Irish Famine.* Oxford: Clarendon, 1995.

Noone, Val, ed. *Melbourne and the Irish Famine: The Unveiling of a New Monument.* Melbourne, Australia: Irish Famine Commemoration Committee, 1998.

O'Brien, Kat. "Na Seacht Scrínte: Macallaí í nGlenn an Diabhail (The Seven Shrines: Echoes in the Devil's Glenn)." *Canadian Woman Studies/ les cahiers de la femme* (Summer/Fall 1997): 96–100.

O'Brien, Kathleen. "GAOL, GAOL: Re-Viewing Silence in Kilmainham Gaol." *Eire/Ireland* 33.3–4, 34.1 (1998–1999): 173–88.

O'Faolain, Nuala. *My Dream of You.* New York: Riverhead, 2001.

O'Gallagher, Marianna. *Grosse Île: Gateway to Canada 1832–1937.* Ste-Foy, Quebec: Carraig, 1984.

O'Gallagher, Marianna, and Rose Masson Dompierre. *Eye Witness: Grosse Île 1847.* Ste-Foy, Quebec: Carraig, 1995.

Owens, Gary. "Nationalist Monuments in Ireland: c1870–1914: Symbolism and Ritual." Kennedy and Gillespie 103–17.

Pennick, Nigel. *The Celtic Cross.* London: Blandford, 1997.

Quigley, Michael. "Grosse Île: The Most Important and Provocative Great Famine Site Outside of Ireland." *The Hungry Stream: Essays on Emigration and Famine.* Ed. E. Margaret Crawford.: Inst. of Irish Studies and Queens U Belfast, 1995.

Quine, Dany. "Au coeur du cercle celte." *Le Soleil.* 26 septembre 1998, D13.

Rolston, Bill. *Drawing Support 2: Murals of War and Peace.* Belfast, Northern Ireland: Beyond the Pale, 1995.

The Skibbereen Walking Tour: An Historical Walking Tour. Skibbereen: Irish Famine Commemoration, 1995.

Chapter Thirteen

Le Mémorial:
An Irish Memorial at Grosse Île in Quebec

SYLVIE GAUTHIER

On 20 August 1998, a new monument, simply called *Le Mémorial*, was inaugurated on Grosse Île, an island in the middle of the St. Lawrence River in the province of Quebec. This monument was the third major one built there in 150 years. The first one was erected in memory of the physicians who died while tending the sick in 1847. The second was erected in 1909 in memory of individual clergymen and lay people who ministered to the sick and dying, and of the "thousands of Irish emigrants who . . . ended here their sorrowful pilgrimage."[1] Unlike these two older monuments, the new one does not officially commemorate the Irish Famine of 1846 to 1850 but has been erected to remember all the people who were buried on the island from 1832 to 1937, the years the island functioned as a Quarantine Station for immigrants to Canada. Funding for a memorial was authorized some years after Parks Canada revealed its plans to develop a national historic site on Grosse Île, on the theme of immigration. At the time, Irish-Canadian groups held a countrywide postcard campaign to petition the Canadian Government for special recognition of the thousands of Irish who lie in mass graves on Grosse Île. The message on the postcard read as follows:

Dear Prime Minister: I urge you to intervene personally to ensure that the Irish mass graves at Grosse Ile are perpetuated as the main theme of the National Historic Park, and as a reminder of the Irish role in the building of Canada. The Canadian Government must correct the historical misrepresentations in the Grosse Ile Development Concept.

Subsequently, the Canadian government renamed the island *Grosse Île and the Irish Memorial National Historic Site* and commissioned a new memorial that would acknowledge, among others, the large number of Irish who died in transit. The team chosen was commissioned to build a monument to all people buried on Grosse Île. However, while the names of the dead suggest the diverse cultural backgrounds of immigrants who came to Canada via Grosse Île from 1832 to 1937, as well as those of the sailors and island employees who died on or near the island, the visual impression of the monument is Irish. The circumstances surrounding the design of the 1909 Celtic cross and the 1998 memorial, and the unveiling ceremonies held for both monuments will be examined. Possible interpretations for the different components of the newest monument will be considered.

Until the new memorial was built, the largest monument on Grosse Île was a tall stone Celtic cross, unveiled in 1909 after twelve years of campaigning and fund-raising by the Ancient Order of Hibernians (AOH). At that time, the National AOH was a North American organization comprised of a Canadian and an American division (Jordan 9). On a pilgrimage to the island in 1897 to commemorate the fiftieth anniversary of the worst year of the Famine, AOH members from Québec had found the gravesites neglected and thus undertook an initiative to mark the site. In May 1899, in response to a petition asking him to allow this endeavour to move forward, the Canadian Deputy Minister of Agriculture gave the AOH conditional permission to "erect a Memorial Monument on a suitable site at the Grosse Île Quarantine Station for the purpose of honouring the graves and perpetuating the memory of their kinsmen who fell victims to ship fever in 1847 and '48" (O'Gallagher 84). The County President of Quebec Division No.1, AOH was Jeremiah Gallagher. In her book *Grosse Île, Gateway to Canada*, his granddaughter Marianna O'Gallagher, herself a local historian, described him as follows: "a civil engineer, a Gaelic speaker, assistant waterworks engineer at City Hall in Québec, he had, from the time of his arrival in Canada in 1859, become as ardent a Quebecer as he was an Irish nationalist" (85). He wrote to John Keating, National President of the AOH, suggesting a collection of ten cents from each member of the organization, to be attributed to the monument fund. In his letter, Gallagher stated:

it is our duty to see that this hallowed spot where so many thousands of our country people are buried should be reclaimed, be becomingly enclosed and have a befitting monument with suitable inscriptions (in Gaelic, Latin, French, and English) not only in memorium of the unhappy Irish exiles but also as a protest against the misgovernment of which they were the victims. (O'Gallagher 84)

Gallagher's vision of the monument was much more political than envisaged by the government.

The AOH formed the Grosse Île Monument Committee, which raised the funds required to build the monument through public subscriptions in both Canada and the United States. Jeremiah Gallagher provided the final design, based on the submissions the Committee received from various monument makers, all of whom had used differing representations of the Celtic cross in their drawings. The 46-foot tall cross is made of granite from Stanstead, Quebec, a small town about 100 miles from Grosse Île in the mostly Anglophone Eastern Townships on the American border. The Fallon Brothers of Cornwall, Ontario, were given the contract to cut the stone, transport it to Grosse Île and build the monument on the chosen site (O'Gallagher 85).

The cross stands on Telegraph Hill, the highest point on the island. On this spot in 1832, the year in which Grosse Île was set up as a quarantine station, a mast had been raised "to semaphore messages to Montmagny and hence by overland relay to the Citadel in Québec City" (MacKay 134). The cross faces west "towards Québec City and the new life the thousands who died there never experienced" (Quigley, "Canada's Famine Memorial" 20–40), thus sending out its own message of remembrance into the Quebec landscape. The Monument Committee organized an unveiling ceremony to take place on 15 August 1909, the Feast of the Assumption, a prescribed holy day in Roman Catholic countries. This day celebrated the Virgin Mary's rising into heaven body and soul as a sign of her purity. According to Kevin Danaher, in Ireland the main activity on this Feast day was to hold "Patterns"[2] at local shrines of the Virgin Mary. In addition, the day was an opportunity for "excursions and other outdoor pursuits" in many areas of the country. However, in parts of the north of Ireland where Orange parades were held on the twelfth of July, "the Ancient Order of Hibernians, and other similar groups, held rival marches on 15 August" (Danaher 178). These dual connotations overtly linked the unveiling of the Grosse Île monument with both Roman catholicism and Irish nationalism.

About 9,000 people from across Canada and the United States attended the event, including a Madame Roberge, one of the hundreds of orphaned Irish children adopted into French-Canadian families. Her name had been Mary Cox but when her parents died on the island, she was taken and brought up by a French-Canadian family. At the ceremony, it was said that she and her two daughters spoke only French (Jordan 98).

In addition to the unveiling of the highly political messages carved on the ebony panels (see O'Brien), a requiem mass was celebrated in the field where thousands are buried and speeches were given on "well known aspects of the history of Ireland and of the Irish of Canada and the U.S." (O'Gallagher 87). Among the speakers were several high-ranking representatives of the Catholic Church, such as Mgr. Sbaretti, the Papal Delegate, who talked about the link that joined French Canadians and many of the Irish who came to Grosse Île:

> Both peoples, Irish and French, have suffered much and fought valiantly in the cause of holy religion. Almighty God in his mercy has aroused their struggles both here in this country side by side, in prosperity and peace, enjoying the blessings of civil and religious liberty. As they were united in the hour of affliction so I earnestly hope and ardently pray that they may be always one, and, both scions of noble Catholic races, that they may go forward hand in hand for the welfare of their religion and their common country. (Jordan 88)

Other church representatives in attendance were Mgr. Bégin of Québec City and Father Maguire, the parish priest of Sillery and Provincial Chaplain of the AOH. Also present were prominent French and Irish Canadians including Sir C.A.P. Pelletier, Lieutenant-Governor of Quebec; Mr. Beauchamp, President of the Saint-Jean Baptiste Society; Sir Charles Fitzpatrick, Chief Justice of the Supreme Court of Canada; and Secretary of State, Charles Murphy, who, in his highly political speech, referred to Robert Emmet, Charles Stewart Parnell, Michael Davitt, and the Wild Geese. In addition, in his address to the crowd the National President of the AOH, Mr. Matthew Cummings, spoke of the political aspects of the Famine and of the strong historical links between the Irish and the French. Finally, Joseph Turcotte, Member of Parliament for Quebec County, spoke to the gathering in French, and an American Major, Mr. A. T. MacCrystal, addressed the crowd in Gaelic (Jordan 76–98).

In 1989, at a ceremony marking the eightieth anniversary of the Celtic cross unveiling, the Irish ambassador to Canada, Dr. Edward J. Brennan, spoke of the Famine as "Ireland's holocaust" and the Irish as "the first boat people of modern Europe" (Quigley, "Most Important" 25–40). Five years later, on 21 August 1994, speaking at a commemoration of the victims of 1847 while on an unofficial visit to Grosse Île, Irish President Mary Robinson said that while the failure of the potato was a "natural disaster" across Europe, "in Ireland it took place in a political, economic and social framework that was oppressive and unjust." She noted that "ailleurs sur le continent, on fermait les portes contre les Irlandais."[3] She reflected, in Irish and French, that Grosse Île—Oileán na nGael—l'île des Irlandais is a "hallowed place."

In 1992, the Federal Government released a proposal on how Grosse Île could be developed. Hardly a mention was made of the importance of this site for the Irish community in Canada and around the world. Indeed, it was suggested that "there should not be too much emphasis on the tragic aspects of the history of Grosse Île. On the contrary, the painful events of 1832 and 1847, which have often been overemphasized in the past, need to be put back into perspective, without robbing them of their importance" (Environment Canada 62). Following a long, laborious campaign led by Toronto-based Action Grosse Île and Irish-Canadian communities to highlight, preserve, and acknowledge what might be the Famine's largest single mass grave in the world,[4] Canadian deputy Prime Minister and Minister of Heritage Sheila Copps announced, in 1996, that the Grosse Île National Historic Site would be officially recognized as the Irish Memorial (Quigley, "Canada's Famine Memorial 20–40). Soon afterward, the Department of Canadian Heritage of the Canadian Government sent out a notice across Canada announcing a competition for the "creation of a commemorative work in the form of a memorial" at Grosse Île (Notice to Companies and Artists). The Instructions for Bidders stated that a memorial would be erected:

> to honour the memory of the immigrants—mainly of Irish origin—and quarantine employees who were buried on the island between 1832 and 1937. . . . It will be placed near the island's main burial ground and witness to the scope of the 1847 tragedy, and will be required to blend in and harmonize with the sector's cultural landscape, and to express the signification of the commemoration. [T]he work will be inscribed with nearly 6,000 names divided into two categories . . . [which] will be treated separately and distinctly, to enable visitors to distinguish between A) The immigrants buried on the island (for the year 1847, there will be an inscription stating that 2,200 unidentified people who died on ships in quarantine were buried on Grosse Île); and B) The quarantine station employees and the members of their families buried on the island. The names will be presented and inscribed in chronological order (by year of burial), and in alphabetical order. It must also be possible to add new names to the memorial, as they are identified by new historical research.

The Canadian Government provided all the funding for the monument. No money was raised through private subscriptions.

In all, 64 proposals were received from Canadians throughout the country. Five projects were chosen for Phase I, and the designers were asked to develop and clarify their plans and build maquettes. The seven-member jury was composed of two representatives from the Department of Canadian Heritage, two from the artistic and architectural communities, two from Canada's Irish community, and one from the federal Department of Public Works and Government Services. It was chaired by a representative of Canadian Heritage. In December 1997, the jury chose the Québec City consortium of Émile Gilbert et associés, architects, and Lucienne Cornet, artist (Government of Canada). In announcing the $300,000 contract for the monument in April 1998, Canadian Heritage described the Memorial as follows: "Located near the Irish cemetery, the memorial takes the form of corridors which, through a series of passages, lead into the earth, a symbol of darkness, and then re-emerge into the light."

As with the older monument, the date chosen for the unveiling was in August. However, the modest ceremonies took place on Thursday, 20 August, because that was the date on which Minister of Canadian Heritage Sheila Copps was available (Boudreau). Had the event been held on the Feast of the Assumption, it could have been symbolically linked with the 1909 unveiling of the Celtic cross. Also, since the Feast day fell on a Saturday in 1998, the ceremony could have stimulated more community participation. In addition, only a small number of government officials and clergy were present at the inauguration.

Although the cultural composition of the group of dignitaries present at the event differed greatly from that of ninety years earlier, the structure of the inauguration ceremony was somewhat similar, with welcoming remarks by Jean-Claude Marsan, the Representative of the Historic Sites and Monuments Board of Canada and Member of the Selection Board for the Memorial, and speeches by Larkin Kerwin, Chair of the Advisory Panel on Grosse Île and Member of the Selection Board; Ron Irwin, Canadian Ambassador to Ireland; and Sheila Copps, who also officially inaugurated the monument. Gilbert Normand, Secretary of State (Agriculture and Agri-Food) (Fisheries and Oceans) offered historical notes, and the Bishops of the Anglican Diocese of Quebec and of Sainte-Anne-de-la-Pocatière, the Right Reverend Bruce Stavert and the Most Reverend Clément Fecteau, blessed the memorial (Commission des lieux). Perhaps a reflection of government as opposed to community involvement, only about a hundred people attended the event, 8,900 less than attended the unveiling of the Celtic cross.

The design team for the new memorial was composed of three people: France Laberge, a French-Canadian architect from the Québec City region; César Herrera, an architect originally from Mexico; and Lucienne Cornet, an artist who immigrated from France. None had any known Irish family connections, and all were neophytes regarding the history of Ireland and of Grosse Île prior to their extensive background research for the competition. They delved into Irish history and examined Irish immigration patterns, particularly during the Famine years. The group considered the geography of Ireland, the lives of its people, and their hopes and setbacks. The designers also noted that many visitors to the island had described it as a very emotional place, a type of holy ground. The team strove to incorporate all these elements into the design, which resulted in a monument commemorating individuals rather than an event. In their plans for the structure, the designers noted that the topography of the Grosse Île site was reminiscent of that of Ireland, an island with rocky cliffs and green undulating fields and that the east-west axis of Grosse Île paralleled the immigrants' east-west voyage. As they became more and more familiar with the history of Ireland and that of the Famine, the team made a conscious decision to "stay away from politics" (Cornet), unlike Jeremiah Gallagher, whose intent was politically motivated, as indicated in the French/English/Irish text panels on the Celtic cross (see O'Brien).

FIG. 13.1. CEMETERY

In reference to Ireland's distant past, instead of the contentious politics of the Famine era, the designers settled on the idea of stone circles and megalithic passage graves as a "spiritual expression of the people of Ireland" (Herrera). The monument's pathways lead downward to the center of the structure, labeled "the crypt" by the design team, a place where viewers can channel their feelings. The memorial is situated between the hill where the 1909 Celtic cross stands and the field of unmarked mass graves of thousands of Irish migrants, eerily shaped like the many abandoned potato beds in rural Ireland after the Famine [see fig. 13.1]. The dry stone walls of the circular monument were built by workers of Portuguese and Bosnian origin and are made of local stone from a quarry about fifteen miles north of Québec City, a largely French-speaking area. Much of Québec City's architecture is built from this stone. The walls are also reminiscent of the thousands of stone walls seen throughout the west of Ireland. By using stone from this quarry, the memorial and the people it commemorates become symbolically rooted in the local geography and culture.

The monument's east-west corridor, charting the passage from the old world to the new, cuts through the structure. One half of the funereal monument is filled with schist from the rocky cliff against which it rests. This half represents the land of arrival and integration of the newly arrived into Quebec and Canadian society. The other half is topped with moss, representing Ireland, the land of departure. Perpendicular to the passageway, a steel wing-like structure emerges from the stone-filled half and cuts through the other half, effectively partitioning this section in two parts and forming a walk-through Celtic cross laying on the ground, a reconfiguration of the traditional symbol [see fig. 13.2]. The Celtic cross has been used in Famine commemorations in Ireland, North America, and more recently, Australia. In addition, it is a symbol that has been appropriated by diverse Irish nationalist groups and organizations at different times in Irish history. However, though the artists had surely seen this image during their initial research, they clearly indicated there was no deliberate intent to construct a Celtic cross. In discussing this reading of the monument, they attributed the emergence of this imagery to the subconscious, "the consequence of an inner force" (Laberge and Cornet). With the 1909 Celtic cross looming over the site, the new memorial has inadvertently become a type of shadow of the earlier monument, perhaps a reflection of the increased secularisation of contemporary society in Quebec and Ireland.

In their dossier to Parks Canada and during my interview with them, the three designers did not attribute any significance to the split in the

FIG. 13.2. MONUMENT FROM ABOVE

FIG. 13.3. CORRIDOR

green mossy "Irish" half of the structure, and they denied any intent to portray a divided Ireland. They made no intentional connection with politics in the Famine era or more contemporary divisions and violence in Ireland. Despite a visual correspondence to the metal peace wall in Belfast or the violent connotations of the sharp jutting edges, the steel wing springing forth from the new land toward the mass graves is simply meant to suggest life emerging from the earth, an energy contrasting the inertia of the dead, an energy that ensures survival [see fig. 13.4]. For the artists, it represents the pre-eminence of life over death, the hope of a new life.

The narrow east-west passage brings the viewer on a symbolic voyage to the constricted center of the circle [see fig. 13.3]. This

FIG. 13.4. STEEL WING

voyage is meant to suggest the pain and suffering of the migrants as well as the hope and faith they may have felt upon arriving in a new land. Their journey is also recalled in four niches integrated into the southern wall and reminiscent of similar constructions found in both Ireland and Quebec. Each small alcove contains a cast bronze image that can poignantly evoke absence, elements of the life left behind by the immigrants, or the dream of a new life in a new country. The niches invoke the personal experiences, lifestyles, and culture of the poorer immigrants instead of referring to a more elite group or to the event itself.

When looking at these sculptures, the viewer is stimulated to imagine what the individual lives of the immigrants may have been like; the possibilities are intentionally left open-ended. The first niche depicts a house floating above a small boat resting on a face [see Fig. 5A, 5B]. It

FIG. 13.5A. TWO NICHES

FIG. 13.5B. THE FACE

may imply an immigrant's dream of building a house, a symbolic attachment or anchoring in a new place. The boat could be the one taken by the immigrants from Ireland to Grosse Île or can suggest passage to the world beyond. The face, an island disconnected from its body, can be interpreted as an isolated individual, the mother country, or perhaps the new motherland. A reproduction of this piece is on display in the Strokestown Famine Museum in Co. Roscommon; it was part of the exchange when Grosse Île was twinned with this site in May 1998 ("Grosse Île"). The official document twinning the sites states that many of Mahon's tenants sailed to Quebec and that of the "more than 1000 immigrants from Strokestown, many fell ill and now lie in the communal graves at Grosse Île" (Memorendum).

The second niche, situated just below the first one, depicts a piece of material that is draped on a chair and over a cradle and cascades over the edge of the bronze piece, suggesting that perhaps the fabric had belonged to someone who left it behind or simply laid it down. The flowing material can imply a path leading into the future, the continuity of life, or the finality of death.

In the third niche is a tree, perhaps the tree of life or the tree of liberty, a symbol associated with the United Irishmen and Irish rebellions (Whelan), or a more general reference to a personal relationship with the earth. A coat hangs from the tree and a shovel rests against its trunk next to a mound of earth. More specifically, this image was inspired by an old tree that was standing next to the site where the memorial is now located. Unexpectedly, Parks Canada workers cut down the diseased tree just as construction on the memorial was about to start. The sculptor modelled the bronze tree after this one, which had stood as a sort of silent witness for more than a hundred years. The inference in this piece can be read many ways. Perhaps the earth has been prepared for planting or to bury someone; or perhaps when the field was dug up and found barren, the family left these objects behind as they got on board the ship.

In the last little alcove are smaller objects of an individual life: an open book—maybe a journal, a Bible, or a travel log; a candle holder—perhaps a personalized beacon or guiding light; a spoon and glass—simple objects from a simple life, an analogy to the food and water needed to survive. These objects could be things that immigrants brought on their voyage or left behind. The viewer can imagine that behind each stone lies another niche, another scene from another life, one for each person included on the monument's panels. Through glimpses into everyday life, the viewer can link the events of the Irish Famine with individuals and imagine the human faces on this tragedy.

The last component of the memorial is the one that most distinguishes it from the anonymity of other commemorative monuments associated with the Famine and connects the stone structure with the individuals who are buried close by. Between the stone circle and the gravesite stand twelve glass panels that echo the circular motif of the stone structure and act as the vehicle on which long lists of names are visually suspended between the viewer and the mass graves, giving back to the dead some measure of identity.

The small white crosses marking the gravesites are seen through these panels. Reminiscent of the Vietnam Veterans Memorial, the glass panels are etched with about 6,000 names, the majority Irish. Also, a small boat is engraved in the glass for each of the estimated 2,200 deceased who have never been identified. In remembrance of these people who died and remained unnamed, and of the island employees and sailors who lost their lives at or near Grosse Île, three poetic dedications, in French and English, are engraved and read as follows:

Inconnus, l'histoire n'a pas encore dévoilé le secret de votre identité
Votre dévouement dans la souffrance, le don de vos vies
Compagnons de la dernière traversée, le destin à la barre

Unknown but not forgotten, your names not yet surrendered from the past
Your dedication to life, yours given 'till the end
Waves, shivering; the sea, binding fates

Most viewers, Irish or not, who walk through this very moving section of the monument search and sometimes find familiar names. During an official visit to Grosse Île in 1998, President Mary MacAleese was photographed looking at her own name after spotting it on one of the panels. Visitors who come on a pilgrimage to this site often experience some similar kind of personal connection.

Today, official tours of Grosse Île present the Irish story as a small part of the island's history, and visitors are often confused by a lack of clarity regarding the time frame of events that occurred in different periods of the island's history (see Blair). But although the initial intent of Parks Canada was to make Grosse Île an apolitical national immigration site dedicated to all peoples who migrated to Canada, the nature of the island and of the visual markers scattered about the island has made it impossible to detach it from a focus on Irish immigration and the tragedies that prompted those waves of immigration. *Le Mémorial*, like several other monuments and plaques found on the island, clearly accentuates the Irish connection, especially the difficult period of the Famine years. Although the designers attempted to avoid specific political connotations in their design of the monument, viewers approaching the monument with a knowledge of Irish history and of the ongoing political conflict in Northern Ireland can understand the monument on various levels.

Strong links between the Irish who came to Quebec and French Canadians are re-emerging as a result of the new focus on Grosse Île. It has been estimated that perhaps as many as 40 percent of French Canadians may have Irish roots, but because of intermarriage and name changes, their Irish ancestry has become invisible. For example, when preparing for my interview with the design team, I looked at photographs I had taken on a previous visit to the new memorial some months earlier. To my astonishment, I found the names of my great-great-grandmother's parents who, unbeknownst to me, my mother, and her family, seemingly died on Grosse Ile in 1847. At least one of their daughters survived, had a child, and married into a French-Canadian family. My research indicates the child's name changed from Brady to Gauthier to Lanctôt [see fig. 13.6]

Le Mémorial functions on several levels. It is a site of remembrance and meditation, a place of hope, continuity, and discovery, and a valuable source of information. The design team felt that theirs was a "duty of memory," that they wanted to bring to light an important part of the history and heritage of Canada and Quebec that had been neglected in hope that it will be re-learned, remembered, and passed on to future generations. They created a memorial and now it is up to the

FIGURE 13.6. NAMES

public to move forward and continue the work of remembrance. As it is slowly uncovered, the story of the Irish in Canada, and particularly in French Quebec, will undoubtedly unveil a different facet of the Irish diaspora and deepen the understanding of the contributions of the Irish outside Ireland. This monument represents a step in this direction.

Photos by L. Cornet/É. Gilbert (1,2,3,5a) and S. Gauthier (4,5b,6)
Notes
1. Part of the inscription on the English language panel on the monument. For a more detailed discussion of the monument and the text engraved on its four sides, see O'Brien.
2. Celebration of the patron saint.

3. "Elsewhere on the continent, the doors were closed to the Irish" (my translation).

4. Estimates are as high as 12,000. See Jordan 25–40.

Works Cited

Blair, L. "(De)Constructing the Irish Famine Memorial in Contemporary Québec." *Ireland's Great Hunger: Silence, Memory, and Commemoration.* Ed. D. Valone and C. Kinealy. Lanham, Md.: University Press of America, 2002.

Boudreau, L. Personal Communication. Parks Canada.

Canadian Heritage. News Release. *Contract Announced for the Construction of a Memorial at Grosse Île and the Irish Memorial National Historic Site.* P-04/98-4, CC980058.

Commission des lieux et monuments historiques du Canada. Programme de l'inauguration du Mémorial. Août 1998.

Cornet, Lucienne. Interview with France Laberge, César Herrera, and Lucienne Cornet, 6 November 1999, Québec City. (My translation.)

Danaher, Kevin. *The Year in Ireland. Irish Calendar Customs.* Cork: Mercier, 1972.

Environment Canada, Parks Service. *Public Consultation. Grosse Île National Historic Site. Development Concept.* Ottawa: Minister of the Environment, 1992.

Government of Canada. Canadian Heritage. *News Release.* 16 April 1998: P-04/98-4, CC980058.

"Grosse Île twinned with museum." *The Irish Times.* May 30, 1998.

Herrera, César. Interview with France Laberge, César Herrera, and Lucienne Cornet, 6 November 1999, Québec City. (My translation.)

Instructions for Bidders. Project to create a memorial at the Grosse Île and Irish Memorial National Historic Site. Department of Canadian Heritage, 1997.

Jordan, J. A. *The Grosse-Isle Tragedy and the Monument to the Irish Fever Victims, 1847.* Quebec: Telegraph, 1909.

Laberge, France, and Lucienne Cornet. Interview with France Laberge, César Herrera, and Lucienne Cornet, 6 November 1999, Québec City. (My translation.)

MacKay, Donald. *Flight from Famine. The Coming of the Irish to Canada.* Toronto: McClelland and Stewart, 1992.

Memorendum of Understanding for the twinning of the Grosse Île and the Irish Memorial National Historic Site, Quebec, Canada with Strokestown Park and the Famine Museum, Roscommon Co., Ireland.

Notice to Companies and Artists, Department of Canadian Heritage, 1997.

O'Brien, Kathleen. "Famine Commemorations: Visual Dialogues, Visual Silences." *Ireland's Great Hunger: Silence, Memory, and Commemoration*. Ed. D. Valone and C. Kinealy. Lanham, Md.: University Press of America, 2002.

O'Gallagher, Marianna. *Grosse Île. Gateway to Canada 1832–1937*. Québec: Carraig, 1984.

Quigley, Michael. "Grosse Île: 'The Most Important and Evocative Great Famine Site outside of Ireland.'" *The Hungry Stream*. Ed. E. Margaret Crawford. Belfast: Queen's Univ. Press, 1997.

---. "Grosse Île: Canada's Famine Memorial," *Éire-Ireland* (Earrach/Spring 1997): 20–40.

Robinson, Mary. *Address by the President, Mary Robinson, at Grosse Île on 21st August 1994*.

Whelan, Kevin. *The Tree of Liberty. Radicalism, Catholicism and the Construction of Irish Identity 1760–1830*. Notre Dame, IN: Univ. of Notre Dame Press, 1996.

Chapter Fourteen

(De)Constructing the Irish Famine Memorial in Contemporary Quebec

LORRIE BLAIR

I. Background to the Study

Selling the past to the present is one of the most profitable aspects of the tourist, or more specifically, the heritage industry. In this context, heritage is a contemporary concept describing a marketable experience based on the interpretation of historical events. Interpretation is the selection from archival materials, architecture, relics, monuments, and so forth, and the packaging and presentation of such a selection to the consumer, in this case, the tourist. As a tourist product, heritage is largely market driven in that the interpretation of history is determined by consumer demand, not necessarily by the raw materials that went into its construction (see, e.g., Ashworth and Voogd 1–14). Thus myths, legends, folk memory, and fictional accounts can be, and often are, woven into the interpretative tale.[1]

In Canada, Parks Canada administers the heritage industry, and their mandate is "to commemorate, protect and present places which are significant examples of Canada's cultural and national heritage in ways that encourage public understanding, appreciation and enjoyment of this heritage in a sustainable manner" (qtd. in *Grosse Île: Proposed Development* 4). The national historic site system began with the 1917 opening of Fort Anne in Nova Scotia and now encompasses 130 sites, including such diverse examples as a prehistoric burial grounds in

Newfoundland, two North West Company fur trade posts in Saskatchewan, and the remains of Kitwanga, a fortified native village in British Columbia. In 1992, Grosse Île, Canada's first and largest Quarantine Station was officially added to this vast mosaic of heritage sites. Parks Canada proposed to spend about 11 million dollars to restore buildings, open a new visitor's center, and clean the three cemeteries. Grosse Île, an isolated island in the middle of the St. Lawrence River some 30 miles downstream of Québec City, was designated as a Quarantine Station in 1832, in response to a cholera epidemic. Grosse Île also played a major role in 1847, when 90,000 immigrants arrived in Canada. From 1832 to 1860, the Irish accounted for 52 percent of new arrivals, and many died while at Grosse Île. The estimated number of those buried there differs greatly from source to source. Parks Canada, in their visitor's guide, claims that 7,480 are buried at Grosse Île, and that more than 6,000 are buried in the Irish Cemetery (12). However, historian Michael Quigley sets the number for one cemetery as "no fewer than 7,000 people" and refers to it as "almost certainly the largest Great Famine mass grave site in the world" (20).

After 1860, 60 percent of arrivals came from England. The remainder came from a number of areas, including Scandinavia, Russia, Italy, France, and Iceland. As medical knowledge about contagious diseases progressed, the need for a Quarantine Station diminished. The station closed completely in 1937, and afterward, the island housed the Defence Research Board, which used the site as an experimental station for bacteriological warfare. Here, advanced research was conducted on the anthrax bacillus. Shortly after World War II, the research station was closed and only a caretaker remained on the island. In the 1950s and 1960s, Grosse Île, under the auspices of the Department of Agriculture, was used for studying animal disease, and from 1965, it was used as a winter storage for imported animals. The island remained closed to the public until 1984 when its governance was transferred to the Canadian Parks Service.

Given that the key purpose of a heritage site is to provide a venue to preserve widely shared memories and values, those who construct these sites must be able to achieve a broad public consensus on their ideological and emotional content. However, any account of so vast a tragedy that took place on this island was bound to be politically fraught, and achieving consensus vexed developers from the outset. After studying Grosse Île's architectural, archaeological, and ethnographical resources, Parks Canada, in collaboration with l'Écart-type, a marketing research firm, conducted a market survey of potential visitors. L'Écart-type employees made questionnaires in either French or English available to each of the 5,152 people who had visited Grosse Île during the 1990 season and, of that group, 289 responded. In addition to providing information such as age, gender, and level of schooling, respondents rated their level of interest in the following four subjects: history of 1832 to 1937, history of 1937 to present day, quarantine, and immigration. Some 86 percent rated their interest in history of 1832 to 1937 as "high or very high." Immigration was ranked last with a rating of 76 percent (l'Écart-type 45). In a second questionnaire given immediately after a visit to Grosse Île, visitors were asked to similarly rate their attitudes and motivations concerning trips and vacations in general. For example, a sample item from this questionnaire is, "When you are travelling for touristic or recreational reasons . . . how important is it to visit places where there's a lot of different things to see and do" (l'Écart-type annexe 7).

The next phase of the study involved a number of focus groups to test various "visit experience" scenarios and included 95 persons selected by l'Écart.[2] Each group was relatively homogenous and was made up of individuals who could potentially promote tourism at Grosse Île. For example, one group consisted of travel agents and experts in tourism, and another consisted of representatives from secondary and elementary schools. While l'Écart-type reported that one group consisted of eight individuals of European origin who were recent immigrants to Canada, the report of the group's discussion provided as an annex revealed otherwise (l'Écart-type 56). The group consisted of Madeleine, who is identified as *québécoise pure laine;*[3] Yvon, an immigrant from Brittany who has lived in Quebec for forty years; Bernard, an immigrant from Africa; Juanna, a immigrant from Peru; and Allen, a Montrealer whose family immigrated from the Ukraine. Three others, Laurent, Alain, and Félix, joined the group late and did not participate in the discussion (l'Écart-type a3–39). It is important to note, further, that only two people who participated in these group discussions indicated that they were of Irish decent, and no group included a representative from any Irish-Canadian community. Despite the fact that the market study showed that "both current and potential clienteles clearly stated that the theme of immigration has little impact," Parks Canada released to the public its development plan promoting the island as an immigration center using the theme "Canada: Land of Welcome and Hope" (*Grosse Île: Proposed Development* 47). In reviewing this March 1992 document, it seems as though Parks Canada had long intended to create a Canadian equivalent to Ellis Island and since 1974 had been looking for an appropriate site to highlight immigration (*Grosse Île: Proposed Development* 5). Starting with the premise that Grosse Île played a significant role in the history of Canadian immigration, and given the number of in situ architectural resources, Parks Canada declared Grosse Île to be the ideal location. Not everyone agreed.

Action Grosse Île, a committee created in June 1992 by Irish community representatives from Toronto and other Ontario cities, was perhaps the most vocal group to oppose the plan. The committee's overarching goal was to "ensure that the mass graves of the of the Irish Famine victims of 1847 [were] perpetuated as the main theme of the National Historic Park on Grosse Île and as a permanent monument to the Irish role in the building of Canada."[4] During public hearings on the development plan, members of Action Grosse Île accused Parks Canada of attempting to rewrite history because Grosse Île was never used as an immigration center. Michael Quigley, the group's co-founder and historian, in an interview for *Hunger's Children,* a documentary about Grosse Île that was aired several times on the CBC, expressed astonishment to consider how a place containing mass graves could possibly be conceived of as a place of either hope or welcome. Others reacted strongly to Parks Canada's market study referring specifically to the "infamous passage on page 62," which stated that "there should not be too much emphasis on the tragic aspects of the history of Grosse Île. On the contrary, the painful events of 1832 and 1847, which have often been overemphasised in the past, need to be put back into perspective, without robbing them of their importance" (*Grosse Île: Proposed Development* 62). Even Parks Canada's use of the word "theme" drew fire, particularly from the press (see, e.g., Lyons H10). No doubt, it was a poor word choice because of its association with amusement parks typified by Disneyland.

This is certainly not to suggest that the Irish community was represented by a single, united voice. Cecil Houston, in the abovementioned CBC documentary, criticized the motives of Action Grosse Île stating, "They want to make sure that the British colonial experience is heightened in the understanding of Grosse Île. So, the Canadian government is often presented as being party to some sort of secret deal to keep Grosse Île out of the realm of discussion of the perfidity of the English." He continued, "Grosse Île is not to be created to right some wrong that was done, or perceived to be done, in another part of the world. We can't do that sort of thing. You can't extend that sort of responsibility into the past."[5] At their root, these arguments represent an ideological division about British government's responsibility for the Famine. Moreover, they reveal a lack of consensus on whether Grosse Île is the end or the extension of the Irish Famine story, or the beginning of a Canadian immigration story. Parks Canada chose the latter option, stating that it wished to commemorate, not interpret history, and maintained its original plans to focus on aspects of immigration at Grosse Île. In a supplement to the initial plan, Parks Canada issued the following statement:

> It is proposed that the larger story told at Grosse Île be one of arrival and dispersal of various immigrant groups over a long period of time, including the Irish for whom arrival often involved death or treatment for illness, and for whom the island has special meaning. The Service wishes to show all possible sensitivity to those members of the public who attach special importance to the struggles and hardships of their own ancestors, but it is not intended to use any historic site in the national system to tell the history of people in their original homelands beyond the borders of Canada. (21)

II. The Study

During the past three years, I have been taking part in the guided tours of Grosse Île in order to collect data on how the employees of the Canadian Parks Service contextualize historical documents, buildings, archaeological remains, and artworks to inform the public about aspects of Irish immigration and the Irish Famine. I began this study with the assumption that Parks Canada's treatment of Grosse Île as a heritage site is a form of education and, as such, plays a crucial role in shaping conceptions about Irish identity and history in Québec. The data I have collected thus far will inform this discussion.

For this study, I rely on a method of critical analysis, which crosses several disciplines, including museum, heritage, and tourism studies, and draws on ideas from art criticism. I am largely concerned with the narrative topology of the Parks Canada guided tour. Defined briefly by David Brett, narrative topology is the arrangement of spaces and the connection between them and is concerned with circulation, as it is a form of social ordering (88). Brett maintains that a narrative topology is a form of rhetoric, which seeks to persuade the viewer. He states, ". . . our experience of a site is mediated by our journey through it and the meanings we derive from it cannot be separated from the particular order in which we encounter its parts" (91). Brett makes the distinction between directive topologies, which one must follow, and indirective, which allows individual variations. The Parks Canada tour is largely directive. Although the Parks Canada brochure promises that one can visit "[o]n your own or in the company of a guide," touring independently is not an option. In fact, its *Proposed Development Concept* states, "At the present time, all visitors must join groups led by tour guides who are Parks Canada employees. Individual tours are not permitted" (64).

III. The Tour

While the park is open seven days a week from May through mid-October, it is not always possible for a single visitor to go there. The only access to Grosse Île is by chartered boats, and it is simply not cost effective for boat operators to make the thirty- or forty-minute passage for a small number of visitors. A critical mass of about one hundred visitors is achieved when a group of people travel together as part of a larger tour of the Québec region and visit Grosse Île as part of the package. The time visitors are permitted to spend on the island is strictly determined by the boat operator's schedules. This is limited to a three-hour tour with an additional half-hour allowed for lunch.

As the boat slowly inches its way to the wharf, Parks Canada employees line the shores to greet visitors. Once safely on shore, visitors are separated into two groups: one for francophones, and another for anglophones.[6] All tours begin with an approximately fifteen-minute introductory lecture given by the guide. During this lecture, the history of Grosse Île as a Quarantine Station is told to visitors who sit on benches or stand in small groups in front of the guide. The quality and tone of these opening lectures depend on a number of factors, including the guide's facility with the language, his or her comfort with the material presented, and the audience's questions or comments. Guides do not work from scripts. However, some anecdotes have been repeated verbatim by several guides.

While the content of the opening lectures varies greatly, the guides place some emphasis on what they refer to as Grosse Île's "two black periods of 1832 and 1847," periods both associated with an influx of Irish to Canada. In my experience, the word *famine* has never been used during an opening lecture. Instead, the causes of cholera and typhus epidemics of 1832 and 1847 are attributed to overpopulation, poor hygienic living conditions, and poor hygiene on board the ships bringing immigrants.[7] While visitors are told that in 1847, 100,000 immigrants, mostly Irish, arrived at Grosse Île, they are not told why they left Ireland. Some guides describe the conditions on the "coffin ships" and refer to those on board as "human ballast." One guide assured her group that, "The majority of people who came to Canada were not sick and the majority of the sick survived."

Western Section

The tour is divided into three parts, each taking slightly less than an hour. The first part involves a walking tour of the western sector of the island. It begins immediately after the opening lecture, when visitors are led into a large, rectangular building known as the "Third-class

Hotel." This structure, built in 1914, is the most recent of the three hotels on Grosse Île, and its name refers to the travel class of those who lodged in it. The choice to begin here has a practical purpose in that this building houses the cafeteria where lunch will be served mid-way through the tour. The discussion here is generally about the social status of the immigrants who arrived in the early 1900s and the small amount of space given to each person. A brightly embroidered costume in a glass case prompts visitors' questions, but the guides provide little or no information except that it belonged to the Doukhobors who were exiled to Canada from Russia and stayed briefly at Grosse Île.[8]

The group exits this building and walks along a dirt road in the direction of the Celtic cross. Along the way, the guide points out the various unrestored buildings such as the bakery, the kitchen, and wash house. The guide invites group members to peer through the windows into the rooms of the First-class Hotel. This hotel was built in 1912 to provide better accommodation for healthy immigrants. Here, immigrants were assigned one person to a room.

Next, the tour continues with a walk up a steep gravel road, then veers off to the left to take the pathway uphill to the Celtic cross. Designed by Jeremiah Gallagher and erected by the Ancient Order of Hibernians (AOH) in 1909, the fifteen meter high monument is indeed an impressive sight. Before the group is invited to carefully walk around the base to read the trilingual transcription, brief explanations of its origin and the choice of location are given. The guide also points out at this time that the texts differ according to language and recalls from memory the Gaelic inscription translated as, "Children of the Gael died in their thousands on this island fleeing from the laws of foreign tyrants and an artificial famine in the years 1847–48. God's blessing on them. May this monument be a token to their name and honor from the Gaels of America. God save Ireland." Usually, a visitor with some knowledge of the Irish language will correct the last line, "*Go saoraigh Dia Éire*" as "God free Ireland." Here, the guides simultaneously must deal with politically loaded terms such as "artificial famine" and "foreign tyrants" and try to keep visitors from venturing off the edge of the cliff. The explanation for the Famine usually given is that the Irish were only allowed to eat potatoes, and that the potato crop failed. After allowing a few minutes for photographs, members of the group are asked politely to move to the next attraction—the Irish cemetery.

After a short walk along a wooded path, the group reaches the site of the mass graves. The long rows are lined with simple white wooden crosses, and this rippled terrain is often compared to Ireland's abandoned lazy beds in which potatoes were grown. At the edge of the cemetery, the St. Lawrence sparkles in the sunlight. The guide, who stands on the road between the visitors and the gravesite, breaks the silence. She tells visitors that the crosses were placed there in 1986 and that 5,424 people are buried here. The number given corresponds to that carved on the Douglas monument. Carved from a marble stele, which is decorated with a cornice and topped with an urn, this small memorial overlooks the cemetery. On the north and south side of the memorial, the inscription lists the doctors who died of cholera in 1832 and of typhus in 1847. On the east side, facing the cemetery, the inscription reads, "In this secluded spot, lie the mortal remains of 5424 persons, who fleeing from pestilence and famine in Ireland, in the year 1847, found, in America, but a grave." Visitors are told that Dr. George Douglas, the first superintendent of the Quarantine Station and a native of Scotland, served at Grosse Île from 1832 until his death in 1864. He commissioned the Medical Officers' Monument around 1853 to honor six of his colleagues who died while in service on the island and to recall the Irish immigrants who died during the summer of 1847.

During each tour, the issue of mass graves is carefully explained. One aspect the guides take care to emphasize is that each person was placed in an individual coffin and given a proper burial. The coffins were placed one on top of the other, three deep, in trenches. This point is also mentioned and punctuated with a black-and-white drawing in the guidebook, which states, "Despite the state of emergency, the dead were buried with the greatest respect" (Parks Canada, *Grosse Île and the Irish Memorial* 12). The second point the guides emphasizes is that a number of immigrant children were adopted into Québécois families, and that these children were allowed to keep their Irish surnames. The average time spent here is ten minutes.

The guide then turns from the cemetery and ushers the group toward the third, and newest, memorial, commissioned by Canadian Parks Service in 1998. Created by Lucienne Cornet and the Émile Gilbert et associés architect firm, the work is situated to the left of the Douglas Memorial and also overlooks the cemetery. The memorial consists of a labyrinth of concentric circles. In the center, one-meter high stone fences create passage from east to west, following the path of the St. Lawrence River. Steel blades, recalling the bow of a ship and the wake behind it, perpendicularly intersect the path. Encircling the stone wall is another, higher stone wall. Imbedded in the stones are tiny steel relief tableaux containing facsimiles of personal effects the immigrants might have carried with them during their voyage or of that they left behind. The names of individuals buried in the cemetery, listed alphabetically in the year of their death, are etched in clear glass panels facing the cemetery. At the entrance of the memorial, a site marker placed by Parks Canada reads, "[E]ach of these stones reverberates with the echoes of the children, women, and men, who filled the horizon with their laughter, cries, singing, tears, and especially their hope for a new life, of a life that ended here. Among them were 7553 immigrants of every nationality, 1545 of whom remain nameless in the face of history, like so many small craft set adrift." No lecture is given, but time here is limited to about five or six minutes.

The group is led back to the cafeteria, completing a loop, and along the way visit a plaque erected in honor of the Doukhobors. Here, one guide told visitors, "This plaque is to say that not only Irish people came to Grosse Île."

The Disinfection Building

After lunch, the tour begins in the disinfection building, which has been restored [see Fig. 14.1]. Built in 1892, the disinfection building housed three large steel disinfection chambers on the first floor and forty-four showers on the second floor. On the ground floor, trolleys loaded with baskets to disinfect immigrants' belongings ran along three tracks that pass through the steam bath area. After a brief lecture introducing visitors to historical methods of disinfection, visitors are asked to don headphones and listen to a narrative that attempts to make them relive the immigrant's disinfection experience. Here, voices, speaking in English with various "foreign accents" tell their immigration story in brief sound bites. The visitor first walks past a display area and views various multimedia displays consisting of reproductions of photographs portraying groups of immigrants, then continues down a long metal corridor flanked on either side by industrial gray showers [see Fig. 14.2]. Sounds of metal doors shutting and of water coming through the showerheads are heard in the earphones. At the end of the tape, visitors hand back the headphones and in exchange, are given a card stamped with the word "DISINFECTED" as a souvenir.

The remainder of the hour devoted to the disinfection building is, as Brett describes, non-directive. Visitors may view two multimedia displays: one providing historical information on diseases such as smallpox, typhus, cholera, and the plague [see Figs. 14.3 and 14.4]; and the other, on the history of the Famine in Ireland, particularly the events leading to emigration [see Figs. 14.5 and 14.6]. Touring these areas mainly involves reading a great deal of discursive text, but there are also displays, enlarged reproductions of works of art, newspaper illustrations, and archival photographs. While the amount of time spent on each display is up to the visitor's discretion, the circulation pattern is not. The movement is one way and visitors must at least walk through the display on disease in order to reach the information on the

Irish. While the display on disease is completed and well lit, the Famine display is still a work in progress. During my visits, the area was poorly lit and the video monitors were either shut off or not working.

The Eastern Sector

Despite its name, Grosse Île is a small island. It is about a mile in width and three miles in length. However, visitors are not permitted to walk about freely. The last portion of the tour involves riding a trolley that makes stops to allow visitors to enter various buildings in the eastern sector of the island. Here, the guides tell stories of the lives of doctors and of their families. The trip has changed over the three years due to the progress made in restoring buildings and opening them to visitors. During my last visit, the trolley made three stops. The first was to see the Catholic chapel, built in 1874, and a second, to view the place that houses an ambulance and ice canoe. Several photographs showing the families who lived at Grosse Île are mounted on the wall.

The last stop of this tour is made at the lazaretto, built in 1847 and one of the key buildings of the Grosse Île tragedy. Referred to in the guidebook as "temporary convalescent accommodations" (Parks Canada, *Grosse Île and the Irish Memorial* 13), this building served as a hospital for the sick and dying in 1847. However, one searching for the "authentic" is bound to be disappointed. Although the brochure shows the exterior of the building unpainted, in reality, Parks Canada has painted it a cheery bright green with yellow trim. One guide said it was restored to its 1937 appearance. Inside, the building is empty and is still being restored. Over time, the lazaretto was used for a variety of purposes including as a place to house chickens; except for the building itself, there are no artifacts to connect it to 1847.[9] With each tour, as more buildings are restored and opened to visitors, increasingly less time is given to visit the lazaretto. After about ten minutes, visitors are herded back on the trolley, which makes a U-turn allowing visitors only a glimpse of another cemetery.

IV. Discussion

The circulation pattern of the Parks Canada tour is circular, starting and ending in the open space in front of the disinfection building. At first, it appears as though movement is one of convenience: the need to move people from place to place and to avoid bottlenecks. However, in doing so, the tour does not follow a chronological or otherwise logical narrative. Time blurs as visitors walk past buildings constructed at very different times and used over time under very different circumstances. Yet, it would be possible to alter the route to create a more flowing narrative. While the lazaretto and Irish cemetery are at the opposite ends of the island, beginning the second part of tour at the lazaretto easily could accommodate the physical, as well as historical, distance. Instead, the tour of the disinfection building follows the tour of the Irish cemetery.

For me, Grosse Île suffers most for what it is—a memorial to those who died here and a monument to modern medicine, and that is most evident in the narrative constructed in the disinfection building. Here, that narrative is based on dichotomies. Canada is a clean, healthy, hygienic place. Immigrants, on the other hand, come from unhealthy, unhygienic places and are dirty. In the disinfection building, a thirty-minute shower, to use a baptism metaphor, cleanses the immigrants and allows them entrance into the Promised Land.[10] While it is true that typhus infection was associated with crowded and unhygienic conditions, viewed through a wider lens, typhus was a disease of disasters. August Hirsch, a German epidemiologist, writing in the nineteenth century, commented that "the history of typhus was the history of human misery" and connected the infection with famines as well as wars (qtd. in Kiple 104). The narrative told in the disinfection building focuses on symptoms but omits causes.

The disinfection building did not exist in 1847; yet the Irish story is very present in the building as Bridget O'Donnell, as well as other Famine icons, graces its walls [see Fig. 14.7]. However, by closely linking the Irish immigration narrative with that of infectious diseases, Parks Canada inadvertently reinforces beliefs that Irish immigrants arrived with diseases and spread them throughout Canada, thus communicating the tacit message that the Irish were a social menace. Perhaps Action Grosse Île anticipated results of this narrative tangle in the beginning it they pointed out that Grosse Île was never an immigrant center.

In its present form, the areas most associated with the Irish and the Famine are at the end of each tour segment, allowing visitors very little time for remembrance or contemplation. Moreover, the tragedy of 1847 is downplayed in the guided tour. For example, while one guide said the majority survived, she did not say that "around 18 percent (17,477) of the 98,649 emigrants who boarded vessels for Québec City in 1847 died before reaching their final destination" (see Charbonneau and Sévigny 15). At the cemetery, instead of admitting that something went terribly wrong here in 1847, events are made palatable by the notion that in Canada, immigrants were given a decent burial. The guidebook's image of individual coffins can be contrasted with well-known Famine images, such as the *Illustrated London News'* image of a Clonakilty woman begging for money to buy a coffin to bury her dead infant. However, sources such as Quigley, Woodham-Smith, and Charbonneau and Sévigny recount harrowing tales of the struggle to bury the dead in the summer heat.

While we cannot fault Parks Canada for wanting to create a positive image for Canada, we can question why events are diminished or omitted from the tour. Is this simply an attempt to attract tourist dollars by creating a banal, feel-good tourist destination? If that is the case, Parks Canada created the exact opposite of what tourists want when they visit a memorial. Tourists want an authentic experience and, during visits to difficult places, they expect or even demand a visceral response.[11] Furthermore, tourists do not avoid emotionally charged places. As examples, both the Vietnam Veterans Memorial and the Holocaust Museum are among the most heavily visited tourist sites in Washington, D.C. However, Parks Canada's handling of the emotional content may have been influenced by the findings of l'Écart-type's market research. Parks Canada and l'Écart-type reported that less than half of those who responded to the questionnaire indicated that they were interested in participating in a "powerful emotional experience."[12] This conclusion was drawn largely from the response visitors gave to one item on the second questionnaire. On the English language form, that question read, "When you are travelling for touristic or recreational reasons . . . how important is it to visit places where we can find thrills and excitement" (l'Écart-type, annexe 7).

More important, we must ask why Parks Canada went forth with their plan to focus on immigration, even after the angry response from the Irish community and a lukewarm reception of the idea indicated by the market study. While some, such as Quigley, suggest they did so to avoid upsetting relations with Britain, I will argue that Britain has little to do with Grosse Île. Grosse Île is a Canadian story, and its path from a mysterious, forbidden island to a national heritage park based on immigration runs parallel to political events concerning Québec. In 1971, after losing party support as a result of his policy on bilingualism, then Prime Minister Pierre Elliott Trudeau initiated a federal policy that recognized and promoted the understanding that multiculturalism reflects the cultural and racial diversity of Canadian society. Former Québec premier René Lévesque was dismissive of the Multicultural Act, calling it "folklore." He further claimed it was "devised to obscure 'the Québec business,' to give the impression that we are all ethnics and do not have to worry about special status for Québec" (qtd. in Colombo). Political scientist Christian Dufour echoed this view. In his book *Le Défi québécois*, he wrote that the Multicultural Act was a way of refusing the bicultural nature of Canada and the political consequences of Québec's special status. He further claimed that, in principle, it reduced the Québecois to an ethnic phenomenon. In other words, this act relegated the Québecois to one immigrant group among the many that made up the Canadian mosaic.

The Multicultural Act authorized the heritage minister to "encourage and assist individuals, organisations, and institutions to project the multicultural reality of Canada in their activities in Canada and abroad." In addition, he or she was given funding to "promote the understanding and creativity that arise from the interaction between individuals and communities of different origins." What better place to promote that than on federally owned land located in the heart of the province of Québec? So, it comes as little surprise that former Heritage Minister Michel Dupuy focused on immigration at Grosse Île and that his successor, Sheila Copps, used the site to deliver a message on national unity. With Canadians still reeling from the results of a second referendum on Québec separation, Copps publicly launched two Parks Canada publications concerning Grosse Île. She stated, "The fantastic thing about the story of Grosse Île is not only the courage of the people who hung on through pestilence and death, but also of the arrival of those children without parents who found homes and hearts in French Canadians who saw a need and were there to meet it."[13] This statement is reiterated in the lectures given by the Parks Canada tour guides at the cemetery.

It is evident when studying their initial development plan that Parks Canada never intended to focus on the Irish at Grosse Île. Instead, the proposed visitor's circuit began at the disinfection building and ended at the lazaretto, which housed not only Irish but immigrants from other nations as well (73). The Irish cemetery, the Celtic cross, and the Douglas monument were all omitted from the tour. The development plan also made it clear that the theme for Grosse Île was foremost immigration with quarantine as a secondary theme. But the Irish got in the way, and, in order to accommodate this vocal group, the Irish Famine story was added. However, it was not integral to the story Parks Canada intended to tell. The title, *Grosse Île and the Irish Memorial,* indicates this, as does the narrative topology of the tour. The Irish story is told at the end of each segment: at the end of the disinfection building, just before lunch, on the way back to the boat. The physical fact of the mass graves and the texts carved into on the memorials forced Parks Canada to place more emphasis on Grosse Île's quarantine operation. Then, in the disinfection building they are able to tell visitors, "Yes, there was a problem here, but we fixed it."

During a guided tour of Grosse Île, narratives become intertwined and have little impact on visitors' understanding of the Famine or immigration. What is lacking at Grosse Île is any thought-provoking insight, analysis, or interpretation from a political, sociological, philosophical, or other perspective. Without more complex explanations, or at the very least, clarifying questions, it is difficult to see how the lessons we learn from Famine history might be relevant to our situation today. This is indeed unfortunate, because Grosse Île could have been so much more. It could serve as both a memorial and a call for action. In her address given at Grosse Île in 1994, Mary Robinson evoked the images of famine in Rwanda and Somalia and stated, "Although we cannot turn the clock back and change the deaths that happened here, at least we can do justice to the reality of the people who died here by taking the meaning of their suffering and connecting it to the present-day challenges to our compassion and involvement" (qtd. in Gray 182). Indeed, the lesson of the Famine needs to be constantly learned and applied until famine ceases to decimate populations around the world. Grosse Île could have been a vital component of this lesson.

Notes

Author's note: I would like to thank Michael Quigley, Tom Boyle, and Thomas O'Grady for their valuable comments and suggestions on this paper.

1. Here I am thinking of Mangan's work *Gerald Keegan's The Famine Diary*. This book created controversy when some critics questioned the authenticity of the diary and claimed the diary was a work of fiction published by Robert Sellar under the title *Summer of Sorrow*. Regardless of evidence that Mangan's book is a work of fiction, it is cited in later texts, such as Laxton, as historical fact.

2. Their report does not mention how individuals were recruited or what criterion was used for their selection.

3. In Québec, this term ("pure wool") has been used in reference to descendants of the original French settlers.

4. This information is written in the program guide for the 1997 Irish Person of the Year Award and was provided to me by Michael Quigley.

5. *Hunger's Children*. The narrator suggests that the arguments about the focus of Grosse Île are "divided along sectarian lines." While I will make no such claims, I will make mention that Cecil Houston is the co-author of *The Sash That Canada Wore: A Historical Geography of the Orange Order in Canada* (Toronto: Univ. of Toronto Press, 1980).

6. This study is limited to the tours given in English.

7. I am aware of the contentious issues surrounding this label. While I agree that *refugee* is more appropriate, I employ immigrant here to remain consistent with Parks Canada's tours and written visitor's guides.

8. In 1899, more than two thousand Doukhobors were quarantined at Grosse Île for 27 days. They eventually settled in Saskatchewan. See, for example, Tarasoff and Ewashed.

9. For a personal account of life on Grosse Île see Masson.

10. I am indebted to Jean-François Frappier for use of the metaphor and for his video documentation of the guided tours.

11. For a more detailed discussion of what tourists want, see MacCannell.

12. Parks Canada, *Grosse Île: Proposed Development* 59; l'Écart-type 63.

13. Although this was reported in major newspapers across Canada, I am quoting from Lasalle A9.

Works Cited

Ashworth, Gregory, and Henk Voogd. "Can Places Be Sold for Tourism?" *Marketing Tourism Places.* Ed. Gregory Ashworth and Brian Goodall. London: Routledge, 1990. 1–14.

Brett, David. *The Construction of Heritage.* Cork: Cork Univ. Press, 1996.

Charbonneau, André, and André Sévigny. *1847 Grosse Île: A Record of Daily Events.* Ottawa: Minister of Public Works and Government Services Canada, 1997.

Colombo. *The Dictionary of Canadian Quotations.* Toronto: Stoddart, 1991.

Dufour, Christian. *Le Défi québecois.* Montréal: 'Hexagone, 1989.

Gray, Peter. *The Irish Famine.* New York: Abrams, 1995.

Illustrated London News, 20 February 1847.

Kiple, Kenneth. *Plague, Pox, and Pestilence: Disease in History.* London: Phoenix Illustrated, 1997.

L'Écart-type. *Étude de marché—LHN de la Grosse Île.* Report drafted for Canadian Parks Service, Québec Region, Policies and Socio-economic Research Section.

Lasalle, Luann. *The Gazette (Montréal)*, 16 August 1997, final ed.: A9.

Laxton, Edward. *The Famine Ships.* London: Bloomsbury, 1996.

Lyons, Nancy. "Meditations on the Tragedy of Grosse Île." *The Gazette,* 17 September 1994: H10.

MacCannell, Dean. *The Tourist: A New Theory of the Leisure Class.* New York: Schocken, 1976.

Mangan, James. *Gerald Keegan's The Famine Diary.* Dublin: Wolfhound, 1991.

Masson, Jeanette Vekeman. *Grand-maman reconte la Grosse Île.* Ottawa: Les Éditions la liberté, 1981.

Parks Canada. *Grosse Île: Proposed Development Concept.* March 1992.

---. *Grosse Île and the Irish Memorial, Visitor's Guide.* Ottawa:
    Minister of Public Works and Government Services Canada, 1997.
---. Information Supplement. 1992.
Quigley, Michael. "Grosse Île: Canada's Famine Memorial." *Éire-
    Ireland* 34.1 (Spring 1997): 20.
Tarasoff, Koozma, and Larry Ewashed. *In Search of Utopia: The
    Doukhobors.* Spirit Wrestler Associates, 1994.

FIG. 14.2. DOOR OF SHOWER

FIG. 14.1. ENTRANCE TO THE DISINFECTION BUILDING

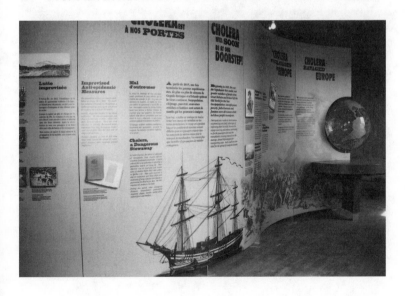

FIG. 14.3. DIDACTIC PANELS ABOUT INFECTIOUS DISEASE

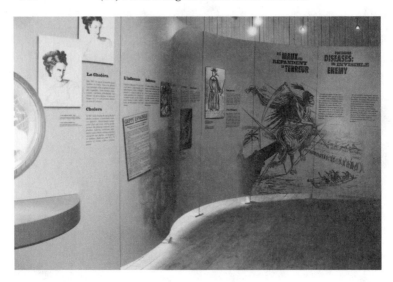

FIG. 14.4. DIDACTIC PANELS ABOUT INFECTIOUS DISEASE

FIG. 14.5. DIDACTIC PANELS ON THE GREAT FAMINE

FIG. 14.6. DIDACTIC PANELS ON THE GREAT FAMINE

FIG. 14.7. DIDACTIC PANEL NEAR THE EXIT OF THE
DISINFECTION BUILDING

Chapter Fifteen

Reflections on the Grosse Île Memorial in Contemporary Quebec: A Response

GREGORY P. GARVEY

The chapters by Lorrie Blair, Sylvie Gauthier, and Kat O'Brien offer a compelling discussion of the motivations behind the monuments commemorating the Irish Famine on Grosse Île in Quebec. The legacy of these memorials represents conflicting intentions, meanings, and interpretations that raise questions concerning who selects what is to be remembered. The three chapters convincingly show how competing political agendas intrude upon and shape the personal and private act of remembrance. Diminished is both the truth of what happened and what may be the lessons we all can learn as famine still afflicts peoples around the world.

Sylvie Gauthier reveals that instructions for those submitting proposals for the design of the most recent memorial were "to honor the memory of the immigrants—mainly of Irish origin—and quarantine employees" (Gauthier 298). The winning design team made a conscious decision to "stay away from politics" (300) and indirectly reference Ireland's distant past. Laurie Blair concludes that Parks Canada chose not to focus on the Irish at Grosse Île but to emphasize the themes of immigration and quarantine. The "Irish got in the way" of a "message on national unity" (Blair 323). Blair suggests that this was part of a broader federal policy to promote multiculturalism in an attempt to reduce the issue of Québecois separatism to "an ethnic phenomenon" (323).

Quebec license plates display the phrase *Je me souviens*—"I remember." It is a collective call to the individual to remember the distinct cultural and historical identity of French Canadians. The chapters by Blair, Gauthier, and O'Brien remind us of the close links between the Irish immigrants and Québecois. Both share the Catholic faith and a history of resistance to British domination. O'Brien notes that the 1909 Celtic cross commemorates the Famine with a distinctly Irish Catholicism. It is "the visual icon of competing voices and silences" (O'Brien 276).

Three "competing" texts in English, French, and Gaelic are found at the base of the Celtic cross. The Gaelic differs from the French and English by being the most politically charged. Even the Gaelic term, *An Gorta Mor*—"the great hunger"—carries a meaning quite different from the English word *famine*. The Gaelic vividly recalls the personal subjective experience of the pain and anguish of starvation. Like the Quebec *Je me souviens*, it reinforces a sense of identity. The English term, the Famine, reduces subjective experience to objective and impersonal events: a crop failure, mass starvation, emigration and population decrease.

Jacques Derrida, the evangelist of deconstruction, asserted *Il n'y a pas de hors-texte*—"there is nothing outside of the text."[1] The most recently constructed memorial on Grosse Île goes beyond mere text, using sculpture, architecture, and the landscape to invoke remembrance and construct meaning. It was commissioned by the Canadian Parks Service in 1998 and was designed by Lucienne Cornet and Emilte Gilbert. Sculptural niches confront the viewer with the essentially unknowable and ineffable subjective experience of those who died on Grosse Île. The natural empathetic response is to imagine the thoughts, feelings, hopes, fears and yearnings of those lived lives. Yet, as Laurie Blair shows, the directed tour given by Parks Canada leaves little time for personal reflection to explore the meanings "outside" the literal interpretation.

In writing on hermeneutics, Hans-Georg Gadamer argues that "All understanding is interpretation, and all interpretation take place within the medium of a language."[2] While the list of names engraved upon the glass are silent reminders of those who died, it explains little of the historical, political, and economic circumstances of their deaths. Informed visitors, especially those of Irish ancestry, bring an understanding that goes beyond the mere fact of the text. Interpretation takes us outside of the given text, the sculpture, and the architecture. Not only is interpretation necessary, but interpretation is also inevitable.

Time diminishes truth, and the truth of the lived experience becomes forever out of reach. It can only be partly recovered and is indirectly referenced by the semiotics of the memorial. The compilation of selected facts point as much to what is left unsaid as to what is said. As Laurie Blair observes, the piecemeal tour of Grosse Île led by Parks Canada obscures the central story of the Irish tragedy while trying to present a whitewashed tourist attraction. She notes the lack of consensus on whether Grosse Île is the end or extension of the Irish Famine story or the beginning of a Canadian immigration story.

Kat O'Brien's recent installations are her response to the problem of interpretation. She has chosen to "personalize a site or event through acknowledgment of the invisible dramas enacted in the anonymous individual lives" (O'Brien 286). In doing so, she presents a truth to be encountered and personally interpreted by each viewer.

Yet a memorial is a collective decision to remember. Sylvie Gauthier notes that the designers of the newest memorial felt they had a duty to remember this history and heritage of the Irish in Quebec and Canada. It is now the responsibility of the public to "public to move forward and continue the work of remembrance" (308). In spite of the confusion of competing voices and silences, visitors to Grosse Île are challenged by the former president of Ireland Mary Robinson's call for "taking the meaning of their suffering and connecting it to the present-day challenges to our compassion and involvement" (qtd. in Blair 324).

Notes

1. See Derrida, *Of Grammatology; Writing and Difference;* and *Dissemination.*

2. *Truth and Method.* 389

Works Cited

Blair, L. "(De)Constructing the Irish Famine Memorial in Contemporary Québec." *Ireland's Great Hunger: Silence, Memory, and Commemoration.* Ed. D. Valone and C. Kinealy. Lanham, Md.: University Press of America, 2002.

Derrida, J. *Dissemination.* Trans. Barbara Johnson. Chicago: Univ. of Chicago Press, 1981.

---. *Of Grammatology.* Trans. Gayatri Chakravorty Spivak. Baltimore: Johns Hopkins Univ. Press, 1976.

---. *Writing and Difference.* Trans. Alan Bass, Chicago: Univ. of Chicago Press, 1978.

Gadamer, H. *Truth and Method.* Second Edition. Trans. Revised Joel Weinsheimer and Donald G. Marshall. New York: Crossroad, 1992.

Gauthier, Sylvie. Le Mémorial: An Irish Memorial at Grosse Île in Quebec." *Ireland's Great Hunger: Silence, Memory, and Commemoration.* Ed. D. Valone and C. Kinealy. Lanham, Md.: University Press of America, 2002.

O'Brien, Kathleen. "Famine Commemorations: Visual Dialogues, Visual Silences." *Ireland's Great Hunger: Silence, Memory, and Commemoration.* Ed. D. Valone and C. Kinealy. Lanham, Md.: University Press of America, 2002.

Chapter Sixteen

The MacGilligan Family and the Great Hunger: Collaborative Strategies in an Irish History Course

KAREN MANNERS SMITH, HOLLY GILLOGLY, JIM RIORDAN

I. Karen Manners Smith on Shaping the Instructional Approach

It would certainly be difficult to remove drama and human tragedy from the history of the Irish Famine, but I have seen textbooks that do just that. Granted, the statistics alone are staggering: more than a million dead, more than one and a half million in flight. Even so, the story of the Famine and its aftermath could get lost in a textbook covering thousands of years of Irish history, or in a one-semester survey course using that textbook, where students are assailed by centuries of unfamiliar material and are, in any case, looking forward somewhat impatiently to the unit on Ireland's troubles in the late twentieth century.

I decided to make the Famine the focal point of an Irish history course in the spring semester, 2000. This was my first Irish history course and the first taught at my small institution for as long as anybody could remember. My task in designing this course had been complicated by the fact that our department's modern European historian was unable to team-teach the course with me, as we had originally planned. As the semester started, I discovered I had nine graduate students in the course, as well as eighteen undergraduates, a large enrollment by our standards. (As many who teach

Irish history in the United States have discovered, the level of interest is high, partly because so many of our students have Irish family backgrounds.) Naturally, I would have to give the graduate students a course that was different from and more demanding than the one for the undergraduates. I was already teaching a course overload, including an evening class on Irish film, so I decided to seek all the collaboration and cooperation I could get. I arranged for some faculty specialists in art, religion, and military history to give several of the lectures, and I delegated the organizing of a field trip to Irish immigrant sites in Kansas City to an extremely competent nontraditional graduate student. The first assignment for the nine graduate students was to prepare a variety of bibliographies for the undergraduates to use in their research projects. They compiled lists of all the Irish history books in our university library, and they searched several databases for recent articles in Irish history. They searched booksellers' Web sites for new and traditional offerings in Irish history and literature, and they located and listed a huge number of Web sites for Irish history. One student compiled an extensive bibliography of Irish music. These materials were filed in my office for both graduates and undergraduates to consult when embarking on research. The next collaborative project was the Famine Families project, whose inspiration was the work of two of the graduate students, Jim Riordan and Holly Gillogly, and whose instructional design was a collaboration between the three of us.

Since I began teaching I have—somewhat oxymoronically—used fiction to make history real to students. In every history course I teach, my students read novels, short stories, and plays in addition to textbooks and monographs. I believe in the power of narrative to elicit empathy for people of the past. For that reason, I have been pleased to see that narrative history, so long a despised ancestor of our current, more interpretive historical writing, seems to be regaining favor.

Historian Marsha Gilpin Ehlers has pointed out that students need "pictures in the their heads," in order to understand past human experiences. I would add that they need voices in their heads as well. Not that I am recommending schizophrenia for students, nor, obviously, am I suggesting that students should not read interpretive history; but I would like their own interpretations to be, as Ehlers suggests, a "dynamic process," a process enriched by their own attempts to empathize with historical subjects and to feel the truth of their lives. In order to enable such evocations, or re-creations, we need not only a picture of the past, we need to hear or to reproduce the voices of the past. I believe that it is in the act of reproducing historical experience that empathy can best be achieved.[1]

Except for the occasional quirky essay exam question, I have never asked college students to write fiction. It is too easy to abuse a fiction writing assignment in a history class or to treat it dismissively. In the case of the Famine Families project, we asked students to invent stories about victims and survivors of the Famine. I hoped that if we built enough safeguards into the project, we might make students treat the assignment with respect, so we made sure each story written by a student was annotated and historically contextualized, and that each was followed by bibliography. Since part of the project required presenting one's story in front of the whole class, there would be additional pressure to respond respectfully to the assignment. I am persuaded that having students write short fictional pieces grounded in historical fact awoke sympathies for those who had passed through the Famine and promoted an understanding of human tragedy and human resilience that these students might otherwise not have gained. I have come to believe what Jim Riordan and Holly Gillogly had demonstrated in their invention of the MacGilligan family: that combining fiction with historical events can be a useful approach to studying history.

II. Project History: Famine Families

The Famine Families project actually began in the fall semester 1999. Holly Gillogly and Jim Riordan, then graduate students at Emporia State University, and two of this article's authors, were taking an environmental history class called Plagues, Plants, and People, taught by Emporia State historian Ron McCoy. The main objective of this class was to introduce students to the role of the environment in human history using an interdisciplinary format. As a final assignment, each student would create a project that related to environmental history. There were no restrictions on the type of project itself. Final presentations included Power Point presentations on the Dust Bowl and on the Bubonic Plague, and more traditionally structured papers on the impact of smallpox on Native Americans and on the nuclear clean-up operations at Hanford, Washington. Jim Riordan and Holly Gillogly initially started out with separate project ideas. Jim had wanted to write a research paper on the potato blight and the Irish Famine, and Holly wanted to do a project that used fictional characters to demonstrate historical events on a personal level. They decided to collaborate, and the Famine Families project was born. Pooling their research, Holly and Jim created a multi-generational fictional Irish family, the MacGilligans, and traced their lives through the Famine era, constructing for each member a life experience based on historical accounts of the Irish people during the Famine and the diaspora.

The basic design of the project consisted of four sections. For the first section, Holly and Jim wrote a background essay on Irish history. The next part of the project was the development of the biographical sketches of the MacGilligan family itself. The two students researched Irish surnames, generated a list, and then selected names at random to create nuclear family units. These groupings of names were then formed into the MacGilligan family tree. Jim and Holly wrote a short biographical sketch for each family member, linking him or her to parents and offspring, and told their stories as well. In creating more than eighty biographical sketches, the two students researched birth and death rates during the Famine years, occupations, morbidity and mortality data, migration rates and destinations, politics, and cultural attitudes. They also read both narrative and interpretive accounts of the Famine. Their concern was to make the family as "real," or plausible, as possible. The last two sections of the project consisted of an essay that highlighted the environmental issues behind the Famine and an appendix of Irish history resources. Finally, the project was organized into a notebook, which included not only the text, but also maps and images related to the Famine. Jim and Holly also produced a large chart of the MacGilligan family tree to facilitate easy use [see Fig. 16.1].

The project attracted interest beyond the class in which it was presented. Several faculty members in our small department were intrigued by what Jim and Holly were doing and asked for a demonstration. As soon as I heard about the Famine Families project, I asked Jim and Holly if they would help me incorporate the MacGilligans into my Irish history class the following semester. Our plan was for the undergraduates in the class to expand on the brief biographical sketches, basing their own stories on additional historical research.

Three months later, in the classroom, Jim and Holly presented the MacGilligan family and the new project guidelines to the undergraduates and then divided them into five groups of three or four each. Each group was assigned a branch of the family. Group members could choose to write about one or more individual family members from their branch or, working as a group, they could build stories for everyone in that branch of the family. They were free to incorporate ideas from the brief sketches about "their" family members, or to start new and different stories, retaining only the names from the family tree. The only major restriction on the students' projects was that the expanded stories had to be based on true experiences of the Irish people, not only in Ireland, but also in the countries to which they emigrated. Each student was expected to provide citations and bibliography for his or her chosen branch of the family or individual. The students were to present their expanded stories to the class in the form of oral reports, dramatizations, illustrated narratives, or Power Point presentations. In the end, the student presentations included—in addition to narratives—"diaries," "letters," and even a highly hypothetical

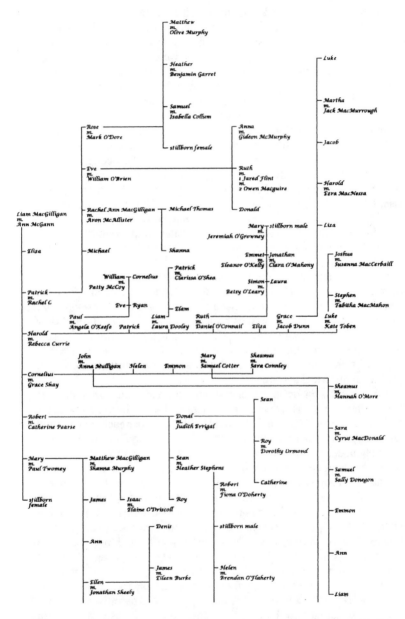

FIG. 16.1. THE FICTIONAL MACGILLIGAN FAMILY TREE

"reunion" of family members long dead or scattered. The students' projects, and the materials that accompanied them, were evaluated on the basis of verisimilitude and the extent of the research.

III. Conclusion

Our undergraduates had a variety of responses to the assignment. Some loved the chance to flex creative muscles, and some natural writers chafed at the restrictions of having to write about people whose outlines had already been drawn. Since there was an option of discarding the sketch biography and writing a new story about a named character, some did that. The Emmon MacGilligan story is an illustration of the work of a truly creative student who took a bare outline and made a powerful and evocative story. In another instance, a student carried her branch of the family forward into the twentieth century, making up descendants of the original family members and telling their stories. Cleverly, she included name changes as these great-grandchildren in the United States begin to intermarry with non-Irish. Yet another student, a fan of soap opera, wrote a set of sensational stories about a branch of the family who moved to Kansas, where one member was killed in a prairie fire; another, her mind distorted by grief, walked into a tornado; and yet another poisoned her unfaithful husband, only to marry a lover and find herself diseased.

As we had anticipated, this assignment proved difficult for some students, and in at least one case the student sought refuge in making his narrative a historical absurdity. For some reason, the Australian diaspora stories were the least successful, perhaps because that country's immigrant history is so much less familiar to us than our own.

Something we did not include this time, but which I hope to emphasize in the next Irish history course, is a general discussion of famine and global responsibility. Empathies awakened on behalf of people of the past can surely be expanded to include people of the present. Students can be encouraged to use the political, environmental, social, and moral lessons of the Irish experience to understand and respond to modern outbreaks of famine anywhere in the world.[2]

Overall, our project was enjoyable, and feedback in student course evaluations indicates it was a success. I intend to use the Famine Families assignment in my next Irish history course—there are still plenty of names on the MacGilligan family tree that need stories. Jim and Holly and I also consider this project something of a prototype. It should be possible to get students to write research-based historical fiction in any number of history courses, and it would be especially useful to encourage empathic fiction writing about historical people whose language, culture, and ethnicity are even more remote from American students than the lives of the Famine Irish, and whose stories are equally compelling.

IV. Web Site

Once the classroom part of the project had been successfully implemented, the three authors of this article decided to create a Web site to make both the original project and the students' biographies available to the public, as well as opening the project to further development. Emporia State University's Web master, Terri Weast, designed the site, and, with her help, we have been adding edited versions of the undergraduate students' stories a few at a time. Students who have seen their work on the Web have been delighted.

The Web site is still being expanded. In the future, we will begin accepting stories from the public to be placed on this site. It is possible that we will expand beyond the MacGilligans, or that we might encourage people to submit renderings of their own ancestors' family stories from the Famine and the diaspora.

The Web site (http://www.emporia.edu/socsci/famine/index.html) begins with a basic introduction, including the history of the project and information about the site. The site has four main links. The first is to the original project's historical essay. Next is a link to information about the site itself as well as a bibliography and a list of related Web sites. The site's main link is to the MacGilligan family tree. Each name on the tree is a link to a biographical sketch. Miniature family-tree "branches" link every individual sketch to other sketches in the same branch of the family. In some cases, sketches include illustrations. A number of the biographical sketches are linked to the expanded stories written by the students in the Irish history course.

Appendix

Examples of Original Biographical Sketches and Expanded Stories

First is the sketch of Liam MacGilligan's life. The following sketches in the project tell the life stories of his surviving children—Mary, Robert, Cornelius, Harold, and Patrick—and further sketches deal with the generations that follow.

Our appendices here contain brief sketches of Emmon MacGilligan (the third child of Cornelius MacGilligan, Liam's second son) and sketches of three of the offspring of Rachel O'Ciaran and Patrick MacGilligan (Liam's youngest surviving child). The four original brief sketches are followed by expanded stories written by Emporia State University students.

Liam MacGilligan (Original Brief Sketch)

Liam MacGilligan, the family progenitor, was born around the year 1773, in the county of Sligo, in the province of Connaught in west Ireland. MacGilligan, a man of medium height and stocky build, was born in a small cottage in a clachan. A clachan was a community of several interrelated families who owned the land around them communally.

By the time Liam was born, Ireland itself had been under the control of England for nearly a hundred years. All the land that Liam's clachan "owned" technically belonged to the Duke of Ambrose, whose grandfather had received title to lands throughout Ireland from William III. Ambrose had never seen his land holdings in Ireland, they were for the most part leased or administered by upper-class Protestant Irish. When Liam was ten, Michael Plunkett, a merchant from Ulster who had made his money in the wool business, rented the land the clachan sat on, as well as the land several miles around it. Plunkett ordered the land broken up into plots to be rented to the locals. Due to the poor quality of the region, the only way Plunkett could make money off the land was to charge rents on it. The break up of Liam's clachan was gradual, but total.

When he was seventeen, Liam married a local woman named Ann McCann. After the marriage, instead of building a hut in the clachan as his father had done, Liam rented fifteen acres of land from Mr. Plunkett. Liam's land was poor at best. It sat at the base of a hill and consisted of rocky uplands at one end and a bog at the other. Liam's hut sat on a relatively flat piece of ground at the edge of the bog and was essentially a stone box with a turf roof. Liam drained part of the bog and planted it with potatoes, the only crop that could be effectively grown on the poor ground. As was the case with most of his neighbors, potatoes were his family's main source of food. Liam paid the rent on the land, which increased a little every year, with a combination of entrepreneurial schemes. Liam grazed between four and five pigs on the uplands of his farm. With the money from selling the pigs, he was able to pay his rent and had a little left over to buy some barley. Although making alcohol was technically illegal, Liam distilled the barley into liquor, and sold it throughout the community. Liam's wife, Ann, also contributed to the support of the family by spinning woolen thread, which was sold to local merchants who supplied wool to the textile industry of Ulster in the northeast. With the extra money from these schemes, Liam and his family were able to supplement their diet of potatoes with milk and bread, and, on rare occasions, meat.

In spite of their difficult lives, Liam and Ann had a total of seven children. The first child, a girl, died at birth. Because she had not yet been baptized, she could not be buried on the consecrated ground of the local church. Instead, the MacGilligans' first child was buried in Liam's bog. Liam and Ann's second child was also a girl, whom they named Mary. She was born in the winter of 1791. Much to Liam's joy, the next four children, who were born over a five-year period, were all boys: Robert, Cornelius, Harold, and Patrick. Liam and Ann's final child, a girl they named Eliza, survived her infancy. However, at age ten, she was caught in a rain storm while tending to the pigs. The next day, she had a raging fever with a wheezing cough. There were no doctors in the area and, even if there had been, the MacGilligans could not have afforded one. A local midwife was called upon, and she administered several local remedies in exchange for a quart of Liam's homemade whisky. Most of the remedies were made by mixing local roots and herbs with a large portion of turpentine. In spite of the remedies, within a week of Eliza's first fever, she died of what was commonly referred to as consumption, but was probably pneumonia. She may also have been tubercular, as the disease was common in nineteenth-century Ireland, as elsewhere.

Emmon MacGilligan (Original Brief Sketch)

Emmon, Cornelius MacGilligan's third child, became a wanderer. Very little is known of him. There is no indication that he had a wife or a child. In fact, the only thing that is known about him is his final day in Ireland. Emmon ended up in Belfast, an industrial city, and went down to the docks to look for work. While he was wandering around the docks, a press gang clubbed him over the head and carried him off for service in her majesty's Royal Navy. In the eighteenth and early nineteenth centuries, captains in the Royal Navy were responsible for getting their own crews for their ships. If they were unable to find enough bodies through enlistment, they sent out press gangs to kidnap "volunteers." Thus was the fate of Emmon MacGilligan, and that was the last anyone heard of him.

EMMON MACGILLIGAN (EXPANDED BIOGRAPHY BY EMPORIA STATE UNIVERSITY STUDENT MICHAEL WIENANDT)

Emmon MacGilligan was the third child of Cornelius MacGilligan and Grace Shay. He lived in western Ireland, where the effects of the Famine were extremely devastating. Emmon kept a journal of his life, but when the Famine came he lost track of dates because his survival depended on food not dates, but he continued to write. His Famine story begins with the eviction of his family from their home.

My father died when I was ten years old. He struggled to grow wheat in the barren, rocky soil of western Ireland rather than potatoes as everyone else did. His death came from being overly determined to tame the wild land and grow grain. I was forced into taking over where my father left off, but this work made me strong and healthy, and, in retrospect, I believe this is what kept me alive through the toughest years of the Famine. However, the landlord we were tenants for came to evict us from our home in March of 1846. He had with him a band of Irish "housewreckers," evicted tenants themselves who were doing anything to survive the Famine (Gallagher 46–48; "Great Famine"), and a group of British officers to keep the peace. My family was evicted because we could not pay the rent. Parliamentary policy had made us destitute, yet the landlord was still trying to extract money from us. This hated system caused many secret societies throughout Ireland to form and to terrorize the landlords and anybody who supported the Parliament (K. Wright).

As I sat watching the housewreckers tear apart our only means of shelter, I lashed out at them and the landlord verbally, coming under a sense of humiliation, degradation, contempt, and hunger. We were given the opportunity to take away the wood and thatch from the crumpled roof, which we did (Gallagher 51). I found myself moving along a dusty road in a daze, whether from the weight of the wood on my sore back or the hunger pangs in my stomach, or both, I do not know. But I did know that I was sick of being hungry and sick of being treated as an inferior, subhuman being. My family and I stopped in a ditch along the roadside at dusk. We built a crude, cramped, lean-to structure that became our only refuge from the cold, the wind, and the rain (Gallagher 51; "Great Irish Famine" unit III).

The hunger and humiliation made me a selfish person. The following morning I abandoned my family by the roadside and headed east in search of food and work. As I walked, I noticed many frail creatures stumbling forward and many who had fallen into ditches and not gotten up. I stopped a man to ask him how far the nearest town was. His clothes were in tatters and the child on his back was nearly naked. Blood ran in tiny streams all along its fragile legs, maybe from being scratched or from the cold. All the father could do was lament about his starving children, so I left him to himself and continued on my way ("Great Irish Famine" unit IV). I had heard of roaming bands of armed men who attacked relief wagons laden with food.[3] It became my top priority to find such a group and join it. I did not care what penalties Parliament impressed upon those who were caught in such an act, but I knew they would be harsh. I had heard of a man being exiled to Australia for seven years for stealing glue (K. Wright).

I walked on, resting every time I became dizzy in the head and weak in the knees. I made it into a town and stumbled from house to house looking for a resting place. The children I saw not only looked as if they were newly raised from a grave to life, but also as if they had just been thawed out of ice where they had been embedded until their blood turned to water ("Starvation"). I retreated into a dark house but immediately ran back into the street, the heavy stench of death having invaded my nostrils. I resorted to lying down beside a house for the night. The following days were a wash of hunger, fatigue, and isolation. I wandered the countryside along the roads looking for those elusive roaming bands of men. I came into another town, but having become aware of two men following me, I stopped and turned around. The men came up and jumped back in astonishment. I sat down in the road and rested. I listened to the men as they stood there describing my appearance. Tall and sinewy, bowed down, sunken cheeks, and sallow-colored skin as if death was upon me: these were the words that rang in my ears. Was this true? Had the Famine already deteriorated me to the state of a walking dead man?[4]

I awoke the next morning to the shouting and cursing of a mob of starving men and women. I saw they stood in front of a store, which seemingly was stocked with bread, potatoes, and other foodstuffs, but none of it for sale to the mob. I quickly joined in the shouting until the mass of people stormed the entrance to the store, then it became a free-for-all as everybody contorted their bodies in every which way to grab food from the shelves and the floor. What became of the storeowner was not my business; I attended to my depleted body and fed to it the bread and milk that I had stolen (Woodham-Smith 373).

Some time passed before I finally joined a band of thieving men. We walked out of town heading to a crossroads where we were told a relief wagon would make a stop. Along the way I commented on the many frail bodies stumbling about in the cold, watery bogs. I was told they were Famine victims who had been employed by the Office of Public Works. In order to receive aid, they were required to build a road through the bog to an unknown destination.[5]

"They are no better off than we," said a companion. "They're working on a road for the meager, piss-poor wages those the English will give them. You know, I heard this old lady say that the most miserable of English paupers is better fed and clothed than the most prosperous of Irish laborers" ("Irish Famine," Irish Famine).

I was appalled. How could one society exert so much hatred onto another with such ease? My thoughts were interrupted when I saw one of my companions stand up, curse a passing wagon, and run after it. I heard a shot rip through the air and cringed. I understood that the Famine caused peaceful men to do unjust things, but I never imagined murder would be one of them. I stumbled over to where our fellow Famine victim stood over a lifeless body. The blood ran warm and thick across the road and into a pool at the bottom of the ditch. Someone told me that the slain man was the landlord of the starved man who had killed him ("Irish Famine," Housing and Landlords).

I had seen young children huddled together in their death rags, I had witnessed the bodies of men and women thrown into the streets as their burial, and I had seen shallow graves with the soil barely covering the dead.[6] I had seen pale, gaunt, walking skeletons, but never had I seen the true horridness of murder. I cannot help but think that this Famine has not only destroyed our main food staple, but it has also destroyed our humanity, our dignity, our souls, and has left behind battered, lifeless forms that search day and night for food and work but instead get handed a shovel to dig their own graves, or a handful of imported grain that makes them ill, not full (Moody and Martin 270–71).

During the year of 1847, I spent the days "housewrecking" my own people's shelters. My starvation led me into a state of sheer desperation; I would do and say anything to be fed or paid. One house I was supposed to help tear down was already crumpled when the entourage of landlord, British officers, and housewreckers arrived. It seemed to the tenants that if they helped to destroy their own homes, then the government would give them a little bonus for sparing the housewreckers the toil of the job. All these wretched creatures got was mockery and a deeper sense of humiliation and degradation. The towns I traveled through were wracked with desolation and disease. The onslaught of famine fever carried with it typhus, dysentery, cholera, and diarrhea. The imported grain caused massive illness, and the cramped living quarters of the victims spread disease like wildfire (Moody and Martin 270–71). In one town, the wet ground almost seemed to smoke beneath the victims' feet, burning with the famine fever ("Starvation"). When I looked into these suffering people's homes, I noticed many huddled in the darkest corner, so as to hide themselves in their pitiful state, choosing to die in the shadows of life.

I left my employment as a housewrecker and sought refuge in a workhouse. I applied, fully knowing that I had no money, no food, and to my recollection, no family. I was instantly denied. The operators told me their workhouse was full, and they were fearful of me spreading disease throughout the workhouse. I had come to this wretched building as a last resort.[7] I wanted to live. I wanted the satisfaction of knowing that the British would have to murder me if they hated me so much and wished me dead. But what was I to do now? I could not even get into a workhouse.

I have yet not realized how I survived the next months. They were a blur of hunger, pain, disease, rioting, and death. One day I came across a band of armed men who were talking excitedly. They said they were waiting for more of their fighting brothers of the recently formed Young Ireland. They were beginning the emancipation of the Irish peasant today, they said. I caught word a day later that their revolt was crushed and many of them were to be hung. The Widow McCormack's homestead in Co. Tipperary was their first and last stand (Neill 114). I did not care for this group; I only wanted my life back.

Belfast, I believed, teemed with work and food. I had exhausted myself looking for help in the desolate countryside, which had became intolerable to me, with its daily scenes of crime, inhumanity, death, disease, and suffering. Belfast seemed to offer a chance to restabilize my life, but I was not alone. Hundreds of starving peasants flocked there and to other cities. looking for work (Desmond Chap. 10). However, Belfast's economic expansion created problems for us Famine victims. Seeing us as Catholics and not as starving people, the Protestants tried to drive us out of town. What ensued was as repulsive as what I had seen in the countryside—a complete disregard for human life just to prove one faith was right and another was wrong. Bloody fights and riots resulted from this closed-minded attitude.

While I was in Belfast, I heard little bits of political talk. I cared little for politics but one conversation held my interest for a while. I overheard that a man in Parliament was standing up for the Irish, opposing Britain's economic philosophy, and supporting the idea that Parliament was covering up the mortality rates of the Famine victims in Ireland. This man, I heard, was Lord George Bentinck. One man even quoted from a newspaper a passage from a speech Bentinck had given to Parliament: "They know the people have been dying by their thousands and I dare them to inquire what has been the number of those who have died through their mismanagement, by their principles of free trade. Yes, free trade in the lives of the Irish people" (Kinealy, sec. Mortality).

These words gave me a feeling of despair. Only if the whole of Parliament would support what Bentinck was saying would I be able to feel a sense of happiness or even relief. Then I might be able to believe that the Famine was just a natural phenomenon and not a natural event exploited by a hate-filled, greedy, and ignorant society in order to rid the land of a supposed subhuman species.

Emmon's Famine story does not end with him finding work and restabilizing his life. It ends with him being attacked by a British press gang. This was a group of British sailors who sought men to take captive and force them to serve in the Royal Navy of Britain. The attack on Emmon was not especially brutal, but his frail bones snapped like thin twigs under the clubs and what was left of his blood drained from cuts on his head. The press gang, seeing Emmon in such a state of wretchedness and fragility, left him for dead in a dark, lonely Belfast alley.

The last journal entry Emmon wrote before he was attacked was undated, but conveyed a sense of hope. The survivors of the Famine may have held this same hope, but for Emmon, despite his faith, death came at the hands of human beings.

"I started to end this entry, but I just have to wonder—why is this happening? Some say it is punishment for our sins. But I have a hard time believing that. God is made of love, not hate. And hate is death. Death is what is happening now. He wouldn't make this happen" ("Journal").

Rachel Ann MacGilligan McAllister (Original Brief Sketch)

Rachel Ann, Patrick and Rachel MacGilligan's second child, married a farmer named Aron McAllister. They had two children, Michael and Shanna. Unfortunately, when the Famine struck, they were unable to pay the rent on their farm, and they were evicted by the English landlord's agent. Most English absentee landlords were more than happy to get rid of the Irish peasants living on their land. When Ireland had been taken over by the English, the English landlords had not minded the Irish peasants living on the land that grain could not be grown on. However, as the textile industry grew in England, there was greater demand for wool. Sheep could easily be grazed on much of the land that was occupied by the Irish peasants, so many landlords looked upon the Famine as an opportunity to rid themselves of unwanted Irish peasants. The McAllisters did their best to survive as potato gleaners, but in the end all four starved to death.

RACHEL ANN MACGILLIGAN MCALLISTER (EXPANDED BIOGRAPHY BY EMPORIA STATE UNIVERSITY STUDENT ANTHONY HARTMAN)

Rachel Ann was the second child of Patrick and Rachel MacGilligan. She helped raise her younger sisters Eve and Rose. She and her older brother Michael helped their mother with the farm while their father worked as a traveling laborer. She enjoyed taking care of her sisters and tolerated her work on the farm. Michael taught her to read in what spare time they had in the evenings. Rachel Ann taught herself to write and grew to resent not being able to go to school. She longed to become a schoolteacher, and Michael encouraged her in that. They would keep in contact on and off throughout their lives. The MacGilligans attended mass on the days their father was home from work. These were some of the only times the children saw their father, and Rachel disliked spending much of that time in church. On one of the rare times her family attended mass, Rachel Ann met a young man named Aron McAllister. He was in town a while seeing a friend off to America, and he decided to stay after he met Rachel Ann. They were married after several months and moved to his farm, north of Donegal, to live in a cabin on a small tract of land. Aron was barely older than Rachel, who was nineteen at the time of their marriage. He was no longer on speaking terms with any members of his family and refused to talk about it with anyone. Before he had broken with his family, Aron had inherited the tenancy of the land his potato farm was on. The common Irish practices of subdividing land and marrying young gave the young couple just enough land to make a meager profit when times were good (Magnusson 84).

Aron worked around Donegal sharpening blades and farming instruments. He used his income and any other profit they made to buy several pigs. During the winter, the pigs lived in one corner of the one-room cabin, and Rachel Ann and Aron lived in the other. Rachel Ann tended a small garden near the house that produced cabbage when they could afford the seeds. She also grew potatoes and tended to the farm while Aron worked around the county. Rachel Ann found herself in a marriage that mirrored her childhood. She had grown up essentially without a father, and she felt alone in marriage as well. Aron and Rachel Ann had decided to limit themselves to one child, knowing that their fairly comfortable lifestyle couldn't support more than one addition to the family. But their good intentions did not make a foolproof birth control plan. Michael Thomas was born in 1835 and Shanna two years later. The children placed an emotional and economic strain on the marriage that distanced Rachel Ann from Aron. The couple discussed giving one of the children up for adoption, but neither could bear the prospect of choosing which one. The McAllisters were contributing to the booming population of Ireland, which had risen to 8 million by 1841, almost twice that of just forty years earlier (Magnusson 83). That growth strained the resources and brought about the further subdivision of the land.

When the McAllister children were old enough, they helped their mother on the farm. In the afternoons Michael Thomas collected turf nearby. He and Shanna helped their mother in the field. She taught them to read and write in the evenings. Before bedtime, the family gathered around the fire and the children took turns reading from the newspaper. Rachel Ann helped with their pronunciation of the difficult words and kept Aron from laughing. The children fell asleep to the warmth of the turf fire and the snuffles of pigs.

The *Gardener's Chronicle* of 13 September 1845 carried the news: "We stop the press with very great regret to announce that the potato murrain has unequivocally declared itself in Ireland. The crops about Dublin are suddenly perishing." The word spread quickly, and the murrain followed shortly. A foul smell given off by the affected crops was the first sign of its arrival. With hardly a warning, the whole crop withered and rotted (Magnusson 84). The blight returned the following year and the year after that.

The potato blight not only took away the McAllisters' main source of food, but it also took away their only source of income. After they had sold all their pigs, they lapsed on their rent payments. The landlord's agent lowered the rent slightly and gave them three months to catch up. The English landlord had already rid himself of many of his tenants, combining their land into larger, more workable sections. The devastating effects of previous potato blights threatened an already struggling population of Irish peasants. The immediate response of the government saw the establishment of Relief Committees. Guidelines put forth by the Relief Office required that landowners satisfy the Committees of their destitution before they would be admitted to workhouses (Magnusson 88). Because Aron still held his itinerant blade-sharpening job, the McAllisters were denied admittance. They made it through the winter only by begging and gleaning the fields for scraps of food left behind.

The family was evicted that spring by bailiffs at the request of the landlord's agent. Their cabin was burned, and the family huddled around the fire that night for heat. The next several weeks, they followed behind Aron while he worked, but soon no one could afford to have anything sharpened, and his boss had to fire him. The McAllisters were out of food and had no source of income; they were miles from any Relief Committee. For months following their eviction, they wandered the countryside looking for food and shelter from the cold nights. They found an abandoned barn a little way from a small village and slept in the straw, huddled together under a single blanket. Aron lacked the energy to glean the fields for food, depriving himself for months so his family could eat. He died of starvation that spring. Michael Thomas dragged him to the side of a nearby road and half covered him with stones until exhaustion overcame him. Rachel wept at nights over her husband and their horrible condition. The children took turns comforting their mother and begging for food from any passing journalists or photographers. Michael told Shanna not to leave their mother alone while he was in the field, for fear of what she would do in her depressed state. He often resorted to stealing from a farmer's garden nearby. Rachel Ann eventually improved and went with Shanna to beg for food. They sometimes received small bits of bread or a cup of soup at the gate of a nearby landlord's agent. The leaky roof of the barn collapsed one day, but no one was inside. When they returned, they gathered the wood from the roof to use as firewood. Soon they all lacked the energy to beg or walk the fields, and they sat together outside the ruined barn. Rachel Ann took ill with a very high fever. She asked Michael to bring her some water from a stream nearby, but he didn't have the energy to go. She recovered in a couple of days but was completely drained of energy. Michael and Shanna caught cholera after eating rotten potatoes, despite their mother's warnings. They became seriously ill very quickly, and Rachel Ann worried about who would pay for their coffins. There she sat against the remains of the barn with her children lying at her feet, groaning. A passing journalist from Dublin stopped when he heard the children's moaning. After photographing them, he told a nearby farmer of their condition. The farmer decided he would help them get to a Relief

Committee. When he and his son went to help them onto his cart, they discovered that Rachel Ann had been gone for some time already. It was common practice for the sick and dying to go the Relief Committee for a proper burial at the expense of the government (Magnusson 90). The Relief Committee admitted the children to an infirmary run by several nuns. Shanna fainted on receiving food. She awoke a day later, only to die after a few hours of consciousness. Michael hung on slightly longer, dying shortly after Shanna's burial. Michael was eleven; Shanna was nine.

Rose MacGilligan O'Dore (Original Brief Sketch)

Rose, Patrick and Rachel MacGilligan's last child, emigrated to the United States at age eighteen. She worked as a laundress and a seamstress in the Irish slums of New York. She married a laborer named Mark O'Dore. When the Civil War broke out, Mark joined to earn money. He got more than he bargained for out of the army. At the first battle of Bull Run he was shot in the leg. When the doctors finally got to him, the only thing they could do was amputate. The doctors were very skilled and the amputation took less than two minutes. They dipped the stump in hot pitch to cauterize the wound. Luckily the shock of the amputation, which was done without anesthetic, did not kill Mark, nor did he develop an infection afterward. Mark spent the rest of his life tending bar in the Five Points section of New York. All told, Mark and Rose had four children, Matthew, Heather, Samuel, and a female child that was stillborn.

ROSE MACGILLIGAN O'DORE (EXPANDED BIOGRAPHY BY EMPORIA STATE UNIVERSITY STUDENT MATT BLACK)

Rose MacGilligan, the last child of Patrick and Rachel MacGilligan, was born in Connaught in the year 1825. Her childhood was spent helping her mother and three siblings plant potatoes on their small plot of rented land while her father was away on a traveling labor force. When Rose was seventeen, she became engaged to a Brian Murphy. But when her father Patrick heard the news, he discouraged the wedding because Brian did not rent any land, let alone own any. He claimed that it would not be a "good marriage" (Miller 54–55).

With much resentment for her father, Rose borrowed money from her brother Michael in order to go to America. In 1843, at the age of eighteen, Rose emigrated to New York City where she was able to find work as a laundress and seamstress. Living by herself was extremely hard, since her wages were just enough to pay for her room and board. This was all to change when she met Mark O'Dore. Mark was a native New Yorker whose his parents had emigrated from Ireland in 1823, the year before he was born. Mark worked as a laborer, but surprisingly he always seemed to have plenty of extra money to spend.

The two were married the same year. Life became a lot easier with the combination of their wages and Mark's extra income, which came from Mark's lucrative hobby of petty burglary and picking pockets (Cook 168–70). Within six years the O'Dores had several children, three of whom survived. Matthew was born in 1845, Heather in 1849, and Samuel in 1851.

The O'Dores lived fairly comfortably despite the geography of their residence. In 1853, Mark O'Dore met a radical immigrant named Thomas Francis Meagher, an Irish nationalist who had fled the English following his attempts to form a rebellion. This friendship between Mark O'Dore and Thomas Meagher would set the tone for the later evolution of the O'Dore family. Meagher obtained a law degree and advanced quickly through the New York political system. Through his influence, Mark became active in politics and the Irish nationalist cause. When the American Civil War broke out in 1861, Mark was quick to join with his friend Meagher, who would enter the Union Army as a Brigadier General (Ranelagh 119–20). With Meagher's help, Mark was given the rank of sergeant and commissioned to the first serious battle of the war, Bull Run. During the battle, Mark was shot in the leg. With their limited medical knowledge, the field surgeons were unable to save his leg and were forced to amputate it. Separated from his friend and no longer able to fight, Mark was sent home to his family in New York. He could not hold a laborer's job; instead he found work as a bartender at a local saloon. With this job he was able to ascend the ladder of political power in the Irish community. Mark, along with son Matthew (now sixteen), got involved with the Tammany political powers (Blanshard 282). The father and son became quite powerful with their recruitment and enlistment of Irish-Catholic immigrants to the Democratic Party. Together they gathered a vast number of constituents for whom they provided services in return for political support. This support was acknowledged with money from such political bosses as Peter Sweeney and Richard Connolly (who in turn worked under William "Boss" Tweed). Matthew and his cohorts also sustained Democratic power by roughing up the opposing voters in order to keep them away from the polls (Miller 330). The O'Dores reaped the benefits of the political system.

In 1863, following the issue of the draft by the Union Army, riots broke out in the city. Matthew was now eighteen, and with the success that he and his father were having in the political system, he had no wish to fight in the war. He was able to bribe his way out of service. During the next several years, Matthew continued to gain political power while working for his father. In 1870, he married Olive Murphy, and in the same year he became ward boss. Matthew O'Dore solidified his political career through patronage. He provided jobs, services, and other favors that in turn provided him with votes.

Several other events took place that year for the O'Dore family. Matthew's younger sister Heather married a newspaper editor by the name of Benjamin Garret. This angered the rest of her family for two reasons. Garret was an English Protestant, and on top of that, his paper was notorious for digging up dirt on certain corrupt politicians. Also, Heather would make a rare conversion to the Protestant religion. To add insult to injury, the youngest O'Dore brother, Samuel, began working on the presses of Garret's paper. Samuel had aspirations of one day becoming a reporter, which he eventually did. The events of 1870 caused great turmoil and division within the O'Dore family (Blanshard 164).

Heather and Samuel became the black sheep of the family following these events. Despite being ostracized for taking the job at the paper, Samuel respected his family. He expressed this respect by steering clear of reporting on any corruption or graft that involved his father and brother. Heather did her part to keep her husband, Benjamin, away from the saloon where the O'Dores' illegal political maneuvering took place. Meanwhile, Matthew and Mark were still experiencing great success in politics. Mark and Rose, along with Matthew and his wife Olive, were able to move out of the slums to an environment that reflected their increased status. However, they still operated their business in the same area, where Irish immigrant poverty was rampant. Much of the extra money that they made was donated to the Catholic Church to be given to the poor, but Mark would also send a monthly fund back to Rose's brother Michael in Dublin. Michael used this money to help finance the struggle for Irish Independence. Rose had always felt indebted to her brother the priest for his help on her journey to America and felt the least they could do was to support his cause.

By the mid-1870s, young Samuel O'Dore had become quite successful. The main reason for this was his estranged brother Matthew. Even though the two never spoke, Samuel still received money from Matthew for overlooking his corrupt practices. With his newly acquired wealth, Samuel married a well-to-do woman named Isabella Collum.

The O'Dore families held on to their cold relationships. Even though the family had been divided, everyone went about their business with relative comfort. Heather and Samuel no longer communicated with their parents or their brother, yet each side tentatively trusted the other.

This would soon change. On 5 October 1877, Matthew was indicted on charges of corruption. The newspapers went mad trying to dig up dirt on the politician. Samuel O'Dore and Benjamin Garret now had their chance. They knew that they possessed information that would launch their sales. By exposing Matthew O'Dore, they would solidify their positions in newspaper history. That night Samuel and Benjamin stayed at the presses until the early hours of the morning. They never returned home. Investigations yielded no clues as to the whereabouts of the two newspapermen, yet it was common knowledge around the area what had become of them. No documentation of the story they were working on survived.

In the coming months, and in the absence of evidence against him, Matthew O'Dore was acquitted of his charges of corruption. Heather Garret lived in fear, though. This fear kept her from going to the authorities with any incriminating information about her brother. She would later suffer a nervous breakdown and be forced into a mental institution.

In 1879, Mark O'Dore retired from his position at the saloon to be with Rose. At the same time, Rose received a letter from her brother Michael in Dublin. In the letter, Michael disclosed information on the whereabouts of her sister Eve, who had emigrated from Ireland to America and settled in Kansas. Rose wrote a letter to her sister. Rose's letter was quite simple. She told her the story of her life in America. But the only family she mentioned was her loving husband Mark and her wonderful son Matthew.

Eve MacGilligan O'Brien (Original Brief Sketch)

Eve MacGilligan married a fairly well-to-do farmer named William O'Brien. William had enough land to grow wheat for export to England. In spite of this, the Famine caused enough economic problems for him that he immigrated to the United States with his wife. Unlike most Irish, William, Eve, and their first child, Anna, did not stay long in the slums of a large city. William took advantage of the Homestead Act and acquired 130 acres of land in what is today Ottawa County, Kansas. In Kansas, the O'Briens had two other children, Ruth and Donald, called Donal.

EVE MACGILLIGAN O'BRIEN (EXPANDED BIOGRAPHY BY EMPORIA STATE UNIVERSITY STUDENT ANNALEE M. S. COY)

Patrick and Rachel MacGilligan could certainly be proud of their third child, Eve. Eve has managed to secure herself a place in Irish-American history through the extensive letters she left behind as well as other documentation provided by her children. We know much about the lives of this branch of the MacGilligan clan thanks to this recorded history of Eve.

Eve MacGilligan married William O'Brien soon after her sister Rose's engagement was called off. Rose resented Eve's marriage because their father had been so set against Rose's fiancé. Eve was fortunate enough to marry a man with a fairly large amount of land. This land ensured that the O'Briens were able to earn money through wheat. As we all know, England continued to export crops grown in Ireland throughout the

Famine. Eve and William were able to fill their bellies and save some
money, too, from the profits provided by the wheat crop. When Eve
became pregnant with their first child, the O'Briens decided to leave
Ireland immediately. It had been too difficult to watch Rachel's family be
torn apart by starvation and death. Eve wanted something better for her
child: a chance to survive. The O'Briens decided that the best way to
ensure survival was to go to the United States.

It is during the crossing of the Atlantic Ocean that we first experience
life through Eve's pen:

Dearest Mama,
May 4, 1859

    Oh! It has been so difficult leaving you all. I despaired greatly over this
decision, but I know this is best for the life growing inside me now. I
sometimes cannot figure out if I have seasickness or morning sickness. Either
way, I know I spend a lot of time with my head over the rails. William
worries over the baby and me too much, though. He is already fretting over
where to live once we arrive. The cost of this passage has nearly depleted
our savings. I pray everyday that God will take care of Ireland and us.
Love, Your Evie

Dearest Mama and Papa,
September 25, 1859

    William has been able to find a little work. He won't let me help to make
money with the baby being so close. I do have to admit that this belly of mine
is just a bit large to be doing too much. I just hate being stuck here in this
awful building. I want to be able to get out of here soon. Neither of us is fond
of city life. We dream of owning our own farm again someday. We keep
hearing whispers about going West. If what they say is true about free land,
we just may go after the baby is old enough to travel. If my dear brother
Mike visits with you soon, please have him write me soon. I am longing to
hear some news about my home.
Love and Prayers, Evie

Dear Grandmama and Poppa,
November 12, 1859

    This is the first moment I have had time to sit down and write. Did you
notice the greeting? Your granddaughter, Anna Kathleen O'Brien, was born
on October 25th. She is so beautiful and sometimes, so loud. Anna likes a lot
of attention, which her father happily gives. We have even more motivation

now to get out of these slums soon. Anna deserves better, she needs to have
room to run and grow. We are going West as soon as possible. I have written
Michael. It sounds as though things are still going pretty rough around
there. I was thrilled to hear about Seamus and Evelyn. I pray that more
homes in Ireland open their doors for the poor orphaned children. God bless
Michael!

Love, William, Eve, and Anna Kathleen O'Brien

There is now a gap in Eve's letters. Based on what is about to happen in
her letters, I believe that William and Eve worked hard for the next two
years. With their hoarded money, they jumped on an offer. On 20 May 1862,
President Lincoln signed the Homestead Act. This act offered that "any
person, the head of a family, or 21 years of age, whether a citizen or intended
citizen, could take up a quarter section of the public domain" (Gates 6).
William fit this description to a "T." The O'Briens only had to live on and
improve the land for five years and the title would be theirs.

Dearest Michael,
December 28, 1862

Sorry it has been so long since I have contacted you. I am sitting here in
the back of our wagon trying to sleep. I am too excited to even close my eyes.
We are only miles away from our new farm. It is not really ours until
January 1, 1863, but it makes my heart peaceful to know our dreams for
Anna are almost a reality. The timing of this opportunity is a bit
inconvenient; all of this hard work coming up is going to be difficult with a
new baby. Yes, I am going to give birth to the second O'Brien any day now. I
will mail this letter after it arrives so that you can spread the good news.
Love, Evie

P.S. Ruth Rachel O'Brien sure knows how to make an entrance. She
decided it was time to be born while her daddy was out staking our claim on
the 1st of this new year. Anna has been a great help with her, although she
wants to know where her brother is! I hope she can be happy for now with a
sister.

Dear Rose MacGilligan,
July 15, 1865

I truly hope this is my sister Rose MacGilligan. It has been too long for us.
I pray that this letter finds you happy and well. I am living in Kansas.
William and I are doing well. We have three beautiful children, Anna, Ruth,
and a brand new son Donal. A young couple rolled through our farm with
news from New York and they know a Rose O'Dore from our town in

Ireland. I hope that you will write to me soon. Michael is worried about you too!
Love, Eve MacGilligan O'Brien

Dearest Rose,
December 7, 1865

Praise the Lord that you are well! The whole family has been very worried about you. Papa has not been the same since you left. I am thankful that you have forgiven him, and me, for the circumstances in your life. I am so happy that you have married and have been blessed with children. Even over all the miles, we will always be family and always be Irish. I am reminded of a song I heard on the ship coming here to America:

I'll never deny I'm from
Ireland,
It's my birthplace, and proud
I'm to own
That I love it, the bog and
mireland
I'm Irish to the backbone.
(R. Wright 102)

My dear sister, we must not ever let differences make us forget who we are and where we come from. Tell those beautiful children of yours about home so that we don't forget.
Love, Evie

Eve and William lived a wonderful, hard-working life up until 1873. At this time, the pain and tragedy they sought to escape found them even on the prairies of Kansas. From an article in a small church newsletter, we can read about the O'Brien accident:

A tragedy has befallen one of our beloved lambs. Donal O'Brien is with our Lord in Heaven following his recent death. The prairie fire that destroyed many of our lands also destroyed this young life. Donal was a slight lad of only eight years and was unable to outrun the raging flames. Let us remember his family in our prayers.

Sadly, this incident forever changed Eve. She closed off nearly all contact with her family from Ireland. William tried desperately to please his depressed wife, but she never really snapped out of it. We learn about her death from her daughter Anna.

Anna had decided that she wanted to become a schoolteacher. Her father agreed to let her attend the Kansas State Normal School at Emporia, Kansas, shortly after her mother's death. The circumstances surrounding Eve's death are recorded in an essay written by Anna O'Brien. The following is an excerpt from this essay:

My mother was a beautiful woman, with an ugly mind following my brother's accident. Donal was only eight years old when he burned to death in a freak grass fire accident. Mother blamed the wind that caused the fire to consume so quickly. Whenever there would be a storm with lots of wind, Mother would sit on the porch and wail. Last April, there was a terrible storm with howling winds. For some reason, this time Mother was not content with just sitting on the porch and crying over her lost son. A bolt of lightening streaked across the black sky and I saw her take off running across our yard. Mother was screaming and shaking her fist in the wild wind. Suddenly, another bolt illuminated the yard and I saw the approaching funnel. I hollered for my mama to come back, but I don't know if she even heard me. I thought she did because she stopped abruptly, but she only raised both of her arms to the heavens. I watched as the twister returned her embrace and whisked her away.

Anna graduated from the Kansas State Normal School and moved to Louisburg to teach. It was there she met her future husband, Gideon McMurphy. Gideon was a Civil War veteran and considerably older than Anna. Anna enjoyed her job teaching and was torn between that and her love for Gideon. She hesitated too long and lost her job teaching at the middle school because some of the parents did not approve of her choice in men. The decision made for her, Anna married Gideon. This marriage did not provide the happy ending for this poor girl. While consummating their marriage, Gideon suffered a heart attack and died. Anna spent the remainder of her life back at her family farm helping her father.

Ruth left the farm when Anna returned. She had only stayed so that her father would not be alone, but she could now head to the big city, Kansas City. She was fortunate to secure a job at a clothing store. Because of the long hours of standing, Ruth soon tired of the "working girl" life and married one of the male clerks there. Jared and Ruth Flint's marriage was a strained one. Ruth stayed home all day and ate. She figured that she had worked hard enough in her lifetime, so her husband should take care of her. On a quick trip to the market for more cheese, Ruth met Owen Maguire. Owen worked the graveyard shift at the Armor meat-packing plant. The two fell madly in love and began a sordid affair. There was only one thing standing between Ruth and Owen's happiness: Jared Flint. One evening, Jared came home to a lovely scene of dinner on the table and a smiling wife. This wonderful scene of loving domesticity was the last thing Jared ever saw. From Ruth's journal we have the plot:

> *Owen and I cannot live another day apart. I finally voiced what we both had been thinking. Jared has just got to go! We talked it over and decided to poison him. Owen is going to poison a can of potted meat at the plant and bring it to me. I will fix Jared dinner, and he'll go to sleep with a full belly and a smile. I don't know if I will be able to make love to him one more time, but Owen says that the poison will circulate through his blood faster if he exercises. I will just have to picture my wonderful Owen.*
> *Soon . . .*

The plan was a successful one. After waiting a year following Jared's "tragic food poisoning," Owen and Ruth married. The Maguires lived a somewhat happy life together. They were unable to have any children because of a disease Ruth contracted from her now-dead husband on their last night of passion. In my research, I found a letter from Jared Flint to Erin Quinn, another clerk where Jared worked. It turns out the two had been having an affair. Erin had loved a lot of different men; Jared contracted the disease from Erin and gave it to Ruth.

Eve MacGilligan O'Brien and her offspring left for us a compelling story of life for an Irish immigrant. Tragically, there are no direct descendants of this line of the MacGilligan family.

Notes

1. Marsha Gilpin Ehlers, "'No Pictures in My Head:' The Uses of Literature in the Development of Historical Understanding," The O.A.H. Magazine of History, Vol. 13, No.2 Winter 1999.

2. Tom Hayden, ed. Irish Hunger: Personal Reflections on the Legacy of the Famine. Roberts Rinehart, NY 1998. This book contains a number of essays and poems on the emotional legacy of the Famine. It also stresses the relevance of the Famine and its consequences for discussions of modern-day starvation, and in the formulation and implementation of policies to cope with world hunger.

3. See "Famine in Ireland"; K. Wright; "Irish Famine"; Woodham-Smith 140.

4. Somerville, excerpt of a letter from Longford, 5 March 1847.

5. Gallagher 42, 92; "Irish Famine," Relief and Public Works; "Great Famine."

6. "Irish Famine," Death and Disease; Gallagher 105–12; " Great Famine."

7. "Carrick-on-Shannon"; "Great Famine"; Gallagher 46.

Works Cited

Blanshard, Paul. *The Irish and Catholic Power: An American Interpretation*. Boston: Beacon, 1953.

Brown, Thomas N. *Irish-American Nationalism*. Philadelphia: Lippincott, 1966.

"Carrick-on-Shannon Workhouse and The Great Famine." <http://vassun.Vassar.edu/`sstaylor/FAMINE/Journey/Narrative.html>.

Cook, Cittell, Mack. *City Life: 1865–1900*. New York: Praeger, 1973.

Desmond, Jerry. "Desmond's Concise History of Ireland." <http://members.tripod.com/`JerryDesmond/index-2.html>.

Ehlers, Marsha Gilpin. "'No Pictures in My Head': The Uses of Literature in the Development of Historical Understanding." *The O.A.H. Magazine of History* 13.2 (Winter 1999).

"Famine in Ireland." <http://vassun.Vassar.edu/`sstaylor/FAMINE/PT/Famine.html>.

Gallagher, Thomas. *Paddy's Lament: Ireland 1846–1847 Prelude to Hatred*. New York: Harcourt Brace, 1982.

Gates, Paul W. *Free Homesteads for All Americans*. Washington, D.C.: Civil War Centennial Commission, 1962.

Geographical. 70.1 (January 1998): 53–56.

"The Great Famine: 1845–1849 in Co. Mayo, Ireland." <http://www.mayo-ireland.ie/Mayo/History/Famine.html>.

"The Great Irish Famine." <http://www.nde.state.ne.us/SS/irish/irish_pf.html>.

Hayden, Tom, ed. *Irish Hunger: Personal Reflections on the Legacy of the Famine*. New York: Rinehart, 1998.

"The Irish Famine." <wysiwyg://16/http://www.geocities....ill/Congress/2807/irishfamine.html>.

"The Journal of Maggie O'Connell." <http://rmgtech.com/fam/Caitlin/ipfjrn12.html>.

Kemp, P. K. *The History of The Royal Navy*. New York: Putnam, 1969.

Kinealy, Christine. *This Great Calamity: The Irish Famine 1845–52*. Boulder, Colo.: Rinehart, 1995.

Lewis, Michael. *The Navy in Transition: 1814–1864 A Social History*. London: Hodder and Stoughton, 1965.

Limerick Chronicle. 5 February 1847.

Magnusson, Magnus. *Landlord or Tenant? A View of Irish History*. London: Bodley Head, 1978.

McQuillan, D. Aidan. *Prevailing over Time: Ethnic Adjustment on the Kansas Prairies*. Lincoln: Univ. of Nebraska Press, 1990.

Miller, Kerby A. *Emigrants and Exiles: Ireland and the Irish Exodus to North America.* New York: Oxford Univ. Press, 1985.

Monthly Review. 47.11 (April 1996): 11(9).

Moody, T. W., and F. X. Martin. *The Course of Irish History.* New York: Weybright and Talley, 1967.

Neill, Kenneth. *The Irish People: An Illustrated History.* New York: Mayflower, 1979.

Ranelagh, John O'Beirne. *A Short History of Ireland.* New York: Cambridge Univ. Press, 1983.

Somerville, Alexander. "Letters from Ireland during the Famine of 1847."
    <http://www.people.Virginia.EDU/`eas5e/Irish/Somerville.html>.

"The Starvation in Ireland."
    <http://www.toad.net/`sticker/nosurrender/NYEvePost.html>.

Woodham-Smith, Cecil. *The Great Hunger: Ireland 1845–1849.* New York: Harper, 1962.

Wright, Karis. "The 19th Century: The Great Famine."
    <http://www.humboldt1.com/history/lexiso/famine.html>.

Wright, Robert L., ed. *Irish Immigrant Ballads and Songs.* Bowling Green, OH: Bowling Green Univ. Popular Press, 1975.

Chapter Seventeen

Designing the New York State Great Irish Famine Curriculum Guide

MAUREEN MURPHY, MAUREEN MCCANN MILETTA, ALAN SINGER

PART ONE: Studying the Famine in the Secondary School Curriculum

I. Why Is It Important to Study the Great Irish Famine?

In 1997, the people of Ireland and of Irish descent around the world observed the 150th anniversary of the worst year (1847) of the Great Irish Famine, a catastrophe precipitated by a fungus that destroyed the potato harvests of 1845, 1846, 1848, and 1849. To mark the Great Irish Famine commemoration in New York State, the state legislature voted that study of the Famine in Ireland be included in the Human Rights curriculum required in the state's public schools. The curriculum already includes the study of slavery in the Americas and the European Holocaust.

The State Education Department selected the Hofstra University Department of Curriculum and Teaching to coordinate the development of interdisciplinary units, lesson plans, and teaching materials for grades 4 through 12 that are designed within the framework of the New

York State Learning Standards. The final product will be available as a curriculum guide, on the world wide web, and as a CD-ROM.

The consequences of the Great Irish Famine altered more than the course of Irish history; the Irish diaspora changed the shape of world history, especially that of the United States, Canada, Australia, and England. In the 1990 federal census, 44 million Americans voluntarily reported their ethnicity as Irish. Irish immigrants and Irish Americans have made significant contributions to every phase of American life, including politics, labor, sports, religion, arts, entertainment, and business. They have produced American mayors, governors, and presidents. They invented both the submarine and Mickey Mouse; making fortunes and Fords. They earned more Congressional Medals of Honor than any other ethnic group, and they helped build the American labor movement. They wrote about the American Dream, and they lived it. Irish immigrants have also known discrimination, poverty, and hunger, and the harrowing details of their lives have been described by Irish-American writers.

New York State is especially proud of its Irish heritage. In 1855, 26 percent of the population of Manhattan was born in Ireland. By 1900, 60 percent of the population was of Irish descent. Today, thousands of New Yorkers trace their ancestry to Famine-era immigrants who helped develop the infrastructure, economy, and social and political institutions of our state.

The Great Irish Famine occurred in a period where England, countries in continental Europe, and the United States were developing industrially and as modern states. The Famine challenged the British government, international humanitarian organizations, and philanthropic private individuals to provide aid to massive numbers of poor Irish, many living in remote areas, who were suffering from starvation and Famine-related disease. The degree to which those involved responded continues to draw praise and condemnation more than a century later. The ideas they debated about the responsibility of government are still being discussed today.

Studies of the Great Irish Famine suggest that Famine-related deaths and the accompanying mass emigration were the result of multiple causes, including a food shortage, the lack of individual resources to obtain food, and the failure of the government to adequately regulate markets and provide sufficient support. It is important to note that the economy of England in the 1840s was probably roughly equivalent to the economy of Indonesia today, while economic conditions in Ireland were probably very similar to contemporary Somalia.

One of the most vexing questions about the Great Irish Famine is the question of the availability of food. Mary Daly has calculated that by

1846 there was a significant food shortage with sufficient provisions for only five or six million of Ireland's population of more than eight million people. While there is no question that there were serious food shortages, other commentators have argued that starvation was more the result of the inability of the poor to obtain existing food. Significantly, the 1998 Nobel Laureate economist Amartya Sen has presented the same case for the Indian famines of the 1940s.

Perhaps the most compelling reason to study the Great Irish Famine is that hunger and homelessness are still with us; that there is want in a world of wealth. The Famine's legacy has affected the psyches of the Irish and the Irish of the diaspora, teaching us that distress and dislocation have long-term consequences on its victims and its descendants. The lessons of the Great Irish Famine have a claim on our fundamental humanity; they remind us that we have an opportunity to help our neighbors who face similar suffering. Students studying the Great Irish Famine in the context of other famines will develop a better understanding of the factors that contribute to famine in today's world and will, as a result, become actively concerned about the human right to adequate nourishment.

In addition, study of the Great Irish Famine provides a case history for exploring key social studies and science concepts, including culture, religion, economics, scarcity, democracy, citizenship, public policy, and demographics. Science topics include nutrition and the environment. Language Arts lessons consider the literature of the Great Irish Famine and other famines in a comparative context and explore how the Great Irish Famine continues to provide themes, metaphors, and symbols for contemporary Irish writers. The arts explore the visual, musical, and dramatic representations of the Great Irish Famine. Overall, the curriculum enables students to examine and understand the intersection of art, music, and literature with science, culture, and history.

II. The Great Irish Famine (1845–1852): A Historical Introduction

The main goal of this curriculum guide is to make accessible to public school students in New York State the history of Ireland, particularly the history of the Great Irish Famine. The curriculum writers have attempted to present in a variety of units, lessons, and projects material drawn from the best and most up-to-date historical scholarship. Their work has been reviewed by teams of historians and literary scholars in Ireland, as well as in the United States. This section offers a historical introduction providing teachers with a brief summary of events during the Famine years. Much is still not known about the human impact of the Great Irish Famine, and debate continues about certain interpretations of events. Even the dates assigned to the Great

Irish Famine vary. The dates of 1845–1852 chosen for the curriculum are based on Joel Mokyr's work on Famine-related deaths. Teachers need to help students understand that history involves both research and constant reevaluation. Selected historical sources are provided at the end of this essay. There is a longer Great Irish Famine Bibliography and Media Resource List in one of the guide's appendices.

The Great Irish Famine was a human catastrophe precipitated by a potato blight, a fungus that destroyed the harvests of 1845, 1846, 1848, and 1849. As a result of the ensuing Famine, the official population of Ireland declined from 8,175,124 in 1841 to 6,552,385 in 1851, a loss of more than 1.6 million people to Famine-related deaths and emigration. The official numbers are only an estimate, probably under-reporting the actual number of people who lived in Ireland in 1841 and minimizing the impact of the Famine on the Irish people. Many of Ireland's poorest and most vulnerable residents, people on the west coast and in the interior, especially Gaelic speakers, were either skipped over by census enumerators or avoided being counted. These people disappeared without leaving any permanent record. Even using the official census count, one person in four disappeared between 1841 and 1851.

What was responsible for the Great Irish Famine? The causes of the Famine that accompanied the failure of the potato crops were rooted in Ireland's troubled history as a colony of Great Britain. After the unsuccessful Irish rebellion of 1798, a rebellion inspired in part by the success of the American Revolution, the Act of Union between Great Britain and Ireland canceled Ireland's short period of autonomy in 1801. As a result, Ireland reverted to direct rule by the British parliament.

During the first decades of the nineteenth century, Irish politics were dominated by Daniel O'Connell, who helped secure some civil rights for Catholics and other religious minorities, including the right to serve in parliament. O'Connell was unsuccessful, however, in his campaign for the repeal of the Act of Union. An important O'Connell legacy was his parish-based organizational strategy that became the model for Irish constitutional nationalism and American urban ward politics.

Political events in this period masked more serious demographic and economic problems. Some 10,000 English and Irish landlords, many of whom were absentees, owned nearly all the Irish land, which they rented out through a series of tenants and subtenants. During the Napoleonic wars, there was a strong demand for grain and for agricultural laborers. In response, the Irish population rose quickly; people, especially poorer people, married relatively young, and fathers distributed the right to their rented land among their sons. By 1841, nearly half of the Irish (45 percent) lived as tenants, subtenants, or nondocumented homesteaders on holdings of less than five acres. In the poorest, more desolate and densely populated areas of the west, the percentage was even higher. The pressure for land and food drove the Irish poor onto more and more marginal land. Fuel came from turf harvested from the surrounding bogs. Eventually the word *bog* became associated with poverty, and poor Irish were derisively called "bog-trotters."

Apart from the agricultural sector of the economy, there were few regular employment opportunities for Irish workers, an economic imbalance that contributed to later problems. Irish businessmen could not compete with British manufacturing concerns that were beginning to dominate world markets. The domestic textile industry, which had been a major source of rural income in the eighteenth century, suffered a major decline. In 1815, when grain prices dropped after peace was restored with France, the agricultural market became depressed and there were no alternative sources of employment to replace it. Visitors to Ireland before the Famine, like the American traveler Asenath Nicholson, observed how desperate the Irish were for regular, rather than seasonal, employment. Nicholson met many Irish who had been to America, had children in America, or who hoped to go to America. Pre-Famine emigrants were artisans (often displaced textile workers), farmers, servants, and unskilled laborers who left Ireland for better economic opportunities in the booming economies of Lancashire in England and of the East Coast of the United States. Pre-Famine Irish laborers in New York State worked digging the Erie Canal system and building the state's railroad network. Many women entered domestic service. Both Irish men and women entered the rapidly expanding textile industry in the mill towns of New York and New England.

Under normal circumstances, the Irish cottiers, agricultural laborers, and their families lived on a monotonous but nutritious diet of potatoes and buttermilk. But no year was ever really normal. In pre-Famine Ireland, there were regularly periods of want, the "hungry months" of summer before the new potato crop came in. There had also been a major famine in 1741 and, periodically, other crop failures; however, in all of those cases, healthy potatoes returned the following season, and life continued as usual. While these earlier experiences should have provided some warning that a sustained period of crop failure could happen, the government and the country at large were quite unprepared for the catastrophe that occurred when the potato crop failed four times in five years from 1845 to 1849. While the potato failed elsewhere in Europe, only the Irish relied on it as their principle source of food. Indeed, they relied on only one kind of potato, a particularly high-yield variety called the "lumper."

The potato blight was reported first in Ireland in the *Dublin Evening Post* on 9 September 1845. Overnight, healthy green fields of potatoes turned black, and there was an overpowering, sickening sweetish smell of rot. The cause, unknown at the time, was a fungus called *phytophthora infestans,* which causes blight. It probably arrived in Europe from North America where there had been blight in Maine in 1842. The blight spread quickly through Holland and Belgium to Ireland.

The first official Irish response to the potato blight was to try to estimate the extent of the damage. The police were instructed to report the losses weekly; experts were asked to investigate the situation, and an official committee was convened to assess the extent of the crop failure and to suggest possible remedies for what the government thought would be a short-term problem.

As the blight spread throughout the country, British Prime Minister Sir Robert Peel authorized the purchase of American Indian corn, a commodity that did not interfere with the protected English agricultural market. Peel also appointed a committee to administer a government relief plan that supplemented the assistance provided under the 1838 Poor Law Relief Act.

In January 1846, the government enacted its first Famine relief measure, a Public Works Bill that authorized small-scale, county-based, relief projects. In March 1846, a bill passed to encourage the fishing industry by providing grants to construct piers and harbors. These measure gave work to able-bodied men, women, and boys of afflicted households, but they offered no assistance to the elderly, to the infirm, or to young children. In response to the outbreak of infectious diseases, including typhus, the government directed local Poor Law Guardians to designate separate facilities as fever hospitals and dispensaries and to segregate the sick. At the time, there was no effective treatment for Famine-related diseases.

In April 1846, government food depots were established in areas of great need, particularly in the west and southwest. In June, Parliament repealed the Corn Laws, the legislation that protected the United Kingdom's markets from cheaper imported grain. This last action was unpopular in Peel's political party and precipitated the collapse of his government.

Lord John Russell, himself an Irish landlord, replaced Robert Peel as Prime Minister in June 1846; he would remain in office for the duration of the Famine. By the summer and fall of 1846, it was clear that the disaster precipitated by the potato blight had become a famine. The 1845 infestation destroyed 30 percent of the potato crop, and the fall 1846 crop was almost a total failure. As in earlier emergencies, people tried to cope with rising food prices by selling their livestock and their possessions, even their clothing. During this period there were also thefts of food reported.

Under Russell, the government returned to a relatively orthodox laissez-faire economic policy in Ireland. It did not intervene to prevent speculators from profiting from food shortages, prohibit the diversion of grain from the food supply to distilleries, or block the export of grain from Ireland to England. While some individuals no doubt profited from the lack of government regulation, Cormac Ó Gráda's analysis of contemporary economic data suggest that no group—merchants, money lenders, or landlords—benefited during the years of the Great Irish Famine itself.

There was opposition to Russell's policies in Ireland, such as a food riot when a shipload of oats left Youghal on 25 September 1846; however, active Irish resistance to the British government's failing policies was never more than scattered. The extent of Irish resistance to the British government's Famine policy is a question that continues to puzzle historians, as well as people concerned with what appears to be patterns of passive acceptance by victims throughout history of policies that threaten their survival. In Famine-era Ireland, this may have been because the Irish people, who had survived similar agricultural cycles in the past, believed they could weather this storm. Another explanation is that after centuries of colonial domination, the Irish had been forced to accept their status as a subjected people unable to influence governmental decisions. Whatever the case, no one was able to anticipate two more years of crop failure. Eventually, the strongest emigrated, while others grew weak and either concentrated on daily survival or lost hope.

In an effort to provide a temporary solution to Famine suffering, the Russell government passed a new Poor Law for Ireland. It was based on the assumption that Ireland would be held responsible for Irish relief. The law authorized relief projects financed by treasury loans that would be repaid by local Poor Law Rates (taxes) levied on the landlords of a union (district). The impact of the new law was limited. Only the poorest were eligible for relief work. The wages on the work projects were kept at or below market level so they would not compete with private employers. Poorer districts often lacked resident landlords willing or able to apply for and support the work. When public works projects were put into operation, wages were insufficient to meet the rising cost of food. The work projects also prevented able-bodied members of households from farming, fishing, or developing other food sources. Finally, conditions were made even more unbearable by the unusually severe winter of 1846–1847, a winter of perishing cold, snow, and icy winds.

As it became clear that the government response was inadequate, private relief organizations mobilized to meet the Famine crisis. The Irish Quakers met in Dublin on 1 November 1846 to found the Central Relief Committee (CRC) of the Society of Friends. They set up soup kitchens where a quart of nourishing soup was available for a penny. Soup tickets could be purchased and distributed to the poor. In this private effort there was little of the demeaning bureaucracy that characterized government programs. The CRC's practical and generous intervention is still remembered today, and the Irish government issued a stamp in their honor during the 1997 Famine commemoration year. The Irish Quaker abolitionists, who had previously worked with their American counterparts in the struggle to end slavery in the United States, used their contacts to bring the news of Irish suffering to the United States where American Quakers set up their own relief committees. Irish emigrants and other people of good will used the CRC as a way to send contributions of food, money, and clothes to Ireland.

The Quakers tended to channel relief funds to local Protestant clergy who often had wives and children to help with relief efforts. In many places Protestant and Catholic clergy worked cooperatively; however some evangelical Protestant missionaries in Ireland, like Rev. Edward Nangle of Achill, Co. Mayo, regarded the Famine as an opportunity to win converts with meals. While this type of proselytism remained vivid in Irish folk memory, the reality was that most conversions were temporary.

The Roman Catholic church's role in Famine relief involved priests working among the poor of their parishes while their bishops appealed for relief from Irish immigrants abroad and from Catholic Europe. On 25 March 1847, Pope Pius IX issued his encyclical *Praedessores Nostros,* which called on the world's Roman Catholics to pray for those suffering from the Famine and to contribute funds to relieve the Irish poor. As the Famine continued, the voice of the Irish hierarchy grew increasingly critical of the British government's response to the crisis, particularly its toleration of eviction.

The U.S.-based committee, the General Relief Committee (GRC) of the City of New York, convened in February 1847, coordinated other American aid to Ireland. The GRC sent $250,000 to Ireland, much of the money raised from generous New Yorkers from all over the state. The committee also received a donation from the Cherokee nation who collected $170 for the Irish poor.

Despite the help from abroad, death raged during the winter of 1846–1847, especially in the south and west of Ireland where the high price of food, the lack of local resources and employment, and the region's distance from alternative food sources intensified the suffering. By 1847, the British public was aroused by the press reports of the Famine, especially accounts in *The Illustrated London News* with their graphic illustrations. On 1 January 1847, British merchant bankers and philanthropic individuals formed the British Association for Relief of Extreme Distress in Remote Parishes of Ireland and Scotland. They established a special fund to feed children on a diet of ten ounces of bread and a half pint of meat or fish soup per day.

At the end of January 1847, the Russell government enacted a series of limited interventions that were insufficient to meet the crisis of a year that has come to be remembered as "Black '47." The measures included temporarily suspending duties on imported grain until the next potato harvest, substituting soup kitchens for the public works projects, and permitting direct relief to the elderly, the infirm, the sick poor, and women with two or more dependents. Able-bodied workers could also receive aid for a limited period of time.

Official government policy continued to misread the gravity of the situation. The government continued to maintain that Ireland's poor were Ireland's problem, and that local landlords were responsible for funding relief programs. The 1847 Poor Law Relief Act (Ireland) carried the Gregory Clause, a provision that excluded people who lived on more than one-quarter acre of land from government assistance. In effect, this law also provided landlords with a legal justification for the eviction of tenants.

The Temporary Relief Act (the Soup Kitchen Act), while a humanitarian departure from the government's previous practice, was terribly inadequate for a hungry and weakened population struggling to survive the second winter of the Famine. Enacted in February 1847, it was not operational until March. A model soup kitchen was opened in Dublin in April, but the soup kitchen for County Galway's Clifden Union was delayed until the middle of May 1847. Once again, those most in need came last.

The quality of government soup became the subject of satiric ballads because it was less nutritious than the soup offered by the Quakers. Inadequate as they were, the soup kitchens did feed three million people, and the Irish considered them an improvement over overcrowded workhouses where families were separated and people were treated like prisoners. By the spring of 1847, the workhouses had become death houses, especially for women and children who perished from dysentery and infectious diseases that killed care-givers—doctors, clergy, landlords, and workhouse personnel—as well as the poor.

By 1847, local landlords, even those most willing to aid starving tenant farmers, found it difficult to pay the Poor Law tax rates. The Poor Law did not distinguish between resident landlords who used their own means to provide employment and relief to their tenants and the absentee landlords who ignored the crisis. All were charged the same rate. While he was critical of the entire landlord system, John Mitchel distinguished between the responsible resident landlord and the absentee.

Unable to collect their rents, an increasing number of landlords began evicting tenants who had fallen into arrears. On some estates, landlords used the Famine as an excuse to consolidate land holdings and to clear off their tenants with programs of assisted emigration. During the Famine years, at least 500,000 people were driven from their homes. While mass evictions did not begin with the Great Irish Famine, most of the nineteenth-century evictions took place during the Famine decade. A haunting image in Irish folk memory is the specter of evictions of tenants dying of starvation or disease—at least 500,000 of them—and their little cabins destroyed so people could not move back in. Evicted with no place to go, many of the homeless and landless sought refuge in ditches alongside the roads.

While some migration to the United States, Canada, England, and Australia was promoted and even assisted by landlords, most emigrants had to make their own way to new lands; therefore, it was generally the able-bodied Irish with some resources who left. In their weakened state, many died of fever en route, prompting the renaming of emigrant ships as "coffin ships." Thousands also died in a makeshift fever hospital in Grosse Isle, Quebec, in the St. Lawrence River. Famine immigrants crowded into Boston, Philadelphia, and New York where they worked at unskilled labor and endured anti-Irish and anti-Catholic nativism. By the 1850 United States census, there were 961,719 Irish-born residents, 42.8 percent of the foreign-born population.

While 1847 is regarded as the worst year of the Famine, the crisis was not over. The 1847 potato crop was healthy, but scant, owing to the scarcity of seed and the employment of able-bodied workers on the public works projects. The government pressed the Quakers to continue their soup kitchens, but their resources and workers were exhausted. They closed their soup kitchens in July 1847 and spent the rest of the Famine working on projects to encourage employment. Declaring the Famine "over," Treasury Under-Secretary Charles Trevelyan, the official in charge of Famine relief policy, closed the government soup kitchens open on 1 October 1847.

The government's declaration, while suffering was still wide-spread, prompted collective responses by Irish religious leaders and nationalists. Roman Catholic bishops met in Dublin and issued their strongest statement criticizing the government for putting the rights of property before the rights of human life. On 2 November 1847, Major Denis Mahon, whose efforts to clear tenant farmers off of his estate had started before the Famine, was assassinated; he was one of a half dozen landlords who were killed in the winter of 1847–1848. The official response to Mahon's death was a call to protect landlords and their middlemen from a tenantry that was viewed as desperate and lawless.

In 1847, Daniel O'Connell died. By the time of his death, two years of Famine had seriously weakened support for his politics of constitutional nationalism. In early 1848, the nationalist John Mitchel, who indicted government laissez-faire economic policies with the words, "Ireland died of political economy," began to call for an armed rebellion. In July 1848, the nationalist Young Irelanders, who had split with O'Connell over the question of using of physical force, staged a brief and unsuccessful rebellion near Ballingarry, County Tipperary. The rebellion leaders were convicted of treason and transported to Tasmania. Among the leaders who would play a significant role in U.S. history was Thomas Francis Meagher who escaped to America in 1852 where he became a journalist and a member of the New York Bar. During the American Civil War, Meagher recruited New Yorkers for an Irish Brigade that took heavy casualties at the Battle of Fredericksburg in December 1862. By the end of the war, Meagher was a Brigadier-General. He was later appointed acting governor of the Montana Territory.

The gallantry of units like the Irish Brigade helped to reduce anti-Irish nativism; however, as the losses in Irish regiments mounted, the Irish community became hostile to the war, especially to the 1863 draft law with its provision that drafted men could purchase substitutes for $300, an option beyond the resources of poor Irish immigrants. Irish bitterness against the law erupted in the July 1863 draft riots in New York City that lasted five days and scapegoated the city's African-American population; eleven African Americans were killed by rioters and an orphanage for black children was destroyed by fire. Order was finally restored by New York City police and the military, which included many Irish soldiers.

The fall of 1848 was made more miserable with the recurrence of cholera in Ireland and an acceleration in evictions. The government passed the Encumbered Estates Act to facilitate the sale of lands by landlords who were bankrupted by the Famine. Many landlords preferred to sell out rather than be pressed to support the poor;

however, there were a few landlords like Mary Letitia Martin, the "Princess of Connemara," who inherited a heavily mortgaged estate of 20,000 acres, spent large sums on relief and employment, defaulted on her mortgage, and lost her land. Almost destitute, like thousands of Irish, she emigrated to New York where she died in childbirth in 1850. The new landowners frequently evicted tenants to maximize the return on their investments. In 1849, there were 13,384 officially recorded evictions, twice the number from the previous year. This figure probably represents half of the actual number of those who were evicted.

By the 1850s, the Great Irish Famine had produced changes in Ireland that would alter the course of Irish and world history. In Ireland, the bottom third of the economic order, poor people and the landless, were largely removed. The cottier class was destroyed. The potato remained a staple food for the Irish, but the rural population was no longer dependent on a single crop. While the decline of Irish as the country's spoken language did not begin with the Famine, Irish-speaking areas were hardest hit and those casualties accelerated the silence of the language in the Irish countryside. The practice of dividing land among all sons was replaced by a system of a single inheriting son and a single dowered daughter. The other siblings had little option except to emigrate. The Great Irish Famine altered the balance of the population. There were many fewer landless families and families with very small holdings and a relatively larger middle-class population with more conservative attitudes. Because of the important role the Irish played in shaping Roman Catholicism in the nineteenth-century United States, this conservative ethos came to predominate in the U.S. church.

A long-term result of the Great Irish Famine was the nurturing of Irish nationalism, both among those who never accepted the Union between Great Britain and Ireland and those embittered by perceived British indifference to Irish suffering. In the twentieth century, nationalists, supported by aid from Irish living abroad who considered themselves political or economic exiles, finally secured political independence and a democratic society for the majority of the Irish people.

III. Addressing Controversial Historical Issues through the Study of the Great Irish Famine

Studying about the Great Irish Famine provides teachers and students with an opportunity to explore controversial issues in global history. Our approach in the Great Irish Famine curriculum is to emphasize the complexity of history by presenting multiple perspectives about the causes and significance of events. The Great Irish Famine Curriculum guide makes available to teachers and students a variety of primary and secondary source documents and lesson plans. Questions and activities that accompany the documents and lessons encourage students to think, write, and speak as historians, to analyze historical material, to question their assumptions, to gather and organize evidence before reaching conclusions, to discover connections between events, to recognize parallel developments that may not be directly related, and to realize that conclusions are subject to change as new evidence and more integrative theories emerge. As they study about the Great Irish Famine, students should come to realize that historians do not have all the answers about the past or present and that they do not always agree.

The Great Irish Famine curriculum guide gives students and teachers an opportunity to examine a number of essential social studies and historical questions that are also major components of the New York State Social Studies Learning Standards. Examples of essential questions include (1) Are there historical or philosophical connections between slavery and the African Slave Trade, the Great Irish Famine, and the European Holocaust—subjects that are focal points in the New York State Human Rights curriculum but that happened in different eras? (2) What are the relationships between these events and broader historical developments? (3) What types of injustice and oppression constitute genocide? (4) Is there such a thing as human nature, and if so, what is it? (5) Why have some groups of people been victimized in the past? (6) How do people survive, resist, and maintain human dignity under inhumane circumstance? (7) Why do some people become rescuers while others collaborate with oppressors? (8) Should historians assign blame for historical events? (9) Should a focus for historians be to identify individuals or groups as villains or should it be to examine the social, economic, and political systems that generate human rights violations? (10) What criteria, if any, should be used to evaluate actions by individuals, groups, and societies? (11) Who should be considered citizens of a country, and what rights and responsibilities should accompany citizenship? (12) What are the relationships between history and geography? (13) When should the cause of a catastrophe be considered an act of nature, and when should it be considered the responsibility of human institutions?

Following is a discussion of some historical controversies that can help teachers think about issues related to the Great Irish Famine before they begin to examine specific lessons and documents.

A Point of View about History

The definition of history is complicated because it refers to a series of distinct but related ideas: (1) events from the past—"facts," (2) the process of gathering and organizing information from the past—historical research, (3) explanations about the relationships between specific historical events, and (4) broader explanations or "theories" about how and why change takes place. In other words, history is simultaneously the past, the study of the past, explanations about the past, and explanations about human nature and the nature of society.

The pedagogy that informs the organization of the social studies lesson material in the Great Irish Famine Curriculum Guide draws on this broad understanding of history. It is not a list of facts to memorize though it tries to incorporate a considerable amount of historical information. While we believe that drawing conclusions about the past is a vital part of the historical process, we try not to make a narrow ideological presentation. We hope the material in this guide allows room for widespread debate and promotes a broad dialogue on what makes us human and what is the responsibility of society.

To achieve these goals, we are offering a document-based curriculum guide for social studies lessons that is organized to promote an inquiry approach to learning history. We want students and teachers to become historians, to sift through the past, to examine different data and interpretations, and to draw their own conclusions based on a variety of evidence.

We also recognize that teachers play the crucial role in the creation of curriculum because they choose the material that will ultimately be presented in their classrooms. We want to facilitate, not usurp, this function. Instead of dictating what should be taught, the curriculum guide offers teachers a broad range of primary source documents, interpretive passages, worksheets, literary resources, and individual and group projects.

Drawing Connections between Historical Events

Study of the Great Irish Famine is part of a New York Human Rights curriculum that includes the study of slavery in the Americas, the Atlantic slave trade, and the World War II era European Holocaust. Part of the task confronting teachers is to help students examine potential connections and/or parallels between these historical events. This involves students in exploring theories of historical change and ideas about human nature, culture and civilization, the role of government, and the political and economic organization of societies.

A difficulty in making direct comparisons between these events is that they happened in different historical eras, had different goals, and occurred in different social and economic systems. While studying slavery and the Atlantic slave trade, students need to examine and understand the magnitude and specific historical context of a system that, between 1500 and the end of the nineteenth century, enslaved millions of Africans and transported them across the Atlantic Ocean to the Americas where they and their descendants were defined as nonhumans and were expected to provide unpaid labor in perpetuity. Historians have argued that this system of human exploitation played a central role in European colonial expansion around the world and that the labor of enslaved Africans was crucial to the development of commercial capitalism and the start of the industrial revolution.

On the other hand, while the social, political, and economic conditions that contributed to both the Great Irish Famine and the European Holocaust had deep historical roots, these events happened in much narrower time frames and more restricted locales and had different impacts on the affected peoples. The first year of the Great Irish Famine was 1845, the last failure of the potato crop was in 1849, and Famine-related deaths tapered off by 1852. The Famine occurred in part of the United Kingdom, the most powerful and prosperous country during the early part of the Industrial era, and while Ireland suffered from a severe population decline during this period, most of it was the result of emigration rather than death.

The European Holocaust is generally studied in connection with the growth of Nazi ideology and power in Germany prior to and during World War II. It was precipitated by a culturally, technologically, and industrially advanced nation that in the middle of the twentieth century sought to exterminate an entire group of people.

A problem teachers should consider when comparing these events is that historians prefer to limit the use of historical terms to specific, relatively narrow, historical contexts. These distinctions may or may not be appropriate in elementary, middle, or high school social studies lessons. Examples of terms with complex and changing meanings that also have narrower technical definitions are *racism* and *imperialism*.

Racism is popularly used to define any form of prejudice or discrimination that is based on the belief that some hereditary groups are superior or inferior to others. In the United States during the era of slavery, enslaved Africans were defined as chattel, a non-human form of property. Any person with a single African ancestor was considered non-white, and in the South, laws were passed to prevent manumission (the freeing of slaves). In Nazi Germany, an effort was made to apply quasi-scientific notions of genetics and Social Darwinism to outlaw racial mixing between Aryans (Germans) and people who were deemed to be racially inferior, particularly Jews. In both situations, Africans and Jews were subject to severe restrictions and could not legally change their racial classification.

English observers of the Irish before and during the Famine also describe the Irish as an inferior race and often argue that their inferiority was the primary reason for the devastation caused by the Famine. However, the focus in these documents tends to be on the culture, religion, and work habits of the Irish, rather than their biological heredity. Some observers even suggested that if the Irish renounced their way of life and lived like Englishmen, they would no longer be racially inferior. In this view of race, which is different from the ones employed in the United States during the era of slavery and in Nazi Germany, it is possible for individuals and entire groups to change their racial status. Students need to examine similarities and differences in the way the term *racism* is used in different settings and to decide where and when they believe it is applicable.

Imperialism generally is used to describe empire-building and the exploitation of one nation over another to obtain economic, military, and political benefits. In its broadest sense, it includes colonialism, the practice of creating permanent settlements in other lands, and mercantilism, the regulation of colonial economies to benefit the dominant power. It has also been used to describe the relationship between a dominant group that holds political power in a country and ethnic minorities that are subject to their power. Using this general definition, the term *imperialism* can be used to describe the historic relationship between England and Ireland.

Historians, however, tend to differentiate between forms of national domination, especially during different historical periods. The term *imperialism* and the designation "Age of Imperialism," are often reserved for describing the expansion of European influence in Africa and Asia as European nationalism and the needs of industrial economies spurred competition for markets and raw materials between 1870 and the start of World War I. Classroom teachers need to consider whether making this type of distinction will be meaningful for their students and, if so, how best to address it.

Addressing the Political Debate

The meaning of the Great Irish Famine has been contested by political activists and historians from the 1850s to the present day. The Great Irish Famine has been the source of nationalist anger, a historical problem to be coolly dissected and demythologized, and a reminder of the realities of hunger and poverty in the modern world. Mary Robinson, the former president of the Republic of Ireland, argues that reflection on the Great Irish Famine should spur action to prevent similar catastrophes in the present and future. We hope the Great Irish Famine Curriculum Guide will promote discussion about access to food and health care as human rights, and an examination of the responsibility of governments to meet the needs of people in modern, democratic, industrial, and post-industrial societies—topics that are fundamental parts of the New York State Social Studies Standards and the Economics and Participation in Government curricula.

A highly contentious political debate is over whether the government of Great Britain consciously pursued genocidal policies designed to depopulate Ireland through death and emigration. While we do not believe that British policies during the Great Irish Famine meet the criteria for genocide established by the United Nations (1951) in a treaty signed by the United States, we believe it is a legitimate subject for discussion.

One way to approach the political debates is to explore the differences between the goals of political activists and historians. The primary concern of activists is to win support for their political positions in an effort to bring about political, social, and economic changes in society. While historians also have political views and goals, their professional commitment requires that they examine events from multiple perspectives and that they hold themselves to a higher standard when they draw conclusions based on evidence. As students read excerpts from primary source documents and interpretations of the causes of the Great Irish Famine and the reasons for British policies, they need to consider the following questions: (1) Is this commentator writing as a political activist or a historian? (2) What is her or his point of view about the Great Irish Famine and other events in Irish history? (3) Does that point of view aid in an examination of events or interfere with his or her analysis? (4) How could the argument be made more effective? (5) Can someone be impartial when researching and writing about a topic like the Great Irish Famine?

The authors of the Great Irish Famine Curriculum acknowledge that we have individual, and a collective, points of view, and we recognize that our views influence our interpretations of Famine history and the way we selected documents, organized lessons, and framed questions. In general, we believe the Great Irish Famine was the result of multiple causes, including a natural ecological disaster, rapid population growth, religious and cultural prejudice, a British imperial ideology that legitimized colonialism, government relief programs that were inadequate to the magnitude of need, and policies that favored English political and economic interests, especially the interests of emerging English industrial capitalism. To limit the impact of our biases on the curriculum guide, international committees of historians, literary scholars, and educators reviewed the package at different stages in its development. We do not expect all teachers and students to share our conclusions. Hopefully the documents will enable people to discuss alternative explanations and reach their own conclusions.

Significance of Religion

The United States has a long and valued tradition of a "wall of separation" between church and state. This tradition, and the laws that support it, protects religious beliefs and church organizations from government regulations that might be used to stifle religious practice. They also prevent powerful religious groups from determining government policies, gaining unfair advantages, or stigmatizing families who choose not to believe.

In public education, the wall of separation has been redefined over the years. It now means that public schools cannot sponsor Bible readings or prayers and cannot present one set of religious beliefs as a norm that every moral person should follow. However, while public schools cannot teach religion, teachers are free to, and in some cases expected to, teach about religion.

Because of the importance of the wall of separation, many public school teachers hesitate to teach about religion. They fear that adherents to these beliefs might feel they are being presented incorrectly, or that people from other religious backgrounds, or those who reject all religions, will object to what their children are being taught. This presents a dilemma when teaching about Ireland and the Great Irish Famine, because the history and culture of Ireland cannot be separated easily from the religious beliefs of the people of Ireland. In many parts of the world, the mid-nineteenth century was a profoundly religious era when people were concerned about their salvation and that of others. While their beliefs were genuinely held, occasionally their zeal led them to adopt attitudes that today would be regarded as evidence of bigotry and religious prejudice.

We have tried to address these issues in the Great Irish Famine Curriculum Guide in two ways. First, we acknowledge the complexity of the matter of religion in Famine historiography and address that complexity in our examination of the way Irish of different religious traditions responded to the Famine crisis. Roman Catholic institutions, leaders, and practices played a major role in the daily life of most Irish, in resistance to British colonialism, and in providing support during the Famine years. Customs, oral traditions, and folk arts reflect religious heritage. Rather than ignoring important aspects of Irish culture and history, we think the role of religion in Irish life should be examined. Students on all grade levels can use an examination of religion in Irish life to help them explore the role of religion in human history and why groups of people have often expressed their most fundamental values and beliefs through religion.

Second, the Great Irish Famine Curriculum Guide does not demonize Protestants as proselytizers. It pays tribute to rescuers from all religious denominations who aided in relief efforts. Some Protestant denominations, especially the Quakers, played a crucial role in providing Famine relief. While the authors believe that anti-Catholic prejudice played a major role in justifying injustice, lessons encourage students to explore the role of religious and cultural prejudice in the joint history of Ireland and Great Britain and to draw their own conclusions.

Validity of Sources

The historical reliability of some of the material presented in this curriculum guide has been challenged, either because of its point of view, or because of its clouded origins. Instead of removing these documents, we want teachers and students, acting as historians, to evaluate their validity and historical significance. For example, John Mitchel and Charles Trevelyan are political leaders who are either attacking or defending British government policies. Readers must take that into account when evaluating their explanation of events. Newspaper accounts also contain political and social biases.

The authenticity of some Famine journals have been challenged. Critics question whether Gerald Keegan's diary, first published in 1895, is an actual historical account or a work of fiction. Because of the intensity of debate surrounding the Keegan diary, and because other, better established, primary source documents are available for examination, we decided not to include excerpts from the Keegan diary.

Global Perspective

In designing the Great Irish Famine Curriculum Guide, we decided that a narrow focus on the events between 1845 and 1852 did a disservice to history, students, and the victims of the Great Hunger. We have tried to place events in a broad global context, while developing lesson material that fits into the New York State ninth and tenth grade Global History calendar and can be used in Language Arts and Literature and Arts education classes.

The historical narrative begins with the origins of Ireland and the Irish and early ties between Ireland and Great Britain. The guide makes it possible to include sections on Ireland in the study of the Columbian Exchange, colonialism, early industrialization, the development of modern economic thought, the growth of nineteenth-century imperialism, nineteenth-century trans-Atlantic migration, the origins of the modern state, U.S. history and instances of famine in the world today.

Because of our concerns with examining essential social studies and historical questions, connecting the history of Ireland to other events in the past and present, and exploring themes in the New York State Social Studies Learning Standards, the guide includes a section that addresses the UN Convention on the Prevention and Punishment of the Crime of Genocide and other human rights issues in global history and the contemporary world.

Selected Bibliography

Bottigheimer, K. *Ireland and the Irish: A Short History*. New York: Columbia Univ. Press, 1982.

Daly, M. *The Famine in Ireland*. Dundalk, Ireland: Dundalgan Dublin Hist. Assoc., 1986.

Donnelly, J. "The Great Famine, 1845–51." *A New History of Ireland, V(1), Ireland under the Union, 1801–1870*. Ed. W. Vaughn. Oxford: Clarendon, 1989.

Edwards, R., and Williams, T., eds. *The Great Famine, Studies in Irish History*. Dublin: Lilliput, 1994.

Gray, P. *The Irish Famine*. New York: Abrams, 1995.

Kelleher, M. *The Feminization of Famine*. Cork: Cork Univ. Press, 1997.

Killen, J., ed. *The Famine Decade*. Belfast: Blackstaff, 1995.

Kinealy, C. *This Great Calamity*. Dublin: Gill and Macmillan, 1994.

Kissane, N., ed. *The Irish Famine. A Documentary History*. Dublin: Nat. Lib. of Ireland, 1991.

Litton, H. *The Irish Famine, An Illustrated History*. Dublin: Wolfhound, 1994.

McCaffrey, L. *The Irish Diaspora in America*. Bloomington: Indiana Univ. Press, 1976.

Miller, K. *Emigration and Exile*. New York: Oxford Univ. Press, 1985.

Mokyr, J. *Why Ireland Starved*. New York: Routledge, 1983.

Nicholson, A. *Annals of the Famine in Ireland*. Ed. M. Murphy. Dublin: Lilliput Press, 1998.

Ó Gráda, C. *Black '47 and Beyond: The Great Irish Famine in History*. Princeton, NJ: Princeton Univ. Press, 1999.

---. *The Great Irish Famine*. New York: Macmillan, 1989.

Póirtéir, C. *The Great Irish Famine*. Dublin: Mercier, 1995.

Scally, R. *The End of Hidden Ireland*. New York: Oxford Univ. Press, 1995.

Woodham-Smith, C. *The Great Hunger*. London: Hamish Hamilton, 1962.

PART II: What Are the *Big* Questions? An Essential Questions Approach to Understanding the Great Irish Famine and World History

In March 2001, an educational columnist for *Newsday* (New York) dismissed the new New York State Great Irish Famine Curriculum guide as another effort to promote ethnocentric history and the idea that the United States is little more than "a pastiche of different peoples, linked mostly by a Constitution and a system of interstate highways." The columnist cited Chester Finn Jr., a long-term opponent of multiculturalism, who insisted, "[i]f we invite every faction in our society to insert their own best or worst episode from history, there will be no end of it" (Hildebrand A32).

The *New York Times* had a different take on the curriculum guide (Zernike B7). According to the *Times:*

> If all goes according to plan, those Irish clichés (shamrocks and leprechauns) would be replaced by appreciation for 'the amazing potato'; the famine-ravaged town of Skibbereen; Annie Moore, the first immigrant processed through Ellis Island; and the modern historical view that the potato famine of the 1840s resulted not just from a natural calamity but from Britain's policy of exporting other crops that could have kept its Irish colonial subjects alive.

The article also credited the curriculum with drawing connections between events in Ireland in the 1840s and current issues, "including starvation in African nations, homelessness, immigration—as well as the history of other cultures."

As the primary authors of the New York State Great Irish Famine Curriculum guide, we certainly liked the *New York Times* review better; but the reality is that neither newspaper captured what we tried to do, and believe we have done, with the curriculum. Our primary goals were to write Ireland into the world history, not create a separate course of study; to offer teachers model standards-driven document-based lesson plans, projects, and assessments; and to design a curriculum centered around addressing the *big*, or essential questions, in world history (Murphy, Militia, and Singer).

The curriculum uses the history of Ireland as a case study for understanding world history from the Columbian exchange (when Europeans are introduced to the "amazing potato") through twentieth-century human catastrophes. Major academic goals include encouraging students to think critically about historical events and primary sources, to draw conclusions based on criteria and evidence, and to debate fundamental questions about the responsibilities of government and individuals in times of crisis.

In its final form, the guide will include 150 interdisciplinary lessons for grades 4 through 12 that draw on science, literature and the arts, as well as social studies and history. It will be available in book form, as a CD, and on the World Wide Web. The lessons are divided into units that address four major historical questions: (1) What forces were shaping Ireland and the world before the Great Irish Famine (e.g., the Columbian exchange, the Reformation in Europe, and Colonialism)? (2) Was the Great Irish Famine an act of nature? (3) How did the Great Irish Famine change Ireland and the world? (4) What is the legacy of the Great Irish Famine? Within the four areas defined by these *very large questions,* the guide addresses a collection of essential questions that permeate the study of world history.

Whether intended or not, both newspaper articles did touch on essential historical questions. In his attack on ethnic history and multiculturalism, the *Newsday* columnist was really trying to define the American experience, and asking, "What does it mean to be an American?" The *Times* article, which presented the debate over Britain's role, introduced two essential questions, one related to historical causality and the other to government responsibility. These are exactly the kind of questions we want students to consider.

As we designed the curriculum, we found that an examination of Irish history constantly forced us to think about essential historical questions. For example, in 1861, Irish nationalist John Mitchel charged that "[N]o sack of Magdeburg, or ravage of the Palatinate ever approached the horror and dislocation to the slaughters done in Ireland by mere official red tape and stationery, and the principles of political economy. . . . The Almighty sent the potato blight, but the English created the famine" (Kissane).

Whether or not you agree with Mitchel's accusation about British policy in Ireland during the Great Irish Famine, his statement contains a number of key ideas about Irish, British, and world history. The sack of Magdeburg, a German Protestant city, in 1631 by the forces of the Catholic League, which included Italy, France, and Spain, was part of the One Hundred Year War in Reformation Europe. The ravaging of the Palatinate, also in Germany, by the forces of Louis XIV of France from 1688 to 1697, was more directly related to imperial ambition during an era of European colonial expansion. Both of these conquests, as well as the British conquest and rule over Ireland, force students and historians to consider human nature, especially human behavior during times of war, the legitimacy of religions and religious leaders who urge war to promote or enforce beliefs, and the relationship between large powers and their smaller, vulnerable neighbors. Significantly, these are all major questions confronting the world today—for example, the Balkans and central Africa (war), Southwest Asia and Afghanistan (religion), and the U.S. role in the Americas (use of power). In addition, Mitchel is asking us to explore causality in history, the workings of a laissez-faire political economy, the nature of bureaucracy, and collective responsibility for government action (or inaction). One small quote unleashes a slew of major issues and powerful questions.

An essential questions approach to Irish and world history draws on Grant Wiggins's work on social studies teaching methods, Paulo Freire's belief that education must involve students in posing and examining questions about the problems facing their own communities, the focus on social issues presented by the National Council for the Social Studies in the *Handbook on Teaching Social Issues,* and Alan Singer's use of current events to help high school students and teachers frame and examine complex and controversial questions about the contemporary world, and use these questions to direct their examination of the past.[1]

Wiggins argues that teachers should present students with broad questions without simple answers that are reintroduced over and over throughout the curriculum. For social studies, he suggests questions like: Is there enough to go around (i.e., food, clothes, water)? Is history a history of progress? When is law unjust? Who owns what and why? Singer has students develop their own questions about the past, present, and future. He starts the school year with teams of students searching through newspapers and selecting articles they believe report on important issues facing the contemporary world. Teams categorize the issues, identify underlying problems, and formulate the questions they want to answer. Their essential questions are placed on poster boards, hung prominently around the room, and referred to continuously.

As with Wiggins's approach, the Great Irish Famine Curriculum starts with essential questions; however, it is designed so that new questions continually emerge as students explore global history. These essential questions include:

1. How can a small thing or event transform the world?
2. What role does religion play in human history? Can we understand history without discussing religion?
3. What is human nature?
4. How did the Industrial Revolution change the way people live and work?
5. Are famines acts of nature or the result of decisions made by people with power?
6. What is the cost of prejudice?
7. What is the responsibility of government?

8. What are the responsibilities of individuals to respond to injustice or calamity?
9. Is imperialism caused by racism?
10. What are human rights?
11. What is genocide?
12. Can groups and individuals shape the future?

How can a small thing or event transform the world?

Students are asked to think of a small thing or event that transformed the world. The class "brainstorms" ideas, which are written on the board, and discusses how these things or events brought about change. Popular choices are Rosa Parks sitting down on a bus in Montgomery, Alabama; the invention of the printing press; Columbus's voyage; the discovery of agriculture (seeds); and the invention of computer chips. At this point the teacher holds up a potato and asks how something like the potato could change the world. The lesson includes an activity sheet on the potato and charts or graphs showing Irish population growth from the mid-seventeenth century (when the potato was introduced) through 1841 (the last census prior to the arrival of a potato-destroying fungus) and population collapse from 1841 through 1871. As a follow-up activity, students compare their choices about events that changed the world with a list prepared by the Time-Life Company for the millennium celebration.[2]   Interestingly, the Time-Life list ranked Europe's learning about the potato from the Inca in 1537 as the thirty-ninth most significant event of the last 1,000 years.

Time-Life Top Ten Events of the Last Millennium
1. Gutenberg Prints the Christian Bible, Germany, 1455
2. Columbian Encounter, Spain, 1492
3. Protestant Reformation, Germany, 1517
4. James Watt patents the steam engine, England, 1769
5. Galileo establishes sun-centered solar system, Italy, 1610
6. Robert Koch develops germ theory of disease, Germany, 1882
7. Gunpowder used in weapons, China, 1100
8. Declaration of Independence, United States, 1776
9. Nazis come to power, Germany, 1933
10. Compass used to navigate, China, 1117

Potato Facts and Legends
1. About three thousand years ago, native peoples in the Andes Mountains, in what is now known as Peru, found a plant with a short, fleshy underground root that was good to eat. They called this vegetable

papa. These native peoples learned how to grow different types of potatoes in different climates and soils.

2. The Inca, who developed an empire in this region, preserved potatoes for future use by letting them freeze on the ground overnight. The next day, men, women, and children stamped on the potatoes in their bare feet to drive out the moisture. This was repeated for four or five days until they were left with a dry white flour they called chuno.

3. An Inca Prayer: "O Creator! Lord of the ends of the earth! Oh, most merciful! Thou who givest life to all things, and has made men that they might live, and eat and multiply. Multiply also the fruits of the earth, the papas [potatoes] and other food that thou has made that men may not suffer from hunger and misery."

4. In the 1530s, Spanish soldiers encountered potatoes high in the Andes Mountains when they invaded Peru. The potato was introduced in Europe about 1565. By 1570, potatoes were being sold in the marketplace in Seville, Spain. In 1586, a boat commanded by Sir Francis Drake stopped in Cartegena, Colombia, to pick up food and other supplies. The crew brought potatoes back with them to England.

5. There is more than one story about how potatoes reached Ireland. The most likely possibility is that the potato arrived in Ireland in 1588 when an invading Spanish fleet was damaged by storms off the coast. The crews were killed or captured by the Irish, who took what they found on board, which probably included potatoes. After potato cultivation spread in Ireland, many English refused to eat them because they were seen as food fit only for Irish peasants.

6. During the seventeenth century, many European herbalists thought potatoes could cure medical problems like tuberculosis, diarrhea, impotence in men, and barrenness in women. Other writers were afraid that potatoes would cause diseases like leprosy. Some people feared eating potatoes because they were not mentioned in the Jewish or Christian Bibles. In 1653, Bernabé Cobo of Spain, a historian, wrote about how to plant a potato crop, make potato flour, and cook potatoes.

7. European peasant folk beliefs included: Wear a dry potato around your neck to protect yourself from rheumatism; keep a peeled potato in your pocket to cure a toothache; if a pregnant woman eats a potato, she will have a child with a small head.

8. In 1719, Irish Protestant settlers in the British colony of New Hampshire brought the potato to North America. In the 1740s, Emperor Frederick II of Prussia ordered German peasants to grow potatoes. In the 1750s, a pharmacist named Antoine Parmentier popularized eating potatoes in France. When Thomas Jefferson returned to the United States from France in 1789, he brought home a love for potatoes. When he became president, he served potatoes in the White House.

9. In 1776, a strange new fungus ruined the potato crop in the Netherlands. In 1842, it struck American potatoes. From 1845 through 1849, the potato blight destroyed the Irish potato crop.

10. Today, the value of the potato crop worldwide is about $100 billion a year. This is about three times greater than all the gold and silver Spain took from the Americas during colonial times (Meltzer; Daly).

What role does religion play in human history? Can we understand history without discussing religion?

Throughout recorded history, people from the ancient Romans through the contemporary Taliban have done noble and horrible things in the name of God. However, because of the importance of the wall of separation between church and state in the United States, many public school teachers hesitate to teach about religion. They fear that adherents to these beliefs might feel they are being presented incorrectly, or that people from other religious backgrounds, or those who reject all religions, will object to what their children are being taught.

This presents a dilemma for social studies teachers because religious beliefs and institutions have played a central role in most of recorded human history. As one example, the history and culture of Ireland cannot be easily separated from the religious beliefs of the people of Ireland. In 1649, Protestant forces from Great Britain under Oliver Cromwell invaded overwhelmingly Roman Catholic Ireland. They defeated Irish rebels and slaughtered or displaced many Irish civilians. In an infamous statement that has spurred on generations of Irish nationalists, Cromwell declared that Catholic landowners had the choice of "hell or Connacht"—Connacht symbolizing rocky, unproductive lands on the Atlantic coast. As a result of this invasion, the English parliament abolished the Irish parliament and confiscated Irish estates. By 1688, only 22 percent of the land of Ireland was owned by Irish Catholics (Gray 14–15; Moody and Martin 201).

The Great Irish Famine Curriculum guide acknowledges the complex role of religious institutions and beliefs in pre-Famine Irish history, Irish resistance to British colonialism, and the way people from different religious traditions responded to the Famine crisis. Rather than ignoring important aspects of culture and history, we think the role of religion in history must be examined. Students on all grade levels can use an examination of religion in Irish history to help them explore the role of religion in human history and why groups of people have often expressed their most fundamental values and beliefs through religion.

3. What is human nature?

As noted above, the study of the role of religion in history introduces both the noble and the horrible. In doing this, it forces us to think about our essential nature and beliefs as human beings. The history of Ireland during the Great Famine is the story of human indifference and of human sacrifice to help others survive. It is a story that helps students examine their own human potential and the choices we make as historical actors.

How did the Industrial Revolution change the way people live and work?

According to the song, "Pat Works on the Railway," in 1841 Paddy "puts his corduroy breeches on" and starts his migration from Ireland to the United States (Folke and Glazer 84). That is five years before the potato crop fails in Ireland in September 1846. Either the song was prophetic or something else was going on. Actually, the wave of Irish emigration to the United States and England precedes the Great Irish Famine by at least twenty-five years and is related to a number of complex factors affecting rural populations across Europe. These include long-term population growth that strains rural resources, an agricultural depression following the Napoleonic wars, new jobs in industrializing centers, and moves to eliminate traditional agrarian land tenure. In many ways, the Great Irish Famine can be best understood as part of nineteenth-century industrial development.

From this perspective, the indifference shown by British government officials toward the Irish is not so different from the attitude of elites toward peasants, the working-class, and the poor in other parts of the world. Conditions were so bad in England's industrial centers that in 1840 the "average age at death" for "labourers, mechanics and servants" in Liverpool was only fifteen years. In Manchester, nearly 54 percent of workers' children died before their fifth birthday (Engels).

Are famines acts of nature or the result of decisions made by people with power?

In 1798, the Reverend Thomas Malthus wrote that famine is "the last, the most dreadful resource of nature." Malthus believed that "[t]he power of population is so superior to the power of the earth to produce subsistence for man, that premature death must in some shape or other visit the human race. . . . [G]igantic inevitable famine stalks in the rear, and with one mighty blow levels the population with the food of the world." Malthus's prediction is one of the reasons that economics is known as the dismal science. Yet despite numerous natural disasters, wars, and periodic famines, Malthus's prediction has proven to be wrong. The world's population now exceeds six billion people and continues to grow along with its supply of food and a wealth of new technologies.

In the last decade, Nobel Prize–winning economist, Amartya Sen has argued that, at least in the twentieth century, famine has been the result of the inability of starving people to buy food that exists and the unwillingness of governments to overrule market forces and appropriate and distribute it (Sen 160–88). Where democratic governments responsible to local populations are in control, they have responded to natural disasters and avoided massive human misery. Significantly, Sen's position parallels Mitchel's claims about the Great Irish Famine.

What is the cost of prejudice?

Social studies students in the United States today are usually sensitive to the problem of stereotyping and prejudice and their impact on individuals, but are not as well informed about its social cost. The Great Irish Famine Curriculum uses political cartoons and contemporary commentaries to examine how the dehumanizing of the Irish by the English created conditions for ignoring or minimizing their plight during the Famine years. These lessons provide a context for examining the dehumanization of Jews under the Nazi regime in Germany, nativist and racist campaigns and practices in U.S. history, and contemporary attitudes toward immigrants in many parts of the world.

What is the responsibility of government?

In the midst of the Famine, an editorial in the *London Times* claimed, "Human agency is now denounced as instrumental in adding to the calamity inflicted by Heaven. It is no longer submission to Providence, but a murmur against the Government" (Gray 154–55). The editorial defended the British response to conditions in Ireland and argued that the

> Government provided work for a people who love it not. It made this the absolute condition of relief. The Government was required to ward off starvation, not to pamper indolence; its duty was to encourage industry, not to stifle it; to stimulate others to give employment, not to outbid them, or drive them from the labor markets. Alas! the Irish peasant had tasted of famine and found that it was good.

The editorial goes on to denounce the "Irish character" and declare "the potato blight as a blessing."

Students who examine this editorial and British government policy have immediately drawn parallels with attitudes toward the poor and people receiving government assistance in the United States today.

Famine lessons repeatedly introduce students to debates over government responses to emergencies and long-term structural social inequality.

What are the responsibilities of individuals to respond to injustice or calamity?

Whether governments take responsible actions or not, individuals must also consider their own choices. During the European Holocaust, numbers of individuals and groups placed themselves at risk to defy Nazi orders and assist Jews and other targeted people, while other individuals and communities complied. During the Great Irish Famine, people made similar, though perhaps not as dramatic choices of whether to collaborate or resist. One of the more disturbing aspects of the Famine in Ireland was the way that absentee and Anglo-Irish (Protestant) landlords took advantage of economic hardship to evict tenant farmers and end their traditional claims to the land. Between 1846 and 1854, almost 200,000 Irish families were "ejected" (O'Neill 29–58). At the same time, numerous individuals, especially Quakers, supported and worked in soup kitchens, and some risked their own lives caring for people in fever-infested work houses. One of the more touching stories of human generosity is commemorated in a children's book, *The Long March* (Fitzpatrick). It recounts the decision by the Choctaw people of Oklahoma, themselves victims of a government relocation program, to donate scarce tribal funds to Famine relief efforts.

Is imperialism caused by racism?

This question emerged during a lesson in a high school where most of the students are African American, Caribbean, and Latino/a. After studying nineteenth-century British colonial policy in India and imperialist ambitions in China and Africa, students concluded that imperialism was motivated by racism. After their teacher introduced the history of Ireland, especially the British response to the Famine, the students were startled that "white people could do this to white people." This led to discussion of the meaning of race in both nineteenth-century and contemporary terms and a more systematic exploration of imperialism as a product of capitalist expansion.

What are human rights?

As we progress into the twenty-first century, the question of what constitutes a human right, and the issue of protecting human rights around the world, seems to be developing greater importance. The Great Irish Famine Curriculum introduces the idea of access to food as a basic human right and asks students to consider whether human rights, especially under emergency circumstances, should take precedence over the rights of property holders.

One of the most powerful lessons in the curriculum has students examine Frederick Douglass's visit to Famine-era Ireland. In his autobiography, Douglass, a leading African-American abolitionist, compares the sorrow expressed in the songs of the Irish with the sorrow he remembered from his days as a slave in the American South. The passage makes clear that both freedom and access to food and shelter must be respected as fundamental human rights.

What is genocide?

In field-testing the Great Irish Famine curriculum, we frequently introduced this question as a culminating discussion following study of the decimation of the Native American population, the Atlantic slave trade, the Great Irish Famine, Armenia during World War I, the European Holocaust during World War II, and post–World War II efforts to exterminate people in the Balkins and central Africa. Students examined the United Nations definition of genocide, which requires intent but also identifies as forms of genocide, "causing serious bodily or mental harm to members of the group"; "deliberately inflicting on the group conditions of life calculated to bring about its physical destruction in whole or in part"; "imposing measures intended to prevent births within the group"; and, "forcibly transferring children of the group to another group." Students questioned both the requirement of intent and the number of different categories, and then used the United Nations definition to decide, based on its criteria, which events in human history should be classified as genocidal.

Can groups and individuals shape the future?

The lessons in the Great Irish Famine curriculum, as they help students consider possibilities for the future, directly address National Council for Social Studies thematic strands, especially "ways that individuals and societies make decisions about rights, rules, relationships, and priorities"; "roles played by social institutions like schools and families in a society and their impact on individuals and groups"; and "the relationship between the expressed beliefs of a society and the implementation of these beliefs in actual practice."

Our last essential question is our most important. It is part of an exploration of the legacy of the Great Irish Famine and other human tragedies. If future generations learn from them and act accordingly, the victims will not have died in vain. The greatest tragedy is if their losses are forgotten.

Notes

1. Wiggins 44–48; Wiggins and McTighe 28–32; Shor and Friere; Evans and Saxe; Singer 28–31.

2. www.lifemag.com/Life/millennium/events.

Works Cited

Daly, Douglas. "The Leaf That Launched a Thousand Ships." *Natural History* January 1996.

Douglass, Frederick. *My Bondage and My Freedom.* New York: Dover, 1969.

Engels, Frederick. *Condition of the Working Class in England.* Trans. and ed. W. Henderson and W. Chaloner. New York: Macmillan, 1958.

Evans, Ronald, and David Saxe. *Handbook on Teaching Social Issues, NCSS Bulletin 93.* Washington, D.C.: Nat. Council for the Social Studies, 1996.

Fitzpatrick , M. *The Long March: A Famine Gift for Ireland.* Dublin: Wolfhound, 1998.

Folke, Edith, and Joe Glazer. *Songs of Work and Protest.* New York: Dover, 1973.

Gray, Peter. *The Irish Famine.* New York: Abrams, 1995.

Hildebrand, John. "Story of Famine Stirs Educational Melting Pot." *Newsday* 13 March 2001: A32.

Kissane, Noel. *The Irish Famine, A Documentary History.* Dublin: Nat. Lib. of Ireland, 1995.

Malthus, Thomas. *Essay on the Principle of Population.* Ann Arbor: Univ. of Michigan Press, 1959.

Meltzer, Milton. *The Amazing Potato.* New York: HarperCollins, 1992.

Moody, T., and F. Martin. *The Course of Irish History.* Boulder, Colo.: Rinehart, 1994.

Murphy, Maureen, Maureen Militia, and Alan Singer, eds. *New York State Great Irish Famine Curriculum Guide.* Albany, N.Y.: State Department of Education, in production.

National Council for the Social Studies. "Curriculum Standards for Social Studies: Expectations of Excellence." *NCSS Bulletin 89.* Washington, D.C.: NCSS, 1994.

O'Neill, Tim P. "Famine Evictions." *Famine, Land and Culture in Ireland.* Ed. Carla King. Dublin: Univ. College Dublin Press, 2000.

Sen, Amartya. *Development as Freedom.* New York: Knopf, 1999.

Shor, Ira, and Paulo Friere. *A Pedagogy for Liberation: Dialogues on Transforming Education.* South Hadley, Mass.: Bergin and Garvey, 1987.

Singer, Alan. "Teaching Multicultural Social Studies in an Era of Political Eclipse." *Social Education* 63(1): 28–31.

United Nations. Convention on the Prevention and Punishment of the Crime of Genocide. 9 December 1948.

Wiggins, Grant, and Jay McTighe. *Understanding by Design.* Alexandria, Va.: ASCD, 1998.

Wiggins, Grant. "The Futility of Trying to Teach Everything of Importance." *Educational Leadership* 47 (November 1989): 44–48.

www.lifemag.com/Life/millennium/events.

Zernike, Kate. "Using the Irish Famine to Explore Current Events" *New York Times* 21 March 2001: B7.

List of Contributors

Lorrie Blair is an Associate Professor in the Department of Art Education at Concordia University.

The **Rev. Jerome Joseph Day, O.S.B.**, is a member of the Benedictine monastic community at Saint Anselm College, Manchester, New Hampshire, where he teaches English and communications. He earned his Ph.D. degree in communications from McGill University, Montreal. Father Jerome's dissertation examined the discursive construction of the Irish Famine in literary and dramatic texts from 1845 to 2000.

Mary Lee Dunn works for the graduate Department of Work Environment at the University of Massachusetts Lowell. Dunn is co-president of the Ballykilcline Society (www.ballykilcline.com), an organization of descendants of Kilglass families. She is a co-editor of *The Cotton Dust Papers*, a book about the social history of byssinosis as a disease of U.S. textile workers (Baywood Publishing Co., 2002). Contact her at MaryLDunn@aol.com.

Gregory P. Garvey is an Associate Professor in the Department of Computer Science and Interactive Digital Design at Quinnipiac University. He previously held appointments as Associate Artist of the Digital Media Center for the Arts at Yale University, Chair of the Department of Design Art at Concordia University and Fellow at the Center for Advanced Visual Studies at MIT.

Sylvie Gauthier is a translator working in public health and a student in history and Irish studies at Concordia University in Montréal. Recently, she and Kathleen O'Brien co-authored a photo essay entitled "Montréal: re-imagining the traces/les traces évocatrices" published in the *Canadian Journal of Irish Studies*.

Holly Gillogly has an MA in Library Science from Emporia State University and is completing a Masters degree in History at the same institution.

David T. Gleeson is an assistant professor of history at the College of Charleston in Charleston, South Carolina. He is the author of *The Irish in the South, 1815-1877* published by the University of North Carolina Press.

Michael R. Hutcheson is Associate Professor of Humanities at Landmark College in Putney, Vermont. He previously taught at Bradford College and Merrimack College. His academic specialty is early modern Ireland, with a particular focus on environmental and landscape history.

Rached Khalifa is completing his Ph.D. thesis "W. B Yeats: A Poetics of Ideology" at the University of Essex. His dissertation addresses the problem of ideology in Yeats's poetry, contextualizing it within the "modernist predicament.

Christine Kinealy is a Reader in History at the University of Central Lancaster. She is the author and co-author of several books on the Great Hunger, including *This Great Calamity: The Irish Famine 1845-1852* and *A Death-Dealing Famine: The Great Hunger in Ireland.*

Connie Ann Kirk is a second generation Irish-American who writes frequently about American literature, history, and culture. Her publications include a forthcoming biography of Dickinson from Greenwood Press. She is currently working on a book about Irish domestic workers and 19th Century American writers.

MaryAnn Matthews is a research affiliate of the Gilder Lehrman Center for the Study of Slavery, Resistance and Abolition at Yale University. With the support of the Gilder Lehrman Center, she developed the Tangled Roots web site.

Edward T. McCarron is Associate Professor and Chair of the History Department at Stonehill College. He is the author of several articles on Irish immigration and is currently completing a book on the Irish in northern New England.

Maureen McCann Miletta, a former elementary school teacher, is an associate professor of elementary education at Hofstra University and an associate director of the New York State Great Irish Famine Curriculum.

Maureen Murphy is a professor of secondary education and the coordinator of the Language Arts and English certification program at Hofstra University, Hempstead, NY and the director of the New York York State Great Irish Famine Curriculum.

Kathleen O'Brien is an installation Artist and Associate Professor in fine Arts at Concordia University in Montreal where she also teaches in Irish Studies. She is co-editor of book reviews and associate editor of visual culture for the *Canadian Journal of Irish Studies*. She is currently writing a book on caoineadh, politics of the female voice, and famine commemorations in Ireland, Canada and the United States.

Thomas O'Grady is Professor of English and Director of Irish Studies at the University of Massachusetts Boston. His essays on Irish writers have been published in *Éire-Ireland, New Hibernia Review, James Joyce Quarterly*, and many other journals. He is currently completing a book-length study of William Carleton, Patrick Kavanagh and Benedict Kiely.

Deborah Peck received her doctoral degree in Clinical Psychology from the Massachusetts School of Professional Psychology. Her dissertation traced the historically and psychologically traumatic aspects of the Great Irish Hunger (1845-1852) across several generations of Irish Famine descendants.

James R. Riordan has Masters degrees in Library Science and History from Emporia State University. He is a doctoral candidate in labor history at the University of Massachusetts, Amherst.

William B. Rogers is Associate Dean of the Caspersen School of Graduate Studies at Drew University in Madison, NJ. He teaches graduate and undergraduate courses in 19th century American history (particularly the Civil War), the impact of war on American society, and Irish/Irish-American history and literature.

Alan Singer is an associate professor of secondary education at Hofstra University and editor of *Social Science Docket*, a joint publication of the New York and New Jersey Councils for the Social Studies. His is also associate director of the New York State Great Irish Famine Curriculum.

Robert A. Smart is the Director for Ireland Studies and Associate Professor of English at Quinnipiac University. He is the author of *The Nonfiction Novel* and Founding Editor of *The Writing Teacher* (National Poetry Foundation).

Karen Manners Smith is an associate professor of American, British, and Irish history at Emporia State University in Kansas. She is the author of *New Paths to Power: American Women 1890-1920*.

David A. Valone is a Visiting Assistant Professor of History at Quinnipiac University. He has published widely on the educational, linguistic, and medical history of Britain and the United States during the nineteenth and twentieth centuries.